Real Florida

Key Lime Pies,
Worm Fiddlers,
A Man Called Frog
and Other Endangered Species

Jeff Klinkenberg

ISBN 1-878086-22-7

Library of Congress Catalog Card Number
93-071406

Printed in the United States of America

Cover and inside artwork: Scott Hiestand
Book design: Elizabeth House

Down Home Press
P.O. Box 4126
Asheboro, N.C. 27204

For Suzanne, Kristin, Peter, Katie,

and Grandma Bea

with all my love

Acknowledgements

The stories in this book were drawn from *St. Petersburg Times* columns written between 1977 and 1993. Most are reprinted here as originally published; some have been revised slightly to eliminate references to events long past, to improve clarity, or to correct goofs in grammar and style that make me blush every time I encounter them. A few of these stories appeared in an earlier collection of my work, *Blind Dog in a Smokehouse*.

I'd like to thank people who helped make this book possible with their editing, advice or encouragement over the years: Gene Patterson, Andy Barnes, Mike Foley, Neville Green, Bob Haiman, Sandra Thompson, Gretchen Letterman, Jeanne Grinstead, Nancy Waclawek, Dave Scheiber, Kelly Scott, Jack Reed, Mary Jane Park, Anne Glover, Anne Hull, Sheryl James, Chris Lavin, Bill Landrey, Barbara Hijek, Karen Dean, Christopher Scanlan, Jeanne Malmgren, Howell Raines, Lum Pennington, Gabe Horn (White Deer of Autumn), Don Murray, William Howarth, Bob Silver, Scott Hiestand, Don Fry, John Crittenden, Al Levine, Horance C. "Buddy" Davis Jr. and Jerry Bledsoe.

Special thanks to Roy Peter Clark and Tom French, the best friends anyone could ever hope to have.

Contents

Fall

Winter

Spring

Summer

Permissions

Recommended reading: *Walden*, *Cape Cod*, and *Journal* by Henry David Thoreau.

Introduction

I'm the world's luckiest fellow. My parents moved to Florida when I was two and brought me along. They were big-city midwesterners, but they became real Floridians, in attitude, and so did I. In 1952, even in Miami, real Florida came naturally.

In the real Florida of my youth, people went barefoot and paid attention to the rhythms of nature. They worked backyard gardens before work in the morning. In the evening, the old couple behind us sat on their porch and told wonderful stories in beautiful southern accents. At night, through my open bedroom window, I heard owls hooting from the top branch of the poinciana tree.

Television hardly mattered in real Florida. There was no Disney World. There were no video games. For fun, a boy ran to the canal at the end of the street and caught snook and jack and snapper on his fish pole. In between bites I studied sea cows, our name for the lumbering manatees, common then but an endangered species today.

A lot of real Florida and real Floridians, from manatees to the folks who try to live simple and natural lives, are endangered now. Among the fastest growing states, modern Florida has 13-million citizens, subdivisions stretching to the horizon, behemoth shopping centers, terrifying traffic, and pavement everywhere. For some people, I guess it's a kind of progress. For some of us, it's a step backward. Real Florida is in danger of disappearing.

In our big cities, you still can find it, but you have to look hard. In the country, real Florida is easier to come across, but even there it's on the wane. Sometimes you have to drive far out of town to hear frogs serenading or count fireflies or look at the Milky Way.

But like I say, I'm the world's luckiest fellow. I got to grow up in real Florida, and the *St. Petersburg Times*, the newspaper I work for, has let me write about the real Florida that remains. Looking for it, I've wandered the state from the Keys to the Panhandle, warmed my backside at numerous campfires, been asked in for supper, and for the most part never have had to wear a necktie or talk to a lawyer.

I've divided this book into seasons, because the time of year is usually important in real Florida. For example, in the fall we start looking for hawks and other migratory birds and we plant our gardens. In the winter, we watch for the snowbirds who are otherwise known as tourists and spend as much time as we can outdoors. In the spring we take our shoes off, maybe plant some melons, and go to baseball games. In the summer, we fish, swelter, fish, swelter, and worry about hurricanes.

Real Floridians have taught me how to fiddle for earthworms, build fine cigars, call turkeys, reel in tarpon, make lye soap, and appreciate the nature of gossip in a fancy town like Palm Beach. I got to meet a man called Frog. I chewed the fat with a woman who may bake the last authentic Key lime pie in the state. I looked for the Bardin Booger, Florida's bigfoot. I visited with Milt Sosin, a legendary newspaper reporter who covered Florida when it was mostly real Florida. I went to a wedding where the bride and groom were married under crossed fly rods. Along the way I've attended some funerals, too. They have reminded me of friends and loved ones, real Floridians, long dead.

What I've tried to do, in my newspaper columns and now in this book, is preserve the color and flavor of real Florida. I hope you like what you find in these pages.

Fall

Fall

Fall does not march into Florida like a brass band. That happens in New England or North Carolina, where blazing leaves are a tourist attraction. In our state, fall more or less slips through the back door a month after many people have all but given up on its arrival.

Fall comes whistling softly.

Forget what the calendar says about the autumnal equinox. In Florida, the seasons are all messed up. Fall starts in mid-October, at the earliest, and says goodbye in mid-December. Winter has come and gone by March. Spring lasts a little longer, until about the middle of May, when humidity and temperature shoot up and the rains begin. Summer, the longest season, stays five months until we yell for mercy.

We curse our lawns, which won't stop growing. We curse the TV weather forecasters, who won't tell us to turn off our air-conditioners. As we watch the World Series on our televisions in late October, we hate the lucky northern stiffs who are wearing coats and mufflers while watching baseball. Even those of us who would live nowhere else begin entertaining Rocky Mountain fantasies.

Then one day it rains, and when the rain is over, it's a degree cooler. It rains again five days later and cools another degree. We notice a kestrel, a sparrow hawk, that has migrated from the north, perched on the telephone wires. We see mullet bunching up in the bayous. In the woods, or on the roadsides, we see wildflowers. In Florida, fall sneaks up on you.

It's a subtle thing, which is why so many Florida transplants complain about how much they miss the changing seasons of the northern latitudes. They don't know about the hawks or mullet or flowers. They are used to admiring flashy leaves. In Florida, dying leaves do not flash like neon lights.

But if you're observant, if you're willing to venture into the out-of-doors, if you'll work a little, the signs of fall are small but unmistakable. Blink and you may miss them.

The leaves of certain trees do change. It's not the spectacular, get-the-camera-out phenomenon of New England, but it's something anyone can see if they look.

In our swamps, the leaves of maples first turn yellow and then scarlet. Leaves from laurel and water oaks change color and die; live oaks simply stop putting out new growth. On higher ground, pines shed their needles. Golden rain produces yellow flowers that turn salmon pink before death.

Cast your eyes downward and behold your lawn. St. Augustine grass finally (and thankfully) shifts into low gear, sparing weekend gardeners the most hated task known to civilized men and women – mowing. In the woods, in areas where sunlight can penetrate, wildflowers bloom twice a year. Spring and now.

Fall.

At Boyd Hill, a city nature park near my St. Petersburg home, goldenrod blossoms are dying in early November. So are blazing star and tickweed. Carphephorus, topped with rosy-purple flowers, have been covered by bumblebees for a couple of weeks now.

Bend down, if you dare, and look closely at those flowers. See the big green thing that could almost be another stem? A praying mantis, it hopes to pick off any insect made careless by the orgy of pollination.

Songbirds, hovering above, are more than willing to gobble the praying mantises. Above the songbirds, up in the trees, are hawks. They've been arriving for a couple weeks now from points north. They will eat small birds that have come to eat the big insects that have shown up to eat the small ones that arrive to sip the nectar from wildflowers that bloom in the fall.

Snakes will also eat birds if they get the chance. In the fall, snakes do. In summer, snakes are sluggish and in hiding, like people, and unwilling to move much. Now it's cooler, their juices are flowing, and they are out cruising for anything foolish enough to stay still too long in the same spot. Birds, toads and insects are on the menu, as well as mice that skip through wildflower fields looking for seeds.

In West Central Florida, where I live, fishers are often the first to notice the arrival of fall. As the Gulf of Mexico cools, fish migrations begin. Kingfish are not as plentiful as they once were due to overfishing and pollution, but a few schools do swing by our coast in the fall.

An angler who baits a hook with a sardine, and drops it into a deep hole a mile or so off the coast, may be rewarded with a kingfish weighing 60 pounds or more. Kingfish herald fall.

So do redfish. Big ones migrate into Tampa Bay, like clockwork, in the fall. Try this: Bait a hook with a live shrimp, and sneak out onto a dock, walking lightly to avoid alerting fish hiding underneath. Drop your line next to a piling, and hang on to your pole. During fall, some of our Tampa Bay reds weigh 30 pounds.

You don't have to be an angler to see mullet. You need only open your eyes and look at the bay. More than anything, more than changing leaves, wildflowers and bird migrations, mullet mean fall has arrived.

I drove to the bay before work the other morning to look for them. The wind hadn't picked up yet, and the water's surface was calm, except for where several thousand mullet were bunched together. Their noses poked out of the water. Their bodies pushed a wake.

In the fall, right before they spawn, they gather by the hundreds, thousands, millions. They are fat with roe and so thickly schooled you think you could walk on them. Swimming along the shorelines, they head up our bayous, creeks and canals. Then they wait.

By early December, cold fronts arrive with regularity. Each seems cooler than the last. Each night, the moon grows larger in the sky. Now here comes a cold front in about the middle of December; there is the moon, fat. The full moon stirs something in the mullet. Always has. Always will.

They move, by the millions, in what is one of nature's awesome migrations. They swim out of the bayous, creeks and canals into Tampa Bay. Dolphin slash into them. Big predatory fish feed on them from below. Commercial fishers encircle them with long nets.

Still the mullet press on, in enormous schools, for the mouth of the bay, and the Gulf of Mexico beyond, for what they were born to do.

Reproduce their species.

When the mullet return to the bay a few weeks later, they are weak and skinny, their roe spent. Winter will have arrived.

The woods of Elmo Boone

The woods are cold and dark but not quiet. Not on the night before hunting season. On the night before hunting season you hear dogs yowling from portable cages and from the backs of pickup trucks. You hear the excited voices of men crowded around campfires that flicker through the trees. In the Phillips 66 gas station-grocery, you eavesdrop as hunters in camouflaged coats chew the fat while picking through last-minute vittles that include canned chili, sardines and pickled sausage.

Just off U.S. 98, near North Florida's Aucilla Wildlife Management Area, Elmo Boone is getting his hunting camp ready. Elmo is particular about his hunting camp. He scouted out the woods weeks ago and picked a site on the edge of a small cypress swamp close to the island where he will hunt deer and hog.

He has pitched two tents and dug a fire pit. He has built a table and cut firewood. He has installed a clothes line from which he hangs a battery of lanterns. The air smells of frying food. There is nothing like the night before hunting season.

Elmo is 65, though he looks younger. He is tall with salt-and-pepper hair hidden by a cap sporting a camouflage pattern and ear flaps that stick out like airplane wings. He has long sideburns and bushy black eyebrows. He is built as solidly as an old oak stump.

Born in Miami, he fled the city with his parents after the 1926 hurricane blew down their house and forced them to spend the storm beneath a tomato truck. They moved to north Florida's Oklawaha River, where hurricanes were scarce and their neighbors were a family named the Barkers who were headed by a nice woman everybody just called Ma.

One day, to Elmo's surprise, the FBI showed up and gunned down Ma Barker and her boys. To him, they were not criminals, just pleasant folks who liked the bass he gave them.

Elmo lived in St. Petersburg for a spell and worked a half century in the nursery business. Retired, he lives now on a Citrus County lake where he hopes to catch a world record bass. Fall is his favorite time, when he can camp, hunt and enjoy the company of like-minded men.

"You don't come into the woods to shoot things," he tells one of his guests, a city boy. Elmo is thawing out soft-shell turtle for supper. "You want to get a hog or deer, but you're here for the friendship and the camping and the food and the stories."

At dusk, other men arrive at Elmo's hunting camp. There's Tommy and Rob from St. Pete, and Jim, Elmo's next door neighbor. Guns are cleaned and oiled. Sleeping bags are fluffed up on cots inside tents. Ice sloshes in huge plastic cups brimming with ginger ale and Rebel Yell sour mash whiskey. At 7:11 p.m., Elmo Boone fires up the Coleman stove.

"I'm going to fry some cooter," he says. Cooter is Elmo's name for the softshell turtle commonly found in fresh water Florida lakes. Elmo catches them during summer, butchers them and freezes them for hunting season. He likes to feed his men something special. Tomorrow night he plans Louisiana-style baked bass. The following day he will fix mullet roe and baby lima beans so powerful the men will have to carry toilet paper into their tree stands.

When the oil is boiling he dips turtle pieces into flour mixed with black pepper, and tosses them into the cast-iron kettle he has used for two decades. The sizzle is loud enough to be heard above the tape recording to which he has listened for the last half hour. It's a tape of Jim's son, calling turkeys.

When the turtle is ready, and the potatoes and broccoli, Elmo pours cups of the homemade wine he calls Wild Plum Crazy. He waits anxiously for compliments and is visibly relieved when they come. Relaxed, the men sit at the fire and eat and tell stories. When you visit Elmo Boone's hunting camp, you tells stories or listen to them. That is the way it always has been.

You hear about last year's opening day hunt, how Tommy shot a 400-pound hog 15 minutes after dawn, how the hog was so big Elmo had to saw it in two so four men could haul it five and a half miles through the cypress swamp to camp, and how they were so tired nobody hunted the rest of the day.

"Those boys give me a hard time for spoiling their hunt," Tommy says. "But that hog sure ate good."

"There's bigger hogs in that swamp," Elmo says. "Today when we were scouting I saw where a hog rubbed mud off himself four and a half feet up a palm! That's a six-hundred-pound hog to do that! His tracks was eighteen inches deep in the mud!"

The talk turns to bears. A man says he'd never shoot a bear, unless it attacked, and Florida black bears just do not attack. They only want to eat bugs and plants and maybe a farmer's beehives. A man talks about panthers. He disagrees with wildlife biologists who claim panthers exist only in the Everglades. He says he saw one three years ago in Citrus County, near a rockpit, with a chicken in its mouth.

"You see all kinds of things in the woods," Elmo says. He tells his bigfoot story. He believes bigfoot – Florida's version of the abominable snowman – does exist. One time he was wading in the swamp not far from here and got water in his waders. He headed for an island where he could dry out. On the island he noticed a clearing under a palmetto thicket. Something big, bigger than a bear, had slept there.

"There was this neat pile of manure this high," Elmo says, his hands a foot apart. "Now most animals have no toilet manners, but this animal had piled it up neatly, away from where he slept! I was taken by that, and then I saw his prints. Now I wear a nine and a half double E. His print was twice as wide as my foot and about four inches longer. And there was a depression in the heel, like he had some kind of horn or spike there."

The conversation turns from bigfoot to alligators. They are right quick, according to Elmo. One time, he was trying to show some city boys how you could put a gator to sleep by turning it over and rubbing its belly. The four-and-a-half-footer woke. Elmo still has the scar.

7

"He struck like a rattlesnake," Elmo says. "I had to choke him to make him let go."

The rattlesnake mention inspires another Elmo story. In this one, Elmo was fishing in a canal when he was bitten by a venomous water moccasin. At the hospital, his hand swelled like Popeye's forearm. The big thing, Elmo says, was that he did not panic. He was back to work in two days.

"This fella from Georgia told me about the night he heard a frog a-hollering," Elmo says. "He went over and saw the frog in a moccasin's mouth. He felt real sorry for the frog and pulled him away from the moccasin. Now he felt sorry for the moccasin and poured a pint of whiskey down the moccasin's throat. A little while later, something bumped the fella in the leg. It was the moccasin. He had brought another frog."

The men laugh. Elmo had them going for a minute. They drink more sour mash and tell stories about ghosts and UFOs. One by one, the men say good night and crawl into their tents, except for one man who has fallen asleep sitting in his chair. Elmo shakes him gently and tells him it's late, go to bed.

Elmo shovels sand onto the fire. He turns out the lanterns and crawls into his own tent. You can hear his voice for a while – he's telling another story to his sleepy companion – and then there's silence, except for the dogs in the distance, baying at the moon.

Tommie's soap

Tommie Smith put pine saplings under the black kettle to keep the fire going. She dumped pork fat into the kettle, and as it melted she added water and lye and stirred with a wood spoon. The mixture was neither too thick nor too liquid. She could tell it was going to be a good batch.

The smoke curled into the oaks and pines above and into Tommie's face. She blinked and stepped back. Then the wind shifted and she attacked the kettle again with her spoon. Her large arms showed muscle as she stirred hard. She wanted everything to be just right for the people who had come to north Florida's Stephen Foster State Folk Culture Center here to watch her make her specialty – lye soap.

"This is what five generations of my family have done," she told a dozen spectators in her high reedy voice. "My mother teached me to make soap, and my grandmother teached my mother. I teached my daughters and now my granddaughters are learning how."

She was born 67 years ago in Hamilton County, not far from the Georgia border, in the deep woods. Her ancestors, stolen from Africa by white slavers, worked the soil. A self-sufficient people, they made their own clothes and provided their own food. They wasted nothing, not bacon grease or the fat cracklings from pork chops. Fat went into soap.

"When I was a child, you just couldn't go to the store and get what you needed," Tommie explained to the schoolchildren gathered around. "There was no money, and the store was a long way off, and the only way to get there was by wagon and mule. Everybody made soap – white and colored, rich and poor."

Tommie Smith spat snuff juice into the pine needles at her feet. She stirred the kettle again. The soap had the consistency of oatmeal. She spooned it into a shallow pan and patted it dry with a towel and said she would let it sit for a spell. Then it would be ready.

"The soap is good for just about everything," she said. When she spoke, the schoolchildren listening automatically hushed. Tommie Smith had a commanding presence. A large woman, she wore jeans, a smock and an apron the color of the sky. She wore a white hat that at first glance seemed to be made from an animal's fur. It was cloth, but it made her look all the more like a pioneer.

"Now you can use this soap in your bath," she said. "If you melt it, and pour it on your clothes, you'll get them cleaner and fresher smelling than with any soap you buy from the store. Yes, it will! Sometimes I run out of my own soap and have to buy some." She grimaced. "I don't like store-bought soap."

As Tommie talked, her adult daughters, Clementine and Sarah, poked at the fire and took turns stirring the kettle.

"If you have psoriasis in your hair, lye soap will cure it," Tommie said. "If you got poison ivy, wash yourself with lye soap. You'll feel a lot better."

Tommie Smith reeled off other reasons for using lye soap. It soothes mosquito and flea bites. If softens chapped hands. Even though it originates as animal fat, as soap it makes a body smell fresh and clean. Yet, cut up into small chunks, it's a fine catfish bait.

"And if you melt lye soap into your pig's slop, you'll worm him. When you slaughter him, he'll have the prettiest liver and intestines you ever did see."

Some children listening giggled at the thought of pretty pig livers and intestines. For the most part they were city children whose parents drive to the supermarket to buy meat that some anonymous worker has killed and some anonymous butcher has carved and packaged in plastic. Things were different when Tommie Smith was a child, and they are different for her now.

"Times was hard," she said. Tommie was one of 11 children raised on a farm in the middle of the woods. She and her brothers and sisters did without material things and grew up in a society that for the most part did not welcome African-Americans. Yet she remembers a happy childhood, and her family never went hungry.

"Lordy, no! We grew corn and tomatoes and okra and beans and peas. We hunted and fished. Back then, you could go anywhere you wanted and help yourself to what was in the water and the woods. Now, somebody owns everything."

Back when there were few fences, and fish and wildlife were plentiful, Tommie's father and brothers caught bass, catfish, bream and turtles in the lakes and rivers. In the woods they shot rabbits, squirrels, deer and turkey. Sometimes they got a possum or a raccoon, which Tommie's mother baked with black pepper and onions.

Tommie learned cooking and other chores, including soap making, from her mother. And Tommie helped her father in the fields. As she told the wide-eyed boys and girls listening to her: "They worked children early in those days."

She had to walk to a small school two miles away through the pines. There were few doctors in the area, and when somebody got sick, and no professional help was available, her mother did the healing with folk remedies she had learned from her own mother. Corn shucks, boiled into a tea, were used to cure illnesses that included measles. Folk medicine worked: Tommie's mother and grandmother lived into their 90s.

Whenever the moon approached full, Tommie's mother made soap. Like many country people, Tommie's mother planned important chores around the moon, which was thought to have a strong influence on the world.

Tommie abides by the same notion. "Full moon soap isn't too hard and it isn't too soft," she said to her audience. "New moon soap just isn't as good."

She got married and had nine children. She and her husband Evrt have kept up all the family traditions, from farming to making soap.

Like her mother and grandmother, Tommie is a self-sufficient woman. Unlike most Floridians, she seldom pays somebody to do what she can do herself. She makes her own clothes and preserves her own food. The word "waste" is missing from her vocabulary.

She saves fat left over from cooking, stores it in cans and waits for the moon to get right. She builds a small fire outside and scoops six pounds of fat into her worn kettle. When the fat has melted, she pours in two and a half pints of water. In one of her few concessions to modern life, she adds the contents of a small can of lye. Years ago, she made her own lye by mixing water with the ashes of oak and hickory and letting it sit overnight.

"Now children," she said to the newest group of youngsters who had gathered round."You be careful with lye. It could blind you sure as anything! Even on your hands, it'll burn you good."

After 35 minutes of cooking and a couple hours of cooling, she cut the soap into two dozen chunks and sold them for 50 cents each. Although children bought soap, adults seemed genuinely thrilled with it. In Tommie Smith's homemade lye soap, they had a souvenir of a pioneer past that most modern Floridians don't know existed.

"I think everybody should know how to make soap," Tommie was telling a city man late in the afternoon. "Who knows? We might see hard times again. Oh my yes! Those hard times might come back one day and we should be ready."

The last Key lime pie

It was the middle of the afternoon. Hungry, I felt irritable as I passed one fast-food chain after another. When you are in the Keys, you don't want fast food. You want native.

Then I saw it, out of the corner of my eye, from 50 mph. It was a rectangular concrete building with gray peeling paint that had once been white. I made a U-turn and stopped in front of the Key Lime Grill.

The faded lettering on the building said "Lime Ade – Key Lime Pie – World Famous" and I knew for once I might get lucky. I parked, opened the screen door and plopped down at the counter. I looked the old woman in the eye and told her I'd have a Key lime pie. It was the real thing.

Yowza.

The state of Florida should stop bragging about our beaches and weather and promote Key lime pie instead. In the United States, Key limes are found only in Florida. They are tiny, round and yellow, thin skinned and juicy, very tart to the taste. Key lime pie is to Florida what gumbo is to New Orleans. You can't get the real thing anywhere else.

Here's the disgrace: It's almost impossible to find authentic Key lime pie in Florida. Even in the Keys, Key lime trees are as scarce as gold nuggets.

Yet every restaurant and bakery here sells Key lime pies by the dozen, mostly to naive tourists. The truth is that such Key lime pies are almost always made from other kinds of limes, which means they are not Key lime pies.

Most bakeries, in fact, buy from companies that import a blend of Persian and Key lime juice from Central America, the Dominican Republic and Mexico. Key limes, sometimes called West Indian limes, are even hard to find in the West Indies.

"The Key lime is unique," says Rick Biddle, who owns a juice business. "The taste just lingers longer. The pie it makes is just damn good. I wish I could get more limes."

In the Keys, where the limes used to be common, it's easier to find crocodiles. The large commercial groves that once supplied the United States were destroyed by hurricanes in the 1920s and 1930s. Most were never replanted. Replanted groves didn't survive the 1970s, when real estate in the Keys became too valuable to waste on trees. Today, only a few trees remain, mostly in backyards.

As I sat alone at the counter at the Key Lime Grill, watching the ceiling fan stir the warm air, and scraping the last pie crumb from my plate, I wondered how one

12

ramshackle eatery, 90 miles from Miami, had survived. I asked for lime-ade and the elderly woman who owns the place got up from where she was crocheting and got it for me.

I took out my business card and notebook and asked about Key lime pie. I told her I wanted to write a story about how her grill might be the last restaurant in the Keys to serve authentic Key lime pie. She smiled. She was tall with curly hair and horn-rimmed glasses, but it was her smile that got to me. She said, "Naw."

Naw? I said what do you mean naw. Most restaurants kill for publicity. "I mean I don't want publicity," she said. "I been making pies for thirty-one years. I want to retire. I don't need people from Tampa coming down here and making more business." She smiled again.

Knowing how old-time Conchs are often suspicious of strangers, I tried to win her over. I said her product was unusual, a part of Keys culture, and somebody should write about it before it was gone. She shook her head and smiled, as if it were the dumbest idea she had ever heard. I said, at least give me your name. Her smile turned into a grin. I will call her the Pie Woman.

The screen door banged open. A commercial fisherman who called himself Steve strolled in. He ordered lime-ade and said hello to everybody. He complimented the Pie Woman on her lime-ade. He knew it was the real thing, too.

Pouting and plotting, I thought maybe Steve could help me talk sense into the Pie Woman. I introduced myself and told Steve how the Pie Woman wouldn't talk. He said, "What do you wanna know?" I explained I needed to know more about her business, how she liked selling pies, how she managed to last, and, why not – what it meant to society.

The Pie Woman interrupted. "I told you thirty-one years I been makin' pies." Steve turned to me and said, "Thirty-one years."

I said to the Pie Woman: But you won't tell me anything more. Steve said, "Let him write the story!"

She smiled and said, "It's a free country."

Steve ordered another juice. I took out my notebook again. Steve ordered a slice of pie. He wolfed it down and ordered a whole pie. He asked for a slice to eat in his truck, too. I asked how much juice she put into pies.

The Pie Woman smiled. "It depends on how hard I squeeze the limes."

I told you she was good.

The Pie Woman said, "You want my recipe! I'm not going to tell you my recipe!"

Steve and I told her we didn't want her recipe. You can find the recipe in most any cookbook. A nine-inch pie contains six egg yolks, a can of sweetened condensed milk and a half cup of Key lime juice. Steve and I asked about her own history, and she was tough. She budged little, only admitting that a Mister Tift had opened the restaurant after World War II and he had sold pies, too. Then she took over and had been making and selling pies ever since.

Trying to scare her into being cooperative, I asked Steve if he knew of any other places that might sell real Key lime pies. Steve thought a moment and named a bakery. The Pie Woman shook her head sadly.

She said, "She don't even squeeze her own limes!" I mentioned another place. The Pie Woman said, "They use food coloring!" She found fault with the new bakery behind the marina. "It's for the tourists. She has to buy lime juice like the others."

I asked, well, where do you get your limes? She pointed toward the back of the restaurant. "There's a grove of trees. I got the only grove around here."

Steve left with his box of pie. We heard his truck drive around back. The Pie Woman walked to the window and said, "What's he doin'?" It was clear she feared he wanted to steal her limes. He was only looking, but she watched until he was gone.

After that I tried to make small talk about her crocheting. She didn't thaw. I gave her my opinion on tourism. She looked bored. I complimented her menu, even though she only sells three things: lime-ade, pie and grilled cheese sandwiches. I hoped I could butter her up by ordering a sandwich.

She smiled and said, "I don't have any."

I smiled and drove on to Miami.

Making music
for earthworms

Jack Palmer thought it was a shame people in his town had forgotten a basic skill of Florida crackerhood. They couldn't fiddle up a mess of earthworms to save their lives.

They couldn't recognize a worm's sign when they saw it. They didn't know how to hammer a wood stake into the ground, rub an ax back and forth against it like a bow on a fiddle, and create a God-awful vibration that drives sensitive worms out of their burrows and into the tin cans of eager fishermen.

Worm fiddling had no part in the lives of modern Floridians tempted by television, fancy cars and shopping. For Palmer, a crusty 53-year-old city councilman, fire chief and worm maestro, it was unendurable.

He had grown up in this panhandle town 20 miles from the Alabama border, and he had fiddled worms. Everyone he knew had done it. Fiddling worms was a way of life, as important as knowing how to hunt and fish.

"There was no bait shops, so if you wanted to fish, you sure enough had to get your own worms," said Palmer, one of nine children of a professional alligator hunter and his wife.

"I sold worms to the commercial fishermens for a penny apiece. Shoot, when I was a boy I always had money enough for a pocketful of penny suckers, or an Ike and Mike Cake and a big old RC Cola."

Times changed. When the state years ago prohibited commercial fishing for most freshwater species, the demand for earthworms by professional fishers diminished and reduced the need for fiddlers. Today, modern sport anglers buy worms raised by farmers. Only old-timers such as Palmer carry on the fiddling tradition.

Palmer, a self-sufficient man who feels most comfortable in the woods or on the water, thought it was high time modern folks learned the joys of worm fiddling, too.

In 1974, with his support and supervision, Caryville held its first worm-fiddling contest. By 1976, the town of 600 people was calling itself the Worm-Fiddling Capital of Florida. And nobody argued.

A few weeks ago, about 300 people tolerated pouring rain to watch the best worm fiddlers in the state make their weird music. On a sunny day, who knows how many spectators would have crowded the field next to city hall?

"We've had as many as five hundred," said Palmer, a stocky man who covers his white hair under a fire department cap. "Next year I'm gonna try to get some paratroopers to parachute in. That would really draw a crowd. As it is, we've had people here from New York. England. We've had 'em from everywhere."

Proceeds from worm-fiddling contests helped build a ballfield for Caryville. Future contests may pay for a new firehouse while exposing a new generation to worm fiddling.

"We're bringing it back," Jack Palmer said.

Palmer has taught a number of new people the art, including his wife JoAn, who had the misfortune of growing up in Indiana, where people didn't know diddly about fiddling. JoAn, who had watched her husband fiddle up fish bait for years, entered the 1978 contest and called up a state record 246 worms in less than 15 minutes.

"I was on TV after that one, but they never showed my face," JoAn Palmer said. "When you're worming, you're down on your hands and knees. All they showed of me on TV was my rear end. Well, at least I got a trophy."

This year's contestants also took home trophies. Billy Joe and Ashley Pate fiddled up 35 worms to win men's division, Shirley and Pat Bailey won women's with two and William Clayton Bailey and Roger Gay got nine to win the children's category. During the grand championship, which matched the three division winners, the children took top honors with six worms.

Jack Palmer judged the contest, knowing it would be unfair to compete against worm-fiddling dilettantes. "Shoot, when I was a boy, I could fill me a gallon bucket in no time. I used to get 16- and 18-inch worms! You'd a thought a snake was coming up, some of 'em was so big."

An expert can fiddle up snakes, in fact. At least Palmer has done so. Fiddling for worms on the edge of a swamp, Palmer once was startled by the ominous rattle of a nearby diamondback, apparently angry about the vibrations created by the maestro. Palmer didn't cotton to the presence of the uninvited snake either.

"When I see a rattler I get me a limb and whomp him one."

Birds and squirrels chirp and chatter when Palmer starts to make his music. Alligators, some people claim, have been known to grunt in response. Not that the maestro wants alligator. He is alligatored out.

"When I was little, and my daddy was hunting alligators, we ate more gator than I could tell you. We even had it for breakfast with biscuits!"

These days, Palmer wants only to provoke worms, and most people around here agree that he has few peers – at least by today's sorry worm-fiddling standards. His grandmother was equally skilled, and in his grandfather's hands, an ax head and stake was a Stradivarius. But how his grandparents learned the art, Palmer knows not. Worm fiddling, like grits, is a southern mystery.

"I can't even tell you who discovered it would work on worms. I've always heard that one day somebody happened to notice that vibrations from an idling Model T or a tractor bothered worms enough to make 'em come out of the ground."

This much is known: The best time for fiddling is early morning or late afternoon when the ground is cooler and worms are shallow. After a rain is good, as long as it wasn't a downpour, and the slightly damp earth of a shady swamp is worm paradise. Jack Palmer regards winter worm fiddling a waste of time because worms are hibernating. Besides, he would rather hunt deer than bass fish once the air turns crisp.

"There are probably worms in this here field," Palmer said, getting out the ax and stake he always carries in his battered pickup truck.

"I call stakes 'stobs,' and I prefer to call worm fiddling 'snoring' or 'grunting,' " he said. "But it don't matter what you call it. We say fiddling in Caryville 'cause it makes it easier for the people to make sense of it. It kind of reminds people of somebody playing a fiddle."

He fingered the stake.

"This here stob is white pine, and I'd rather have cedar, 'cause you get a better vibration, but white pine will have to do."

He snuffed out his Pall Mall, fell to his knees and stared at the hard ground. "I knew it," he said, touching a tiny mound of dirt. "We got worm sign here."

On a stifling hot day in a field near his home, the maestro was about to compose another movement in his earthworm symphony.

He drove the stake into the ground and picked up the ax. Then, like an artist playing Beethoven's Violin Concerto, he rubbed the ax head against the stake, and the quiet country afternoon was shattered by a cacophony of squeaks, grunts and rumbles that shook the ground for 15 feet around.

Head bowed, eyes half shut in concentration, Palmer played his instrument, constantly changing the angle to get different tones, sometimes stopping to pour sand on the top of the stake to create a grittier pitch. Suddenly, on the ground surrounding Jack Palmer, it happened: Earthworms squirmed into the sunlight. If worms had hands and ears, those hands would have been covering those ears. Doing everything but begging for mercy, the worms writhed in what can only be described as agony.

"Them worms don't want to go back in the ground," Jack Palmer said. "Worm fiddling, it just drives 'em crazy."

Carmela's cigars

TAMPA 12/10/86

The old cigarmakers are dying now, or they have been replaced by machines, or by young people who do not wish to make cigars a career or get their hands dirty. This is sad news to Carmela Varsalona. She says, "Listen, honey: Cigarmakers are getting short. They're all dead."

She was 16 when she rolled her first cigar. At 78, she still is rolling cigars, by hand, 40 hours a week. She has no plans to retire. Who would replace her? A machine operated by a smart-aleck kid? Carmela Varsalona does not like to think of a machine, or an uninterested youth, doing her work.

"Machines, they are always breaking down," Carmela says, in an Italian accent as musical as her name. "Machines do not pick the thread or dirt or whatever out of the tobacco – machines just jam it into a cigar. And the young people don't want to get tobacco on their fingers or smell cigars. They want to work machines.

"I make fine cigar, by hand. You say that in the paper. Say 'Carmela still make a fine cigar.'"

Once upon a time in Tampa, cigars were king. In 1886, a man named Martinez Ybor began a cigar business. A neighborhood grew around it, and eventually there were 50 factories that employed 20,000 cigarmakers in Ybor City.

"Back then, if you made cigars, you were considered a craftsman," says Bill Elliott, Carmela's boss at the Maniscalco Cigar factory in Ybor City. "Now there can't be more than 35 people left in all of Tampa who know how to make a cigar by hand. If you make a cigar by hand, you're an artist. It's a dying art."

Today, about 600 people work in about a half dozen cigar factories, in a city very different from the one Martinez Ybor found. Tampa has skyscrapers, suburban sprawl and ambitious young people who do not wish to make cigars their life's work. Automation has replaced many workers. There may even be less of a demand for cigars because people are quitting smoking for fear of cancer.

The men and women who make cigars by hand, for the most part, are elderly Cubans, Spanish and Italians who have known no other life and who barely speak the English language. A few are older than Carmela. Every year, a few more die and with them goes another piece of Florida history.

It will be a while before Carmela Varsalona is finished with cigars, though. She looks younger than her age. She wears a pretty green flowered dress and earrings. Her hair is full and dark with little gray. Her hands are graceful and steady. On a good day, she can turn out 500 cigars.

When she is not making cigars at the factory, she can be found making them for relatives who have tobacco or smoke shops. Once a week she works for a nephew who has a smoke shop at Tampa International Airport. On Fridays, she rolls cigars for her grandson at a tobacco shop in a Tampa hotel.

Her grandson, Jim Tyre, has installed a cigarmaker's desk next to a window in his store. He has secured a license which, in essence, declares his little store a cigar factory. Passers-by stop and look through the window at Carmela Varsalona, who glances up and smiles, greets them in Italian and then returns to her cigars.

"I can make a whole cigar," she says. "When I was a girl, my father said, 'Learn how to make the whole cigar and you'll never have to worry about being laid off.' I can do that. Most people, they can't. There is a lot that goes into making a cigar, and most people only learn how to do just one part."

Her father made cigars and her mother made cigars, and when she was old enough, she was expected to make cigars as well. She quit school and went to work at her mother's elbow. Everything she learned, she says she learned from her mother, Maria.

"It took a year to learn how to make a fine cigar," Carmela says. "One day, my father come by and say to me, 'You make a good cigar now. Now you have to make them faster.' The more you make, the more you get paid."

Most cigarmakers earn about four cents for every cigar. In a good week, Carmela makes about $80. She won't accept money from her grandson or nephew. She won't take money from family.

"If you make cigars, you do it because you like it."

People tell her that her cigars taste very good. She wouldn't know. She has never smoked one. "I don't even like cigarette smoke. They say you can get cancer. I'll make them but never smoke them."

From the desk drawer she removes a clump of Cuban tobacco, grown in the Dominican Republic, and shapes it into a greenish cylinder. She places it in a press that shapes it into a crude cigar. She takes a tobacco leaf – the Rare Corojo leaf she tells her grandson to buy – and wraps it tightly around the crude cigar. She applies tobacco paste here and there, until she is satisfied she has crafted a perfect cigar.

"Her cigars always have the same quality," says her grandson, who sells her cigars for $1.50 each. "They are wrapped tightly, which is what you want, yet they draw and burn evenly. It's a hard combination to get. I'm prejudiced, but I consider her a true master."

Carmela Varsalona smiles when she hears such praise. She says, "I make a cigar pretty. I can make them long and skinny or short and fat. I'm a nice cigarmaker. I been making them my whole life. Honey, it's all I know."

Chairmaker

LAKE WORTH   **12/9/87**

Robert James Rudd never considered himself an artist. To him, an artist was someone who painted you a pretty picture – not some Florida country boy building tables and chairs in a barn in the woods.

As usual, it was his wife Betty who told him straight. Of course, you're an artist, Robert James, she said. What else could you be?

You get up early, you drive 250 miles to North Florida, you put on snake boots, you wade into the swamp, you cut a bunch of cypress trees, you haul them back to the truck, you drive home, then you spend weeks creating furniture so beautiful it makes a body want to cry. And then you sell them for next to nothing.

"If that's not an artist," Betty Rudd said recently, "I don't know what is."

"Well, I don't know," Robert James said, and he wasn't being modest, that's just how he is. "Mama, I just don't know. I just know I like making these things as good as I can."

Robert James, who is 61, has been making furniture as good as he can in rural Palm Beach County since he was a little boy. His daddy made Florida furniture before him, and his granddaddy made furniture back in Georgia. If you were a Rudd, that's what you did.

Last year, through the Florida Department of State's Bureau of Florida Folklife, Robert James got a small grant to teach his 15-year-old grandson, Neil Brooks, to make cypress furniture, too. The grants go to folk artists who are passing on old traditions to younger persons. Some people will tell you that all this makes Robert James Rudd a piece of Florida history.

Years ago, many men used native woods to build furniture in Florida. Cypress, a tall stately tree that grows in southern swamps, was often the material of choice. It was hard and durable but pliable enough to work without sophisticated tools. And when it was cut properly, it grew back like a giant weed. Cypress was the perfect renewable resource.

Florida's building boom changed everything. Swamps, considered the breeding grounds for mosquitoes, were drained to eliminate malaria and to provide new land for homes. Other swamps went dry as nearby development sucked water from the ground.

There are fewer cypress trees than in the past, so there are fewer people building cypress furniture. There also are factories that can turn out hundreds of pieces of high-profit low-cost furniture in a day. Working alone from dawn until dusk in a drafty barn next to his house, Rudd can build a single piece in a day. He isn't a starving artist, but he won't vacation in Hawaii next summer either.

"There's no money in this," Robert James said. When he was younger, in fact, he had to work long spells as a carpenter to support his wife and five children. Then, when he caught up, he'd return to his furniture.

"I don't know if my grandson will be able to do this or not," he said. "He'll have to make a living somehow."

Rudd manages to eke out a modest living now that his children are grown and the house is paid for. Ironically, the development that has diminished the number of cypress trees has helped his business.

Once, traffic on nearby Lake Worth Road near the Florida Turnpike consisted mostly of rusty produce trucks roaring through the Everglades. Now the highway is filled with shiny station wagons and vans heading for new subdivisions.

Travelers see his *Rudd Twigs* sign and they see the totem pole he carved and they stop to buy and to place orders. Others who stop have seen his picture in the paper, or discovered him on a TV news feature, or heard about him through their children who are occasionally bused to Rudd's on school field trips. Busier now than he ever was, Rudd is three months behind on his orders.

"I wish he wouldn't do custom work at all," says 60-year-old Betty Rudd, as talkative as her husband is quiet.

"They don't appreciate what he does. They don't appreciate the medium he works with. He's using sticks that are green and wet and bent. It's not going to look like the furniture you buy in the store. But he'll work and work to satisfy them with special orders. I wish he'd just build basic furniture and put it out and let them take it or leave it."

"I don't want people to have a piece of furniture if they're not perfectly satisfied with it," said her husband, relaxing in a cypress chair. "I'd rather give them their money back."

They met when she was in third grade. She thought he was mean. No lady's man, Robert James began what turned out to be a courtship by trashing her playhouse. He calmed down enough to marry her in 1946.

He began learning the furniture trade at age 10 when his daddy made him go into the swamp to help cut cypress. The swamp, in Boynton Beach, is now a landfill. When Robert James wants cypress today, he has to drive.

He leases land from a North Florida timber company that usually bulldozes cypress to get to the more profitable pine. Rudd pays the company to let him take care of the cypress. He's careful with his cuts. Some of the stumps he'll leave this year will sprout new growth next year. Cypress can be farmed.

He and Betty and their grandson go on cypress trips in a Ford panel truck every six weeks. Rudd carries two chain saws, stoves, lanterns and camping equipment. He doesn't leave until he's found what he needs.

"He'll walk for miles through hundreds and hundreds of trees just to pick out fifty or sixty trees that are small and straight enough for him," his wife said.

Then he cuts and drags them through the water to the trailer he pulls behind the truck. Sometimes, as he wades, he shoots venomous water moccasins that strike at him. Last time out, he was stung by wasps. He and Betty also saw six deer and two turkeys.

"The only way you can enjoy the woods now is if you got a job in them," Robert James said. "Otherwise, there's No Trespassing signs everywhere you look."

At home he dumps the logs in a one-and-a-half-acre yard filled with cypress shavings, an airboat used for frogging, a rusty car whose tires are hidden by weeds, a van supported by concrete blocks, a trailer nobody uses, and the house he built almost 20 years ago.

He cuts the logs into the small pieces he will need for furniture. He takes out one of his knives – he has many, including several owned by his late father – and removes the outer bark. Summer cypress is lighter in color than winter cypress. He doesn't know why. Both are beautiful.

"Cypress is a perfect wood," he said, standing outside a barn filled with cypress poles, a frog gig, saws, machinery, furniture, model airplanes, saddles, sling shots, bird feathers, deer antlers, a wild hog's jawbone, a worn-out felt hat, an ashtray full of cigar butts, and a dusty stereo on which he plays Conway Twitty tapes.

"Now your pine has got resin in it, and if you make furniture with it, it's always bleeding resin. Cypress is resin-free. It's hard, but it's soft enough to work with. I can bend it, which is the hard part of making furniture. And it don't crack! You can work it right close to the edge and it won't split.

"It holds up real good with no finish. You shouldn't varnish it or nothing! That would keep the wood from breathing. Just rubbing up against it with your body as you stand up and sit down is enough to give it a real nice shine."

Pretty soon now, and Robert James is unsure when, he is going to move from his rural Palm Beach County home. He and Betty used to talk about living there forever, but their plans have changed.

Somebody stole a totem pole from their yard. Somebody snuck onto their property when they were away and caught the big bass out of their pond. The sheriff found auto thieves stripping stolen cars in the pasture behind their property.

A nursing home is planned for behind their acreage. Next to the nursing home will be a subdivision. The cypress trees behind their house died a long time ago for want of water. Every time Robert James goes on one of his cypress trips he discovers a new shopping center along the road.

"My husband never leaves our property except to get wood," Betty Rudd said. "He even has things like nails delivered. In a way, he's kind of like a hermit. We have to get away from this place. It's not the same anymore."

"I need to be closer to my wood," Robert James said. "There's some good wood left in Florida. But it's a long, long way away from here."

The dark skies of Billy Dodd

The mosquitoes hover over Billy Dodd like Martian spacecraft poised for an invasion of the Earth. Billy ignores them. A barred owl hoots in the woods. Billy ignores bird calls. He stands in the darkness and stares through his giant telescope at outer space.

He concentrates on Jupiter, the largest planet in the solar system. "All right," he says when he focuses the telescope. His scope, about six feet long and as big around as a cannon, reveals four moons, some cloud bands and the red spot, a giant storm that perpetually circles Jupiter's surface.

"You don't always see the red spot," he says with satisfaction.

Next he studies a nebula and peeks at a star cluster. He peers at a galaxy. At midnight, when other astronomers near Billy search through their powerful telescopes for Halley's Comet, invisible to the naked eye, Billy does not look.

He saw the famous comet, which orbits near the earth about every 75 years, the other night. He describes it as a disappointing sight, as small as a pencil eraser smudge on paper.

"It was nothing," he says. "Everybody's in a big hoodoo about Halley's Comet. They're expecting a big barn burner like in 1910. Well, it ain't gonna happen."

This year the orbits of earth and comet are farther apart, which means the comet will be smaller and dimmer. And during its brightest phase next spring, he complains, the comet may still be invisible to earthlings in big cities where lights wash out the skies.

"Light pollution," Billy mutters.

A man can't set up his telescope in his own backyard anymore, if he lives in West Central Florida's crowded Pinellas County, as Billy does, and expect to see diddly squat. And if you want to take color pictures through your scope, as Billy does, forget it.

For Billy, too much light means time and trouble. About eight times a month, when the moon is missing from the night, or dim enough to please him, he takes a road trip to find dark skies. He packs his van with sodas, his TV, his radio, his portable toilet, his maps of the sky, his tools, his $5,000 worth of astronomy cameras, his $15,000 worth of telescopes and drives about 75 miles.

Ninety minutes later he leaves the interstate, whips around a sharp curve, drives for a while on a two-lane country road that is as potholed as a moon crater, and finally bounces into Hickory Hill. Then, standing in an old orange grove, at peace under dark skies, Billy studies his universe.

Billy Dodd has worked as a baker for 22 years. At age 43, he is plump as Pillsbury Doughboy. He has black hair, a jutting jaw and the pale skin of a man whose job and hobby preclude much daylight activities. From 3:00 a.m to 11:00 a.m., he bakes rolls and cakes at a supermarket in St. Petersburg. When he puts away apron and rolling pin, his head turns to the stars.

"Billy is the most advanced amateur astronomer in this area of the state," says St. Petersburg's Ronnie Beck, who sells telescopes. "His photography is way beyond a lot of what you see in the magazines. We have a lot of people on this coast who are very advanced, but when they have questions they call Billy."

Though he remembers barely getting through high school, Billy's knowledge of astronomy, his technical know-how, his ability to take difficult pictures of faint objects through his telescope and his well-known eccentricities have given him almost legendary status among Florida astronomers.

"There are all kinds of astronomers," says Beck. "And then there's Billy."

Billy is different. It starts with his name. No one calls him Mister Dodd or plain Dodd or Bill. It's Billy, even in the phone book. In his wallet, where other people might display family photographs, he carries favorite snapshots he has taken of galaxies, star clusters and planetary nebula. He has trained himself to sleep in two-hour snatches to have more time for stars, and he doesn't mind slapping himself on the face to keep awake while driving home. His dedication to his hobby is so great he once spent Christmas Eve alone stargazing on Hickory Hill.

"It was my wife's idea," he says. "It was a Christmas present."

He has been married to Alice, a supermarket meat packer, since 1961. They have three sons, a nice two-story house in Largo and a $15,000 swimming pool that Billy had built for Alice as a tradeoff for his buying a $10,000 telescope.

"I don't use the house money for any of my hobbies," he explains to the curious who wonder how a baker can afford to be so extravagant. "When I want something, I take on extra baking jobs and photograph weddings and things."

Alice, whom Billy calls "Momma," would kill him if he snitched cookie jar money. Though they clearly love each other and next year will renew their marriage vows to celebrate their 25th anniversary, Billy and Alice don't always see eye-to-eye.

Yes, Alice may have given him Christmas Eve for a present, but it doesn't mean she understands her husband's strange passion. "I like to sleep," Alice says. "I can't understand why anybody would want to go out all night long and look at the stars when you could be asleep."

"Well, at least she knows where I am," Billy counters. "I'm not in some bar. I'm looking through my scope."

When not stargazing, he's likely to be attending three different astronomy club meetings or reading his photography and astronomy magazines. Every month he devours *Astronomy*, *Sky and Telescope*, *Deep Sky* and *Astro Graph* and stacks them on his bedside table. On the bedside table lamp, Alice has drawn a mark eight inches high. When Billy's magazines reach the mark, the magazines go.

"I pitch 'em," Alice says. "See, Billy saves everything. If I didn't pitch 'em, I'd have a house full of magazines."

Ralph Kramden, Jackie Gleason's Honeymooners character, might say, "To the moon, Alice!", but Billy knows he could be neater. Upstairs, in a spare bedroom, he has built a sophisticated darkroom stocked with a computer color photo enlarger, cameras and film. Pictures of stars and planets hang helter-skelter from the walls. Magazines are scattered like leaves. Alice calls Billy's darkroom The Pit.

"I won't go in there," she says.

Several times a year she encourages Billy to do the dirty work himself. Billy drags a couple of empty citrus crates upstairs and sadly sifts through his magazines. Last time he had a humdinger of a cleanup.

"I filled three crates," Billy says. "Paper is real heavy. Them magazines musta weighed two hundred pounds. I almost got a hernia."

Billy Dodd was born in southern Illinois and grew up on a farm with dark skies. "You'd lay in a haystack and look up," Billy says. "You couldn't help but be interested in the skies."

He remembers liking fishing, hunting and girls even more than stars. School interested him little. "I wasn't any good in science," he tells people who are sure he was a boy genius. At 17, he joined the Navy and served as a boiler tender on a ship.

"I was always working in some dark hole or another. It was nice when I could get out and stand on the fantail of the ship." Stars shone down from the dark skies like lasers.

Well, he met Alice in New Jersey, and when he was 18 and she 17 they married. He took her to live on the farm in Highland and got a job at the steel mill, and the babies started coming. Billy hated the steel mill and took up baking. He thought they'd have a better future near a big city, so he and Alice moved to Florida and crowded Pinellas County.

In 1975, a neighbor called and asked Billy to help set up a little telescope. Soon Billy was visiting the neighbor nightly to look at the stars. Alice, taking pity on her husband, bought him a telescope for Father's Day. Billy read everything he could on astronomy. He talked to professionals and experienced amateurs. He wasn't embarrassed to ask questions. He lived and breathed the subject.

Soon, the little telescope was insufficient for what Billy wanted to do. He bought a larger one. He eventually took on extra baking jobs and spent a couple grand on a scope with a lens 10 inches across. Then he started thumbing through catalogs and daydreaming about larger instruments. In 1983, he bought a top-of-the line telescope, the Cadillac of telescopes, for $10,000. It is the largest portable telescope available. The lens is 14 inches across and gathers light like a black hole. It can magnify images 900 times and weighs about 200 pounds.

"I'm just glad it don't eat," Billy says.

Billy bought the telescope to take pictures he could show Alice and the boys at the bakery. The Schmidt camera-telescope he also had bought was fine, but he wanted something bigger and better.

Billy has always enjoyed photographing the skies. Even sunsets appeal to him. One afternoon he rose from his nap and saw a dilly behind his house. He ran for his camera, then shinnied up his ham radio tower in back. The sight of Billy climbing the tower must have been a shock to Alice. Billy, who has eaten a doughnut or two, is not built for speed.

"Momma thought I'd gone loony on her," Billy says.

He got even more spectacular pictures of the stars with his big scope. It took practice. "I made every mistake that can be made," admits Billy, who has never tried to sell his astronomy photographs. "When people ask me questions, it's because I've made all the mistakes."

The other night, Billy sat in the back of the room while Ronnie Beck taught a telescope course at his St. Petersburg store. People asked questions, but mostly they watched color slides of the moon, planets and stars. Some slides were fine, but others were green instead of blue and loaded upside down or sideways in the projector. They were near impossible to identify.

"That's M13," Billy piped up from the back of the room. He recognized the star cluster from the constellation Hercules even if it were green and upside down. Later, he identified moon craters – by name.

Billy has never taught formally. He is not the professorial type. Sometimes, when he talks, sentences come out that might stun English teachers. But if people want to know how to set up a telescope or where to find a faint star cluster or how to take a picture of the Andromeda galaxy, Billy can and will tell them.

Astrophotography is an art not easily learned. For one, the exposures must be long because of the dim light. Two, everything in the sky is moving. If the telescopes fails to follow the star in perfect time, the picture is blurred.

"What I like about it is the challenge," Billy says. "I think if everybody took pictures, I wouldn't. I've never liked things that were too easy."

For some pictures, Billy learned to modify film so he could make even longer exposures. Billy freezes his film to 40 degrees below zero with dry ice contained in a special camera compartment. The cold film allows marathon exposures.

"It gets complicated."

Because of the difficulty, few amateurs bother. They are content to set up backyard telescopes and admire the moon and maybe Jupiter and then go inside to the television.

Billy seldom watches television, except for the weather radar on cable, which supplies him with the kind of technical information he needs to plan his evenings. If Billy spends 90 minutes on an exposure, he doesn't want a 3:00 a.m. cloud to spoil the image.

"Things can go wrong in a second," he says. "Most nights I'm lucky to get one decent picture."

Before he built a dark room, he let drug stores develop his negatives. Drug stores didn't know what to make of Billy's star photos.

"If you give them a picture of a boy and girl, they can handle it," Billy grumbles. "If you give them a picture of stars they'll give you a note explaining what went wrong with your picture."

The notes Billy received said: "Dust specks."

Billy Dodd likes getting to Hickory Hill before dark. The Hill, in farm and citrus country, offers Billy the dark skies he no longer gets in the city.

He loathes the city's sodium vapor street lamps because they give his backyard photographs a reddish tint and make it hard to find faint objects. Even worse are nights when the sheriff's department helicopter spotlight, searching for prowlers, finds Billy and his telescope instead.

Billy wants peaceful, dark skies. The St. Petersburg and Tampa astronomy clubs rent a farmhouse at Hickory Hill and a piece of land in the orange groves. Billy, often the first to arrive, unloads his trunks of equipment from the customized Ford van and gets busy. It takes 45 minutes to erect his big telescope and about that long to get a polar alignment on Polaris, the north star.

If the part of the tripod on which the telescope is mounted is not pointed at true north, about a degree away from Polaris, the scope can't track stars Billy photographs. The moving stars will ruin the picture.

Billy is never satisfied with even perfect polar alignment. Though his telescope should track perfectly, he doesn't trust it. He bends and squints through the eyepiece for the hour or two he photographs. Should the worst happen and a star stray, he can push a button to keep it centered in his telescope.

Next to his scope is a table holding suitcases containing $1,500 worth of eyepieces, $500 worth of astronomy books and his trusty *Atlas of the Heavens*. The maps give coordinates of stars and enable him to find the faintest objects. Billy's atlas, about 10 years old, is stained with insect corpses and coffee.

During cold weather, insects are no problem. Billy likes cold because skies are usually clear and crisp. The Christmas Eve Alice gave Billy for Christmas was the best night of his career.

It was 20 degrees, with ice in the grass, on his windshield and on parts of his telescope. Images were so steady in the dry atmosphere Billy hardly felt the cold. Of course, he was wearing the longjohns, jacket and thick socks he keeps in the van.

"You've got to be prepared."

On this late night, he is prepared for everything but the damp and heavy air. "The atmosphere is boiling," is how Billy explains it. The other dozen or so astronomers also grumble. Billy still picks out favorite galaxies, star clusters and the space gas called nebula and helps people with their telescopes and photography, but he doesn't bother taking pictures himself.

The night is not good enough for Billy. Too many scattered clouds. Too much unsteady air. He never even has to make his speech to Hickory Hill rookies. When he plans a photo session, he doesn't tolerate car headlights. They ruin photographs. If somebody wants to leave, Billy warns, please leave before we start making pictures.

"As long as people live by the code, there's no problem," he explains reasonably.

People do cause problems. For one, they need more and more room in the cities. Next thing you know, houses and shopping centers and wretched lights are going up, and dark skies are ruined.

It has already happened in Pinellas, the state's most densely populated county, where skies are tainted with red glow and Billy has to live. And Citrus and Hernando, 90 minutes north, near Hickory Hill, are among Florida's fastest-growing counties and may be next. What will happen to Hickory Hill when condos spring up along the interstate and those sodium vapor street lights Billy hates are installed? What will he do then?

Well, he already has been scouting the state for dark skies. He's got things pretty well figured. Alice may take early retirement in a year or so, and Billy knows a baker can find work just about anywhere. His eye is on remote country between the South Florida cities of LaBelle and Clewiston. Or maybe Chiefland up there by the Suwannee River.

Out there in the swamp, or by the river, there's nothing but alligators and mosquitoes.

The dark skies go on forever.

In 1990, I visited Billy at his new Suwannee River ranch about 20 miles from the northwest Florida town of Chiefland. He had built a small observatory, and the stars shone down on us like lasers.

Flamingos

"I Need Money!"

The disheveled woman holding the sign stared into the eyes of passing motorists, who pretended she was not there. It was Sunday morning outside the gates of South Florida's strangest paradise, where the realities of modern urban life clash with the surreal mixture of lushly tropical vegetation, old-world architecture – and hot-pink flamingos.

Hialeah Park, the state's oldest horse racing palace, is an island of green and pink in the middle of a solid blue-collar city, around the corner from package stores, button factories and widget shops with bars on the windows and razor wire on top of the back fence. It's the beauty meeting the beast, a metaphor in some ways for Florida. It has those spectacular flamingos, of all things, flamingos which for some people symbolize a sub-tropical world that no longer exists.

"Not a day goes by when I don't watch the flamingos through my binoculars," said Dennis Testa, the superintendent of the 220-acre park. Testa has watched, worried and cared for flamingos since he was seven years old. He grew up following around his father, Angelo, the superintendent before him. The Testas were, and are, responsible for maintaining the beautiful grounds and the flamingos.

Dennis Testa, 40, is a practical man whose college background is in geology, architecture and engineering. Though he is in the pari-mutuel business – a business some people might regard as crass and cold-hearted – he is also considered an authority on what may be the planet's most otherworldly flamboyant creature, the flamingo. Nothing is ever what it seems at Hialeah Park.

"It is a circus, a fashion show, an entertainment with the prospect of profit," wrote John Crittenden in his elegant history of the place, "a sorority and a fraternity, a celebration, a horse show, an escape, a sporting event with the emphasis on event, a Camelot with betting windows, a confection, an island of architectural and horticultural permanence in South Florida's landscape of change."

It's Alice in Wonderland country, in other words, a dream world where the sight of a stout cigar-smoking gambler just might metamorphose after the seventh race into a blinding flock of pink flamingos. Even Alice used a flamingo for a croquet mallet.

In 1931, six years after the park opened, flamingos were brought here from Cuba and released. By the next morning, all 14 birds were gone. The wings of the next batch were clipped. The new flamingos stayed put. When they first reproduced in 1937, Smithsonian officials dashed down from Washington to help celebrate.

Today, not a wing is clipped nor feather pulled. The flamingos, for the most part, consider the 12-acre infield lake at Hialeah Park their home. Last time Dennis Testa counted, he counted 705 flamingos. Hialeah has more than any zoological park in the world. In fact, Hialeah lends flamingos to zoos.

Testa is invited to ornithological gatherings to talk about flamingos. Most zoos find it almost impossible to get flamingos to reproduce in captivity. At Hialeah Park, love is in the air every spring. Even now male flamingos are beginning to court at lakeside. They are bobbing their ridiculously long necks seductively. With pink and black wings held wide, they are showing off by strolling about on stilt-like legs. In short, they're strutting like big-time studs.

"They kind of remind me of the bachelors who stand around at wedding receptions waiting to catch the bridal bouquet," Testa said.

So it goes at Hialeah Park. As horses gallop around the track, as gamblers cheer and wail and curse and tear up betting slips, as vendors sell beer and hard liquor, as an ambulance helicopter whirs across the sky toward a distant hospital, flamingos in paradise dream of reproducing their species.

Greater flamingos probably have never reproduced in the Florida wilds. But they do in the Yucatan, off Venezuela and in the Southern Bahamas. During the last century, though, flamingos by the thousands regularly visited the southern tip of the state.

Today, flamingos are a rarity in the Florida wilds, though lucky birders occasionally discover a few in Everglades National Park. Last year, a few eagle-eyed naturalists even saw one in Tampa Bay. Ornithologists say those flamingos either flew over from the Bahamas or are escapees from zoos or Hialeah Park.

"I'm convinced those flamingos come from Hialeah Park," said Sandy Sprunt, a National Audubon vice president who works in the Florida Keys. "Flamingos often fly at night. So they wouldn't be noticed."

"It's possible we lose a few," said Dennis Testa. At Hialeah Park, flamingos aren't tagged or banded. On weekends during the two-month racing season flamingos are flushed from their lakeside habitat after the seventh race. They take to the air, circle the track and awe spectators. One or two might even forget to come down.

"I've seen them go so high you could hardly see them," Testa said. "They're free of flight, so I can't say they never leave here."

After the racing season, Hialeah Park remains open to the public. It's an Audubon Society-approved bird sanctuary. Ten Canada geese arrived here recently and stayed. There are also blue-winged teal, shoveler ducks and other migrant waterfowl. Once in a while, somebody sights an osprey fishing for catfish and bass in the lake. One very lucky spectator saw a bald eagle.

"If I was a bird, I'd stop here too," said Testa. "This is a beautiful place."

Hialeah Park was carved out of the Everglades during the great Florida boom of 1925. Soon the race track was considered among the most beautiful in the pari-mutuel world, with its French Mediterranean clubhouse, terraces, gardens, lakes and flamingos.

The park attracted beautiful and important people, too. Winston Churchill gambled here. So did presidents named Truman and Nixon. Every day during winter, a special train arrived here from Palm Beach, carrying Joseph Kennedy and cronies. The name "Vanderbilt" was familiar here.

Angelo Testa's job was to see that the park remained beautiful. He quit his New Jersey race track job and started work at Hialeah on January 20, 1959, at 3:00 p.m. Like his son Dennis, Angelo has a head for details.

Angelo, 71, still comes to the park every day to help Dennis. They talk to each other constantly over short-wave radios. They finish each other's sentences as if they know what the other is thinking or is about to say. It's as strange as their park.

Angelo, like his son, knows every leaf, every blade of grass, every clump of clay, at Hialeah Park. He supervised the construction of the five-terraced dining room. He overhauled the beautiful paddock. He saw to it that the statue of Citation, the famous race horse, was perfect.

He dispatched trucks to Florida City to buy the royal palm trees that are everywhere at Hialeah now. The trees were so large only one could be trucked and planted a day. It took 100 days.

Dissatisfied with the clay of the race track, Angelo developed his own formula. Angelo's base was native marl. He mixed it with topsoil trucked in from remote sites. He grew soybeans in a corner of the park, ground them and added them to the topsoil and marl. The last ingredient was the ashes of more than 200 horseplayers who had requested an eternal resting place in paradise. The racing surface at Hialeah Park is the envy of the horse-racing world.

The welfare of flamingos was always on Angelo's mind. For years, he'd fed them a mixture of shrimp paste and boiled rice. Suddenly, the price of shrimp paste went sky high –"and that was if I could even find it!" He experimented and experimented and found a food the flamingos seemed to like even better. Every day they eat 192.86 pounds of high-protein dog chow, poultry feed, whole wheat, cracked corn and the vitamin beta carotene.

Angelo was also considered the Dr. Ruth of the flamingo world. In 1971, when Hialeah's usual winter racing dates were moved to spring – flamingo mating season – the timid birds were so disconcerted they lost interest in sex. Within a few years, their population dropped in half to about 300. Angelo worried himself sick.

He talked to experts. He talked to more experts. To jog flamingo memories of sex, he built the volcano-like flamingo nests. He used plaster of paris and one of his wife's stocking containers to build artificial eggs. The flamingos were unimpressed. And then the drought hit, the worst drought in Florida history. Anyway, Hialeah flamingos stayed celibate for nine years.

"Then one day I was up in the press box," Angelo said. "And we got a little shower. The flamingos started strutting around like they do when they're going to mate. But they stopped when the rain stopped. That gave me an idea."

He draped hoses from the palms. The fine mist simulated rain. Flamingos began mating again. Eggs hatched. Dennis Testa bought cigars and passed them out. Last spring, almost 100 flamingos were hatched.

"This was such a wonderful place to grow up," said Dennis Testa. He was walking around the track. Everywhere he looked he saw an old memory. Not far from the grandstand is a banyan tree that bears his carved initials and those of a girl named Maggie. The teen-age Dennis was in love with her.

When he was a boy, he buried a box of horseshoes and coins in a pile of clay. He looks for the box every year without success. He still likes driving heavy equipment. When he was a teen-ager, he'd hop onto unattended tractors and speed away from the workers.

When he was a boy, he'd stand behind the infield tote board – the scoreboard that provides gambling details – and fish for bass. Sometimes he and other employees would sit inside the tote board and eat fried bass during races. Then he'd peek through a hole in the tote board and watch the horses and the gamblers.

"Look," he said. "The hole is still here."

He grew up watching flamingos. "They're as good as watchdogs," he said. He could always tell if a raccoon or stray dog had invaded the park. The flamingos would raise a ruckus. One night, when he heard the honking, he found a hungry alligator. Without hesitation he killed it with a .22. When law authorities arrived to arrest him, his father took the blame. The charges eventually were dropped. But the Testas were willing to do anything to protect flamingos.

They still are. In 1983, Dennis Testa and the bird curator of Miami Metrozoo formed the Hialeah Park Flamingo Consortium. The consortium, with the blessing of the federal government, loans flamingos to zoos all over the world with the understanding that those flamingos, and half of their chicks, could be recalled should disaster ever befall Hialeah's flock.

"My father always said not to put all my eggs in one basket," said Dennis, who remembers the decade when flamingos stopped mating. Anything, he knows, could happen.

The same could be said, in general, about Hialeah Park. Although the race track is as beautiful as ever, the community outside has changed a great deal. No longer a small town, Hialeah has 200,000 people. For most of them, English is a second language. Cubans, according to conventional wisdom here, prefer to gamble at Jai-Alai and dogs. They are irregular patrons at Hialeah.

So are some of the wealthy people who once flocked here every winter. The train no longer runs from Palm Beach. Some well-to-do folks, frankly, are afraid to come to this section of Hialeah, with its barbed wire, barred windows and working-class citizenry. Two years ago, the park actually closed for lack of business.

But it reopened in November. More than 30,000 customers filed in. It was the largest opening-day crowd in 45 years. Even the flamingos were taken by surprise. Many failed to go airborne when they were flushed, by tradition, after the seventh race. They were out of condition.

They are as strong as ever now.

After the seventh race the other day, Hialeah flamingo flusher Dinonisio Campo did his job. He climbed into the little skiff behind the tote board and rowed across the lake toward flamingo island.

Suddenly, all flamingo heads swiveled toward him. The birds hopped around nervously. They honked. Then they took to the air.

In the late afternoon sun, 705 flamingos turned the sky pink. Following the race course below, they climbed. They climbed 50 feet, 100 feet, 200 feet. They broke off into smaller flocks. They climbed even higher, over Hialeah Park, over the industrial neighborhood, over the crowded roads.

Pink, wonderful, flamingos.

"Hey, Vasquez!"

Down on Earth, just before the eighth race, an unhappy bettor was screaming at a passing jockey. "You're a crook. When are you blankety-blank going to retire?"

Vasquez ignored the railbird. So did the flamingos. They remained airborne for another five minutes. A few bettors even watched them.

A man and his mules

GLENNELL   12/12/90

A man and his mules can go a far piece in this life.

Jim Carris and his mules – his wonderful mules – have traveled thousands of miles over the years. He has carried them to equine shows all over the country and won trophies and ribbons. He has worked a plow behind mules and even lassoed cows from them. When he took part in Wyoming's centennial celebration, mules hauled his chuck wagon across the state.

"Now some people go drinkin' and some people chase wimmin," Carris was explaining one morning as his three mules, Homer, Gomer and Molly, listened intently. "Some people hunt and some people fish. Me, I like to get with mules."

Carris, a state livestock inspector who lives on a Hillsborough River ranch about an hour from Tampa, has yet to meet a mule he dislikes. Mules are his passion. He is active in two mule associations, raises mules, sells them, buys them back sometimes and brags a blue streak about them.

"People, they don't understand mules," said Carris, who started messing with mules as a boy in Georgia. "They think mules is dumb. Mules ain't dumb. They got common sense. They won't do what's not right for them."

Carris, defender of mules everywhere, was warming to his favorite subject.

"I'll take a mule over a horse any day," he announced. "You turn a horse loose in a feed lot and he'll eat until he's bloated and sick. A horse'll drink until he's wallowin'. But a mule has sense. When a mule is full, he stops eatin'. He drinks to satisfy his thirst. He won't make himself sick."

Carris, a burly fellow who would look naked without a cowboy hat and a cheekful of tobacco, looked around to see if anyone would disagree. Nobody did.

"A horse, he'll run right into a fence! A mule will stop and check out the fence. A horse'll try to cross a river even if the water's too deep! A mule will look for the shallow spot. Sometimes a mule seems stubborn, but usually it's just their common sense. Mules is people, too."

A mule, actually, is not a people. A mule, technically, is the sterile hybrid child of a male donkey, or jackass, and a female horse. This is no science report, but mules lack the right number of chromosomes, those do-hickies within sex cells that have to be perfectly matched to make a life. Anyway, a mule ends up with half the characteristics of its parents. Heads and faces are usually donkeyish; from the neck down mules more or less resemble Ma.

But they don't act like Ma, that horse. As Carris would say: Shoot fire! No!

"The thing I like about a mule is that a mule can outwork a horse. They can't outrun a horse for short distances. But at the end of a workday, see who's still runnin', and it'll be a mule."

Mules have been around for 3,000 years, give or take a century, and nobody knows, for sure, how they came about. But they were a featured animal in the Old Testament, and Asian cultures depended on them for heavy labor. They played a prominent role in civilizing North America, especially the South, where they hauled timber and plows. They towed families in wagons across western prairies. In war, they hauled cannons and ammunition.

Hard-core mule men get misty-eyed thinking about the 20-mule teams that towed tons of borax across Death Valley during the last century. Borax wagons weighed four tons, held 36 tons, and carried cargo 165 miles through the closest place to hell on Earth. So listen: Don't talk to a mule man about horses. He'll laugh at you.

Last spring, Carris got a taste of what a mule can do under trying conditions. He joined a wagon train that traveled the prairies and mountains of Wyoming. A horse – somebody's else's horse – kicked him and broke his leg. But his mules, Homer and Gomer, performed magnificently. They pulled his wagon up and down those mountains, through bogs and swamps, and they never tired.

"You can start workin' a mule in the mornin' and he'll still be workin' at sundown," Jim Carris said. "A mule is a four-wheel drive vehicle on four legs."

Yet mules are in relatively short supply these days. Tractors and other modern machinery started displacing them about 40 years ago. Mules, for most people, became irrelevant.

The reputation of mules has suffered since. Some people, especially horse people, look down on mules. Others, believing all the stereotypes, think mules are stubborn or plain dumb.

"A mule looks kinda dumb, don't he?" Carris said. "Look at those big nostrils! Look at those big ears! But let me tell you. He's got big nostrils so he can breathe hard when he's workin'. And those big ears help keep him cool. Plus, a mule can hear a four-way conversation."

Carris' female mule, Molly, did seem to be listening to two different conversations. One ear was pointed at Carris and another at a stranger who carried a notebook. Molly looked nervous.

"That's another thing I like about a mule," Carris said. "They're a little suspicious of strangers. They'll look you in the eye – I like an animal that will look you in the eye! – and take your measure. Anyway, a mule won't come up on a stranger right off and get stolen like a horse will."

Carris was eight when he went mule crazy. He and his Uncle Aubrey drove the family pickup to a farm to get a mule with which they hoped to plow the family garden. The mule took its sweet time walking the 10 miles back to the Carris homestead. Uncle Aubrey was agitated, but his nephew was fascinated.

"He was an ornery mule, but he knew his mind, and I've loved mules since."

His mules are not run-of-the-mill animals. When Carris is in the market, he wants a mule whose jackass dad was smart and strong and whose mother was a big, beautiful but gentle Belgian mare. The result is a mule that has size, appearance, strength and intelligence. His mules weigh more than 1,000 pounds, are easy on the eyes and more or less obedient. They're worth about as much as a compact pickup truck – about five grand.

Though mule competitions and mule-men meetings have yet to show up on ESPN, the mule circuit is a busy one. The American Donkey and Mule Society, headquartered near Dallas, boasts more than 2,000 members. The Florida Draft Horse, Pony and Mule Association is smaller, but it sponsors competitions throughout the state. So do the Florida Whips.

At equine shows, Carris and his mules compete against other people and their mules – and sometimes against other people and their horses. His mules have whipped horses. His mules can jump a fence. They can trot in a perfect figure eight. They can do about anything a judge would like. Carris has owned national and world champions, and he has the trophies to prove it.

"I love going to shows so I can aggravate horse people."

Sometimes he is the one aggravated. For some folks, mules are a curiosity, like a Model-T Ford. People confront him at equine shows and tell him about the mules their families owned – stupid, stubborn mules that only beatings would motivate. Carris winces at the thought of abused mules.

"The only bad mules is ones that get beat," Carris said. "And anybody who'd beat a mule is the dumb one. A mule demands your respect. It can also kick you over a pine tree."

Carris and his wife Katie never had children, so Carris treats his mules as if they were his offspring. He keeps them in a large piece of fenced-in woods near Hillsborough River. They don't have to plow. They don't have to haul borax through a desert. They run free, more or less, and seem to enjoy their independence. They also keep Carris on his cowboy-boot toes.

"I'm going to catch them right now," he said, walking through the gate. "But the trick with mules is you can't let them know you're fixin' to catch them. They'll sense it, and they won't let you. You have to ease up on them."

Carris walked nonchalantly through the woods toward his mules. They nonchalantly walked the exact amount of feet away from him.

"That's what I like about mules," Carris yelled from a distance. "Smart."

He took out his secret weapon: a pail of grain. His mules came to him, though the matter was in doubt until the end. They allowed Carris to put a halter on them. Then nuzzled him and seemed to delight in his touch.

Carris, eventually, reluctantly, removed their halters and told them "Git." Homer and Gomer galloped in a straight line to the front gate. They butted the gate with their heads. They bit at the lock.

Yes, mules can open gates. You think a horse can open a gate? Shoot fire! No.

The Bardin Booger

If you want to know about the Bardin Booger, Florida's Abominable Snowman, you need to stop and talk with Bud Key at his grocery.

Bud, who has lived in rural Putnam County for most of his six decades, collects Booger lore and legend. He has never seen the creature, which is supposed to be big and hairy, but he would like to believe it exists.

Before you can talk to Bud, though, and get the lowdown on the Booger, you first have to find his country grocery, which is not necessarily easy. Bardin, missing from most maps, is more or less stuck between Gainesville and Palatka on an unmarked road that cuts through a forest. You have to work a little.

Bud's is in the middle of deep woods where red-tailed hawks call from the trees, skunks lie squashed on the two-lane blacktop and speed limit signs have been blasted by buckshot. Bud's is just down the road from the three Baptist churches and the two spooky cemeteries that serve the 500 families sprinkled through the pines, oaks and cypress.

It's logging country as well as Booger country.

But if you've been paying attention, and if you've been lucky enough to notice the unmarked Bardin road, you'll eventually see Bud's up ahead, on the left, in an opening in the trees. There are gas pumps out front, trucks parked on one side, and bales of hay on the other. Park your vehicle, walk past the sleeping dog at the door, and enter. At a back counter, next to the jars of pickled sausage, you'll find Bud slicing meat. Sure, he'll talk about the Booger.

"There are a lot of stories," he says, wiping his hands on a blue jumpsuit.

The Bardin Booger is six to eight feet tall, according to most accounts Bud has heard. Booger's footprints are 14 to 18 inches long and six to eight inches wide. He has long legs and walks upright like a human. He is as hairy as all get out. He stinks bad.

Bardin's version of the boogerman is sometimes seen near the graveyards, but he also favors the creeks that meander through the woods to the St. Johns River. Fox hunters, prowling the pines at night, report him from time to time. So do motorists who drive the remote roads. Known for a healthy appetite, the Booger is suspected of eating corn left out at night by farmers for their hogs.

In one infamous story, he picked up a truck with a hunter in it and shook it like a rag. In another, he drooled over a farmer's hunting dogs while they cowered in their kennel. Those two stories, which were reported in 1982 in the lively supermarket tabloid, the *Weekly World News*, under the headline "We Live With Bigfoot," were

37

apparently all wrong. So wrong that two Bardin Booger spotters quoted by the *Weekly World News* no longer talk to the media.

But there are many who do.

"It kind of looked like a big monkey," says Jackie Cone, a carpenter who has lived in Bardin for all of his 43 years. Five years ago he had his close encounter with what he is sure was the Bardin Booger. "A bunch of us were driving around in a truck one night. Down there, just past the church house by Bud's, we saw a Booger. He went right across the road into the creek."

Steve Wilkinson, a baby-faced 18-year-old mechanic at Bud's, was the last person to report the Bardin Booger. Last June, he and his uncle were driving Bardin Road about 10:00 p.m. Sure enough, the Booger hotfooted it across the highway.

"I speeded up," Wilkinson says earnestly, "and got a pretty good look. Well, he looked like a hairy gorilla. My uncle wanted to get out and shoot him, but I said 'Leave him be! Stay put!' I was scared. The Booger stepped over a fence like it was nothing and walked into the woods. Long legs."

The Bardin Booger has been around a long time. Bud Key, born in 1928, heard tales about the Booger when he was a boy. "And it had been around for a long time before me," he'll tell you. "When I was coming up, I was always scared to go in the woods. One time, I thought I saw him through the screen door. But my daddy convinced me it was just leaves moving."

Bardin is the kind of place that feeds the imagination. It seems a million miles from what most people would call "civilized Florida." There are no malls, no apartment complexes, no beauty parlors, no bookstores. Just woods, river marshes, little houses with tin roofs, small wood churches, mobile homes, graveyards and a gun shop.

And lots of animals. Hunters delight in the deer, turkey and squirrel. Every pickup truck comes complete with a gun rack. Bears keep things interesting for the beekeepers in the area. And when night comes, and the moon rises, and the wind starts rattling the trees, some people claim to see and hear critters that aren't on any game lists.

In that, Bardin's Booger-watchers are no different from other Floridians. Monsters have been reported all over the state for years. In 1942, a man driving a dirt road near the Suwannee River claimed a giant ape jumped onto his car's running board and stayed there, staring into the window, for half a mile. A few years later, a Manatee County commercial fisher swore he had a tug-of-war with an apelike creature over a net full of mullet near Tampa Bay.

In 1948, huge tracks were found on Clearwater Beach. During the next two decades they were discovered on beaches from Tampa Bay to the Suwannee River. Alas, the Clearwater Monster was eventually uncovered as a fraud. A prankster had been hiking beaches wearing giant footware.

In 1971, Hernando County, an hour north from Tampa, had ape problems with no practical jokers in sight. A rancher reported that an eight-foot hairy animal terrorized his horses. A St. Petersburg man, the late Gordon Prescott, formed an organization known as the "Yeti Research Society" and went to investigate. Prescott announced that the creature almost certainly had to be the "missing link" between monkey and *Homo sapiens*. He even estimated that Florida had at least 100 ape-men.

South Florida, meanwhile, was also an ape-man paradise. There, the creature was known as the Skunk Ape because of its alleged body odor.

In 1971, the Skunk Ape made national headlines when a woman living on the edge of the Everglades said some kind of weird gorilla peeped into her window. A police search failed to turn up the five-foot tall visitor, though an animal control officer discovered strange footprints that measured about 12 inches long.

In 1974, a near-hysterical motorist driving a remote Everglades road late at night reported hitting an eight-foot tall creature. Police, who used a searchlight-equipped helicopter in their hunt, found nothing. An hour later, five miles away, another motorist called the police about a huge, two-legged animal that limped across the road into the trees. It too eluded the law officers.

Florida has a number of large predators, including black bears and panthers. The panther is the state's rarest and most elusive animal. A panther may weigh 150 pounds, is light brown in color, has a long, graceful tail and walks on all fours like all cats. Black bears may weigh as much as 600 pounds and typically walk on all fours. When they occasionally stand on hind legs, they might measure seven feet and be mistaken for a Booger.

"I don't know what to think of the reports," says Don Wood, endangered species specialist for the Florida Game and Fresh Water Fish Commission. "We've never really investigated, though I've got a little file on Yetis, Skunk Apes, whatever you want to call them. One time somebody sent us some hair that was supposedly from a skunk ape. But it turned out to be Spanish moss."

Bardin has been a hotbed of stories throughout the 1980s. A farmer named Randy Medlock was the source for many. An avid fox hunter, he spent most of his nights in the woods, and one night saw something that gave him the creeps. At first, he said nothing about it, because he was afraid people would doubt him. But the cousin who was with him had loose lips, and word got out. The Associated Press found Medlock.

"This thing came out of the woods," The Associated Press quoted him as saying. "It was big and hairy and looked like a bear, but it had a pug nose and walked upright, like a man. The way it walks, a bear couldn't walk like that. Its arms were swinging, just the way you and I walk. It walked across about thirty feet in front of the car. We were on a big sand hill. It looked sideways at us and kept walking. I knew it was strong because when it walked back into the woods, it just slapped these pine saplings out of its way like they were nothing."

Medlock said he got out of his truck and looked at the tracks. They were larger than his size 13 feet.

The supermarket tabloids, when they found out about Medlock, had a field day with the unfortunate farmer, who says he was badly misquoted in their bigfoot stories. If you call Medlock now, his wife answers, and she will not even summon her husband to the phone. "He doesn't talk about Boogers anymore," she says.

But over at Bud Key's grocery, the Bardin Booger is alive and thriving. Bud, a white-haired man who is the honorary mayor, keeps a scrapbook of clippings about Booger comings and goings. He has a drawing of the Bardin Booger in his front window. The Bardin Booger caps and T-shirts he sells go almost as fast as his pickled eggs, beef jerky and chain saws. He can hardly keep them in stock.

"I like the Bardin Booger," he says. "I've never seen him, but he's good for my business."

Somebody is always showing up looking for the Booger, and Bud does his best to accommodate. While he can't guarantee a Booger sighting, he can direct an interested party to a known Booger-infested area. And he can make the introductions to the lucky few who have seen a Booger and lived to tell about it.

CBS showed up at Bud's a few years ago, shot some footage in the woods and made a three-minute Booger documentary it broadcast in between Saturday morning cartoons. Seven years ago, Palatka's Billy Crain came over to Bud's and wrote, produced and sang a country record about the Booger.

Turned out there was a market for Booger Music: Crain has sold more than 6,000 copies so far. "Hey, Mr. Bardin Booger, Bardin is your home and every day you love to roam," Crain croons. "You run through the bushes and you run through the trees. Hey, Mr. Bardin Booger, don't get me, please."

The Booger has never harmed a hair on a single head.

"I was scared when I saw him," says Steve Wilkinson, Bud's mechanic, who had his moment with the Booger last June. "But I don't think he's dangerous."

A few nights after he saw his Booger cross the road, Wilkinson loaded his hog feeder with corn and went to bed. In the morning, the corn was gone. But the ground was covered with great big Booger tracks.

"My daddy and I talked about shooting him," Wilkinson says. "But we didn't know if that would be against the law or not. Finally, we just decided to let him roam these woods.

"He's out there now."

Spirits in the night

"...whatever walked there, walked alone."
— Shirley Jackson, *The Haunting of the House on the Hill.*

ROCKLEDGE   **10/29/86**

There must be a logical reason for what happens at Ashley's Cafe and Lounge. At least that's what everybody says – during the day. Why, there are no such things as ghosts. It must be a draft that opens and closes doors. Maybe it's vibrations from passing trains that make things move around. It's just a quirk in the electrical system that makes lights and appliances go on and off on their own. People just let their imaginations get the best of them.

"Down at the bowling alley, people always ask me if my restaurant is haunted," says Greg Parker, 30, who with his wife Susan bought Ashley's last year. "What am I going to say? Yes, it's haunted? And yes, I'm a fruitcake? I'm not a believer in ghosts."

Then the sun goes down, and the 56-year-old restaurant near Cocoa and Cape Canaveral grows dark. The floors creak. The mirrors in the restroom play funny tricks. A train does shake the whole building. Waitresses start looking at their watches and over their shoulders. Suddenly, people are less sure about logical explanations.

How do you explain jars that fly off a shelf on their own? Strange whisperings? An exhaust fan that turns itself on? A cash register that spews receipts around the bar in the middle of the night? All by itself? Glasses that crumple in customers' hands? The feeling that somebody is standing next to you when no one is there? A woman who supposedly materializes in the ladies' room?

"To be honest I believe the place is haunted," says Scott Faucher over the telephone. Faucher, 36, owned Ashley's before Greg Parker bought it. Now he sells real estate in New York. He says he sells real estate because running a restaurant took too much time away from his family. He says he didn't sell the restaurant because of the incident on top of the stairs.

"I was up there late at night. God, this sounds crazy now. All of a sudden a gust of wind went past me, as if somebody had whizzed by me real close. The windows were closed, so there was no wind. The air conditioners were thirty feet away, so you couldn't feel them. I was alone. Nobody was there but me. It was the most overpowering experience."

Ashley's is Florida's most famous haunt. In 1982, the *Florida Today* newspaper did a story about the restaurant and published what the author says was probably

41

a picture of a ghost. Sure enough, the *National Enquirer* was next, publishing the same photo and running a story of its own. Last month, Contemporary Books published Arthur Myers' *The Ghostly Register*. The book features a chapter on Ashley's.

Much of Ashley's chapter is based on the reporting of *Florida Today's* Billy Cox, who spent two months investigating the restaurant. He examined old records. He talked to police officers. He talked to customers. He talked to employees. He brought in two psychics.

There is no history of customers or employees being harmed. But Cox says, "Strange things do seem to happen."

One psychic described the alleged, unsolved murder of a young woman found on a riverbank in the 1930s. The psychic said the victim was stabbed in the restaurant's storage room, and haunts Ashley's today. The psychic told Cox about the ghost of a child, struck by a car on U.S. 1, who walks the restaurant.

During *Florida Today's* investigation, photographer Malcolm Denemark took hundreds of pictures. In one, he discovered a man who he says was not present when the photograph was taken. In the fuzzy black-and-white picture, reproduced in the Myers' book, the man is standing next to the salad bar. He cast no shadow in a picture that has plenty of shadows. Reporter Billy Cox insists the photo was not faked. He also admits he and Denemark sold the picture to the *Enquirer*.

"It was just a phenomenal photo," Cox says over the telephone.

Does he believe the restaurant is haunted?

"It's fun to think there are ghosts, but who really knows? I wanted to have an experience in there, but I never did, although there were a couple of times I felt the hair on my neck standing on end. But I think that was from the power of suggestion more than anything else.

"I did come away from the story thinking that it's nice to have mysteries in life. They keep life from getting boring."

The restaurant never has been boring. Since 1930 it has been owned by many people and had many names. Gentleman Jim's. The Loose Caboose. The Mad Duchess. The Sparrow Hawk. At times it has been a family restaurant; at times, a juke joint, where customers carried sharp knives and enjoyed using them.

In recent years, Ashley's has catered to families and young single people who enjoy meeting other single people on weekends. Fridays are big, and so are most Mondays, when football dominates the television over the bar.

Strange things continually happen. Once, not long ago, a woman suddenly stripped off her clothes at the bar on Saturday night and had to be taken away by police. On a recent occasion, a car skidded off U.S. 1 and crashed through the front door. Bartenders who say they blow out all candles at closing time sometimes find candles lit in the morning. For a while, they also found cash register receipts strewn around the bar.

"Twice when I owned the restaurant the police called me in the middle of the night," former owner Scout Faucher says. "They'd say, 'We're going into your restaurant. The lights are on and there's movement inside.' They'd go in with dogs. Nothing. Nothing stolen. Nobody there."

By contemporary standards, Ashley's is a mysterious-looking place. Across the street is a 7-11, a hospital and the usual fast-food stops. Ashley's architecture is English Tudor, built of wood, full of crazy angles. A flower box in front looks as if it's going to fall any second, but it was made that way.

Inside, Ashley's seats 115 people. It could be an antique store, with its aged wood banisters, tables and floors, and high ceilings. It is also very dark, especially at night, when lamps and candles cast long shadows.

Upstairs, there are tables and a small office and storage room. Restaurant employees avoid the storage room. They say they sometimes sense the presence of people who aren't really there. A waitress named Arlene once went up after closing and came down "white as a ghost," according to a current bartender, Ruthie Holtz. "She said a lady was sitting at the desk."

That's no surprise to waitress Marianne Menta. Two weeks ago she went into the room on a Friday night for an iced tea glass. As she stretched for the glass, she says she extended a leg behind her for balance. "I kicked somebody. You know when you've kicked somebody. I turned around to apologize. Nobody was there. That gave me a start."

Restaurant employees are also uneasy about the downstairs storage room, the place the psychic claimed was a murder scene. "I had one bartender who said the lights started flashing on and off in there one night," former owner Scott Faucher says. "When she walked over to investigate, the swinging doors kicked out at her. She didn't go in."

Next to the bar is the ladies room. Judy Cowles, who managed the restaurant between 1979 and 1984, says she was sitting in the ladies room when she noticed a pair of feet in the adjacent stall. The feet were adorned in high-heeled, high-button boots that had been unfashionable for half a century. Cowles left her stall and turned to admire the boots one last time. She says nobody was in the stall.

A cook named Jan says a similar thing happened to her this year. Like some people with ghostly experiences, Jan won't give her last name. "I'm embarrassed about this," she says. "People think you're crazy. But once I was in the ladies room and sitting in a stall. I heard all this rustling in the next stall. It was so loud, I made a wise-crack. There was no answer. I came out of my stall and looked at the other one. The door was closed and locked, but nobody was in there."

Two years ago, a customer ran screaming from the ladies room. She told former restaurant owner Scott Faucher that the toilet had exploded. Faucher says, "The toilet was in about seven pieces. She didn't look strong enough to kick apart a toilet. And she wasn't carrying a baseball bat."

Next to the bathroom is the kitchen. It could be any restaurant kitchen, with its stainless steel sinks, ovens, refrigerator and counters. There's nothing spooky about it at all. One morning a cook walked in to find about 100 bread baskets scattered on the floor. She had stacked them neatly the night before.

George Heppler, another cook, talks about the time a jar flew off the counter all by itself. "It didn't scare me," he says. "It was just weird. One of the things that happen here."

At lunch I eat a spinach salad and talk to Greg Parker, the current owner. In the last year he has spent about $10,000 on his restaurant. His goal is to make it more modern without changing it too much. He's been in the restaurant business for most of his life, but this is the first he's owned and he's nervous about it.

"It's a prime location," he says, "right on U.S.1. It's attractive. I think we have pretty good food. It should go over pretty well. Shouldn't it?"

He hasn't advertised his restaurant as a haunted house. "It would be pretty good publicity," he says. "I've thought about it." On Halloween, he has asked his employees to wear costumes.

"But I don't know about this ghost business," he says. "Like I say, I'm not a believer."

I ask if he's experienced anything unusual.

"Well, there was one thing. Me and this cook, Bob, were getting ready for lunch in the kitchen. Suddenly, the exhaust fans went on by themselves. There are two switches you have to throw. We were twenty feet from them. We didn't touch them.

"Like I say, I'm a logical person. There's got to be a logical explanation that we haven't discovered yet. If you want stories, talk to my bartenders. They're afraid to close up the place at night when they're alone. With their tip money they pay a guy to stay with them."

Dana Holtslander, 26, is daytime bartender today. She has worked at Ashley's for two years. She says the restaurant is haunted.

"Once I was in the ladies room combing my hair. In the mirror, I see the two doors to the ladies room open. I also notice nobody has come in. I say to myself, 'Okay. I'll just leave.' I go over to the door. It's a swinging door. Easiest thing in the world to open, okay? The door won't open. It feels like it's nailed shut. I go, 'Oooookay.' I take my hands off the door, then try again. This time it opens. Nobody's there.

"The other time was late at night. I had to go upstairs into that storage room by the office. There's a waitress station in there. There's glasses stacked on a shelf. I go in there and suddenly the glasses start clinking together. I don't mean vibrating like when the trains go by. There was no train. These were really clinking together.

"It was chilling, but, like, I'm not afraid of these ghosts. They've never hurt anybody. It's just weird. I'm only nervous at night. Are you coming back tonight?"

The moon is rising as I park outside of Ashley's. Traffic is already dwindling on U.S. 1. Inside, a waitress shows me to an upstairs table. With the dim hanging lights and the candles, it's so dark I fear I'll trip on the stairs. I eat a salad, baked potato and lobster.

The food is good and reasonably priced, but I'm one of the only customers seated on the second floor, and I'm nervous. I now understand about the power of suggestion. I almost expect something to happen.

Finished with supper I go downstairs and sit at the bar and talk to Kathy Aanderud. At 28, she is the night bartender. Married with a small child, she needs her part-time job. She says she didn't know about the restaurant's reputation when she got the job. If she had, she says she would have thought twice. Tonight, she's responsible for closing the restaurant. She is not looking forward to the chore.

"Who wants to close a haunted house by yourself?" she jokes.

I ask if she really believes the place is haunted.

"No," she says. "It's just strange. A lot of things happen. After a while, they mount up."

I ask what's happened to her.

"Nothing really. But the weirdest thing sometimes happens. I'll be pouring a drink and the glass will crumble in my hand. I don't mean break like if you dropped it. I mean crumble into a million pieces. That's happened to a lot of people, including customers.

"I know this sounds stupid – I haven't told anybody – but sometimes when the bar is really crowded, I'll hear my name called. Well, I turn because somebody must be calling my name for a drink. Nobody is. I hear my name called distinctly."

Tonight is slow. A big modern bar down the street is holding a party. A lot of Ashley's regulars are there watching Monday Night Football on the big-screen TV. The one or two loyal customers remaining drain their glasses and say goodnight.

"I hate closing," Kathy says.

Tonight Ted Innes will stay with her. He's the dishwasher bartenders pay to stay. He's tough. A tattoo on his right fist spells out H-A-R-D. L-U-C-K is on the other fist.

Ted says, "I'm not afraid. I've had a glass fall part in my hand, though. One time, when I was cleaning the sink, a lemon wedge shot out of the drain and hit me in the forehead. I was here when the jar flew across the room by itself. But I ain't never seen a ghost. The day I see a ghost, I'm gone."

Ghost talk makes Kathy nervous. At 2:00 a.m, she'll have to lock the front door, come back to the bar, and balance the cash register. Then she'll have to go upstairs, alone, and stash the money in the spooky office. Hustling down the stairs, knowing she must next go into the kitchen, she will try not to think of a cold, invisible hand touching her.

"I hate going into the kitchen more than anything else."

She will first make sure the outside kitchen door is locked, then turn out the lights. The 20 feet across the dark kitchen, she says, take forever. She tries to concentrate on the thin band of light spilling through the tiny kitchen window from the bar. She says if the ghosts in whom she does not believe ever get her, it will be in the kitchen.

With the kitchen door swinging thankfully shut behind her, and Ted watching, she steps into a dark alcove and opens the fuse box. That's how she turns out most of the restaurant lights. Removing a couple of fuses is less frightening than having to switch off dozens of individual lights in every room.

That leaves only the candles on the bar. Ted helps blow them out. One by one.

They stride purposely to the front door and hope nothing touches their ankles on the way. They shut the door behind them and step into the cool night air. She slides the key into the lock.

Click.

If something is left inside Ashley's, it now walks alone.

True grit

That Wes Biggs has managed to live to the advanced age of 42 should be filed under the category "miracle." Three times he has been bitten by rattlesnakes. He was so damaged by a stingray that he almost wanted to make the acquaintance of the grim reaper.

In any number of countries, Montezuma indeed enjoyed revenge on his digestive system. He fell off a cliff once, and on another occasion suffered altitude sickness in the Andes. He's been menaced by Marxist guerrillas in a Guatemalan jungle and he can tell you about the time he outran darts fired by blowgun-bearing Indians in the Amazon.

There was that unpleasant business in California, where Secret Service agents pointed guns at him and asked him to stay away from a president's vacation home. In Arizona, he had to be carried out of a sun-baked canyon after spraining his ankle. He only required knee surgery after tumbling down a Mexican pyramid.

Anything else?

Well, last spring he was shot by a suspected drug dealer in North Florida. The AK-47 slug came inches from blowing off his left arm.

So why is the Orlando resident laughing and joking? He is alive, that's why, and back in the woods, practicing what sounds like the world's most dangerous sport — birdwatching.

"It's really not dangerous," Biggs says, popping a grape into his mouth with his good hand. "And I don't consider myself accident prone. It's just when you spend enough time in the field, things happen to you."

Biggs, a Florida Audubon ornithologist and owner of a nature tour company, is what passes in birding circles for a living legend. He's famous for his ability, his enthusiasm, his yen for travel, his gift of gab, his knowledge of the esoteric, and, probably more than anything, his mishaps.

"If something is going to happen," says Florida Audubon vice president Herbert Kale III, "it's going to happen to Wes."

Biggs, who was born in New York, grew up near Tampa Bay and operates his nature tour business from Orlando, has more or less increased his injury odds by stalking birds from the Arctic Circle to the Falkland Islands. He's birded in every state but two. While many birders spend a lifetime without as much as a bee sting, Biggs five times has been hauled to hospitals by helicopter.

The last was May 31, after a night of owl watching in Osceola National Forest.

He was headed back to Lake City when he pulled off the road to record bird data in a notebook. Police believe a drug dealer may have mistaken him for a narcotics agent, sneaked up to his car and tried to murder him.

The bullet broke a bone near the left elbow, cut an artery, severed a nerve and ripped out muscle before exiting Biggs and the car. A former military medic, Biggs survived by using his belt as a tourniquet and driving himself eight miles to Lake City in the dead of night. A helicopter flew him to Jacksonville, where he spent a month in the hospital recovering from his injury and cracking wise.

"The guy must have been a real slimeball, shooting an endangered species," Biggs said following the first of three surgeries. The "endangered species" of which he spoke was not himself. It was actually a handsome tattoo of a bald eagle on his left arm. The bullet obliterated the eagle's head on its journey through Biggs' flesh.

"We're going to have to have some sort of special plastic surgery to get the head back," said Bettye Biggs, his wife.

Like a bald eagle, Biggs probably should be regarded as a rarity. At a time when many people experience life from the safety of the TV room sofa, Biggs is most comfortable in the woods, on top of mountains, on rivers, in swamps, looking for birds and finding old-fashioned blood-and-guts adventure.

He's had so many, in so many places, he can hardly remember details of them all. He includes the following among his most memorable:

"I was in Peru, in the Andes, where birding was spectacular. Everywhere I looked I saw birds I hadn't seen before." Suddenly, at the 17,000 feet level, he saw stars. He keeled over with altitude sickness. He came to in a hospital.

"In California, when I was in the military, we were having war games. It was at night, and I was using my infrared scope to look for owls. I heard a barred owl and turned and fell thirty feet off a cliff." A helicopter carried him and his aching head to the hospital.

"I was in Panama for war games and looking at birds. Another soldier, a guy about six-foot-six, collapsed after he was bitten by a black widow spider. I was the medic, so I picked him up and tried to carry him up a hill so the helicopter could take him out. I'd had diarrhea for about a week, and I collapsed at the top of the hill." He and the ill-fated spiderman recovered in the hospital.

"In Arizona, I was looking for plain-capped starthroats in a canyon. I slipped and sprained my ankle about as bad as you can sprain an ankle." As he watched for birds, his companion hiked for help. Eventually, a helicopter was summoned.

"I led a tour to the Dry Tortugas. It's one of the great birding spots in the world because of the spring migration." Taking a break from birding, he went snorkeling. The skate he tried to pet turned out to be a Southern stingray. The venomous barb struck him on the hand. He lists it as his most painful injury. When a helicopter arrived to transport the victim of a boating injury to Key West, Biggs hitched a ride to the same hospital.

He was on a trip to see the rare giant grebe in Guatemala when he found himself in the middle of what he assumed was a revolution. "Communist guerrillas held machine guns on me until they figured out what I was doing there." They drove Biggs out of their territory in a Studebaker pickup truck.

"I was in the Amazon with another guy, looking for paradise tanagers, and we must have gotten on somebody's property. I mean, the people who lived there didn't want us there. They shot darts at us through blowguns. We hauled ass. I'm sure they could have hit us if they wanted. I'd seen some guy knock a bird out of a tree with a dart. They were trying to scare us."

Parts of his body have inevitably found their way into the mouths of rattlesnakes. "My fault. I'm one of those people who has to pick up a snake. I don't keep them, I just want to pick them up. It drives my wife crazy."

Even as a child he was different. While other children played baseball, football and Superman, he studied cockroaches, collected butterflies and watched birds. He also recorded his first major injury: Hit by a car, he recovered from broken ribs and a punctured lung.

At 12, he went on his first Audubon birding field trip.

"I may have been the only kid. But within a year I was recruiting other boys."

He'd pedal his bicycle the 10 miles from his Pinellas Park home to where Tampa Bay lapped the shores of St. Petersburg and produced wading birds by the thousands. He'd take the bus to Sawgrass Lake and Boyd Hill nature parks.

"I used to drive the people in the local Audubon chapter crazy," Biggs says now. He was so precocious, and so advanced by the age of 14, that the chapter president called Herb Kale, the Audubon ornithologist. Kale drove from Orlando to meet the boy wonder and to take him birding.

"I was interested in everything having to do with nature," Biggs says. His self studies included ornithology, entomology, herpetology, conchology and a little botany. His sense of adventure was so great he decided, initially, to forget about college and see the world, and maybe a lot of birds, in the Navy.

"I've always been completely enthralled with birds. They're the most graceful, aesthetic creations in nature. Just think of this: There are bee hummingbirds no larger than a dime, with wings beating hundreds of times a second, and there are eight-foot flightless ostriches that could kick the hell out of you, kill you in a single blow. Birds are mind boggling."

In 1969, while stationed in California, he enjoyed birding during personal leaves. San Clemente, a wealthy town famous for a certain famous politician, also boasted a fine population of Anna's hummingbirds. One day, chasing a hummingbird from yard to yard, Biggs hopped a stone wall, crept over to a bush, and prepared to take some photographs of the nest.

"I heard some very stern male voices," he says now. "I looked up and I was surrounded by men with guns." Biggs' first thought — that he had stumbled into a Mafia chieftain's hideout — was mistaken. The Secret Service agents wanted to know what he was doing in Richard Nixon's back yard.

Later, at the University of South Florida, Biggs studied geography — and dropped out. College, among other things, impinged on his sense of freedom. Instead of a scientific career he worked construction, as a ranger at a Pinellas County park and as a nightclub bouncer. Bearded and burly, Biggs may look like a movie motorcycle gang leader, but he talks like a college professor.

"Meeting Wes initially can be overwhelming for most people," says Audubon's

Kale. "Some people take an instant dislike to him. No matter what the subject, he has studied it and has a great knowledge of it. He likes to argue about anything, and if he happens to win you over, he's likely to change his mind and argue the other side. He likes those radio call-in shows. He likes to call in and argue."

Most people who know Biggs, however, agree on one thing: Few birders are better at the sport. He's seen 680 species of birds in North America, which puts him near the top of any list. In Florida, only three birders have a better record than his 416 species. That may be because he's one of those birders who on a moment's notice drops what he's doing and drives across the state to glimpse a new species. Two months after he was shot, Biggs migrated south to Key West to admire a Bahamas mockingbird.

Six years ago, Kale hired Biggs to coordinate one of Florida Audubon's most ambitious projects, the breeding bird atlas for the state. Biggs divided the state into districts and dispatched hundreds of expert birders to discover what species were breeding and where. It's what scientists call "baseline data." Years from now, when another atlas is conducted, ornithologists will know if Florida has gained or lost species. A loss would indicate a troubled environment.

Last May, Biggs and Herb Kale traveled to North Florida to collect data. On May 30, in Osceola National Forest, they spent one of those days in the field that would kill normal people but invigorates Biggs. They started at 4:30 a.m. and quit at 10:00 p.m. At least Kale, who suffers from a heart condition, called it a day.

Biggs did paperwork, went out for supper at 11:00, and then decided he needed to look for owls. At midnight, he cruised back into the forest, which, as he suspected, was rich with screech owls. On his return to Lake City, he stopped to make notes.

Near a municipal airport, and a lonely tavern, he saw a parking lot. He pulled off the road, turned on the light inside the rented Buick and took out pen and paper.

"I was totally absorbed in my notes," he says now. "Suddenly, I heard this strange sound. Like something metallic hitting glass."

He looked to the right. Out the closed passenger-side window he saw a very angry-looking young man. The young man pointed an assault rifle at him through the glass and said something he could not understand. Then the young man smiled and pulled the trigger.

Much later, Biggs would find out about another crime involving an AK-47 assault rifle that had taken place earlier in the evening. Two men, suspected drug dealers, had shot up an apartment. Apparently, their escape route was the very road Biggs chose to do paperwork. "They saw me, this guy making notes with the lights on, and must have decided I was a cop."

At first, Biggs feared that his left arm was gone. Instead of checking, and maybe getting shot again, he turned on the motor, hit the gas and skidded down Highway 90 toward Lake City.

"At that point, I had no idea why somebody was trying to kill me. But I assumed they were going to try and finish the job so I kept looking in the mirror for their lights."

But nobody followed. Biggs stopped and examined his wounds. There was blood on his eyeglasses, on the dashboard and on the left door. There was bone and muscle tissue on the left window. Biggs pulled off his belt, wrapped it tight around what remained of his biceps and sped about 100 mph toward Lake City, where he remembered seeing a hospital. The way he held the end of the belt in his teeth reminded him of an old western, *True Grit*, where John Wayne grips his horse's reins in his teeth to keep his hands free for shooting.

"There are times you have to have true grit."

By the time he reached the main Lake City intersection, his grit was fading. He felt faint and couldn't recall the location of the hospital. He staggered out of his car, in the middle of the road, and waved down the first passing vehicle. The pickup truck skidded around him, then whipped up the road to the nearest police station.

Five minutes later Biggs was in an ambulance headed for the small local hospital for emergency treatment. Forty minutes and a helicopter-ride later, he was in the operating room of the trauma department at University Medical Center in Jacksonville.

"When I woke up from surgery, I didn't know whether I'd have arm or not," Biggs says. "But I thought whatever happened, the important thing was I survived. The bastard didn't kill me."

The surgeons had saved his limb. Subsequent surgeries repaired nerve endings and grafted flesh from his thigh and upper back to his wounded arm. A future operation may restore his ability to open and close his left hand. He goes to physical therapy every day.

"I may be too stupid to worry, but I haven't had any nightmares about what happened to me," Biggs says. "I'm depressed about my injury, and I think society has to do something drastic about drugs and drug dealers, but otherwise I feel okay."

Whoever shot him is still at large. "We do not have a suspect," says Columbia County detective Beryl Mayo. "But I would say Mr. Biggs was at the wrong place at the wrong time."

W es Biggs has been dreaming about his business, Florida Nature Tours, and what he hopes to do with it. Among other things, he plans tours to the Dry Tortugas, to the Caribbean, to Central America – to anywhere in the United States where people might pay him to show them birds. He's seen birds everywhere but Alaska and Hawaii.

Hawaii has volcanoes. Alaska has grizzlies. Wes Biggs will be as careful as can be. You know he will.

Protector of the library

Erich Kesse is a careful man. He lays the heavy manuscript for *The Yearling* on a University of Florida library table and leafs through its yellowed pages as if they were made from angel's wings.

"You can tell a lot about the author by studying a manuscript," Kesse says. "Marjorie Kinnan Rawlings was a smoke fiend! Look at all the cigarette burns in the manuscript! Whew! They're everywhere. She also used very, very cheap typing paper."

It's the paper quality more than the cigarette holes that bothers Kesse, the besieged 28-year-old preservation officer for the state's largest library. His challenging job is protecting the university's 2.5-million books and manuscripts from enemies including voracious insects, heat, humidity, mold, mildew – and cheap paper.

Saving *The Yearling*, the 1938 Pulitzer Prize-winning novel written just south of here at Cross Creek, will mean treating 473 pages, one by one, with an anti-acid spray and sealing them in plastic. Otherwise the book will fall apart – 10 percent of the university's collection is in such danger – and break the heart of the protector of the library.

"Sometimes I feel pretty lonely," says Kesse, who has worked four years as the state's only book preservation specialist.

Disintegrating books are only part of his problem. For years, UF's ancient libraries have served as virtual fast-food restaurants for insects. Mildew and mold, meanwhile, are almost as aggressive.

"Cockroaches eat the starch that's in the covers," says Kesse, who keeps a collection of rubber roaches on his office computer terminal. "Carpet beetles eat the glue that binds books together. Silverfish and termites actually eat the paper."

Kesse relishes the battle. To combat hungry insects, he's had UF's three main library buildings fumigated twice since 1987.

Insect-friendly windows and floor cracks have been sealed. Books obtained from insect-infested Caribbean countries are routinely inspected before being placed on shelves. And Kesse himself has taken to confronting hungry students who break rules by smuggling food into the library.

"If you bring food in here, you're going to have insects," says Kesse, who patrols the library while carrying a collection of insect-eaten books to show snacking students. "Most students apologize and say they didn't realize food was a problem. But some students get angry. They threaten to punch my lights out."

51

Kesse, a slight, soft-spoken blond-haired man who wears roundish spectacles, tries to ignore the threats and go on with his work. Florida is so unkind to books. There is so much to be done, so many brittle books, so many insects, so much mold and mildew.

Rarely does he have to look long for moldy and mildewed books. After any rain they are brought damp and dripping into the library by careless students. Wearing plastic gloves, so he doesn't spread mold to uncontaminated books, he dries them in his office, fanning open the pages and blotting them with paper towels. Sometimes he replaces warped covers, or, in some cases, sends them out for repair or copying. He looks forward to the day the university can buy him a $200,000 freeze drier to suck moisture out of books while killing insects.

"Hot temperatures and high humidity are an especially bad problem for Florida libraries," Kesse says, looking at a warped copy of *Introduction to St. Thomas Aquinas.*

That's one reason he frets much about air conditioning. The UF libraries are old, for the most part, and equipped with temperamental air-conditioning systems. Temperatures frequently exceed the 68-degree temperature he considers safe for books. Then mold and mildew come calling.

He has not forgotten the nightmare day when he discovered a broken air conditioner in the one-room performing arts section of the library. He and his staff had to wipe mold and mildew from 5,000 books.

"Mold grew on the places where people had touched books with greasy fingers," says Kesse, looking almost pale at the memory.

Kesse, who received a master's of library science degree from the University of Kentucky and preservation training from New York's Columbia University, can hardly stomach the thought of mistreated books. He was born in Cincinnati, where he spent boyhood hours hanging around his grandfather, a rare book dealer. As he got older, Kesse's appreciation for fine books grew. A voracious reader, he started his own book collection and wrote poetry.

Kesse has given up writing except for a column in the monthly library newsletter in which he takes on subjects ranging from book-eating bugs to the proper way of removing books from shelves. Most people, he contends, don't know how. They tend to pull a book from the top, thus putting pressure on the binding on the bottom. Erich Kesse advocates a firm, even pull.

"Look at this binding," he says, shaking his head in the Latin American section. Generations of students, sadly, have pulled out *The Female and Male in North America* the wrong way.

"This is shelf damage," Kesse says, examining the tattered volume. "And this mark looks like it was done by somebody's Coke."

The university's libraries are huge and spread out. The East Library, built in 1926, boasts seven floors of books. The West Library, which opened in 1957, is six stories. The Marsden Science Library, two years old, has five book-filled floors. Four colleges on campus also maintain separate libraries. Kesse is responsible for their books, too.

"I don't spend much time in my office," he says, walking a dark hall and stopping near an elevator where a sneaking student has deposited a sticky can of Mountain Dew. Kesse will throw it in the trash outside the library.

He spends most time stalking brittle books. Before 1850, most books were constructed from cotton and made to last. Since 1850, most books have been made from wood pulp, and the fibers and chemicals begin wearing down after about 20 years. Kesse has shelves full of failing books he has earmarked for further examination or treatment. Some books he can test quickly for crumbling potential by folding a page corner a time or two. If the paper breaks, it means he has found a brittle book. Others he tests for brittleness with chemicals.

He recently took apart that crumbling 1936 favorite of the agricultural college, *Bullfrog Farming and Frogging in Florida*, so he could more easily make microfilm copies. One copy was sent to a Pennsylvania data bank for safe, humidity-free underground storage. Another was delivered to a similar Central Florida facility. The last microfilm copy remains at the UF library and is accessible to students. Kesse also was able to reconstruct the original, though he is unsure about how long it will last.

Erich Kesse seldom rests. Night time, he has found, is the right time to work the bug beat. Bugs are most likely to show up after closing when they can eat in peace. Kesse remembers the shocking night he found a 1 1/2-inch palmetto bug – the modern record for the UF library – sashaying across the floor.

"It was probably going from feast to feast," says Kesse, whose heavy shoes made sure the roach had eaten its last supper.

Kesse is always trying to stay one-step ahead of his enemies. He is always thinking of new weapons against insects. He has even considered the pros and cons of employing large insect-eating spiders.

His Gainesville home is blessed with some large and hungry spiders that help keep his own book collection bug free. He thinks they probably would like the UF library fine. He also knows that spiders would frighten browsers searching the stacks for, say, the latest Stephen King thriller. Spiders, anyway, are messy eaters.

"They do eat a lot of roaches, but they leave the carcasses lying around. The carcasses attract carpet beetles, which like the protein. Next thing you know the carpet beetles are in the books eating the animal-based glues."

No, his best weapon against book bugs is poison – poison and educating students about library snacking.

"Last year students were having pizzas delivered," he says with a sigh. "Well, we've stopped that. But I did catch somebody with a bag from McDonald's the other day. We can't have that in the library."

The smallest post office

Driving through the Everglades, I hoped to see a panther, but had to settle for big alligators in the canal along State Road 29. The highway was wet from a late afternoon thunderstorm, and I kept thinking about the reptilian welcome I'd get should my truck skid into the canal.

When I got to U.S. 41, which is also called the Tamiami Trail, I should have gone west, toward my motel in Naples, but I turned east instead. I hadn't visited the heart of the Everglades for a while, and I wanted to see how it was doing.

Well, it seemed to be doing fine. Great blue herons stalked minnows in a roadside ditch, the way they always do, while kingfishers scolded passing cars from the safety of telephone wires. There was the same old place selling airboat rides to tourists, an Indian village and a couple of people fishing for bream with cane poles. And up ahead, in a clearing among the trees, stood the little shack that to me somehow symbolizes the toughness of the people who choose to live in this harsh land.

The little shack in Ochopee is the smallest post office in America, serving a couple of hundred Seminole and Miccosukee Indians, hunters, hermits, wildlife biologists and assorted weirdos who don't mind putting up with mosquitoes, alligators, snakes, floods and fire. The little shack, a lonely man-made bump on the landscape, endures as well.

There was rain ahead, so I pulled into the limestone parking lot of the nation's smallest post office, pushed open the shower curtain that serves as the only door and walked in to meet Evelyn Shealy, postmaster. She was as tough as any alligator.

"Can I help you?"

I introduced myself and told her I write stories about Florida. She nodded but said nothing and made me do all the talking. I told her how I used to drive by the post office when I lived in Miami and liked to fish in Everglades City and how I always intended to stop but never did until now. She nodded, neither friendly nor unfriendly. When I tried to ask about her background, she frowned. Most people like talking about themselves, but she didn't. Her background was none of my business.

She looked at her watch and said, "Let me just give you the facts about this place."

Yes, I said, that would be fine.

"I'm the postmaster. I'm going to celebrate my seventeenth anniversary with the post office on Thursday. The post office is the smallest post office in the United States. It's eight feet four inches by seven feet three inches. It's ten feet six inches high."

I wrote down everything and looked up.

"There used to be a general store here that had a post office. In 1953 the post office burned down. The general store wasn't rebuilt. The building that was used as a shed became the post office."

She interrupted my next question and continued.

"We deliver mail. We have a one-hundred-and-twenty-three-mile route. Geraldine Fish delivers the mail. She's been here seventeen years, too. We have a clerk, Naomi Lewis, who works on Saturdays. We deliver to about two hundred people, including Seminole and Miccosukee Indians. We're located in the Big Cypress National Preserve. Ochopee is Indian for 'Big Field.' "

I asked how many pieces of mail her post office processes.

"I don't know off hand, and I don't have time to check. I'm busy. I'd say we do about twenty-eight-thousand dollars in business a year."

I told her I remembered Charles Kuralt doing one of his *On the Road* segments about her post office.

"That was in the 1970s. CNN did something about us recently. We were in *Time* in July. Channel 4 in Miami did something last week. *People* has been here. We've been written up in *Smithsonian, Family Circle* and the *National Enquirer*. We're in the book *Ripley's Believe It or Not.*"

"I guess you've been asked just about every question."

"I've heard every question," she said and went back to her work.

I looked around the nation's smallest post office, and it didn't take me long to see everything. Outside was a mailbox, an American flag and a rack of postcards showing Everglades scenes and the postmaster standing with a child in front of her post office.

Inside was a counter long enough to serve maybe two people, three at the most. There was a poster of missing children on one wall and two FBI posters of wanted criminals on another. There was a sack of mail. There was a cigar box full of rubber bands and 40 post office boxes. There was a steel bar leaning in a corner. I wondered if the postmaster used the bar on prying reporters. I decided not to ask her age.

Instead I asked if her post office is busy during the Christmas season.

"We're just the same as any post office. We're busy."

I asked if it is a problem storing Christmas packages in such a small place.

"We can handle anything any post office handles."

I asked if she has to store packages outside.

"Did you see that wooden box? If I have to, I put them in there. It's not a problem."

I asked if Everglades residents mail anything unusual.

"They haven't mailed any frogs in twelve years. They don't even mail bees anymore." I thought she was joking about mailing frogs and bees. "No, I'm not. I suppose the people were in the frog leg business or the honey business. They had to ship them by mail. They don't do it anymore."

I asked how she likes living and working in the Everglades.

There's nothing to it, she said. Mosquitoes are bad in June and July, and horseflies are a problem in May. Heat used to be awful, but the government bought her an air conditioner. Now everything is fine. No, no alligators have ever menaced her.

Yes, snakes crawl in the post office on occasion, but she calls her son on the telephone; he drives over and gets rid of them.

I asked if she is ever bored.

She gave me a sharp look. "What do you mean?" I asked if she ever finds herself reading books to pass the time. "I told you we're like any post office. I'm too busy to read. I'm always working. We also have a lot of visitors I have to deal with. They come here in buses. We have people who want Ochopee postmarks on envelopes. They want to take pictures."

I asked if I could take her picture. She nodded and we walked outside. She looked as if she had posed for photographs before. One of her friends arrived as I was focusing my camera and told me I was photographing "the prettiest postmaster in the country."

The postmaster's friend asked me if I wanted my picture taken with the postmaster. Sure. Why not? The postmaster said, "He's not a tourist. He doesn't want his picture taken." But she posed with me without further complaint and even smiled.

I had noticed there were no toilet facilities at the nation's smallest post office. I told her I might blush as I asked the next question, but I was going to ask anyway. She beat me to it.

"Now you want to know where I go to the bathroom."

I felt my face get hot.

"I go home. It's not far. Then I come back. There's nothing to it."

She looked at her watch. She had been looking at her watch a lot.

"Well, if you don't have any other questions, I have work to do."

I thanked her for her time.

"Thank you for stopping."

The mayor is in

WINDLEY KEY   10/12/86

It's another election year, and the television is filled with Candidate A slamming Candidate B, slinging mud and causing a ruckus. This is not Al Flutie's way. Al is running for honorary mayor of Islamorada in the Florida Keys for the fifth time, and his fear is that nobody will run against him, which is what happened last time.

"I'd like to have some fun," he says. "Even if I am the honorary mayor, it's no fun without an election."

In the last election, he hauled a bunch of friends to the polls in the back of a dump truck. The time before he rented a tux and a Cadillac convertible.

This time, his campaign manager plans to take advantage of a thing professional red-white-and blue pols might consider a liability – his Lebanese extraction – and play it up big. On election day, Al is supposed to ride a rented camel.

"I don't know about the camel," his honor says. "I hear they bite. But what the hell. I'll do it."

On election day, here is what will happen: Al, his camel and assorted friends will visit 16 bars around Islamorada. Each bar will have ballots on the counter. If you buy a drink, you get a ballot. If you buy two drinks, you get two ballots. Al will make sure everybody gets plenty of drinks, even if he has to buy them himself. He even arranges for safe drivers. He presumes they will thank him with their votes. Last time he got 900 to his opponent's 300.

"It's sort of like real politics," he says, though you don't read about such things in civic books. "The more money you have, the better off you are."

Down in the Keys, which once threatened to secede from the rest of the state and become the Conch Republic, people do things their own way.

Islamorada, see, has no real mayor. It probably doesn't need one. Its 1,441 citizens can take care of themselves. It's unincorporated. Six years ago though, somebody in the Oceanview Lounge got to thinking how Key West had a mayor, and Monroe County had a mayor, and figured Islamorada needed one, too.

Al and his cronies jumped off their barstools at the thought. Jeff Lohr declared himself the first mayor, but there's been an election every year except 1985, when people knew nobody could beat Al and didn't even try. This year he is encouraging friends to take him on, and he is sure they will.

The mayor is 58. He has been married three times. He has lived in the Keys for 22 years, but he first started visiting regularly in 1934. He is thin and leathery, with a bristly moustache, salt-and-pepper hair combed straight up, and eyes as brown as swamp water.

Everybody knows him. Al Flutie, among other things, is part owner of a bill-board company. He is a fishing guide. He is the public relations man for a Key Largo hotel. He has his own radio program. He has a colorful history: He joined the merchant marine when he was 16, was Mr. Miami Beach when he was 18, and after that joined the Marines and was wounded in Korea. He was a glass blower. He flew a crop dusting airplane until he knocked the landing gear off on a fence. Nobody can dispute he is qualified to be mayor.

Al knows important people. He still fishes with Mickey Mantle and Billy Martin, the former baseball players, when they visit the Keys. He once took Paul Newman to Jack's Bar for some pool. "Everybody liked him," his honor says. "If he missed a shot or knocked the eight-ball in, somebody would say 'Stupid shot' and Paul would laugh and laugh."

In the 1960s or early 1970s – Al forgets – the governor of California and his wife hired him to take them fishing. Al Flutie and Ronald and Nancy Reagan, those peas in a pod, broke bread together, caught spotted seatrout in Florida Bay, and enjoyed the sights. "I got a picture somewhere," Al says.

Remember Sargent Shriver, the Kennedy relative who was George McGovern's running mate in the 1972 presidential election? Al Flutie does. Mayor Al helped Shriver find a pair of favorite pants lost at a laundry. Mayor Al says, "He lost his shirt in the election and lost his pants in Islamorada."

Mayor Al used to see Richard Daley wandering around the Keys, too. The late Chicago mayor was an enthusiastic angler. "Talk about a mayor," Al says. "Whew!"

Al is a different kind of mayor in a different kind of place. His city hall is the Oceanview Lounge. The Oceanview has not had a view of the ocean since 1960 when Hurricane Donna blew it across US 1. For that matter, the Oceanview is located on Windley Key instead of Islamorada. No big deal: The mayor of Islamorada doesn't live in Islamorada either. His home is on Plantation Key.

"They're all in the same area," he explains.

What matters is the sign in the Oceanview, the sign that says "The Mayor Is In" or "Out" or "Sort Of." Al sort of likes the sign, since he considers himself sort of the mayor. He loves city hall.

"Let's face it. The Oceanview is a joint. But more is decided at the Oceanview than at any place I know." At the Oceanview, the mayor and his cronies meet to decide the rules of upcoming fishing and golf tournaments. They decide on fund-raising activities and decide to whom the funds will be given.

Once, to raise money for charity, they roasted Al at the Sheraton in Key Largo and raised $15,000. Once, to raise money, they auctioned off the mayor's smelly fishing shoes. Once they asked Al to emcee a pie-throwing contest. Little did he know he was the target.

Once they auctioned off a rubber chicken. Al bid $1.96, and suddenly, everybody in the room bid against him. He ended up paying $250 for a rubber chicken. When he came out of the men's room later, still shaken, somebody had kidnapped his rubber chicken. He got ransom notes.

Rubber chickens may seem trivial, but serious stuff happens at city hall, too. For one thing, real politicians do call on Al. They want his support because he knows so many people. Al asks them about what they will do to protect the fishing, and what they will do to protect the Keys from the wrong kind of growth. He is for progress, but not if it ruins the Keys. He will support only people who agree with him.

Growth is one thing he talks about during his campaign. Another thing is litter. He is against it. His eyes almost grow moist when he tells the story about a friend who followed a Winnebago 50 miles so he could return the garbage the driver had dumped on U.S.1. The other big issue is the Florida Highway Patrol, which Al is frankly against.

"Once me and a bunch of us left the bar at dawn and were playing football on U.S. 1 by the Texaco station. A highway patrolman stops and says, 'There's gotta be a law against this' and gives me a ticket."

So elect Al. He will control growth. He will stamp out litterbugs. He will rid the Keys of the hated highway patrol and allow football playing on U.S. 1. It is another election year in Florida. Al can promise anything, and anything can happen.

Where the buffalo roam

The bug in my ear, so help me, sounded like a herd of buffalo. I bolted straight up in my sleeping bag and thought my wife might be interested. "Uh, dear," I said. My voice sounded high in the dark of Paynes Prairie State Preserve.

"What is it?" she snarled. "I was almost asleep."

Bison were stampeding in my head, I explained. She wondered if my little problem could wait until morning. I wish I could have cooperated with her wish for 40 winks, but the sound of something grazing on my eardrum always panics me.

"Well, I don't see anything," she grumbled, peering into the appropriate orifice with a flashlight. "Oh, wait a minute. There it is. It's coming out."

Before we could examine the intruder – it would have been nice to know whether it had hooves – I automatically crushed it with my thumb. Nobody stampedes in my ear and lives.

I knew Paynes Prairie was one of the state's richest wildlife parks, but it's ridiculous when the wildlife shows up in your ear. It's strangely thrilling, too. Paynes Prairie is the kind of place that demands your attention. It grabs you by the throat, shakes you, and says: "You aren't in the city anymore."

Paynes Prairie, only 10 miles away from Gainesville in North Florida, seems like a million miles from civilization. Its 18,000 acres include thick pine woods, dark oak hammocks, cypress swamps, grassy marshes and a massive prairie where buffalo – you read right – roam.

American bison, the correct name for what we incorrectly call buffalo in this country, once lived in Florida. "But they made the classic mistake," said Jim Weimer, the preserve's biologist. "They came east over the Appalachian Mountains just as the Europeans were moving west. They were wiped out."

The last native Florida bison disappeared in 1821. In 1975, 10 bison, acquired from an Oklahoma refuge, were reintroduced to Paynes Prairie. In 10 years the herd more than tripled in size. When neighboring cattle came down with brucellosis, a contagious disease affecting bovine reproduction, the state asked that bison be tested. All but four had the disease and were destroyed. The herd is slowly coming back.

"There's six-thousand acres of prairie," said Weimer. "And eight bison. Finding one can be like finding the proverbial needle in a haystack. But the good news is they like to ramble. Sometimes they're very easy to spot."

Too easy by some accounts. Not long ago, two preserve volunteers were dispatched on a routine prairie patrol. They saw a bison bull that might have weighed

1,500 pounds or more. The sight of humans irritated the bison. It came running.

The volunteers did the same. They jumped a fence and climbed a tree until the bison went on to greener pastures.

"We haven't seen those volunteers since," said ranger Susan Carl. "Now I don't consider bison dangerous, but they are unpredictable. I've seen them up close. But I was in a pickup truck."

Bison aren't the only unusual creatures dwelling on the preserve. Descendents of horses brought to the New World by the Spaniards five centuries ago were reintroduced to Paynes Prairie in 1985. They're smaller than domestic stock, scrawnier and wilder. Florida's original Crackers – cow hunters, they called themselves – valued such horses for their spirit and endurance.

Spanish cattle, even more ornery than bison and wild horses, also make their living on the prairie. They're known to be mean and particular about the company they keep. They don't cotton to people.

"I'm more nervous around them than I am the bison," said ranger Howard Adams. "Sometimes we have to go into the prairie, round them up and test them for brucellosis. First of all, they'll hide from you. If you find them, they'll try to hit you or your horse with their horns."

The campground was cold and quiet when my wife and I crept from our tent and walked through the dawn. Vultures refused to leave their roosts until the sun did its work. Dew glistened on the webs of hundreds of spiders. We heard the crack of a dead limb. It turned out to be a careless white-tail deer, a doe. When she noticed us, she fled through the palmettos, her tail standing up like a white flag. All this before breakfast. We returned to camp.

I usually don't enjoy staying overnight in Florida's state parks. They're blessed with abundant wildlife and beauty, true enough, but for the most part the actual campsites are designed for trailers and recreational vehicles. RVs and trailers require less space, privacy and shade than tent campers. We who slumber under cloth often endure cramped conditions, noise and blazing sunlight.

But Paynes Prairie is a happy exception. Its 57 campsites, scattered about an oak hammock, are large, shaded – and generally unused. There's a lake at Paynes, and good bass fishing, but the preserve is known more for wildlife watching than a place for people to cavort and consume. You can't buy a hot dog here, rent a boat or water ski. No outboard motors are allowed in the lake: They would disturb the wildlife and the quiet. The only luxuries are a bathhouse or two and picnic tables. Mosquitoes are numerous and thirsty, but the park doesn't spray poisons willy-nilly.

Paynes Prairie boasts a fine museum, and outstanding hiking and bicycle trails if you are brave enough to use them. I've been lost in the back country here before. The only other stranger I saw was lost, too. We went our separate ways; at least one of us found his way back to the pavement.

Being lost, though, has good points. For one thing, it's a reminder of your own insignificance. For hundreds of years we've done everything possible to tame nature. A little taste of humility, though bitter, is educational. And there's something else: Get lost and you have a story to tell.

Do you think we're going the right way?"

My wife and I had forgotten our map. Major trail turns and intersections were plainly marked. But then we arrived at the first of several unmarked forks. I am known for my ability to instinctively choose the wrong fork.

Our destination was Chacala Pond and its wading birds, waterfowl and bald eagles that come for the fishing. A trip to Chacala requires a hike or ride through thick pines and oaks. Deer tracks littered the sand. I listened for turkey, though the only thing I heard was a nagging voice in my head: "The vultures will pick your bones clean, bozo! You're lost!"

We were saved by a young man on an all-terrain bicycle. He invited us to follow him. "The turn to the pond is right up ahead," he said gaily. A mile later he said, "I guess it's a little farther than I thought." Anyway, we made it, and the pond was lovely. Two sandhill cranes studied us studying them.

The stately sandhill cranes are one of Paynes Prairie's best known inhabitants. They like the great wide open of prairie. If they can see danger coming, they are less likely to be ambushed by bobcats and other predators, including deadly *Homo sapiens*.

In 1773, when William Bartram, the famous botanist and writer, visited the prairie, his Seminole host, Cowkeeper, treated him to a crane feast. Bartram, who had a little poet in him, enjoyed watching cranes more than supping on them.

He wrote: " . . . the sonorous savannah crane, in well disciplined squadrons, now rising from the Earth, mount a loft in spiral circles, far above the dense atmosphere of the humid plain; they again view the glorious sun and the light of day still gleaming on their polished feathers, they sing their evening hymn.."

They look nice when they fly, in other words. And they sing pretty good, too.

Cowkeeper's nephew was Chief Payne, for whom the prairie, and eventually the preserve, was named. Payne's village was attacked by American forces in 1812. The chief's men repelled the invaders, but he died later from wounds. Bad feelings festered for several decades. Osceola, the most famous of all Seminole chiefs, fought the first battle of what was known as the Second Seminole War on the south rim of the prairie in 1835. Osceola later was captured under a flag of truce. He died in prison.

On a breezeless night, when the moon is bright, some people will tell you they can hear him howling. But it's only the coyotes. They, too, haunt Paynes Prairie.

At dusk, we climbed the tower overlooking the prairie. We watched a deer slip through tall grass. A great horned owl hooted from the top branch of a dead tree. The night before we'd been treated to a symphony of barred owls at the campground. We'd seen a barn owl flap just over the oak tops. Screech owls trilled from the thickest underbrush.

We heard no coyotes, though. Relative newcomers to Florida, they're rare on the prairie. For years, they've been extending their range like killer bees with legs. Cattle ranchers hate coyotes – cattle ranchers also unjustly blame wolves, panthers, bobcats and even eagles for calf predation – but coyotes are protected on the prairie.

"We used to have red wolves here," biologist Jim Weimer told me. "But they disappeared in Florida in the early 1900s. We're hoping coyotes will fill their niche."

Nature is neither kind nor cruel. It just is. Fang and claw are part of the circle of life. Great blue herons spear frogs, fish, snakes and baby alligators. Mature alligators ambush herons. A king snake will eat a diamondback rattler, which will eat a rabbit, which nibbles on the grass at dusk while watching the sky for the great horned owl. A raccoon will climb a tree to eat owl eggs.

My children have eyes as sharp as owls'. They saw the wild horses first. Grazing 500 yards out on the prairie, they were brown, black, white. Wild horses. Beyond them, way beyond them, visible through binoculars, were the buildings and towers of Gainesville's University of Florida. My attention was drawn away from civilization back to the prairie, where something huge and black was lumbering through the grass.

A bison.

I really didn't think we would be attacked by bison. Really. But when my son and I carried our all-terrain bicycles over the gate and entered the prairie I couldn't help thinking what an enraged one-ton animal could do to puny human flesh. Though visitors are invited on the prairie, signs posted on the fence warn about unpredictable bison with bad tempers.

And then there were all those campfire stories.

"I was at Glacier National Park in Montana once," biologist Jim Weimer had told me, "and I met this ranger from Yellowstone, where they have bison. He said a park visitor tried to get a close-up Instamatic picture. He ended up being gored in the rear end. In the emergency room, his kid was telling the doctors that 'Daddy, went higher than the truck.' "

I sought comfort in the story told by ranger Susan Carl.

"I had a friend who led an overnight camping trip on the prairie," she said. "They stopped near a wallow made where the bison like to cool off in the mud. The other campers camped as far away from the wallow as they could. My friend put her tent right next to the wallow. She wasn't worried. That wallow was one of many on six-thousand acres. That night, the bison came to that very wallow next to her tent."

And she survived? Yes! Yes! She lived to tell the tale.

My son and I pedaled cautiously along Cone's Dike, the muddy, narrow road lining the prairie's southeast rim. We dodged hills of bison dung. We bounced through bison wallows. Fish crows cawed at our approach – or were they simply warning us: "Go back before it's too late." Imagination is my enemy.

After three bisonless miles, and a lot of beauty – fall wildflowers were in bloom – we turned back because our stomachs were growling for lunch. Sandhill cranes flew just over our heads. A Northern harrier, a kind of marsh hawk, dipped and darted just above the grass tops.

Then, up ahead, to the right, we saw something, something that made our hearts go pitty-pat and our stomachs fall all the way to the pit: A black mountain of an animal was plowing through the grass in our direction.

The bison was bigger than a breadbox, but slightly smaller than a Volkswagen beetle. We stopped to watch.

"He's too far away to see us or smell us," I told my son. Somebody had to say it, and I wanted to believe it. We climbed back on our bikes. We pedaled them as fast as two men can pedal in thick, loose sand. Then the unhappy discovery: To return to the gate, we'd have to make a turn that would bring us uncomfortably close to big boy.

There was no other way back.

The bison was now about a five-iron shot away.

We could see his huge woolly head and horns. The wind, blowing toward us, carried his scent. I'll say this: Hygiene is not a priority in the bison world. In the meantime, as the wind seemed to shift, we wondered whether he could smell last night's Ivory soap and this morning's fear on us.

Are bison nearsighted or farsighted? I couldn't remember.

We looked for a likely place to jump the fence. Just in case. Would a fence stop a bison? Maybe not. How about a sugar maple tree?

But big boy was more interested in filling his belly than crushing human bones and bikes. Ten minutes later, when we dragged our bicycles over the gate, and our hearts still hung a notch too high in our throats, the bison was just a black bump on the prairie.

That night, at the campfire, we roasted marshmallows. It seemed appropriate.

Lord of the flies

Carl Hanson sat in his favorite easy chair, leaned over a table and tied wonderful fishing flies. This one would be good for the palm-sized fish called bream. That one would fool a shark. "I do not believe in large flies," he said in that crisp way of his. "Small flies will take a big fish, and I use barbless hooks on my flies. Yes, I lose more fish. What the hell do I care if I lose a fish?"

Nobody had the answer to his question, and Hanson, 78, returned to his work. His fingers, long and thick, seemed better suited for taking apart diesel truck engines than transforming a delicate feather and a tiny hook into something that looks edible to a fish. But there are people in Florida who look at his flies, who watch him cast, and call him an artist. They call him the Lord of the Flies.

Until recently, the Lord of the Flies was ailing. Last spring, after a day spent fly fishing, he came home and had a heart attack. During bypass surgery, he suffered a stroke. He was unconscious for a month, and when he came to, his fingers hardly worked at all.

Now they do. He is back to tying flies. And one night a week his St. Petersburg home overflows with fly fishers who come calling from all over the state. They gather about him like students at the foot of a Zen Master. He teaches them to tie flies. He takes them out into the yard and teaches them to cast under a street lamp. He teaches them the Carl Hanson philosophy of life: Catch fish, if you like, but let them go.

"A fish is too valuable a commodity to be caught only once. A fly fisherman is never a fish hog. Understand?"

He is a tall man with snowy white hair and a beard that reminds you of either Papa Hemingway or Santa Claus. His eyes are as blue as the Gulf Stream. He has been conducting his free fishing clinics since 1950, missing only during his illness. When Christmas Eve and New Year's Eve happen to fall on a Tuesday, and people show up at his house, Hanson holds his clinic.

On weekends, he ties flies at Bill Jackson's, a department store dedicated to outdoors equipment. Sporting goods shows regularly invite him to put on seminars. Fishing magazines write stories about him. In 1990, he was a featured artist at the Florida Folk Festival.

He has been known to carry favorite flies in the picture compartment of his billfold. When he and Esther married, they exchanged vows under crossed fly rods. Do you think the Lord of the Flies would wed an incompetent caster?

Fly fishing is a religion to him, as it is to many anglers, but he finds it difficult to explain why. He says fly fishing is relaxing. He says fly fishing is fun and cheap. Fly

65

fishing is an absorbing activity that just takes hold of a man.

It might also be the way sunlight plays on the water early in the morning, the pull of the tide against his legs, the appearance of a spotted seatrout behind one of his streamer flies. Or maybe it's something altogether different. As Thoreau wrote: "Many men go fishing all their lives without knowing that it is not fish they are after."

Fly fishing requires more physical coordination than other methods of angling, which have been simplified over the years by space-age technology that does everything but clean and cook the fish. But a fly rod is a stick without brains. Casting one takes finesse and timing and patience. As author Norman Maclean wrote in *A River Runs Through It*: "If you have never picked up a fly rod before, you will soon find it factually and theologically true that man by nature is a damn mess."

Hanson was flirting with middle age when he discovered his calling as the Lord of the Flies. He was born in Massachusetts, where his father and his grandfather were commercial swordfish harpooners. He was a body shop welder. He was a garbage collector. He worked 17 years in a shipyard until the day he and 30,000 other employees were laid off.

In 1950, he loaded his 1941 Plymouth and drove to St. Petersburg to make a fresh start. He got a job repairing reels at a tackle store. One day, over at Lake Maggiore, he met a fly fisher named Doc Howe at the Rod and Gun Club. Doc showed him how to fly fish and how to tie flies.

"Pretty soon I was the best in the club," Hanson said. "I was the best in the club because I worked at it. A man asked if I'd teach him to tie a fly. Of course I would! I invited him over. Pretty soon I had people coming over every night. That was too much. So I had people come over on Tuesday nights."

On Tuesday nights, when Hanson's yard resembles a used car lot, parking places are at a premium. He has had as many as 40 fly fishers packed like Spanish sardines inside his modest home. They come from two blocks away and from 200 miles. One drove from Miami, attended the clinic, and drove home the same night.

Teen-aged boys who eat and sleep fishing hang onto his every word. Women, frequent visitors, sit at his elbow. Hanson says women take the time to learn to tie exceptionally handsome flies because they have more patience than men. One exception in the patience department would be the fellow who has attended the clinic for 42 years.

"If you can tie your shoes, you can tie a fly," Hanson tells his pupils.

Many people, of course, prefer to buy flies for a buck or two at tackle stores. Old-fashioned in the self-sufficiency department, Hanson ties flies because it would never occur to him to spend good money on something he can make better himself.

"A fly costs me – what? Six cents," said Hanson, who uses materials at hand in his fly tying, including unraveling carpet and loose hair from his fluffy Pomeranian dog, Bear. He likes to believe his homemade flies are more effective than store-bought lures because they are designed to work where he fishes.

His white and silver streamer, pulled through the water, looks like a Tampa Bay minnow to spotted seatrout, redfish and ladyfish. His mosquito fly, which has fooled many bream, looks like it might bite an unwary angler. Yet Hanson never gets worked up about realism.

"A fly is nothing more than a caricature," he sniffed. "Anyone who claims otherwise is talking foolishness."

At his clinics, his pupils study his hands as he works. They drink his coffee. They argue among themselves. They listen to fishing stories. Hanson has so many. Listen:

"I was out in Tampa Bay catching trout, eight, ten, twelve inches long. Not big. All of a sudden, an automobile explodes out of the water. Then the automobile crashes back into the water. That's what the tarpon looked like to me. It must have weighed a hundred and twenty-five pounds. And there I am standing with a one-ounce rod and a four-pound test tippet."

Hanson lost the tarpon, but he has landed many others. He has caught large trout and redfish and snook. He has caught large Spanish mackerel and jack crevalle.

"If I never catch another big fish I'll be perfectly happy," he said. "I am just interested in the fishing."

Every Thursday, Hanson fishes with his best friend, Jim St. Pierre. They drive across the bridge that spans Tampa Bay and stalk bream in the Braden River. Hanson, who has fished in most of the state's rivers, loves the Braden. He sees eagles and ospreys and otters. Hanson and St. Pierre have a fishing ritual. Sitting in the boat, watching the eagles, they drink a cup of coffee and eat a doughnut and say: "I wonder what the poor folks are doing today."

Last spring, Hanson returned home from a day on the Braden, lay on the couch and felt the chest pains coming. So began a three-month nightmare. St. Pierre, 63, visited his friend daily in the hospital. When Hanson felt strong enough, St. Pierre brought him outside and handed him a fly rod. From his wheelchair, Hanson practiced casting on the lawn.

Now he is almost back to full strength, and on a recent windy afternoon at Lake Maggiore he put on a fly casting clinic for me and two other men. He waded into the lake and cast a fly that looked like a water bug. Its legs were made with rubber bands that wiggled provocatively.

"Notice my hands," Hanson said as he cast.

We obeyed and noticed his hands. His left hand tugged the line at the precise moment his right hand lifted the rod. The effect was like stepping on the gas while releasing the clutch of a sports car: The line got moving quickly. Line speed makes for a fine cast.

The line shot behind him, stopped dead, then reversed direction as he began his forward cast. Defying gravity, the line floated on the air like a poem about a butterfly.

"Casting is easy," he said. "When it's done right, it's effortless. You do not have to be a big strong man to cast a fly."

He cast the imitation water bug to the edge of the cattails. A fish swam under it and popped it once. Carl Hanson said, "A small bream. Too small to swallow my bug."

He does not care whether he catches a fish or not. He is the Lord of the Flies. To some people, the act of writing poetry is as beautiful as a finished poem.

Sewing up the past

Sallie Jones grew up on the banks of the Suwannee River, grew up on the edge of the piney woods, grew up on her momma's and daddy's farm, where a body learned life's most important lessons, mainly how to grow food, how to build shelter, how to stay warm when it was cold.

"Child, you couldn't 'spect people to take care of you," she said. "When I was comin' up you learned to take care of yourself."

Sallie Jones, 74, was looking at a quilt she had made. Some are so colorful, so beautiful, that people around the Florida-Georgia border consider her a folk artist. Mrs. Jones finds it strange to think of herself as any kind of artist. She made quilts because she wanted her 14 children to sleep warm.

"My momma and daddy had fifteen head of children, so my momma had to make quilts, too," Mrs. Jones said. "She started young, and I started learnin' when I was eighteen."

Mrs. Jones and another quilter, Alma Bailey, were at the Stephen Foster State Folk Culture Center to talk about what comes naturally to them. It was part of the state's annual rural folklife days celebration. Old-timey Floridians such as Mrs. Jones and Mrs. Bailey came out of the woods and demonstrated skills once necessary for successful living.

Life used to be hard in Florida. People who endured were self-sufficient and practical. They woke early, worked with their hands and retired shortly after sundown. Then they started over the next day. If something broke they fixed it. If something wore out, they used it in something else. Nobody had to tell them about recycling.

"The world is getting so fast now," Alma Bailey, 63, said softly. "We have a throwaway society. We buy a lot of things. When I was growing up, we didn't throw away a thing. You took old clothes and you used them in a quilt."

Mrs. Bailey was raised on a farm on the other side of the Suwannee from Mrs. Jones. Mrs. Bailey was 10 when she learned how to make quilts from her mother. At night, after a hard day of farming, Mrs. Bailey's mother would lower the wood frame that hung over the dining room table. On the frame Mrs. Bailey and her mother worked on quilts.

"For a while, I thought we were running out of people who knew how to make quilts," said Mrs. Bailey. "People would tell me, 'Well, my grandma quilted, but my mother doesn't. But I'm learning how.' We seemed to have skipped a generation. Young women are getting back into it. And that makes me proud."

68

Quilting is an old folk art, according to experts at the New England Quilt Museum. Quilting began in China almost eight centuries ago when self-sufficient people learned that sewing together three fabric layers produced an exceptionally warm bed cover. A layer of cotton was placed between a bottom lining and a top that sometimes was colorfully decorated.

"A quilt," Sallie Jones told schoolchildren who visited the Folk Culture Center by the hundreds, "is just like a sandwich. You have your bread and you put a noodle or the meat inside."

In America, quilting flourished during colonial times, and out of a practical activity a folk art was born. Some women, including some who could neither read nor write, told family stories through symbols sewn on quilts. Some learned from their mothers precise patterns and stitching they passed on to daughters who passed the knowledge to their daughters. Quilting, traditionally, has been a women's art.

That's how it was in Sallie Jones' family anyway. Her mother and her mother's sisters – and Sallie, when she was old enough – sometimes gathered after breakfast to make quilts. As many as 10 women worked on a single quilt. It was a social activity, where family and community news was communicated – but the object of the exercise was to turn out quilts.

"When the sun went down," Mrs. Jones said, "sometimes we had four quilts done."

Quilts made by Mrs. Jones' family were different from ones produced by Mrs. Bailey's kinfolk. Mrs. Jones is an African-American, and her quilts are often characterized by bright colors and improvised patterns. Mrs. Bailey, working within the Anglo-American tradition, tends to use subtler colors and symmetrical patterns. Mrs. Bailey's quilts are to Mrs. Jones' quilts what pop music is to jazz.

But the two women have much in common. Like Mrs. Jones, Mrs. Bailey grew up on a farm, learned a wide variety of skills and has traditional values. A "widow woman," in her words, she lives with her son and raises cattle, chickens and corn. She still makes about 40 quilts a year, which she gives to friends and relatives.

Mrs. Jones lives outside of Lake City, and she still works in her garden. She makes about a dozen quilts a year, which, she confessed, is hardly enough to supply her family. When she last counted, she had more than 100 grandchildren and 60 great-grandchildren. So many quilts are needed, and so little time is left to produce them. None of Mrs. Jones' children knows how to quilt.

Unlike Mrs. Bailey, who makes quilts by hand, Mrs. Jones uses her late mother's ancient Singer sewing machine. It lacks electricity; Mrs. Jones powers it by a foot pedal.

"I can't sew with my hands anymore," she said. She was showing her son how to build a room when an unbraced wall fell and damaged her thumb. That was 14 years ago, when she was 60 and still comfortable with saw and hammer.

"Honey, I was always a person who watched other people and learned how to do things. I know how to make lye soap. I made my own hats out of palmetto leaves. I could plow a field behind a mule. I grew my own cane, and ground it, and made my own syrup. I used to grow my own rice, and threshed it, and ate of it. My husband, he used to say, 'Girl, you just set a spell,' but I could never set down. I had to be doin' something. I had to be workin' hard."

She and her late husband, Phillip, worked morning until night. All those babies, she said: All those babies were hungry. "Me and my husband wasn't in the habit of askin' people for help. We just went and did for ourself."

She stood, and leaned against her cane – her knee had been causing misery – and picked up an old quilt. She made it years ago from her children's old clothing. While she reeled off the names of her children, now grown, she pointed to their pants, their shirts and their jackets that went into the quilt. The quilt she held in her hands was, in a way, a history of family.

She said she sleeps well.

"Never with a blanket," she said. "I don't care for nothin' but a quilt on me. I'll lay on a sheet, but I need to keep a quilt next to me."

A love song To Florida

Ross Gardner loved Wyoming. It was cold, and it was wild, but the rugged people knew how to take care of themselves. Ross did, too.

"It was a real frontier," he said. "The streets had wooden sidewalks. There were hitching posts and a house of prostitution on the other side of the tracks. The snow started in September and didn't stop until May. It was something."

Ross Gardner would have been happy finishing his life in the Wild West. But when the heart problems started, the doctor told him straight: Go South, old man. Retire to Florida. Take advantage of the few good years you have left.

Thirty-seven years have passed, and Ross is still taking advantage of Florida's gentle lifestyle. Thursday, in fact, he will celebrate birthday No. 95. He is short of breath on occasion, and his shingles pain him now and again, but he does not complain.

What's to complain about? Wearing glasses, he can gaze out the window of his 20th-floor apartment and see if dolphins are chasing mullet in Tampa Bay. He can putt on the putting green and shuffle on the shuffleboard court. Five minutes from his door he can cast a line from the dock and catch a plump flounder for supper. Wyoming may have had grizzly bears, but it had no tasty flounders.

Wyoming never inspired a song.

Last year, Ross Gardner took out pen and paper and wrote a song about Florida's joys. Ross was a teacher, a bank clerk, a secretary and a lawyer before retirement, but his hobby was songwriting. Sitting in his condo one night, thinking about the state, he wrote down words, and on his mandolin plucked a melody, which he played for his friend Dorothy Feltyberger, who thought of a few ways it could be improved on.

Pretty soon *Home in the Sun, Down Florida Way* was ready for the world.

"Home, home in the sun," Ross Gardner's song sounded something like *Home on the Range*, one of his cowboy favorites. "Where our dreams at last have come true. Where new friends are made as we rest in the shade, and life blossoms out all anew."

Ross' wife Frances liked the song, and so did his friends at the condo, but, well, they might have been prejudiced. Ross wanted objective opinions. He sent copies to the governor and Florida's senators. Now it's official: Heads of state like the song, too.

The governor wrote back a pleasant letter of appreciation. Ross' senator, Lawton Chiles, was even more enthusiastic. Last July 28 at 9:00 a.m. the senator stood in the Senate chamber in Washington, D.C., and made a flattering speech about Ross and his music. Then he read the lyrics of *Home in the Sun, Down Florida Way* into the Congressional Record.

"Well, I'll tell you, I'm real thrilled," Ross said. "I've had some life. I've had some experiences."

Spend time with Ross Gardner and the word "experiences" crops up again and again. That's what 95 years on Earth will do for you. He grew up on a Nebraska farm, learned to play harmonica, went to college, learned to play mandolin, taught in a country school, learned to read music, fought the Germans during World War I, moved to Wyoming, wrote songs, became a bank clerk, went to law school, had his own law practice, moved to Washington, worked as secretary to a Congressman, and returned after World War II to practice law in his beloved Wyoming, where seldom was heard a discouraging word and the skies were not cloudy all day – at least until his heart troubles made him take it easier and prompted his Florida migration.

"I was a real outdoorsman," he said wistfully. "I did a lot of hunting and fishing. I saw grizzly bears. Where I lived I had to chase buffaloes away from my gate. Elk came down from the mountain to eat the hay. A friend of mine shot a wildcat once in a cave, but nobody believed him until they came back and saw the blood."

Cowboys and oilmen rode into town on Saturday night, cashed their paychecks, drank whiskey and beat each other bloody before walking across the tracks to the house of ill repute. People settled arguments with guns. Those were the good old days.

"One time this man who I did some work for thought I cheated him. I didn't, but that's what he thought, and the word was he was coming to kill me. I got out my thirty-eight – I was born with a gun in my hand – and I waited and waited and waited. He didn't come.

"Finally, a couple of days later, he walked in, smiling, and he said, 'You know, I almost killed you the other day.' I said, "No, you didn't. I was waiting for you. And if you had pulled a gun when you came in here today, I'd have shot you right between the eyes. I don't want you in here. I don't want your business. You're too dangerous.' "

Gardner never wrote a song about the incident, but he could have. He is the author of more songs than he can remember. He composes religious tunes, pop and big band music. *There's a Light in a Window in the Sky* was played at a Wyoming funeral. *Waltzing With You*, his only published song, is played at the Friday night dances held at the condominium.

"Sometimes songs come flooding out of you like water," said Ross, who also writes poetry. "I get ideas in the middle of the night and I get out of bed to write them down. If I don't, I forget them. I wish I had a tape recorder to say my lyrics into."

The words to *Home in the Sun, Down Florida Way* came quickly. Ross wanted them to describe the idyllic life of Floridians who spend their retirements shuffling from the golf course to the beach to their favorite fishing hole. When he finished, he knew he had something good, and began working on a melody that reminds people of *Home on the Range*.

"I think my song is pretty good, though I don't think it has enough zip to ever be considered an official state song. But it's nice it's had this attention."

Sitting on the sofa, Ross Gardner picked up one of his many harmonicas and played the melody. He shook his head gently and said, "I used to play the harmonica a lot better," and tried again. This time every note was true. Confidence restored, he tooted a perfect *Joy to the World* and *You Are My Sunshine*. Then he stood and did magic tricks.

"I'm deaf in both ears without my hearing aid," he said a few minutes later. "I'm blind in one eye. I'm bald and I have false teeth, and the other day, when I went down to the putting green, I got out of breath and thought I was going to faint. But let me tell you: I have no complaints. I've had so many experiences. This has been one great life."

Home in the Sun, Down Florida Way

We left the old home and started to roam
Then drifted down Florida way.
Where old people find a life-giving clime
And shufflers just shuffle all day
Home, home in the sun
Where our dreams at last have come true
Where new friends are made as we rest in the shade
And life blossoms out all anew.
The toil and the tears of all the past years
The battle for prestige and wealth
Are soon laid aside while here we abide
Buoyed up with new vigor and health.
Through Florida's gates a paradise waits
For all who seek a peaceful repose.
The shuffleboard lures while good fishing cures
Most all of our griefs and our woes.
The lakes and the streams give vent to our dreams
While golfing builds vigor and vim.
Good beaches abound and are used the year round
Where the old and the young love to swim.
Home, home in the sun
Where our dreams at last have come true.
Where new friends are made as we rest in the shade
And life blossoms out all anew.

Winter

Wild by nature

I can tell they are tourists raised on Walt Disney movies. They act as if they have never seen a big alligator in the flesh, and that a big alligator is a friendly fellow who would never think of eating them for lunch. They canoe very close, too close, and break out their video camera. From where I watch from the bank, I can hear the camera whirring.

The alligators at this park near Sarasota are famous for two reasons. One, there are a lot of them. Two, they grow large because the food supply is clearly ample. As I fished from the river bank at dusk many years ago, I almost stepped on a half blind 12-footer. People called it One-Eyed Jack, I found out later. It was lying on the bank, unmoving, and I came close to stepping on it. A man fishing from the dike warned me.

"Hey, don't you see that alligator?"

I didn't. I was new to fly fishing and had to concentrate on every cast or I'd hook myself in the ear. So I got within feet of stepping on what could have been a very nasty log with one eye and big yellow teeth. Alligators sometimes ambush terrestrial prey by lying still and waiting for the careless. I still shiver at the thought.

Today, tourists step forward to videotape their close encounter with a dinosaur. The alligator is probably asleep. Or maybe last night it devoured a plump piglet that had nothing on its mind but a cool drink. The Lord takes care of foolish tourists and alligators.

Winter is when you see tourists and wildlife in great number in our state parks, especially parks near urban centers. Myakka is only 14 miles east of the pavement, restaurants and shopping centers of Sarasota. Sarasota may no longer be real Florida. Myakka definitely is.

There are anglers on the water hoping for bass, bluegill and pickerel this morning. Most anglers are in canoes. Some, believe it or not, are wading among the pockets of lily pads and alligators. I have never heard of an alligator attack at Myakka. Alligators, fortunately, are mostly nocturnal and mostly afraid of people. But I wouldn't wade here at night.

I bike away from my dark thoughts and pedal through an oak hammock. The ground looks as if it were bulldozed. It actually has been pigdozed. Feral hogs, many generations away from domestic stock, roam woods and swamp. They uproot vegetation, eat snakes and whatever else they can catch. I have seen 300-pound hogs here. The boy with me asks, "What would you do if one attacked?"

I say, "I don't think a normal hog would attack a person. The only guy I know who was attacked was a hunter who'd wounded the hog with his first shot. It charged. He killed it on the second shot. Fell dead at his feet."

"Yeah, but what would YOU do if one charged?"

"Well, I'd fight him off with my Swiss Army knife. Or I'd throw you in his way. Or I'd climb a tree."

You could also try to outrun a hog on your bicycle. Do hogs snap at cyclist ankles the way collies do? Probably not. Hogs are smarter than dogs. They'd rip the spokes with razor-sharp tusks and disable the bike. As you writhed on the pavement, Mr. Pig would have at you. Then the vultures would come in for the scraps. There's nothing like a day in the country to reduce life to the basics:

Who eats and who gets eaten?

The bird migrations peak in January. You ought to see Myakka River and the adjacent lake right now. Both are full of waterfowl. From a lakeside boardwalk I see blue-winged teal, shovelers and ducks I can't identify even through binoculars. There are white and glossy ibis. There are great blue and tri-colored herons. Two sandhill cranes, suspicious of strangers, steal glances at me.

Vultures glide across the sky. They are joined by a red-tailed hawk. Below them, I see two other large hawks skimming over the water. I see the white bar on the tail. They are Northern harriers. Marsh hawks. They flit about like paper airplanes. Suddenly, in unison, they dive-bomb the teal. The teal, half flying and half running across the water, make good a terrified escape.

I dig the *Peterson's* hawk guide from my pack and look up Northern harrier. Peterson says a harrier will take a duck. It will hold the duck under the water until it drowns. Then it's lunch time. Ducks have a hard life. Only the best of them, the wiliest, survive the onslaught of harriers, eagles, peregrine falcons, alligators and hunters with .12-gauge shotguns.

Shifting into low gear, I abandon the pavement. From the fire road, I watch a red-shouldered hawk land on top of an oak. It studies the ground for garter snakes. At the river I stop to eat a box of raisins and to chat with a photographer. His Nikon is attached to what looks like a rifle stock. He aims and fires.

"Look at the wood storks!" he says. Wood storks, an endangered species, feed on minnows in the shallows. They are accompanied by the usual suspects, the sandhill cranes, the ibis, the egrets. "This is a great park for a wildlife photographer," he says.

He lists the results of previous Myakka hunts. He has photographed wild turkeys, deer, owls, eagles and even bobcats. I envy him his bobcats. The only one I ever saw was dead on the road.

"Well, you've got to trick them," the photographer says. "I use a bobcat attractant to bring them in." His bobcat attractant is a tape-recording of a rabbit, squealing in death. Bobcats come running and try not to trip over their bibs.

Late in the afternoon, as the shadows deepen, I return to the river with the boy. He has brought his fishing rod and tackle and he is sure he could catch a bass, which would fry up nice. I sit on a bluff and read an Everglades book by Marjory Stoneman Douglas. With much concentration he works a plastic worm through the lily pads.

Two large alligators sunbathe on the opposite bank. A fat one –10 feet long or so – floats in the middle of the river. The boy kneels on the bank to replace his worm with a gold spoon. I notice the fat alligator has disappeared.

I call to the boy. "Hey, where's the gator?" He doesn't know. The ugly scenario plays through my head. The alligator is coming fast along the bottom. It will explode out of the shallows and take the boy.

"Hey, get away from the bank. That alligator is going to eat you."

"You worry too much, Dad."

I watch a pair of osprey on their nest atop the pole that carries the high-tension wires over the river. A while ago, I saw an osprey swoop low and grab a careless bluegill with its talons. Now it's sitting on a pole, just above the wires, tearing at the fish.

The wires go through osprey paradise toward civilization. The osprey goes "Cheep. Cheep. Cheereek!" as it sups. The wires go "Humma humma humma" as they carry electricity toward distant homes, distant stoves, distant refrigerators. The boy says, "Would you swim across the river for $100?" I say no. Where is that alligator? And is it hungry?

The Sunken Gardens gift shop

ST. PETERSBURG   3/15/87

I own a Panama hat I almost never wear. I bought it in a Key West gift shop in 1985.

I own a hand-carved slingshot. It's gathering dust in my sock drawer. I purchased it in a North Carolina gift shop in 1986.

I spent three bucks for a machete in a Clewiston restaurant gift shop in 1987. I grow no sugar cane in my yard, or banana trees. I am afraid of machetes. As a tourist, I had to have one.

I am walking around the Sunken Gardens Gift Shop in St. Petersburg when I encounter a tourist named Maurice Goodell holding a lamp made of seashells. I do not laugh at shell lamps. As the owner of a machete, slingshot and Panama hat, I understand how these things happen. You don't intend to buy them, you just do.

I nod knowingly when Mr. Goodell tells me: "They suckered me $15 for this."

Mr. Goodell, a 68-year-old visitor from Vermont, is not angry. He's not asking for pity. He's stating fact. Something – a mysterious force that human beings are not meant to understand – made him spend his money on a shell lamp.

"I've been to this gift shop lots of times," he says without rancor. "They've nailed me for $40 or $50 over the years."

I come away from our conversation feeling respect for Mr. Goodell.

He has exactly the right attitude. When you are a tourist, don't fight it. Do your duty. Live up to your destiny. Buy incredibly foolish items. Be proud.

There are lots of people who depend on you. How else are shop owners going to pay for the boy's braces? How else are they going to send their daughter through med school? They obviously need your money.

They need you to buy coconut heads carved to resemble one-eyed pirates. You are required to buy rubber alligators. They will not let you cross the Florida border without buying at least one bumper sticker that says, "Let me tell you about my grandchildren."

As I write this, the Sunshine State boasts 1,600 souvenir gift shops, and they mean big bucks. They employ almost 8,000 people, and take in about $1.4-billion annually. Souvenir shops range in size from little Mom and Pop places on the beach to chain outlets in malls for city slickers.

There is one gift shop, however, that stands out above the rest. It is the world's largest, according to its advertisements, and the claim probably is no exaggeration.

The Sunken Gardens Gift Shop, in St. Petersburg, sprawls across 55,000 square feet, about the size of your average supermarket. During tourist season, some people claim, a radio signal is beamed out of the attic at a frequency only tourists can hear. They may want to go to the beach, or to Disney World, but the radio beam makes them exit at the interstate and go to Sunken Gardens instead.

Unable to help themselves, they drive into the parking lot. Like zombies, they trudge for the door of the Sunken Gardens Gift Shop. About 500,000 people pass through the door every year. They intend to admire the truly astonishing garden in back. Heh, heh. To get to the garden, they first must negotiate the perilous gift shop and its seductive aisles and its million items that they definitely don't need, don't want, shouldn't buy – but must.

"Buy me," shouts the alligator ball-point pen.

"Mister," hisses the saltwater taffy, "did you bring your VISA?"

"Hey, you. Yes, you." You turn slowly. Just as you suspected. You have been summoned by the lint brush.

I introduce myself to Cele Juraska. Cele has worked at the Sunken Gardens Gift Shop for 14 years. She is in charge of sales and also does much of the buying for the store. There's a lot more to Sunken Gardens than coconut heads and rubber alligators, she can tell you. There's fine jewelry and nifty ceramic goods and high-quality hats.

"We have a little bit of everything," she says.

I ask about coconut heads and shell lamps.

"Of course, when we go out buying, we look for items that we think we'll sell a lot of. We keep in mind that most of our tourists are retired people on fixed incomes. What they would like to buy is not necessarily what I would like to buy."

I find Mary Cook of Georgia wandering down an aisle. What does she want to buy?

"I'm hunting for this – I don't know how to describe this – well, it's a tiny animal, a squirrel or skunk or something, that's part of a collection. It's for my grandchild."

Here comes tourist Dave Katz, camera slung over his neck. "I have never seen a gift shop this large in Massachusetts," he says. He picks up a toy. It's a shark's head on the end of a stick. When he squeezes a trigger, the shark's jaws open and close.

Katz and I exchange smiles. We both understand his role as a tourist. He must buy the toy, and when he returns to Massachusetts, the toy must disappear forever in his sock drawer.

So will the dozens of shells I later see him toss into a shopping basket. But I don't tell him that. I see him at a cash register with his VISA card. He is grinning.

After a while, I am grinning too, and I don't know why. Maybe it's because I am hearing things. A cap that says "Darn Seagulls," and looks like it's been splattered with bird dung, beckons. I don't come near. I ignore the cries of the sea horse-shaped soap. I harden my heart when the "Dirty Old Man" coffee mug winks suggestively and begs that I pick him up.

I am one tough cookie.

Then, looming in front of me, is something truly dangerous.

Sponge-rubber flamingo slippers. They don't have bunnies on the toes. They have flamingoes. I run for my life, saying to myself, I will not buy, I will not buy, I will not buy – and then find myself, inevitably, in front of the post card display.

How did the store know I am a sucker for post cards? I sigh and buy a dozen.

My hunger satisfied, the Sunken Gardens Gift Shop now lets me go home.

House of Hemingway

The first thing you notice is the cats, cats said to be descended from the pets he kept so long ago. They are on his stone wall and in his banyan trees, on his front porch and on his veranda above, weird six-toed cats everywhere. You walk through his gate, stepping over a cat, as a matter of fact, and hand over your admission at 10:30 on one of those warm Key West mornings for which tourists pay plenty.

Inside his front door, you are funnelled into his living room, now a gift shop, where you can buy black-and-white prints of his face, T-shirts bearing his likeness, and, of course, the books he wrote. Tourists finger through his novels and his short stories and then leaf through wallets for money to pay the saleswoman who doles out change from what looks like a tacklebox.

Ernest Hemingway slept here. Between 1928 and 1940 he lived in Key West, and from April 29, 1931, until early 1940 the two-story Spanish colonial mansion at 907 Whitehead Street was his home. In a spartan room on the second floor of the backyard guest house, at a crude round table, sitting in an even cruder cigarmaker's chair, writing feverishly with pencil, he produced 75 percent of his life's work.

In Key West he finished *A Farewell to Arms*, his World War I novel, and produced *Death in the Afternoon*, his paean to bullfighting. Here he wrote *To Have and Have Not*, his novel about Key West-Cuban smuggling during the Depression, *The Green Hills of Africa*, his safari novel, and short stories including "The Snows of Kilimanjaro" and "The Short Happy Life of Frances Macomber." He began a long association with *Esquire* magazine during his Key West residency, started his novel about the fascist war in Spain, *For Whom the Bell Tolls* and conceived *The Old Man And the Sea*, the novella that won him the Nobel Prize.

In Key West he also began his love affair with deep-sea fishing, drank like a fish in Sloppy Joe's Bar, visited cockfights and houses of ill repute, beat up critics and homosexuals, drove his second wife to divorce and became the larger-than-life celebrity who called himself "Papa."

On July 2, 1961, 19 days before his 62nd birthday, in his new home in Ketchum, Idaho, he took a double-barreled shotgun, pointed it at his forehead and squeezed both triggers. "Papa Passes," was the headline in the Key West Citizen the next day. Good God. Hemingway, of all people. Dead.

Yet here in his old home, where some say he spent the happiest years of his life, he lives on.

"Even from the grave he attracts people."

Larry Harvey, Hemingway House guide, is talking about tourists who visit the sprawling home every day of the year. He stands on the porch outside the gift shop looking polite but impatient at the same time. In a moment he will lead another tour. He does not wish to keep people waiting.

He is a small man who looks younger than his 60 years, and he has been working here nine years. Before that he was retired in Key West and before that taught literature at a Miami prep school and what later would become the New England School of Law in Boston. His father sold rare first-edition books in Paris, where Larry Harvey, a boy then, first met Hemingway. The last time was in Spain 28 years ago. He says Hemingway remembered him and enjoyed talking of Paris. He says some writers cringe when fans approach, but not Hemingway. He enjoyed celebrity.

"He was a dynamic man with an overwhelming personality," says Harvey, flamboyant in dress and manner himself. He wears a colorful flower shirt open almost halfway to his waist and hip-hugging blue slacks. He walks as if his loafers are a size small. "He had very easy relationships with other people, and I think that, along with his ability to write effortless prose, was part of his appeal.

"People love Mr. Hemingway as much today as at any time," he goes on, in a accent as mixed as seafood gumbo. One moment he sounds like Margaret Mitchell's courtly Ashley Wilkes; in the next he could be Laurence Olivier doing Macbeth; a second later he could be Truman Capote on the Tonight Show. He was born in Virginia, but years in Europe, Boston and Key West have wreaked havoc on his speech.

"There is a great Hemingway renaissance going on, you know," he says, and he lets you know that he believes it is about time today's literary world paid homage to Papa. There was a period, in the late 1960s and early 1970s, when Hemingway did seem to fall from grace. Some critics were bothered by the machismo chest-beating in his work, the frequent attacks on other writers and a spare prose style that to some read more like journalism than art. But in recent years, new biographies have been published, several movies have been made from novels, and there seems to be interest again in Ernest Hemingway.

"I think Ernest Hemingway was a trailblazer," Larry Harvey says, sounding like the schoolteacher he once was. "He set new trends. The sparseness of his language, his wonderful descriptive powers and the way he drew his characters from real life are most refreshing. It was true that he was very macho. But he had his very sentimental side. When he heard about the death of his very good friend, the actor Gary Cooper, you know he burst into tears."

Larry Harvey strolls into the gift shop, claps his hands, and the tour begins. A dozen people gather tightly around him, but they don't have to; his voice carries. He tells how the house was built in 1851 by Asa Tift, how it fell into disrepair, about how Ernest and Pauline Hemingway acquired it in 1931 as an $8,000 wedding present from Pauline's uncle. Larry Harvey talks a little about Hemingway's career, which ended on that fateful day in Idaho, and he says, "but on this tour – for heaven's sake – shall we not speak of happy things?"

Happy thing one: When Hemingway's family sold the house in 1963, Larry Harvey says, Bernice Dickson – "Oh, thank God" – bought it in a closed-bid auction for $80,000. Happy thing two: The following year she opened the mansion to the public. Since then thousands of people have filed through, although Mrs. Dickson won't say how many. Her business, she figures, is her business.

But most other things about the house are public. You follow Larry Harvey through the living room as he points out the zebra-skin couch and this and that. On that wall is a Spanish nobleman's 18th century traveling desk complete with hidden compartments to confound pirates. Hanging from the ceiling is a chandelier, Larry Harvey says, "made from hand-blown Venetian glass from my favorite city in the world other than Key West – fabulous Venice."

In the dining room Larry Harvey takes you to the 18th-century Spanish table, which features chairs that include sword racks. "One didn't want to get tipsy," Larry Harvey says, "and stab your good buddy, over or under the table, merely to make" – he sings the next part in falsetto –"another poiiint..."

He asks if you have seen the fireplace in the corner.

"You notice, of course, that it is off-center, as so many of us are in Key West," says Larry Harvey. Like many who live here, he fell in love with the town, which embraces the artistic as warmly as the tourists eager to part with money. He decided to retire here but then accepted a job that allowed him to take advantage of his flair for the dramatic. The Hemingway House guide, happily off center.

"Let me level with you, dear hearts," he says. "In Key West, we wouldn't have it any other way."

So you go past the off-center dining room fireplace and peek into the kitchen, where Pauline Hemingway had the counters raised four inches so her six-foot-three inch husband could stand straight and fillet his fish and cook without tormenting his bad back.

Larry Harvey invites you upstairs into the bedroom. "Come now, little beanies," he calls. You arrive in time to hear him tell everyone to form a semi-circle around Hemingway's huge bed. "That should turn everybody on," he says, and tells how Papa strapped two double beds together to create one of the first king-sized beds.

Above the bed you see a painting of cats. Hemingway, Larry Harvey says, loved them. The 40 or so on the grounds, he assures you, are "a living testimonial to Ernest Miller Hemingway." They require $600 worth of food and care a month, but refuse to drink from the unusual fountain Hemingway hauled back one night from Sloppy Joe's Bar. The gift to his cats from Papa was a urinal.

You contemplate that paradox – Hemingway, the fisherman and big-game hunter who killed lions for fun, dearly loved his pet cats – as you walk onto the veranda outside of his bedroom. The table at which he breakfasted is still there. He liked to eat kippered herring with toast before tackling his morning's writing.

Hemingway was born in Oak Park, Illinois, on July 21, 1889. His father was a doctor; the boy wanted to be a writer. Declared unfit for military service because of poor eyesight, he was a Red Cross ambulance driver in Italy during World War I. After the war he got a newspaper job with the Kansas City Star, became foreign correspondent for the Toronto Star, and was encouraged to try fiction by writer Gertrude Stein. A short-story collection, *In Our Time*, and *The Sun Also Rises*, followed.

In 1927 novelist John Dos Passos told him he needed a place to "dry out his bones" after those harsh Paris winters and told him about the island 90 miles from Cuba, Key West.

Hemingway was finishing *A Farewell to Arms* when he arrived in 1928. He began fishing immediately and started putting together a collection of friends who would later be known as his "mob." There was Sloppy Josie Russell, the bar owner, who became the model for *To Have and Have Not*'s Capt. Harry Morgan. Another regular was attorney George Brooks, "Bee Lips," of the same novel and one of his closest friends.

Brooks enjoyed provoking Hemingway. Among other things, he delighted in encouraging homosexuals to make passes at Hemingway, who wore his manhood like a badge of honor. In one incident at Sloppy Joe's Bar, according to James McLendon's fine *Papa: Hemingway in Key West*, Hemingway stood, drained of color, and knocked cold the offending gay man.

Hemingway's temper was trigger quick and his right hook near lethal. One day his sister was introduced to a well-known poet named Wallace Stevens, vacationing in Key West. Stevens criticized the work of her brother, and when she defended him, he insulted her. She returned home in tears. Hemingway ran to the cocktail party and broke Stevens' jaw.

When he wasn't fighting, he was fishing. There were barracuda trips to the Dry Tortugas, tarpon at Marquesas Key, yellowtail at 12-Mile Reef and marlin in the Gulf Stream. He was also traveling. During his Key West residency he made many voyages to Cuba in his black mahogany fishing boat, *Pilar*, hunted in Wyoming, researched bullfighting in Spain and went on safaris in Africa. Returning home, his head filled with ideas, he would be ready for writing.

Here is Larry Harvey, waiting for you under the coconut palms by the pool, outside the guest house that contained Hemingway's upstairs studio, where he wrote. He is ready to tell the famous pool story and wants to make sure his people are close enough to hear. You will hear the pool story before you see the studio, he says.

It was the Depression, and Hemingway had spent almost a year in Spain, watching the Loyalists' war against the fascist Franco. He had also fallen out of his love with his wife, Pauline, and into love with a journalist named Martha Gellhorn. Pauline, waiting in Key West for her husband, had decided to build a pool.

There were no pools in Key West in 1936. The coral was too hard to cut, yet no dynamite was allowed. But Pauline insisted on her pool. The 60-foot pool was dug by pick and shovel for $20,000 – more than twice the buying price of their home. Ernest Hemingway returned from Spain, saw the pool and grimaced.

He was, Larry Harvey tells you, "tight with the dollar. He had never forgotten that he ate pigeons as a struggling writer in Paris." Throwing down a penny, Hemingway told Pauline that she might as well spend his last cent. Pauline, who had a sense of humor, had the 1934-D Lincoln pressed into the cement. Covered in plastic, it is the last thing you see before going upstairs.

"You are going to see a typewriter on his desk," Larry Harvey says. "If you ever see a photograph of Ernest Hemingway with a typewriter, it is a promotional photograph. He wrote in longhand. Now go ahead, two at a time, please. Go up the stairs and look. Go, little sparklers. Light up the sky."

So you walk up the stairs, two at a time, and look into the room. A chain across the doorway prevents your entry, but you see the small mounted tarpon fish on one wall and the heads of deer and antelope that grace the other, and you see the small round bamboo table where he wrote until he left his wife and his home and Key West in 1940.

The tour ends after that. The rest of his life is not discussed. Overlooked is his messy divorce from Pauline, his disillusionment with a growing tourist-minded town, his third and fourth marriages, the move to a new Idaho home, the triumph of *The Old Man and the Sea*, followed by what he feared was an erosion of his writing talent, the demons that pecked away at his sanity, poor physical health and what happened that July 1961 morning in Ketchum when he picked up for the last time his .12 gauge.

Some people linger to take photos of the house and the garden and the cats and even Larry Harvey, who bows dramatically and thanks you for listening to him "talk about my old acquaintance, Ernest Miller Hemingway."

Then he is gone to lunch, and you walk back into the gift shop to look at the zebra-skinned couch one last time, and to buy a couple of books that you always meant to read. And sitting there, taking the money, is Bernice Dickson.

"Yes, I knew Ernest Hemingway," says Mrs. Dickson, who owns the house now. She says her husband once even roofed the house for Papa. "Hemingway, you know, had a thing about leaky roofs. But my husband guaranteed the roof for twenty years. And it lasted until 1978."

"You knew him?" an eavesdropping tourist asks. Mrs. Dickson nods.

"He was a suicide, wasn't he?" the tourist asks. "Didn't he kill himself?"

Bernice Dickson cringes.

Marjory Stoneman Douglas

MIAMI   2/9/92

As I barrel through Everglades National Park this morning, watching for eagles and wood storks and snail kites out my truck window, I feel butterflies in my stomach. I'm as nervous as a Little Leaguer on his way to meet Mickey Mantle.

My destination, 40 miles distant, is a small home in the Miami suburb of Coconut Grove. Marjory Stoneman Douglas, the formidable 101-year-old author of *The Everglades: River of Grass*, lives there.

Like Henry Thoreau, Wendell Berry and Marjorie Kinnan Rawlings, Mrs. Douglas is among my heroes. In my opinion, River of Grass, published in 1947, is a masterpiece of nature writing. Her book helped put the Everglades, and the environmental problems of South Florida, on the map of national consciousness. It is filled with beautiful prose, solid reporting and a prickly defense of place.

"The water moves. The sawgrass, pale green to deep-brown ripeness, stands rigid. It is moved only in sluggish rollings by the vast push of the winds across it. Over its endless acres here and there the shadows of the dazzling clouds quicken and slide, purple-brown, plum-brown, mauve-brown, rust-brown, bronze. The bristling, blossoming tops do not bend easily like standing grain. They do not even in their own growth curve all one way but stand in edge clumps, curving against each other, all the massed curving blades making millions of fine arching lines that at a little distance merge to a huge expanse of brown wires, or bristles or, farther beyond, to deep-piled plush. At the horizon they become velvet. The line they make is an edge of velvet against the infinite blue, the blue-and-white, the clear fine primrose yellow, the burning brass and crimson, the molten silver, the deepening hyacinth sky. . . "

Mrs. Douglas, a resident of South Florida since 1915, has enjoyed careers apart from painting unforgettable word-pictures about the river of grass. As a young woman, she was a *Miami Herald* editorial writer who opposed the draining of the Everglades and fought for women's right to vote. In middle age, she free-lanced short stories to some of the nation's most prestigious magazines.

She was 57 when she tried her hand at books. Twenty years later, after *River of Grass* had made her and the Everglades famous, she became the acid-tongued environmental activist who to this day lambastes developers, polluters, bureaucrats and lily-livered politicians.

As she approaches her 102nd birthday, she is almost finished writing a biography of W.H. Hudson, the 19th-century English naturalist whose most famous book was *Green Mansions*. But when the Everglades, with its plants and wildlife and water imperiled by the impact of South Florida's 4.5-million residents, need her help she puts aside other projects.

Looking frail, sometimes pushed in a wheelchair, she is brought to public gatherings when her spiritual strength and authority are needed. She'll rise to her feet, raise her fists and speak in a strong, firm voice – a Joan of Arc in sunglasses, straw hat, sensible cotton dress and trademark string of pearls around her neck.

"I will talk about the Everglades at the drop of a hat," she tells people.

Though she is all but blind, and her hearing is wearing out, and there are days when she feels bone-weary tired, she is still the Grande Dame of the Everglades. When I wrote her, asking for an interview, she answered promptly through a secretary. Of course she would talk about the Everglades.

I don't want to be late. You don't keep Marjory Stoneman Douglas waiting. On the other hand, you don't arrive too early either. Mrs. Douglas has her own schedule. For almost two hours, I sit in a Coconut Grove cafe and reread passages from *River of Grass* and her lively 1987 autobiography, *Marjory Stoneman Douglas, Voice of the River*.

The extra time gives me a chance to prepare further. Mrs. Douglas sometimes objects to answering questions she has answered before. This can be tricky for interviewers, since Mrs. Douglas has walked this Earth since Benjamin Harrison was president, and has been already asked most of the good questions. She's famous for pointing out foolish queries or ending interviews with a devastating sniff and the admonishment to "Read the book!"

And sometimes, despite her good intentions, she's simply in no mood for visitors. Like many public figures, especially very old ones who are feeling tired, there are days when she prefers her own company. There are days when she feels out of sorts with what remains of the 20th century. On those rare occasions, she may come across as indifferent, disoriented, or plain cross.

"Softness around the edges is not one of her qualities, nor a quality she values very highly," U.S. Senator Bob Graham has told me. Graham, who grew up on the outskirts of the Everglades in western Miami, first met Mrs. Douglas when he was a boy. She was already in her 60s. They are good friends.

"If you're not performing up to her standards, she'll tell you about it," says Graham, who supported the Everglades as a state legislator and as governor before moving along to Washington. Whenever he sees Mrs. Douglas he approaches her from behind, covers her eyes with his hands, and says "Guess who?" Mrs. Douglas always guesses correctly. Among other things, only a senator whom Mrs. Douglas calls one of her "Everglades boys" would have the nerve.

Just off Douglas Road – it's not named for her, though there are a number of schools and government buildings in Florida that are – I turn onto her property. With its lush umbrella trees, a rare lignum vitae and a mahogany, her yard is a tiny rain forest. I park on her indifferently kept lawn. She never chose to own a car and has no driveway.

Her house is unlike most South Florida dwellings you see these days. With its many shaded windows, large screened doors, and a high mushroom-shape roof, her home was built to take advantage of any breeze blowing off nearby Biscayne Bay. Unlike modern Floridians, Mrs. Douglas never felt the need for air-conditioning. With its mildewed stucco walls and spider webs in every corner, the house looks old and used but sturdy enough to withstand another dozen or so hurricanes.

I knock on her door in a jaunty shave-and-a-haircut-two-bits rhythm to disguise my case of nerves. I hope Mrs. Douglas will be agreeable.

The door of her old home creaks open.

I swallow hard and step into a dark, slightly musty-smelling living room.

"You're very prompt," the tiny white-haired woman says. I briefly clasp Mrs. Douglas' outstretched hand as gently as I'd squeeze a Cape Sable seaside sparrow. She directs me to a chair in a corner. Despite her failed eyesight, she follows me through a maze of furniture as if she possesses radar.

Sitting in an adjacent chair, she switches on a light so I can see my notes and her. She wears a baby-blue bathrobe that looks recently pressed, slippers and her trademark string of pearls. Even in a bathrobe she's a formal person.

I tell her I've brought a gift, a hand-made rug woven by my wife. It's a thank-you note to a person who has lived an exemplary public life and fought for something both my wife and I love with all our being, the Everglades.

"Thank you!" Mrs. Douglas says. She asks to hold the rug. I had been warned about her vision – she suffers from a hereditary disease called bilateral macular deterioration of the retina – and now I realize how completely it has stolen her eyesight. Though sometimes she wears thick eyeglasses in public, she's legally blind.

"I know just the place for this rug," she says.

"Marjory, the rug is blue, red and green," Michael Blaine, her 47-year-old assistant, shouts so Mrs. Douglas can hear. Blaine has worked for Mrs. Douglas since 1967, when he took one of her history classes at a community college and they became friends.

He hovers about, makes sure she is all right, sometimes prepares and serves her meals, and has the ability to make her laugh. He likes to tell her he has dropped her hearing aid into the toilet, or sold one of her beloved cats to medical research. She looks his way and says, "Oh, go on with you."

Every afternoon, he pours her a glass of Desmond & Duff. "She's particular about her Scotch," Blaine says. "She can tell right away if it's a different brand."

Tiny and frail, Mrs. Douglas looks as if one of those Everglades breezes of hers could knock her for a loop. Suffering from a cold, she asks me to find her shawl. I drape it over her legs. Feeling better, she is kind enough to ask about my background. I don't have to ask hers. It's a matter of public record.

She was born in Minneapolis, on April 7, 1890, the only child of Frank Stoneman and Florence Trefethen. They settled in Rhode Island, her parents separated, and she and her mother moved in with relatives in Taunton, Massachusetts. Her voice and inflections still carry a trace of New England aristocrat.

After graduating from college in 1912, she married Kenneth Douglas, a writer who turned out to be a ne'er-do-well sent to prison for passing bad checks. Mrs. Douglas fled the failed marriage to Miami, where her father had founded the *Miami*

Herald, and where she got a divorce. She has not had sex since 1913. She enjoyed marital relations, but does not miss them.

"I got sex out of the way," she wrote in her autobiography.

She covered general assignments for her father's newspaper. She joined the Naval Reserve. In Europe, she worked for American Red Cross. After the war – World War I – she returned to newspapering in Miami. A renaissance woman even then, she also covered high society, served as gardening editor, and wrote a local-interest column.

High-pressure daily newspaper work, her own perfectionist drive to succeed, and several failed relationships with men set the stage for the first of three nervous breakdowns. She gave up daily journalism and looked into a slower paced career as a free-lance writer. Her stories were published in *Black Mask*, the pulp magazine that would later publish James M. Cain and Dashiell Hammett, and the *Saturday Evening Post*, which sometimes published the short stories of Hemingway and Fitzgerald.

In 1942, her national reputation established, Mrs. Douglas was approached by an editor who asked whether she wanted to contribute to a "Rivers of America" book series. The editor suggested a book about the Miami River. "It's only an inch long," she protested. She made a pitch of her own: The Everglades, she said, was actually a 60-mile wide river of grass.

She knew her Everglades. During construction of the Tamiami Trail highway in the 1920s, she and friends liked riding the two-lane road to where it dead-ended in the swamp.

"We'd cook breakfast over a campfire and watch the birds at sunrise," Mrs. Douglas tells me with a smile. "The moccasin snakes would crawl past us across the road. They're quite blind, you know, and they never bothered us."

But Mrs. Douglas never felt the need to commune very deeply with that grassy river. She studied the Everglades, she knew more about them than most people, she defended them, she loved them, but that didn't mean she wanted to swat mosquitoes, sweat buckets and wet her feet.

"I suppose you could say the Everglades and I have the kind of friendship that doesn't depend on constant physical contact," she tells people.

I like physical contact with the Everglades, where I've camped, fished, canoed, air-boated, swamp-buggied, frogged, snaked and skinny-dipped since I was a boy. I tell Mrs. Douglas about my two previous days cycling through Everglades National Park. She asks what I saw. I talk about the alligators on Old Ingraham Highway – she knows the road well – and my failure, as always, to see a panther at Long Pine Key.

"I saw a panther," she says. It was back in the 1960s at Marco Island, before the Southwest Florida town was rearranged by hotels and condominiums. Mrs. Douglas had been staying at her favorite place, a dirty, run-down hotel that nevertheless served outstanding food.

"I got up early that morning – *before* breakfast. In itself that was unusual." She laughs quietly. "Breakfast was not quite ready, so I went for a walk. Suddenly, a panther emerged from the mangroves, walked across the road and disappeared into the scrub on the other side. I had a wonderful view. I saw the crook in his long tail and was close enough to see the shadows on his face made by the long strands of fur. He had been fishing in the mangroves, you know."

She laughs again.

"Suddenly, I had this thought: What if he were watching me? It made me uncomfortable, and at that point I decided it was time for my breakfast."

I mention seeing three bald eagles at Nine-Mile Pond.

"Do you keep a bird list?" she asks. Unlike some birders, I don't keep a list of the species I've seen.

"I didn't keep a list either. I wish I had. I think it would have been fun. Well," she says, looking my way, "it's not too late for you."

Mrs. Douglas researched her book for five years. In 1947, just before President Harry S. Truman dedicated Everglades National Park, her book appeared in stores. In print for 45 years, it has sold almost 500,000 copies.

The book has been a commercial and artistic success. It is also one of those rare books that stirred things up. Before *River of Grass*, most people saw the Everglades as a wasteland, a worthless swamp, something to be drained and conquered. She saw it as valuable, beautiful, alive.

"Her book caught the essential characteristic of the Everglades," says Sen. Bob Graham. ".... the importance of water and its movement ...."

I compliment Mrs. Douglas on her achievement and wonder how she managed to combine wonderful reporting with such graceful descriptions.

"I went out there. I looked. I came back and wrote about what I saw."

I say her descriptions were better than paintings. She says thank you. I ask how she wrote them. She doesn't understand what I mean and I rephrase the question. I still can't make myself clear.

"Oh, mercy me!" she says, frustrated. "I wrote the book in longhand."

But she had been a newspaperwoman, I protest. A reporter's most important tool is a typewriter.

"That's why I wrote it in longhand, you see. I wanted to get away from that newspaper thing, and writing in longhand made me look at things in a different way."

Mrs. Douglas asks about my family. She seems pleased we spend time outdoors. I tell her about my 12-year-old daughter who likes writing, sometimes works as a volunteer ranger at a local park and is fond of snakes. Mrs. Douglas, who says she was never crazy about snakes, autographs a copy of her book in my daughter's name anyway.

I place *River of Grass* on her lap and position the pen in her hand. She apologizes for her scrawl, which she says was not very good even when she was a sighted person.

After *River of Grass*, she wrote a novel, *Road to the Sun*, followed by five books about the history and nature of Florida and the tropics. In 1968, she started planning her final work, the biography of W.H. Hudson. Four times a week, a secretary visits so Mrs. Douglas can answer mail and dictate the last chapters of her book. "He was the man who made England conscious of birds. He was very important to the conservation movement."

So, it turned out, was Mrs. Douglas.

In 1968, when Dade County wanted to build a new jetport in the Everglades, she thought it was the most foolish idea she had ever heard. The Everglades were already stressed by almost a century's worth of development and drainage by 1,400 miles of canals, dikes and flood control gates. And the Everglades are the recharge area for South Florida's water supply.

She thought about the jetport, and the impact it would have on the birds and the mammals and the Indians and the water, and said: NO. She became a card-carrying environmentalist whose reputation and authority could chill all but the most hard-hearted developer or bureaucrat.

Mrs. Douglas started Friends of the Everglades, and served as president until only recently. Then she summoned Nancy Brown, one of her colleagues, and delivered the news. Says Mrs. Brown: "Marjory said, 'You be president.' You do what she says. She didn't run her organization as a democracy."

Mrs. Brown is president of the 4,000-member Friends, and she tries to keep Mrs. Douglas informed. If truth be told, Mrs. Douglas doesn't keep up with every political Everglades detail, which sometimes seem to change by the hour. Mrs. Douglas knows what she knows, and what she knows is the Everglades are beautiful, worth protecting, worth talking about.

"If we don't keep the Everglades wet, with a proper amount of water, they will dry up," she says. She has spent almost half a century warning politicians and water managers about draining the Everglades. Even now, she's lobbying in behalf of an ambitious restoration program.

"The Everglades will be a desert and nobody will be able to live in South Florida."

I ask to look around her home.

"By all means," she says.

There's a tiny dressing room and a tiny bedroom. There are cat-flaps on her bedroom window for Willie and the plump stray that visits. There is a bathroom painted flamingo pink. Mrs. Douglas' kitchen reflects her life as a busy career woman. On those rare occasions she had time to prepare meals, she cooked them on a hot plate or in a toaster oven. She never owned a stove, never, but friends recently gave her a microwave.

Her living room is a wonder, filled with decades worth of memorabilia and life. One wall is stained by honey, left by bees that periodically build their hive behind the plaster. Trophies and plaques and certificates for her public work are scattered everywhere, including under tables on the floor. There's a coffee table whose cargo includes a toy Slinky.

"I haven't seen her play with it," says Michael Blaine.

Mrs. Douglas has enough books to stock a small classic library. Dickens. Shakespeare. Dostoevsky. I wonder about her literary heroes.

"Oh, mercy me. I don't know. I've read all my life. I started on Dickens when I was eight and read my way through all his work. I read constantly. I was an obsessive reader."

I ask whether she admired Thoreau.

"But of course!"

She was a good friend of Marjorie Kinnan Rawlings. While Mrs. Douglas was

REAL FLORIDA

exploring a region, the Everglades, Mrs. Rawlings was discovering the people and culture of Cracker Florida to the north. Mrs. Douglas found *The Yearling* and *Cross Creek* "remarkable, part of the rare body of genuine Florida literature."

Mrs. Douglas can no longer read because of her eyes. She follows the news through public radio and what visitors tell her. She never owned a television, but Blaine used to bring his set over so they could watch "Upstairs, Downstairs" on Masterpiece Theater. She spends leisure time listening to books on record and cassettes. I notice a recorded copy of her own, *River of Grass*.

Mrs. Douglas is looking tired. I tell her I don't want to impose on her hospitality; she repeats she is always willing to talk about the Everglades. I ask if she's ever discouraged about what happened to her river of grass and what is still happening.

"I'm neither encouraged nor discouraged," she says firmly. "The Everglades must be taken care of. There's a job to do and it must be done."

I leave shortly afterward. We shake hands, and she thanks me for the visit and reminds me to thank my wife for the rug. I had meant to ask her feelings on mortality, but my own time in her presence has run out. Anyway, in her autobiography, she answered the question.

She is agnostic. There may be a greater power out there, but she doesn't know for sure. She knows this much: She does not believe in a kind man with a white beard, or even in an afterlife. When she's dead, she'll be dead, and she isn't afraid of death.

"I'd like Marjory to live forever," Bob Graham had told me. "But I know that's not possible. But if we could be wise enough, and committed enough, the Everglades could live forever. That would be her greatest legacy."

I drive through the crowded streets of Coconut Grove and onto the impossible interstate of Miami. As nightfall settles, and the ugly high-crime lights of the city wink on, I wonder what Mrs. Douglas is doing. I picture her in her comfortable chair, a cat on her lap, Dickens going full blast on her old record player.

I hope she is savoring her Scotch, and it is a vintage aged even more than she.

Looking for a panther

To catch a Florida panther you have to ride a four-wheel drive pickup truck into the deepest wilderness left in the state. When the road gives out, and it will, you climb into a swamp buggy and roll through the mud and the wet on giant tires. When the swamp buggy can go no farther, and that will happen, you load a heavy pack on your back, get out and walk.

"Watch out for snakes," someone mutters, and you do, even though it is too cool for snakes to be about. On an overcast winter morning in wilderness South Florida, hawks ride the thermals and owls hoot from the treetops. An otter crosses a clearing. Then you hear the dogs. You can hear the dogs a half mile away giving chase. They're on the other side of the marsh, among the oaks and pines, barking and howling. They must be closing in on a panther.

Your heart pounds, but not from exertion. Here on the fringes of the Everglades, the Florida panther's only stronghold, fewer than 50 survive. For nature lovers, seeing one is the Holy Grail, a kind of communion with Real Florida.

Dave Maehr, the Florida Game and Fresh Water Fish Commission biologist who studies panthers, has invited me along. Maehr, 37, is in charge of the expedition, which includes two other commission biologists, two U.S. Fish and Wildlife Service employees, a veterinarian, a veterinarian's assistant, and Roy McBride, the lion man.

McBride catches big cats for wildlife researchers all over the world. Born in rural Texas 55 years ago, he is one of those people most at home in the woods. He wears boots, scruffy jeans, a cowboy hat and a wolf head belt buckle. Driving in this morning, McBride saw the tracks of a coyote. At the time we were bouncing down a dirt road at 25 mph.

Yesterday, McBride caught the panther biologists call No. 32. Although it was the first I had seen in the wild, I felt disappointment as much as exhilaration. The chase was short and sweet, nothing like the run through the woods and the exciting capture I long had imagined. And the panther, a sinewy 74 pounds, was so mangy I was afraid to touch her.

Today, we're on the trail of panther No. 50 and I'm hoping for better. McBride and Maehr caught it for the first time last year on the Big Cypress Seminole Indian Reservation. A young male, the panther weighed 65 pounds and received a complete physical from a veterinarian. Maehr placed a radio collar around his neck and let him go.

Maehr wants to replace the collar on No. 50 – the transmitter's battery is wearing out – and see how the panther is getting along. Learning how these Greta Garbos of the animal world behave and how they move is an important part of a state-federal plan to save them.

At dawn, a game commission biologist went up in a Cessna, located No. 50's radio signal and directed Maehr and McBride to the general area. No. 50 is living in wilderness called the Devil's Garden on a sprawling Hendry County ranch west of Lake Okeechobee. With its deep woods and primeval swamps, the ranch is a fast-food restaurant that provides a banquet of deer and hogs for the panther.

McBride, the man trying to catch No. 50, is something of a Greta Garbo, too. Working mostly alone, or sometimes with his sons Rocky and Rowdy, he has been catching lions and their kin going on four decades. Years ago, out west, he tracked and killed them for ranchers who paid bounties for livestock-threatening predators. Now he does most of his catching for wildlife researchers. Florida pays him $29,000 for four months work.

Lions are his calling. He's caught big cats from Canada to South America, from Africa to Mongolia, where he looked for snow leopards. He spends most of his time in the American West, chasing mountain lions, a close panther relative.

He's good at what he does, and shy when talking about it. Ask a question and he almost blushes while saying "yes sir" or "no sir" in a drawl as thick as buttered grits. Or he makes a joke of his answer. Or he doesn't quite answer at all. During the winter, when he works in Florida, McBride lives in a small trailer, near his dogs, in the Florida Panther National Wildlife Refuge, alone. Nobody bothers a man out there.

I ask him the breed of his hounds and he says, "They're just plain dogs. Just mixtures of different dogs." I ask him their names and he says, "I call 'em One and Two." Finally, he says, "Amy and Jody." He has gray hair, steely blue eyes and an aging athlete's still muscular build.

"This is a vacation for Roy," Dave Maehr whispers. "He's used to chasing lions in the mountains."

Maehr sends McBride and dogs ahead of us to comb the pines and the palmettos for signs of the panther. When the dogs find the scent – by the howls in the distance it sounds like they have – McBride releases them.

A panther could kill or outrun any dog, but usually it prefers to escape into a tall tree. Panthers are both lions and pussycats. Yet for three centuries, they were persecuted by white Floridians out of fear. People took a look at their size (up to 150 pounds) and their teeth (long and sharp) and grabbed their rifles. There is no record of an attack by a panther on a human in this state.

The radio crackles to life. McBride speaks quietly, sounding a little winded, as if he has been running. "I think we got him," he says. "The dogs chased him up an oak. He's at the top. I think it's okay to come on in."

Our buggies rumble toward the Devil's Garden across Graham Marsh. Once or twice it feels as if we're stuck, but then the heavy wheels take hold and pull us out of the mud. At the edge of the woods, we get out of the buggies and throw the heavy packs of equipment onto our backs. We hike in quietly. Despite the presence of McBride, despite the howling dogs, a particularly anxious panther will leap from the tree when the rest of the party walks in. Then the chase would have to begin again.

"Sometimes they can be hard to pin down," McBride tells people.

We follow the sounds of the dogs. Finally, through the pines and palmettos and the cabbage palms, we see Roy McBride. He's standing under an oak, looking up. I look up, too.

My Lord. No. 50 is so big and powerful and wild. He's the panther I've always wanted to see. He's 30 feet up the tree, partly obscured by branches, looking more curious than frightened. He neither roars nor meows. He stares at the howling dogs and me.

Maehr, McBride and their assistants go about their business like bored accountants. It's a job they've done many times before. As someone who has poked around the wilds of South Florida for most of his life without seeing panthers, I'm thrilled speechless. I'm a city man who likes his city comforts, but I'm terribly attracted to wilderness, a wilderness that is fast falling prey to civilization in this state of 13-million people. A lion in a tree is an antidote to depression.

McBride kneels and assembles the air rifle that will fire a tranquilizer dart. Veterinarian John Lanier and his assistant, Pauline Nol, open their packs and prepare the sedative. "It looks like he's eaten well," McBride says. Without his usual confidence he estimates the cat's weight at 100 pounds. Tree branches hide too much of him.

Estimating a panther's weight accurately is important. Otherwise, the panther might receive too much or too little of the drug. Too little and the panther is hard to handle. Too much and the panther might be hurt. In 1983, a panther died from a drug reaction, prompting some animal rights advocates to call for an end to the radio collar study. Since then a veterinarian has gone on all panther captures.

Dave Maehr, the other biologists and assistants inflate a giant "crash bag" that will be placed under the tree to cushion the panther when it falls. McBride asks me to watch the panther. If No. 50 starts to move, if he acts as if he's going to jump, I'm supposed to yell bloody murder.

I circle the tree to get a better look. No. 50 turns his head to follow me. McBride circles the tree in the opposite direction with his gun. He's searching for a vantage point from where he can get a clean shot with the dart.

McBride aims and shoots.

The panther flinches.

"Got him," says Roy McBride.

The drug works slowly. We have time to move the crash bag into place. Over it we stretch a thick rope net, and stand around like firefighters waiting for someone to jump from a tall building. We try to guess where the panther is going to fall and move accordingly.

Feeling the drug, the panther licks his lips and shakes his head. He leans drunkenly to the left and we shift the net and crash bag to the left. He leans right and we move right. He slips down, as if he's ready to fall, but catches himself. He lies on the branch and appears to sleep.

"He's not going to fall," commission biologist Jayde Roof says, sounding forlorn. It's his job to climb the tree, attach a rope and lower the panther to the net. Roof screws spikes into his shoes, grabs a rope and ascends. He is 34 and weighs 220 pounds. As he nears the panther, the branch creaks ominously.

Roof reaches for the panther, and the panther rises up and stares him down. "He's still full of fire," Roof yells. Roof advances and retreats several times before he is able to slip a rope around the panther's middle. The panther hisses.

"Get ready!" Roof shouts.

He shoves the panther off the limb.

For a moment, Roof controls the descent with the rope. Then he yells, "He's too big!" and the panther falls fast, tumbling and turning and breaking branches on the way. The panther lands in the net two feet from me.

Pandemonium.

The fall has invigorated the drugged panther. Flexing his claws, he scrambles out of the net and leaps to the ground. McBride runs for his dogs in case they're needed. Dave Maehr, who swims ten miles, plays handball and lifts weights every week, flies across the net, grabs the panther's tail and is dragged across the ground. Up in the tree, Jayde Roof hangs onto the rope and the panther while clinging to the branch with his legs.

Pauline Nol, the veterinarian assistant, must weigh 100 pounds. She hugs the panther around the neck. She is dragged with Maehr. The rest of us try to block the panther's escape. He stops, turns and runs toward me. I extend my notebook and camera – paltry weapons under the circumstances – and retreat behind a pine.

Turning, the panther sprints between the legs of a U.S. Fish and Wildlife employee, Mark Lotz, knocking him over. With Maehr still clinging to the tail, Jayde Roof slides down the tree and tackles the panther across the hips. The panther claws his leg, tearing open his pants, puncturing his knee and drawing blood.

The panther, a watermelon seed with fur, slips from their grasp without even a growl.

Roof and Maehr and Nol dive on the panther again and try to entangle him in the net. John Lanier, the veterinarian, slides on his knees and grabs the panther around the back legs, all the while gripping a hypodermic in his teeth. He injects the panther in the hip. Someone hands him a second tranquilizer. He sticks the panther again.

No. 50 goes to sleep.

We're all panting from the chase. Somebody giggles. Somebody swears, but the curse word comes out sounding like a prayer. So much for being businesslike. Catching a panther, the symbol for wilderness Florida, is a primal act.

We carry No. 50 to a tarp where the veterinarian will do his work. No wonder the cat was rambunctious: We underdrugged him significantly. At 129 pounds, he has doubled his weight in 11 months.

As the vet and his assistant take samples of panther blood, skin, hair, saliva, mucous, urine and fecal matter, as they vaccinate the panther against rabies, feline leukemia, feline immunodeficiency virus and feline upper respiratory disease, while they deworm the panther and inject vitamins, Roy McBride says he wants to look in the bushes. He's interested in what the panther was eating.

I ask to go. McBride nods.

"I'm sure he killed somethin' back there," he says, disappearing into the thick vegetation. "There's plenty of hog activity here. And I saw some vultures hangin' around. Come on."

Trying to keep up, I inch through saw palmettos that cut my hands and grapevines that entangle my legs like tentacles. Tall branches close overhead. McBride plows through the dense brush as if skipping across a field of daisies.

Somewhere ahead of me, I hear him say, "Let's spread out. We can cover more territory that way." As someone who has gotten lost in the 300-acre squirrel-infested park near my St. Petersburg home, I'm unqualified to be treated as an equal by a man who catches lions. I branch out on my own, as instructed, but quickly change course so I can stay close to him.

"Panther will cover up his kill with dirt and leaves and come back to it later," McBride goes on. "Look for a mound now." We find no mound, and a moment later McBride adds: "Listen for the flies." There is something wonderful about traveling with a man so attuned to nature that even the wing beats of insects offer him clues about a larger world. He is a panther on two legs.

We return without hearing the flies that would give away the presence of a decomposing hog.

I kneel and pet No. 50.

From nose to tail he is close to seven feet. He's brown and muscular, rough to the touch. His legs are thick and powerful, and his broad chest rises slowly with every breath. He smells wild, absolutely wild, an alley cat magnified by ten. As we carry him to the edge of the palmettos, and watch as he starts to come to, my goose bumps feel like the Himalayas.

"He's going to be all right," Dave Maehr says, reading my mind. "He'll feel sluggish for a few hours, but he'll be fine."

In the afternoon, Jayde Roof drives me back to my truck in Naples. With the windows rolled tight against the cold, we smell wild and primitive, a combination of sweat and panther. It is most pleasant.

Later, heading home on the interstate, I stop at a convenience store for a soft drink. As I pay for the Pepsi, the woman waiting to buy a lottery ticket gives me a look. The scent of pure wilderness still clings to me like French perfume, a perfume neither of us likely will smell again.

On the Loop Road

The swamp man called Jack was in his yard, working on a tractor, when I pulled my truck off the Loop Road and said hello. He walked over, called off his dogs and offered me a wary handshake.

Swampman Jack seldom gets visitors at Pinecrest, a tiny settlement in South Florida's Big Cypress National Preserve that once was the stomping grounds of loggers, froggers, bootleggers, alligator poachers and hell raisers who disdained city living and city slickers with equal passion.

I told Swampman Jack that I had collected snakes near Pinecrest when I was a teen-ager, and that I had always enjoyed the adventure of driving on the Loop Road, but he still looked at me with suspicion. Few people ever take the backwoods byway that passes his property on the edge of the Everglades.

The Loop Road, as State Road 94 is known, is too remote and scary for most modern Floridians. It loops off the busy Tamiami Trail and cuts deep into the woods and swamp. It's 23 miles of potholes, mud and gravel, a place where alligators grunt in the sloughs and arguments between swamp people have been settled more than once with knives or gunfire.

"There ain't much to say: There's just a few of us left now," said Jack, a 50ish man who has lived here for more than two decades and once ran the only gas station for miles. "Most everybody else has died or left. This place ain't the same."

About 20 people live in the swamps of Pinecrest now, and more than half work for the federal government, which has been buying out landowners and ejecting squatters since 1974. The government plan is to restore the area as it was when Europeans came to the New World.

Today, Pinecrest is part of Big Cypress National Preserve, more than 574,000 acres of cypress, pines, marsh and water that is open to hikers, canoeists, fishermen and hunters. But only people who lived here on their own land before the federal government takeover are allowed to live here now.

Once, about 200 hardy folks lived in and about Pinecrest. A few worked in Miami, 50 miles away, but most made a living from the swamp. They raised orchids, chopped trees, gigged frogs and hunted for the market.

There was a restaurant, a gas station, two bars and a lodge that found it necessary to remind patrons "No Guns or Knives Allowed Inside." Off the dusty road, back in the swamp, there were men tending illegal moonshine stills and skinning illegal alligators.

"It was a pretty wild place," said Swampman Jack, who wouldn't give me his last name. "Those bars were going day or night, and the law was a long way off."

Pinecrest and much of the 60,000 acres within the Loop Road are part of Monroe County of the Florida Keys. But the area is cut off from the county seat – Key West – by Everglades National Park and Florida Bay. The nearest Monroe County sheriff's office is 100 miles away by car and about 50 miles as the heron flies.

Road signs have been riddled by bullets and shotgun blasts or have been vandalized. Speed Limit 30 MPH signs I saw along eight miles of paved road were altered to read Speed Limit 80 MPH. I saw no speed-limit signs on the remaining 15 miles of unpaved road. Those sections are too narrow and potholed for even the most daredevil of drag racers.

One failure of brakes, or nerve, might deliver even skillful drivers to a swampy grave unlikely to be discovered. Certain people still find the swamps of Pinecrest's Loop Road an attractive place to deposit the bodies of enemies.

"There is lots of bodies that have been found here," Swampman Jack said darkly. "And there still is bodies left to be found."

Swampman Jack was not exaggerating. A Big Cypress park ranger later told me that two corpses were found near Pinecrest recently. He said the remote area is a popular dumping spot with Miami drug dealers. Gangster Al Capone, said to have been a frequent visitor to a friend's Pinecrest hunting camp more than half a century ago, would have approved.

"Where Capone supposedly stayed is all gone," Swampman Jack said, taking off his Confederate-flag decorated cap and wiping his forehead. "All that's left is a little old pond."

He walked me to the concrete pond which in Capone's heyday must have been quite an extravagance in the middle of a swamp. Now it was surrounded by old tires, awnings and other rubble left over from when Jack had the gas station. He had not let me take his picture, but he said it was all right to photograph Al Capone's pond.

The Loop Road that goes through Pinecrest was built in the 1920s by the Chevelier Corp., a land sales company that envisioned a new metropolis rising along the road through the swamp. But it was too remote, too buggy and too wet. Loggers liked the road, though, and they liked the pine and cypress that grew so near. Bootleggers also liked the deep woods, and so did alligator trappers and game poachers. The land was so wild and so vast that many people felt free to build ramshackle homes or park trailers wherever they wanted. Who would mind?

Now most of those trailers and homes are gone, at the command of the federal government, or have been reclaimed by the woods. Drive down Loop Road and you see the remains of old camps, houses, trailers and buses. The skeletons of rusted-out pickup trucks dot the landscape.

Not many people take the Loop Road now, of course. Most don't even know it's there. But from Naples drive east on the Tamiami Trail, which is also known as U.S. 41, and you'll find the beginning of Loop Road at Monroe Station, a gas station-restaurant popular with swamp people and other refugees from the developed coasts.

Anyone thinking about driving the Loop Road to Pinecrest probably should stop at Monroe Station first – as a preview of what is to come. Eat a couple of proprietor

REAL FLORIDA

Sweet Sue's sausage sandwiches and soak up the atmosphere. If such signs as "This Place Is Insured By Smith and Wesson" don't offend or frighten you, you're probably brave enough for Loop Road and Pinecrest.

Heading south from Monroe Station, you'll pass a sign that points down the Loop Road. Another sign warns you to drive cautiously. While some of the dusty, unpaved part of the road is graded, other sections feature potholes big enough to break an axle.

During summer, you'll want to drive with windows closed against ferocious mosquitoes. During winter, open them up and listen to the swamp sounds. Great blue herons squawk with displeasure as you pass. Turtles splash into the water from rotting logs. You'll hear barred owls even during the day. During hunting season, you'll hear the roar of airboats and gunshots.

On my way to Swampman Jack's, I saw turkey vultures picking clean the bones of very dead possums, and blacksnakes crossing the road. A park ranger told me he's seen bobcats and otters at night. He's never seen bears, but black bears are Big Cypress residents. So are panthers.

From time to time you'll pass hunting camps on the Loop Road. Some look as temporary as a pioneer lean-to. Others are elaborate and protected by barbed-wire fences whose inside perimeters are patrolled by pit bulls. A friend who hunted the swamp once encountered in the middle of Loop Road a pipe-smoking woman in a rocking chair. She smiled, but didn't move, and my friend had to drive around her.

Heading for Pinecrest, I passed three hard-faced men joyriding on all-terrain vehicles. I saw fishermen cane-poling for catfish and an elderly man picking up trash. As I neared Pinecrest, and began seeing more inhabited houses and trailers, I saw a number of residents watching me. I waved to one, a middle-age woman wearing a long dress and a straw hat, but she didn't wave back.

One resident who returned my wave was E.C. Guise. E.C. Guise owns the only remaining Pinecrest business, the Bumpy Loop Restaurant. He sells soft drinks and sandwiches from a little yellow concrete building that is covered by hand-painted advertisements for food, drink and parking. Hunters generally are his only customers.

Guise, 78, moved to the swamp from Miami in 1947, and I found him as talkative and open as Swampman Jack was quiet and suspicious. He sold me a Diet Coke and said I could park my truck behind his place anytime I wanted – for a dollar a day and a dollar a night.

"I used to make cabinets in Miami for a dollar an hour, but hell, that ain't no living wage, so I come here, and I got it made," he said. "My taxes is low, I don't need much, and I'm so far away from everything that nobody bothers me. I got sugar diabetes, though, which I got from drinking soft drinks and beer, so now I stick to water. I have to swallow this little bitty white pill every day, but I'm okay."

I asked whether he lived alone, and he gave me a hard look. I suddenly wondered whether he thought I might be armed, and I wondered the same about him.

"My daughter is asleep in the trailer back yonder," he said. "It's just me and her." He seemed to relax again as he realized my question was prompted by friendly curiosity.

"I like it here," he went on. "It's pretty quiet, except for hunting season, and then

101

it's pretty loud with all the guns, but I don't mind the hunters. Lot of them park here, and a lot of them are so happy to have a place to park they give me $20 and $25 tips!

"It's different pretty much from the old days. Back in the old days, it could get dangerous out here. A man could get shot."

I asked why people got shot.

"Out here, you didn't need no reason to get shot."

Most of old Pinecrest is gone, hidden behind tall weeds or the rubble of falling-down houses, trailers and hunting camps. I saw no evidence that old Jack Knight's Gator Hook Lodge ever existed, and it was the heart of Pinecrest, especially on Saturday nights, when fiddlers played and couples clogged and loved and fought and bled.

The only remaining sign of the old Pinecrest Restaurant is a sign in the bushes at Swampman Jack's old gas station. When the restaurant closed, he kept the sign, and its menu, as souvenirs. You could get frog legs for $3.25 a plate.

"I love it out here," Swampman Jack said when I visited him one last time. He'd warmed up to me, I thought, probably because I knew a little about hunting and pick-up trucks and Pinecrest's history. "But the government won't be happy till all of us is gone. They're lettin' us hunt, but there's all kinds of rules, and a short season, even though the woods is full of game!

"Yesterday there was a big old bobcat in the road. I ran inside and got my binoculars out, but they was filled with water. Don't ask me how they got filled with water, but they was.

"There's also hogs and deer and millions of alligators. You see them crossing the road! They'll eat your dogs! There's also all kinds of mosquitoes. But the government don't even want you to kill mosquitoes now. They don't want you to kill snakes or step on the spiders. Everything is protected.

"It ain't the same here anymore. The people at Pinecrest are the endangered ones. Not the animals!"

A girl and her pig

The pig named Alexander is a smart one. He has learned to open two latches, escape his pen and flee into the pasture. No matter how many people wave their arms and shout and chase him, Alexander returns only when he is good and ready.

"Alexander is a hyper pig," Karen Strickland explains. "Like, he never walks anywhere. He bops. And he is very intelligent. When you close the pen, he watches your hands to see if you're latching the door. A pig's eyes are so little, but they see a lot."

Strickland, 16, raises pigs. An excitable porker ordinarily causes no alarm at her rural Sarasota County ranch house, but this time of year it's different. Strickland is entering her prize pig in the Youth Swine Competition at the Florida State Fair. Alexander will be judged on his appearance and how well he minds his owner when they parade around a ring filled with other contestants and their pigs.

"If I can keep him calm," Karen Strickland says, "I think we'll do okay."

Strickland, one of Florida's most advanced young swine farmers, understands the pig game. She has raised them since she was seven, first entered a pig in a county fair at nine, and has won more trophies and blue ribbons than you can shake a feed bag at.

She was a multiple winner at the 1985 state fair, going home with two blue ribbons, the Premier Exhibitor trophy, a $200 scholarship toward her college education, and a $400 profit when she sold her pig, Spade, at an auction. The records she keeps on hog raising won her a trip to Chicago and a 10th place trophy in a national swine contest. She has sold seven prize-winning pigs in her career and made $2,371.

"I don't have to babysit to make money," she says.

Hog-raising, some people might say, is in her genes. Don Strickland, her father, is an electrical contractor in Sarasota, but he grew up in rural Florida, raised pigs as a boy, and looks comfortable in cowboy boots as he walks about his five-acre spread 15 miles east of Sarasota. Her mother was born in Florida and works for the Sarasota County Fair in its livestock department. Shelly, Karen's 18-year-old sister, has won county fair ribbons for rabbits and steers. Karen, meanwhile, can turn a pig in a poke into a Picasso.

"When Karen was real little she'd crawl into the pen with her pig Clyde," her mother says. "Clyde would grunt and Karen would talk back to him. It was like they could understand each other. She fell in love with pigs back then."

No longer a little girl, she is a tall, brown-haired high school sophomore who sounds like an adult when she talks about the dollar and cents of pigs. For Strickland pigs are a business. She enjoys the competition at the fair, but she loves the idea of making a profit from selling pigs even more. Long active in 4-H clubs and Future Farmers of America, she intends to make a career out of livestock farming. She's deliberating between studying agriculture at the University of Florida or Georgia's Andrew Baldwin College.

There's money in pigs, she can tell you. Americans eat about 60-million pigs annually, according to some accounts, and that ain't hay. Pigs help keep the besieged American farmer solvent by devouring about half the nation's corn crop. Many people prefer pig hide to cow for clothing and accessories.

Pigs are also important to the medical profession. The only mammals that willingly drink enough alcohol to get drunk, pigs are used in alcoholism studies. Scientists study pig digestive systems because they are similar to human's. Pig skin is used as surrogate skin for human burn victims. The late John Wayne may have been a cowpoke at heart, but he had a pig to thank for extending his life. One of his failed heart valves was replaced by an artificial valve made from pig.

Yet people poke fun at pigs. Stupid swine. Fat pig. Filthy as a pig. Pig sty. Eat like a pig. Karen Strickland bristles at anti-swine slander.

"It's one of my pet peeves," she says.

At Riverview High School, her city acquaintances sometimes talk about her, she says. They wonder what she is up to, back on the ranch, raising pigs. Ever the souls of sensitivity, they joke that Karen must be a hillbilly, a redneck, implying that her interests are somehow less important than those of young city people.

"They don't understand what I do," Strickland says. "But then they hear about me and these contests and they're surprised when they hear what goes into it."

Strickland's day is a long one, beginning at 5:30 a.m. and often ending late at night in the pig pen. On cold nights, she puts space heaters into their pens. She once treated a pig with heatstroke with Gatorade. When her pigs are dirty, she hoses them off. If they have dandruff, she gives them a shampoo, followed by a conditioner. She has been known to powder a white pig with talcum. Before competition, she grooms them with clippers.

"All pigs are different," she says. "They all have distinct personalities."

Alexander, a Yorkshire, is high strung. He runs when other pigs walk. He throws dirt around with his snout. He snorts at the family dog, a dachshund named Brandy, who doesn't like pigs and tries to bite them. Alexander doesn't always obey Strickland. The other day, even the wind excited him, and he raced about wildly, chased by his trotting owner. Yet Strickland says, "I think he might be the best pig I ever had."

She knew he had potential the day she bought him as a four-month piglet in North Florida. "When I select a pig, I'm looking for potential. I want a long pig. He should also have the potential to be fairly tall with big shoulders and a high tail. He should be narrow in the middle. A good pig is hour-glass shaped. He should have good hams. At the same time I'm looking for a spring of ribs. I mean, I want those ribs to flair out wide. That means a lot more meat."

Alexander is completely white, broad shouldered and muscular. In November, he weighed 40 pounds. He weighed 180 pounds last week, and he should weigh about 220 pounds by competition time in 10 days. Pigs do grow heavier, frequently reaching 800 pounds or more. The largest on record, according to *National Geographic*, weighed 1,904 pounds – as hefty as your basic Volkswagen Beetle.

Strickland trains Alexander in the late afternoon, after he has been fed his six pounds of swine feed and corn, and likely to be in good humor. She lets him out of the small concrete pen she paid for with her own money and he runs into a larger pen filled with sand.

She picks up a cane and taps him on the left side of the head. The tap motivates him to move right. She taps him on the right and he moves left. She taps him in the rear and he lunges forward as if stung by a bee. The crook of the cane, held in front of his nose, is supposed to make him stop. It doesn't always work. At fair competition, contestants often get angry at their pigs and strike them smartly. Not Strickland.

"That would bruise the meat."

Bruised meat would hurt at the auction that follows the competition. "I'm always more nervous about the auction than I am about the competition." She doesn't want to lose money on her pigs. She pays $75 for a piglet, and she figures it costs about 70 cents a pound to raise the pig to slaughter. She likes to make at least $200 profit on a prize pig. Bud, a fine Duroc, brought $800 at the Sarasota County Fair in 1984.

Last month she sent letters to prospective pig buyers throughout Florida, letting them know she would have an extraordinary swine for sale at the state fair. She doesn't like to leave things to chance. Some contestants at the state fair have to take a loss. Some fail to sell their pigs. So far, she has been lucky. Every Karen Strickland pig has sold at a profit.

One of her buyers was a considerate man who thought of her afterward. He called and asked if she'd like some of the meat, maybe a ham or something, from Bud. Strickland didn't feel right about eating Bud.

"I eat pork," she says. "But that was something that didn't appeal to me."

Heaven is a barbecue

In the morning you drive through fog that goes from bad to worse. Depressed about a long drive getting longer, you stop for coffee – and then spill it in the truck.

The fog begins lifting in mid-morning and you feel a little better, even though there are coffee stains on your pants and your lower back feels like somebody danced on it in aerobic shoes. Then, heading south on U.S. Highway 27, near Lake Okeechobee, you see the sign that lets you know everything is going to be all right.

The sign is in a field full of cows. The sign is red and white and says: "Ya Know Folks I'm Agin Road Signs." You have to drive another 10th of a mile to see the next in the series: "But How Else You Gonna Know Where To Stop Fer The Best Bar-B-Q In The South." What is the name of this paradise? The next sign tells you: "Old South Bar-B-Q Ranch."

The Old South Bar-B-Q Ranch has been feeding people cornpone and barbecue for a long time. In 1954, a fast-talking entrepreneur named Jim McCorvey bought a little bar and turned it into a barbecue palace that helped put this sugar cane town on the map.

McCorvey thought what a good barbecue place needed was a Wild West motif. He packed his restaurant with antiques. He came up with country-bumpkin sayings and put them inside the restaurant, on the menu and on signs that spiced up roads from the Everglades to the Georgia border. Some are there still.

"Folks Be Sure N Stop," a sign screeches at you somewhere near LaBelle. "So Ya Kin Help Pay Fer Theez Durn Signs."

If you are ever going to be happy, you tell yourself, if you are ever going to get over fog and spilled coffee, you need to stop, today, and eat a mess of barbecue.

Not barbecue from some chain restaurant, where the sauce is mild and you never need more than a single napkin. Not barbecue from a restaurant where the waitresses are nice young city women working their way through law school. No, you want tangy barbecue that requires an inch or so of napkins and is served by some tough-looking mama who wears a six-gun on her hip.

Mind reeling with that image, foot resting heavy on the accelerator, you barrel down a highway that cuts through prairie, cattle ranches and citrus groves. Vultures sit on fence posts and inspect the road for the latest animal fatalities. When you have your mind on barbecue, even squashed armadillos don't ruin your appetite.

"Jest 20 Minutes Down The Road," one sign shouts at you. "Eat Like Helen B. Happy," another commands. "If Yore Mind Goes Blank Be Sure N Turn Off The Sound" is another piece of wisdom.

You whip past the Hoosier's Bass Inn, roar over the Caloosahatchee River Bridge and see, within the next nine miles, "Real Pit Bar-B-Q Is Our Business Son – Not Our Sideline" and "Get Reddy To Tie Up Ya Hosses" and "Don't Yall Be Stoppin At Some Other Confounded Place."

Then, up ahead, in the middle of Clewiston, you see a building painted to look like red brick. You tap the brakes and go sliding into the parking lot at Old South Bar-B-Q Ranch. Those signs have reeled you in like a plump catfish. You don't care.

The Old South Bar-B-Q Ranch is a trash heaven for hungry adults. Outside there are wagon wheels, and dummies dressed as cowpokes, Judge Roy Bean's courthouse and a Boot Hill graveyard where one tombstone tells the sad story of Les More, "Kilt Wit Tu Slugs From A 44. No Les No More."

At the front door, standing on the porch, is a man with black curly hair named Jimmy McDuffie. McDuffie, 43, is the mayor of Clewiston, a town of 6,000 people on the southern shore of Lake Okeechobee. McDuffie runs an electrical business and serves on the volunteer fire department. He is the past president of the Rotary Club and in April will become the Exalted Ruler of the Elks Club. He is the latest owner of Old South Bar-B-Q Ranch. He looks prosperous.

"Yesterday that parking lot was slam full of cars," he tells you. "I mean, people were lined up to get on in. We fed 'em all."

Today, nobody's waiting in line, but it's busy inside. Most of the restaurant's 40 tables are filled, and half the customers look as if they have invested years in the serious business of devouring barbecue. Their stomachs, rising over belts like mountains of beans, are a testament to Old South Bar-B-Q Ranch.

"Everybody knows about this place," McDuffie tells you over coffee. "I was in New York on New Year's Eve and I was at Times Square, you know – the place where the ball comes down. I was talking to this fella from Virginia about where we were from. I said 'Clewiston.' He said, 'I been there. Old South Bar-B-Q.' I said, 'I own it.' " McDuffie is only the third owner since 1956. The original owner went bankrupt trying to franchise the restaurant; the second owner lasted 25 years. Now it's McDuffie, a tough-minded businessman who worries about making improvements to fight off the growing competition from fast-food restaurants.

"I'm going to change a few things," he says. "But not too much. I don't want to change what has worked."

His restaurant is filled with antique washboards, wash basins and cast-iron stoves. There are antique fence-hole diggers, moonshine jugs and a three-barrel gun. There are souvenirs, including a used sugar-cane machete for $3.95 that you just have to own, as well as the famous hush-puppy recipe sold on a post card for 20 cents. At Old South Bar-B-Q Ranch, they don't give away secret recipes free, you know.

Inside the restaurant there is an old-fashioned player piano. There are dancing dolls and a little toy bird that will sing for a dime. You can have your photograph taken next to a cowboy dummy, and you can read dumb signs: "There's Only One Thing Worse N A Wife Who Can Cook An Won't. One Who Can't And Does." There are waitresses who, yes, wear six-guns.

"Back in the old days, they used to shoot them – they were loaded with caps – in the middle of the restaurant," McDuffie says wistfully. "They don't do that now. People are so sue-happy. You'd be afraid to have those guns going off."

You wouldn't mind an explosion or two to go with barbecue, but you know McDuffie is right: Somebody would haul you to court and claim loss of hearing. Saddened, you sit at a table in silence and study the menu.

At Old South, sandwiches cost a couple bucks. Barbecue plates cost double that. You can eat ribs – pork or beef – and chicken. You can eat catfish and hush puppies and apple pie. You can slurp frosty mugs of root beer and what the restaurant claims are the "thickest shakes ya ever saw."

You don't want a shake. You order a Diet Coke and hope the six-gun toting waitress doesn't notice you're a wimp. You order the chicken plate, beans and slaw and look her in the eye.

The chicken tears off the bone easily and isn't overpowered by the sauce. A success. You want your sauce tangy but you also want to taste the chicken. The baked beans are solid baked beans and make you forget about the morning fog. The slaw is creamy cole slaw and makes you forget about the coffee stains on your jeans.

You have used six napkins by meal's end. You are satisfied.

You only wish you had the courage to express yourself with a loud belch. At the Old South Bar-B-Q Ranch, a good burp should be worth a discount.

Harley's banquet

Harley Reynolds made meat balls in the kitchen. He mixed ground elk with cheese and placed the golf-ball-sized munchies on a metal tray. Then he attacked the cider squirrel. Cider squirrel is one of his favorite recipes. He browned squirrel in butter, poured a quart of cider in the pan, and said:

"I found the hard cider in a grocery store. But let me tell you something: Hard cider is hard to find, by God." But Harley found it all right, and now the odor wafted through the apartment.

A slab of venison broiled in beer in the oven. So did the dove. The squirrel pot pie, covered by aluminum foil, heated on a back burner. A small wild hog spun on a rotisserie. Bite-sized cubes of venison, elk and antelope were ready, in bowls, next to the fondue pot.

Harley's son Johnny walked in with an ice chest of oysters, fresh from the Florida Panhandle's Apalachicola Bay. The smoked mullet had not yet arrived, Harley Reynolds explained. Nor had the man from Big Tim's, the barbecue joint Harley paid to prepare the larger chunks of wild hog.

"This is half of hunting for me," said Reynolds, a 54-year-old supervisor of a Pinellas Park tool and die firm. "If I can't eat it, I don't want any part of it."

Men, women and children poured into his St. Petersburg apartment. They had parked their cars next door at the closed Mobil Service station. One couple arrived in a black 1929 Model-A Ford. Most drove pickup trucks. Some people wore coats and ties. One man sported a cowboy hat.

Country music blared from the stereo, pop-tops popped, and a man kneeled at the ice chest and shucked oysters. And Harley Reynolds, the wizard of game, cooked at an electric stove. He cooked for 38 people. His infrequent game dinners are an event, as they say in those gourmet magazines, and when Harley puts out invitations, people come.

"Lot of people don't like the taste of game," he said, poking the squirrel. His eyes watered from the sizzling cider. "They think it tastes funny. But it's a matter of knowing how to cook it. You soak a piece of venison in beef bouillon and it tastes like beef. I can cook a deer, and you'd never know you're not eating beef. But you've got to be careful. Brown but never burn, that's what I say. Anything that turns black I throw away. Patience. That's the main thing. That's what it takes to be a game cook."

It also takes game to be a good game cook. That's the most difficult part. One cannot walk into a grocery and buy venison, squirrel, dove or wild hog. Game isn't legally sold. A man wants game, he goes out and shoots it.

REAL FLORIDA

That's what Harley and 11 of his hunting buddies did. They began hunting in September and quit last month after filling their freezers with seven deer, 17 wild hogs, 40 squirrels and 37 doves. Some other friends who hunted in Montana donated elk and antelope. Now they all wanted to eat. And Harley, who staged a successful game dinner for friends 14 years ago, volunteered to act as chef.

"It'd be hard to put a value on the cost of game," said Reynolds thumbing through a warn copy of Bradford Angier's *Food from the Woods Cooking.* "I just know it's expensive, when you take into account the money you spend on gasoline, motels, restaurants, clothing, ammunition and equipment. And you consider the years that you never even get a shot or get anything. We were lucky this year."

Harley Reynolds wore a Banlon shirt, blue jeans and a white towel wrapped around his waist instead of an apron. He stood at his stove, holding a long fork, and savored the smell of squirrel. He laughed but did not accept a proposal of marriage from Bill Brumfield, a 32-year-old tool and die employee who wore a cowboy hat and sipped a beer.

Brumfield said, "I've been tryin' to get him to marry me for years, the way he cooks and all. But he won't."

Reynolds said, "The thing is, I don't cook when we're at camp. The men see me walking around with Kipper's snacks or a tin of sardines. And at night we go into town for Kentucky fried."

A woman named Tonie Mills walked into the kitchen. Her daughter is married to Harley's son, she explained, while helping Harley with the elk meat balls. She said, "I can throw a cast net and I can shoot a gun. But all my husband wants to do is play golf. He's not like Harley."

Harley said, "Now see it was always different with me. I went through two wives because they couldn't agree with my hunting." Divorced, he now lives alone. He checked the deer that roasted in beer.

It was Harley's own deer. He killed it with a bow and arrow last fall while hunting at the Citrus Wildlife Management Area north of Tampa Bay. "I was in a tree," he said, "and I saw it. I didn't think it would come close enough for a shot. But it walked towards me, then turned just right. I hit it dead in the heart. Later on I counted 26 paces from the tree. The deer ran 87 paces before it dropped dead. It fell only 10 paces from the road where I had the truck. So I didn't have far to drag it."

One of the barbecuing hogs belonged to John Garner. The hog weighed 300 pounds and it was difficult to kill. "I saw him first and fired with a 16-gauge loaded with number one shot. He got hit and turned in a circle, mad. I shot again. Then ran out of ammo. The hog started running. I shouted. The guy next to me shot twice and jammed his gun when he got excited. The guy next to him shot twice and jammed his gun. Then Bill here finally got him."

Bill Brumfield, his head still hidden beneath the cowboy hat, nodded. The men gutted the hog, Brumfield explained, drinking a glass of wine. They cut off the head. That's always the worst part, he said, and then they dragged the remains back to camp. "You hang it, spread eagle, from a tree. You skin it. You oughta see the muscle on a big hog. When you got the skin off you do the butcherin.'"

The butchering seminar was postponed when someone hollered, "Soup's on," even though soup was nowhere on the menu. People got in line, picked up their paper napkins and plastic forks and read the cards Harley placed before each dish.

Bobby, Bill, J.J. and others supplied the ribs, whole ham, squirrel, small hog.

Another sign said:

Elk Meat Ball, Please Take One – What You See Is All There Is.

People filled their plates while Harley stood back and watched. "Ahhh, I forgot to cook the wild rice," he said, but no one noticed, as they feasted on deer, elk, antelope, squirrel, hog and dove. The deer, elk and antelope steaks, as Harley prepared them, were tender and tasted like beef. The elk meat ball was spicy. The hog meat was fatless – wild animals develop muscles more than fat – and chewy. Only one diner found a piece of shot in his meat.

The squirrel sauteed in cider tasted like a cross between chicken and pork. The squirrel pot pie could have been chicken. Nobody complained about a game taste. Harley beamed at the compliments and urged second helpings.

Almost all accepted his invitation. One who declined was Dina Rogers, who attended the dinner with her boyfriend, dove hunter Doug Ruppel. Dina smoked a cigarette that looked like a little cigar and explained how her attendance constituted an act of bravery.

"I told Harley I was going to bring a grilled-cheese sandwich to this thing," she said, laughing. "But I didn't. There's something about game I don't like. I tried the elk meat balls, but it took some time. I couldn't eat any squirrel. I mean, how can you eat a squirrel? But I thought the salad was great."

Talkin' turkey

It is 7:30 when the wild turkeys come in. In a drizzling morning rain they come down a dirt road in twos and threes, hens at first, but then the male turkeys, the gobblers, looking big and feisty and ready to take on the world.

The largest gobbler, a fatso that looks about 18 pounds, stops beneath the oak to peck at corn Lovett Williams Jr. tossed on the ground shortly before daylight. In the distance, we hear the rumble of thunder. Fatso responds immediately, thrusting out his chest, fanning his tail open and gobbling.

"I knew it! I knew it!" Williams whispers. "He's answering the thunder. He thinks he's a big shot. Isn't it amazing?"

It's a thrill for me. Although wild turkeys are relatively common, they are among Florida's wariest birds, usually seen only by accident or by experienced hunters who have invested years in learning how to stalk them.

On this morning it's a matter of luck. I'm watching 21 turkeys from a camouflaged blind while in the company of Williams, among the world's foremost wild turkey experts. At 51, he has studied them for more than half his life, first as a young hunter growing up in North Florida and then as a Florida Game and Fresh Water Fish Commission biologist who later headed the state's research laboratory.

Williams, who has published two books about wild turkeys and produced four cassette tape recordings that feature turkey calls, quit the commission last year. Now he's conducting independent turkey research, writing magazine stories, taking pictures, doing private consulting work and running a hunting camp at Fisheating Creek. Florida's best turkey habitat, the creek offers plenty of food and cover within its thick oak hammocks, piney woods, cypress swamps, palmetto scrub and open fields.

Williams is at home in this wilderness near Lake Okeechobee. Nothing escapes his attention. Driving through a palmetto thicket, he points out the winding track of a large gopher snake in the sand. Walking through the pines, he stops, sticks out his hand to make me stop, and says, "Listen to that." I listen. "It's the cry of a sandhill crane," he says.

Leaning against a cypress tree on a creek bank, chewing on a straw, he hears the hoot of a barred owl. He sits straight and apologizes for what I'm about to hear: "I haven't been calling owls lately. So I'm a little out of practice. But here goes." He clears his throat and hoots. It sounds like, "Who cooks for you? Who cooks for you all?"

The owl hoots back.

112

Reared in Perry, a small town on the edge of a swamp near Tallahassee, Williams spent happy hours in the woods as a boy. He learned to shoot a gun when he was eight and hunted all through high school. He graduated from Florida State, and worked one summer in Montana fighting forest fires. One day, while he was away, a grizzly bear chewed through the walls of his cabin looking for food. From then on he slept with a loaded shotgun.

He earned his master's degree from Auburn and his doctorate from Florida during the time he worked for the game commission. In 1962 he began studying turkeys on behalf of the state. "I'd always been fascinated by them," he says.

Because of overhunting, and a loss of habitat, wild turkeys were nearly extinct only 40 years ago – a shameful fact. When the Pilgrims landed at Plymouth Rock, and enjoyed their drumsticks at the first Thanksgiving in 1621, turkeys numbered in the millions. As colonists expanded their settlements into former turkey habitats, and fed their families, turkeys disappeared. By the end of the last century, turkeys were gone from most of their original 39-state range. Only 30,000 wild turkeys remained after World War II.

There were millions of domestic turkeys, of course, so nobody but wildlife lovers even noticed. Finally, in the 1950s, many states initiated game management programs to save wild turkeys. Today, the birds are found in every state but Alaska. The population is estimated at two million, including about 80,000 in Florida.

Tough game laws – and research by Williams and other scientists – were responsible for the wild turkey's comeback. In the early years of wildlife management, much of what was known about turkeys was guesswork. Efforts to increase the turkey population, based on inaccurate information or studies of domestic birds, usually failed.

Wild turkeys were different from tame, domestic birds, whose stupidity is almost legendary. Wild turkeys avoided people. Blessed with instinctive wariness, exceptional eyesight and the ability to get airborne immediately and fly up to 50 mph, wild turkeys were no easy study. Williams helped devise a reliable way of catching wild turkeys for further study: He drugged their food. Finished with the turkeys, he relocated them in wilderness that had no turkeys.

During his studies Williams practically lived with turkeys. He learned about the turkey's life cycle and their habitat. He followed them. An average turkey walks four miles a day and takes 300,000 steps, he says. He photographed them. Wild turkeys, because they are so wary, are among the hardest wildlife to shoot with a camera or a gun, he says. He eavesdropped on their conversations. Turkeys make at least 29 different calls, each with a different meaning, he says.

They yelp to locate each other. They cluck to announce their presence. They cackle to encourage other turkeys to follow. They make a putt-putt sound when frightened. During spring's mating season, males gobble to attract hens.

In the spring, some gobbles heard in the woods originate, not from turkeys, but hunters trying to fool turkeys into shotgun range. Williams is a talented turkey caller who can yelp, cluck and gobble with the best. On several occasions, he has been too good. Trying to call turkeys, he has instead lured other hunters.

"I'll usually clear my throat if I see a hunter trying to sneak up," he says. "I'll say 'How ya' doin?' Sometimes you don't want to sound too much like a gobbler for darn sure."

There is no chance at being mistaken for a turkey by hunters this morning. Turkey hunting season won't start for two weeks and Williams and I have the woods to ourselves. We awaken at 5:00 a.m. for breakfast and walk through the dark to the blind, a small camouflaged building from which the turkeys can be studied or photographed by two people.

When we arrive, five small wild hogs are rooting under the oak tree for the corn Williams throws out to attract turkeys. He runs at them, grunting like a giant hog, to scare them. He doesn't want hogs eating food intended for turkeys.

Williams worries about the morning rain. It might keep the turkeys at bay. Ordinarily they fly from trees at first light, gather on the ground as a flock and go looking for acorns, seeds and insects. The rain may interrupt the ritual. It will certainly ruin any attempts at photographs.

Williams is wrong about the turkeys, though. They arrive on foot at the oak tree in the largest flock I've ever seen. We count 21. Our whispers, I'm sure, must be audible to them, but as long as they can't see us they don't seem to mind.

We watch through the blind's dark screen, though there are slits for cameras. Williams tells me, "Don't use your fingers to open the slits. They'll see your fingers and that'll be it. They'll be gone."

Although Williams occasionally hunts, he has devoted more time during recent years to photography. "It's a lot harder to get a good picture of a turkey than to shoot one with a gun," he says. "I took a lot of pictures last year and didn't get a decent photo."

If turkeys see his camera move, they run or fly away. Sometimes a photo will be ruined by a crow dive-bombing the turkey or landing in the picture. Sometimes a bush will be in the way, or another turkey. Last spring Williams waited hours for a male turkey to strut, drag its wings and fan its tail open. When it did, some of its tail feathers were missing, lost in a fight.

"Something's always going wrong."

I'm excited to see these turkeys so close, and so is Williams. I'm struck, in fact, by his joy. When a male turkey gobbles or struts, Williams, who might be jaded after seeing thousands of turkeys during his career, still cusses with enthusiasm and whispers a mile a minute when they appear.

"Look at that gobbler strut! Look at him! He wants to mate. See how his head is white? This time of year their heads will turn white. But it's too early for the hens. They won't be ready for a couple of weeks. Hear that crow? Listen, a gobbler will answer, a gobbler will answer anything. DID YOU HEAR THAT?"

Three of our flock's gobblers veer off to check out two other gobblers, strangers to the flock, who may be approaching to get closer to the hens.

"Watch this! Watch this! There's gonna be a fight! There's gonna be a fight! See how they're holding their heads high? That means they're the dominant birds. At least they think they are. Oh, damn, that bird is strutting again! Lookie there. He's showing off. He's like a human who flexes his muscle. Whoa. The other gobblers are leaving. They want to avoid the fight."

Our flock leaves and another arrives. The hogs return.Turkeys and hogs feed side by side in peace. Williams takes out a hollow turkey bone and blows into it, creating a high-pitched yelp. Two turkeys yelp back and look confused.They stare at the blind and wonder why they can't see the other turkey.

Williams says we'll stay in the blind until all turkeys depart the area. He doesn't want them to know the blind is something worth fearing. If they see people leave the blind they might not return. An hour goes by. My bones start to ache. The turkeys stay. Ninety minutes. The turkeys stay. Finally, the turkeys walk into an adjacent field – out of our sight.

We sneak away.

When we edge into the field, well away from the blind, one turkey sees us and raises the alarm. Putt-putt. Now every turkey eye is on us. Cackle cackle. Every turkey sprints into the woods. Every turkey flies, single file, over Fisheating Creek.

As we watch through the mist they disappear into the cypress trees.

Swimming
with the manatees

CRYSTAL RIVER   **2/15/91**

Late Friday afternoon is a lousy time to drive Florida's most hellish road, but sometimes you do what you have to do in order to see manatees. I grit my teeth and point the truck north from St. Petersburg.

Traffic creeps through Pinellas County on U.S. 19, horns honk in Pasco and terrified out-of-town drivers try to change lanes every dozen feet or so in Hernando. As a mean old man, I ignore their pleading eyes and pathetic hand gestures.

Learn to drive – or die.

It's hard to sip the milk of human kindness while driving five mph, while the heat bounces off the pavement and shimmers in the ozone-busting exhaust fumes rising from cars that disappear ahead over the curvature of the Earth. I pass one accident. Then another. A siren wails.

Ambulance.

The sweet music of civilization.

During U.S. 19's "rush hour," a contradiction in terms, it takes more than three hours to drive the 100 miles to Crystal River, the nation's best spot to swim with manatees, the cow-like marine mammals now sinking toward extinction. Manatees do badly in traffic, too. In 1990, a record 206 died in Florida, including 47 that were crushed, cut and diced by boats.

There are 718,000 registered boats in Florida in 1991; more than twice that many will be chewing up state waterways by century's end, according to some reports. Meanwhile, there are about 1,500 manatees remaining, and scientists wonder whether the death rate exceeds the birth rate.

Yet here in Citrus County, where the Crystal River pours out of Kings Bay, manatees are so plentiful it's difficult to believe they are in trouble. From November through March, when cold winds blow, manatees by the hundreds migrate in from the Gulf to bask in the comparatively warm, spring-fed water. From a boat, your chance of seeing one is great. If you're in the water, you may see one close enough to touch.

But their numbers – state biologists counted 166 here recently – can give a false impression. Manatees are huge and lumbering and every once in a while they must surface for air. If a speeding boat happens to crease their wide backs, the propeller can cut deep enough to kill. Meanwhile, well-meaning snorkelers and divers, frantically trying to pet them, sometimes harass them into the paths of boats. There are a number of sanctuaries here, where boats and divers are prohibited, but the waters could use more.

116

The U.S. Fish and Wildlife Service, which administers federal endangered species laws, plans to create new sanctuaries, despite protests from local businesses. Some entrepreneurs here are already whining that additional sanctuaries and regulations will make it harder for people to see manatees.

The terrifying result?

Muted cash registers.

As I lie in a motel bed Friday night, hoping to rest for the morning's manatee swim, I think about how common manatees were in the Miami where I grew up. As a kid, I spent hours hanging around Biscayne Canal, skimming rocks, fishing, crabbing and watching manatees. We called them sea cows. Standing on the bank, trying to spear mullet, I was often startled by a rising sea cow. Some were 12 feet long, and when they surfaced for air, I was sure a horror movie monster had risen from the depths.

One day I saw a boy named Buddy throw a spear into a baby manatee. The neighborhood bully, Buddy was older and bigger than most of us, and was always getting some smaller kid or another in a headlock and giving him a painful noogie.

On the morning Buddy and his spear were on the prowl, a teen-ager named Jaspar was also about. Jaspar threatened to beat up Buddy when he saw what he'd done to the sea cow. Jaspar pushed Buddy and threw Buddy's lunch into the water. As Buddy left, humiliated, we in the peanut gallery cheered his shame. I don't know if the manatee survived, but on that day I understood the meaning of justice.

Growing up in Florida, it never occurred to me to swim with manatees. They were part of the daily environment, just like the bird songs anybody without air conditioning could hear through open windows.

We live in a new age now, and people feel differently. As civilization advances, destroying the natural world, many of us are desperate to connect with the natural world before it vanishes. We go whale watching. We swim with dolphins. We swim with manatees.

We have to be careful with all this animal bonding, though. For all the fun, it can be dangerous for the animal. It's easy to love wildlife to death.

I am going manatee watching with the ecology club from St. Petersburg's Lakewood High School. There are three girls, a boy and three adults. We climb into our rented wet suits even before we leave the marina. A cold front is moving through Florida today, and a chilly wind is blowing. Somebody cranks up the outboard. We maneuver out of the canal. An osprey cries from a cypress. We cruise into the river.

How do you find manatees?

At Crystal River, you look for other boats. We anchor near more than a dozen other vessels that range from skiffs to pontoon boats. At least 50 snorkelers and divers are already in the water, up against the ropes that mark a manatee sanctuary.

I spit into my mask to coat the glass against fogging. I breathe into the snorkel and adjust the fins. I fall overboard. Seventy-four degree water fills the wet suit, chills me briefly, but warms soon enough. At first I can't see far because of the silt stirred up by other swimmers. But visibility improves, for some reason, the closer you get to the sanctuary.

Sheepshead, a wide-bodied fish with black vertical bars, patrol the grass for shrimp and worms. A cloud of mangrove snapper, schooled in what looks like a funnel cloud, watch my passage nervously. I cling to the manatee sanctuary rope and gaze beyond it.

No manatees.

I don't blame them. Too many boats. Too much boat traffic. Too many divers. I don't want to swim here either.

We return to our boat.

The teacher who is running this trip, Lita Weingart, has done this before. She dislikes diving with mobs of other people, too. She prefers to find her own manatees. She advises us to watch for breathing manatees. Their snouts, poking out of the water, look like floating coconuts.

We don't scream when we see our first manatee. We want to celebrate, but we don't. You don't want to draw attention at Crystal River, even on a rainy, windy weekend day, because there are just too many people. Other swimmers will answer your advertisement and crash your party.

We slip into the water and try to swim calmly toward where we last saw the manatee. The water seems as turbid as vegetable soup. How will we ever find it?

The manatee passes below.

Through a swim mask, everything looks bigger than it actually is. I estimate this manatee at 14 feet, which means it probably is closer to 12. Anyway, it looks almost as long as the boat, and as wide, and if it wanted, it probably could make a pancake out of any swimmer. The charm of manatees is that they're harmless. They are among the only true pacifists in the animal world. They are vegetarians. They hardly fight with one another. If they don't like the situation, they split.

Our manatee is brown with algae. Its back is dotted with white spots. It seems to be crawling, rather than swimming, across the bottom. Its pulsating cheeks, puffed with weeds, remind me of a cow chewing its cud. I've read that an adult will consume 100 pounds of weeds a day. I think I hear molars crunching. I definitely hear squeaking. I wonder if this manatee is as content as I am.

This wonderful animal, sort of a cross between a walrus and an elephant, begins to plane toward the surface. We try to get out of the way, but it hardly matters. The manatee seems unconcerned about our presence. We've minded our manners by being quiet and respectful.

I'm at the front. Rising, the manatee stops briefly, just under the surface, and looks at me. Its eyes are round and black and – what? – curious. Can a wild animal be curious about a human? Or is it reproach I see in those eyes? One flipper is gone. Manatees occasionally tangle in crab trap lines and lose limbs.

The manatee, only two feet away, begins its descent. I reach out and pet it.

Smooth and cold, my sea cow does not shrink from my touch. There's something wonderful and miraculous about that. They have good reason to fear us.

Now another appears. And two more. Our area is crawling with manatees. All show evidence of boat encounters. One has three parallel scars across its back – a souvenir from a motorboat propeller.

A manatee cow and her calf swim into view. They surface among us. The teen-agers with us shriek with what sounds like both fright and delight.

I wonder to myself: Can there be anything wrong with this?

The dive boat shows up an hour later. The captain has seen us and understood we are onto manatees. A half-dozen divers crash into the river. I can hear their air-tank regulators percolating from a long way off. Soon I see their bubbles. When the divers discover the manatees, they follow them to the bottom. The divers swim on both sides of the animals as if to escort them across the river. The divers rest their arms across the manatee backs as if they were long lost barroom buddies.

There is nothing natural about what they are doing.

The manatees seem to sense that. They swim faster. The divers frantically try to stay even. The manatees pick up speed. The divers have to give up.

The manatees escape into the deeper part of the river.

The divers go looking for fresh manatees.

The drive home goes much faster than the drive up. It's Saturday, after all, and bad weather has kept at least some motorists at bay. I don't use my horn once, I'm polite to other drivers and I indulge myself by cranking up the stereo.

The Charlie Pickett song somehow seems appropriate:

Can you – hear me crying? Can you – hear me crying? Don't send me out in the wilderness.

In St. Petersburg, where I leave the interstate, a motorcycle is down on the wet pavement. A police officer stands over the unconscious driver, who is lying on his back in the intersection, arms spread wide, rain falling on his face. Civilization is as dangerous for the human race as it is for manatees.

In the distance, a siren wails.

Lady of the border

JENNINGS   **12/26/87**

Some people expect beaches and palm trees the moment they cross the Florida border. They expect alligators and snakes and shootouts between cocaine dealers on the interstate.

What they get is a nice middle-aged woman named Dottie Scaff. She smiles at them. She says hey. She gives them orange juice.

"Welcome," she says, "to Florida."

She is the lead information specialist – a fancy phrase for know-it-all – at the Florida Welcome Center on I-75 just south of the Georgia line. Stop and you will see her at work, soothing weary travelers and talking up the state to excited tourists and new citizens who have just driven in.

Last year, she and 11 other workers greeted 1.2-million visitors and poured them 33,200 gallons of juice. They gave away brochures listing attractions, motels, beaches and churches. They dispensed free maps. They answered questions by the jillions.

Where's the nearest beach?

"Sir, Jacksonville Beach is only one hundred and twenty miles away."

Why don't I see palm trees?

"Ma'am, there's a Sabal palm just outside the door. It's the state tree."

Where is your gun? I thought everyone in Florida would be, uh, wearing a gun.

"Oh no, honey. That's just what you've read in the newspaper."

'Ma'am, Do you uh, do you uh...Listen: Where's the nearest nudist colony?

"Well, sir,'' Dottie Scaff says, "'the nearest nudist colony is in Lake City forty miles away."

Welcoming centers – there are six spread out across the border from Jacksonville to Pensacola – play an important role in Florida tourism. They put a happy face on the state's image of a troubled paradise.

Later on, as tourists drive south, they will be certain to find out about horrendous traffic, high prices, crime and other Florida realities. But they also will carry with them the memory of the kind people at the welcome center who spoke in charming southern accents and answered all their questions.

What's the weather like at Disney World?

"You're a cute little boy, you know that? Don't worry. It's sunny."

Where can I catch a bass?

"Any freshwater river or lake would be fine, sir. Let me give you this brochure. It has the information about fishing license requirements. Our largest lake is Lake Okeechobee. That'll be about three hundred miles from here."

Mrs. Scaff, 48, has worked at the center since 1972. When she was hired, she did what other employees have to do. She sat at a table and studied a Florida atlas. Six months later, she passed an oral exam. Her probation over, she was an official information specialist for the state of Florida.

"It's a good job," she says, "especially if you like people."

In December, her busiest month, she meets a lot of them. There was a day, in 1978, when almost 18,000 came through the door in nine hours. "On days like that, about all you have time for is to smile at them."

Sometimes, of course, even a friendly welcome center information specialist feels like frowning. The weather conspires to embarrass the state. Tourists don't behave themselves. Children show up – and stay and stay.

In 1977, it snowed, for crying out loud. The state, fortunately, lifted the burden of having to explain snow in Florida by closing I-75 on account of ice and sending the information specialists home early.

Sometimes mischievous folks ignore the sign outside the door and walk into the welcome center with their pets. Dogs are bad enough – but iguanas?

Sometimes, and this happens more often than you would think, a large family who has visited the welcome center becomes overwhelmed by the free OJ and the maps and the kindness and leaves without counting noses.

"Yes, they'll forget one of the kids. The kids are usually pretty calm. We take them in back and wait for the parents to come back." She has yet to lose a family.

Citrus piggies can be another problem for the kind women of the welcome center. Dottie Scaff occasionally notes that certain people are whetting their whistles more than once. She tells them – nicely, of course – that the policy at the welcome center is one cup per person.

Some drink the free juice and complain.

"For a few years, all we were serving was grapefruit juice," Dottie Scaff says, sounding embarrassed. "A lot of people, they didn't know what grapefruit juice even tasted like! They hated it! It was like we had ruined their life by giving them grapefruit juice instead of orange. They'd just sulk."

That's as negative as Dottie Scaff gets about tourists. She would much rather tell you how nice they are, how they sometimes bring presents – apples from North Carolina, or goat's milk cookies from who knows where – and how they ask charming questions.

Are there mosquitoes in Florida? I'm going to the Everglades.

"Well, sir, it is the summer, and mosquitoes are a fact of life. But you can buy mosquito repellent."

Will I need snake boots in Florida?

"There are snakes in Florida, but they really aren't a problem. And the alligators pretty much stay in the water."

Me and the lady here want to get married. I mean right now. Where can we get hitched?

"The nearest justice of the peace is at the Hamilton County Courthouse in Jennings. About fifteen miles away."

What? You only have orange and grapefruit juice? I wanted prune juice.

"I'm so sorry. We don't have prune juice."

Miss Harriet

Miss Harriet looked into the rear-view mirror, saw the big blue van on her tail and drove her creaking, rusting Japanese sedan off the pavement. "Guy behind me is from New York," she said. "He's in a hurry."

Miss Harriet, who would probably be known as Harriet Smith if she still resided in a northern city, used to be in a hurry all the time, too. She lived in urban New Hampshire, sold computer equipment and was a seasoned competitor in the rat race.

Ten years ago, she quit the treadmill, sold most of her possessions, loaded a old motor home with what she had left, drove to Florida, worked here and there as a house painter, biological technician and a waitress, and then found Cedar Key.

"I was like a lot of people who come here," she said. "I came, I saw, I stayed."

Cedar Key, population 1,000 on a busy weekend, may be the state's most laid-back place. Most residents of the Northwest Florida coastal town are commercial fishermen who know they will never be millionaires unless they win the lottery. They catch mullet when they can, collect oysters when oysters are available, but spend a lot of time just sitting and staring at the water. Other residents own motels and restaurants and shops that are as likely to be closed as open. Here nobody's overly concerned about clocks and calendars.

Everybody knows just about everybody else in Cedar Key, which is about a three-hour drive north of Tampa Bay. Folks are generally polite and follow the southern tradition of addressing each other by Mister or Miss followed by the first name. Nobody wears a tie, unless it's for a funeral or a wedding, and maybe not even then. The town drunk is more likely to be driven home by the police chief than tossed into the pokey. The town's collective blood pressure is on the low side.

Maybe too low. Miss Harriet, 49, worries about Cedar Key and the innocent people who live here. During the last century it has withstood horrible hurricanes, the merciless logging industry and devastating fish shortages, but now the town faces an even more formidable enemy.

Progress.

People fall in love with Cedar Key and move here. Miss Harriet did in 1984. They tell other people about it, and they sometimes move here, too. On weekends, rich people from all over the state drive up or even land their airplanes on the town's airstrip. Several condos have been built, new tourist gift shops have gone up on the waterfront, and there are plans to develop an island just off Dock Street. The town's sewer system is being expanded, which may allow further growth.

Some folks might call all those things progress, but Miss Harriet worries that too much change will ruin Cedar Key.

"What is progress?" she asked the other day, standing in front of the Island Hotel, the 140-year-old ramshackle inn in the middle of town. "The Soviet Union just got its first McDonald's restaurant. Is that progress?"

Miss Harriet's idea of progress leaves no room for fast-food restaurants, interstates, condominiums or gift shops that sell shell lamps. When she thinks of progress, she thinks of quality of life. Cedar Key is surrounded by salt marshes, water, oysters, fish and birds. The air is clean, and people are kind. She wonders how life could possibly be better.

She is doing her part to explain all this in a weekly four-page newsletter called *The Cedar Key Naturalist*. She writes it, edits it, types it, illustrates it and delivers it every Monday. It costs a quarter and has 25 subscribers so far. Almost every restaurant, grocery and gift shop in town also stocks it. If you want a copy, you throw a quarter into a jar and take one. People here expect honesty.

Miss Harriet writes about what wildflowers you might see at the cemetery, about the ospreys that nest near the airport runway and the fact that white pelicans have shown up by the No. 4 Bridge. She also criticizes politicians for their environmental records, explains why recycling is necessary and gives her readers information that may help them evaluate the full implications of growth.

"Where are the ospreys?" she asked in a recent issue. She suggested the hawk-like birds might be in short supply because fish might be in short supply. The fish may be in short supply because of pollution. If pollution is hurting the fish population, it's also hurting fishermen. Although most people here depend on a healthy environment to make a living, they don't ordinarily think of themselves as environmentalists. Miss Harriet tries to tell them that being an environmentalist is not like being a crazy radical.

"I'm not trying to run the town," she said. "But I want people to think about things that affect them. What happens when we develop that island offshore? Well, it's down current from Corrigan's Reef, where we do a lot of oystering. What about the oil that will spill in the water when boats gas up at the new marina? If the fishing dies here, a whole way of life will die with it. And that will open the doors for full-scale tourism. Cedar Key will change forever.

"Environmental problems impact the economy."

Miss Harriet doesn't seem to worry much about money. When she needs a few bucks to put out a newsletter – it costs about $30 per issue – she paints a house, if she can find one that needs painting, or goes out in her skiff and catches a tubful of crabs and sells them at the fish house. She has no checking account and no financial obligations other than the $83.68 she pays a month for the piece of land where she more or less built her own house with lumber she picked up here and there.

"It's incredible what people throw away," she said.

Harriet Smith was born in Alabama, where she learned to love the outdoors at the side of her father, an avid hunter. She studied engineering at Auburn but dropped out. She married and had three children. She tried to write a novel that just wouldn't come. She lived in Maryland and California. She got divorced. In New Hampshire, she sold $5-million worth of computers a year. She wondered if there was more to life than selling computers. Also, it was cold in New England, and she wanted to live where it was warm.

"I might starve to death in Florida," she said. "But I won't freeze."

She tried Key West. She helped wildlife experts gather data at Central Florida's Archbold Biological Station. She worked as a wildlife technician at Northwest Florida's Tall Timbers Research Station. In Tallahassee, she painted houses. Then one day she drove south and made the west turn that took her toward the Gulf.

The easy rhythms of the coast, the soft wind blowing across the marsh, the way the oysters pop on low tide, the comings and goings of the birds and the friendly ways of the people convinced her that she had made the right choice. She put aside her other life, put on blue jeans and a baggy sweatshirt and became Miss Harriet of Cedar Key.

"How's your wife?" she asked a truck driver the other day. Miss Harriet and the truck driver had stopped their vehicles in the road to chew the fat. The driver said, "Well, she ain't passed that kidney stone yet." Miss Harriet said she'd stop by to visit soon.

"These are wonderful people," Miss Harriet said.

She worries about them because, as wonderful as they might be, they have a history of hurting themselves. Cedar Key once boasted 5,000 people, which made it one of the biggest cities in Florida. In 1855, pencil king Eberhard Faber bought land here because he wanted to harvest the cedar trees that grew everywhere. Cedar Key established no conservation policy, and the timber and the local economy were exhausted by 1900.

Cedar Key was also a major oyster producer at one time. But fishermen took too many oysters and killed their own industry. Oysters returned, though not completely, and these days they are dangerous to eat and illegal to harvest. Salmonella, which can accompany pollution, has made some people sick. Pollution, of course, often goes with growth. Unwise growth could destroy Cedar Key's way of life, Miss Harriet fears.

"People don't come here for the condominiums," she said. "They come here for the lifestyle and the natural resources."

Three years ago, after she rescued a pelican that was snarled in fishing line and fish hooks, she stewed about saving birds. She spent a month at Tampa Bay's Suncoast Seabird Sanctuary, learned as much as she could, and opened Seabird Rescue Center of Cedar Key. A local artist started a fund to pay her expenses, and Harriet was on her way.

In 1987, she published a book, *The Naturalist's Guide to Cedar Key, Florida*. The booklet directs visitors to the natural wonders of the place, and is rich with her personality. "For many people," she wrote, "the Florida outdoors away from air conditioning and swimming pools is a forbidding and foreign place. A friend who formerly lived in Illinois once told me 'I used to hike all the time at home, but everything here seems too strange and scary.' Here's the key to overcoming that feeling: RELAX. STOP. LOOK AROUND. LEARN IT."

Miss Harriet helps as much as she can. Every Friday morning, she has a "breakfast with a naturalist" at Cook's Cafe. She may lecture on the natural history of the stone crab or talk about saving sea turtles. Recently, she looked around her table – there were 20 people – and said, "Okay, if we're going to make shrimpers use those turtle excluder devices in their nets to save turtles, and possibly hurt their business, what are we going to sacrifice to help save the planet? Everybody has to do something."

People squirmed. Miss Harriet said, "Are we going to start recycling? Not use pesticides? Not put fertilizers on our lawn?" One man said taxes should be raised and the money be spent on the environment. "Imagine!" Miss Harriet said the other day. "People saying we should tax ourselves!"

Miss Harriet also leads weekend birding trips for a small fee. The author of *Watching Birds in the Cedar Keys*, she takes people out to see kestrels, white ibis and bald eagles. Most customers are tourists, but some are residents who want to learn more about the place they live in. Miss Harriet is happy to tell them.

Some locals, of course, don't want to know any more than they do. They consider Miss Harriet an outsider who is butting into business that doesn't concern her. But they tolerate her – people are tolerant here – and they don't give her a hard time. Sometimes, though, they just shake their heads.

Not long ago, Miss Harriet walked into the gift shop on the dock that sells seashells, including that cliche of Florida tourism, the shell lamp. Miss Harriet thinks seashells are better left in the sea.

"Ah," Miss Harriet announced when she walked into the store and noticed the shells. "The rape of the sea."

"Oh, go away," the shopkeeper said, but not unkindly.

Miss Harriet is here to stay.

Wonder dog

When I travel, I usually hate to stop for anything but gasoline or to check out a story tip. The other day I got to do both.

Driving through Central Florida, I was looking for a gas station a friend had recommended. A gas station may seem an odd thing to seek out, but I had heard stories that, frankly, seemed too good to be true. I had to know. On U.S. 27 and Oak Street, I turned into a gritty looking, no-nonsense place called Becton's Gulf and Tire Service, and ordered gas. As the attendant pumped the petrol, I got out my money. But the attendant never came around to collect my two bucks.

A dog did.

A mixed-breed Labrador retriever stood there, outside my window, panting and looking a little impatient. Finally, I did what the dog wanted. I held out the small wad of bills, and the dog took the money into her mouth. Then she trotted inside the station and stood on her hind legs at the counter. A woman took the money and then tossed a doggie biscuit into the yawning jaws of the four-legged employee.

My friend had told me about this, but I didn't quite believe her. You may not believe either, so I'll repeat: You give a dog your money, and the dog takes it to the woman at the cash register.

Florida has become a complex place, with frightening growth, crowded schools, rising crime and no clear answers about how to solve the problems. So I'll tell you: It's a relief to be able to write about a dog. Especially one that will take your money and even bring you change, soggy perhaps, but all there down to the last penny.

"We have people who come by every day and buy a couple dollars worth – just so they can see the dog in action," said Peggy Becton, who actually beamed while she bragged. "We have people –winter residents – who show up after being gone all summer, and the first thing they ask is, 'Where's the dog?' "

Gulf Pride, GP for short, is likely to be found lazing on the pavement between the gas pumps and the station. She was abandoned as a puppy at Becton's Gulf in 1980. Today, GP is pleasantly plump and slow moving. Whenever she brings money to the cash register, she is rewarded with an edible treat. In fact, she may be the most spoiled dog in canine history. Customers bring her bones, burgers, even cakes.

"She knows certain cars by sight," said Mrs. Becton, who has owned the station with her husband for nine years. "I think she also recognizes the sound of certain motors. She has learned who she can freeload off of."

GP is Florida's wonder dog. Don Becton, 43, knew it the day he began training her. As a pup, she was quick to grasp the intricacies of sitting up, shaking hands and rolling over. So Becton decided to test her further. Standing by the gas pumps, a dollar in his hand, he called her over. He gave her the dollar, and she carried it to Peggy, who called from inside the station. Soon Don trained her to stand at the counter before presenting the money to Peggy. Then he taught her to stand at the left side of the counter, making it possible for Peggy, who is right handed, to accept the money.

"She'll take a credit card, too," said Mrs. Becton, 43. "But her teeth tend to scratch cards, so we discourage it. We prefer that people pay in cash if they want GP to carry it."

GP is polite about taking your money, too. I was nervous when I handed over my two bucks. GP weighs 120 pounds and has teeth the size of pencil stubs. But her mouth was soft and gentle, and she made no attempt to get too friendly. The Bectons have instructed GP not to lean on cars.

"I don't want her scratching somebody's new Lincoln," Mrs. Becton explained.

GP does more than toil at the gas pumps. When the auto-parts truck arrives, GP is there to greet it. She carries small parts into the station to Don. When the afternoon newspaper hits the pavement, she brings that in, too. GP helps the mechanics as they move cars into an enclosed compound at night. The mechanics throw her car keys, and she brings them into the station so Peggy can hang them on hooks.

"She used to get a little carried away," Mrs. Becton said. "She was stealing lug nuts from the mechanics when they were changing tires. She thought I'd give her a treat if she brought me the nuts because I'd given her treats for the keys."

GP is better known for good deeds than mischief. A customer, reaching for gas money, once accidentally dislodged from his pocket a roll of 50 $1 bills. GP carried the cash into the station, and Mr. Careless was flagged down before he pulled away. On another occasion, GP retrieved a lost payroll check. Peggy called the business that had issued the check and announced that her dog had found it. A few hours later, a grateful worker arrived for his money. He presented GP with a reward, a huge bone.

"Everybody loves GP," Don Becton said. Over the Christmas holidays, she got more cards and presents than her owners. For GP, it's Christmas every day.

One man regularly drops by with a can of dog food. One woman always brings Life Savers. One man gave Don Becton a $15 tip – to be spent on GP. One woman treats GP to Moon Pies. One man brings fast-food. While he waits for his vehicle to be repaired, he eats one double-cheeseburger while GP wolfs down the other.

Children come by to ride on GP's back. Though GP hates cats, she lets Don and Peggy's stray stand on her head. GP also enjoys pushing tires around with her nose. She satisfies her thirst by lapping up a bowl of her favorite beverage, Dr Pepper.

"Actually, she likes just about anything," Don Becton said. Even the lollipops that one customer religiously brings. When GP is finished with her candy, she brings Peggy the stick. "She's leery of putting it in the garbage can," Don said. "She got a few spankings when she was a puppy for getting into the trash."

The Bectons make more money selling tires, brakes and shock absorbers than they do selling gasoline. So from time to time, they think about doing away with the gas pumps. But they haven't. Not as long as GP is alive.

"In a way, we sell gas just for her," Peggy Becton said.

I'm glad they do. I have never had so much fun at a gas station.

There are many wonders in this world.

The boys of winter

ST. PETERSBURG   **2/28/90**

Spring training doesn't start for a couple of weeks yet. So what's a body to do for a baseball fix? You walk over to North Shore Park, sit in the bleachers, and take in the Boys of Winter.

Pitcher Pappy Hill, 77, winds and delivers. Batter Pat Rylee, 78, swings from the heels. He lines a triple between outfielders. He may not run like the wind anymore, but he sweeps around the bases like a stiff breeze.

Since 1930, the Three-Quarter Century Softball Club has been hitting, fielding and throwing in St. Petersburg. Players for the Kids and Kubs, as the club's only two teams are called, are men older than 74. Three times a week from October through March they play nine innings at the park on the bay.

They play the game well. Kubs shortstop John Veleber, 75, races toward second, grabs a hot grounder on the first bounce, and beats the runner to second base to get the out. It's a big-league play. Harry Shironaka, 77, charges a slow rolling ball at third base, grabs it and fires home. Out at the plate. Herm Fenderson, 77, comes to bat with two outs in the ninth and his team behind by one run. He slams a double and drives in two. Kubs win, 11-10.

"Some of these guys will make your eyes pop." That's George Bakewell, 97-year-old catcher, talking. He has played softball for the Kids or the Kubs for 22 years – the same length of time Stan "The Man" Musial performed for the Cardinals.

Bakewell, a retired insurance executive from Missouri, is the oldest player. He has 11 years to go before he can lay claim to the club longevity record. The late Charles Eldridge was still playing at 107. Bakewell typically starts the game at catcher, bats once and is replaced by one of the young whippersnappers, maybe Walt Weller, 78, or Jack Dreyer, 79.

"People are always surprised by the caliber of the play," says Paul Good, 80. He's the president of the Three Quarter Century Softball Club and the Kubs' third baseman. "Sometimes we even surprise ourselves."

Good, like most of the other players, seems younger than he is. He credits clean living and athletics. As a boy, he preferred baseball to girls. As a young man, he played on a semi-professional team in Colorado and once batted against Hall-of-Fame pitcher Grover Cleveland Alexander. "This was after he had retired from the big leagues," Good says. "He didn't have his fastball anymore. He threw these big, sweeping curves that were easy to follow. I got two singles off him."

In 1938 he retired his glove, got married, became a stockbroker and took up golf.

He played three times a week. Five years ago, he decided to try out for the Kids and Kubs and made the roster. "I guess your body remembers," he says. "Your instincts are there. Gosh, I hadn't played for fifty years."

Before the game, Good stretches to limber up. Other players keep rust at bay by walking, throwing and batting. To look at them, you wouldn't know that Joe Gillard, 82, had a total hip replacement in 1976, or that Irv Holzheuter, 74, had a triple bypass in 1988.

"For the most part, players are in really good shape now," Paul Good says. "Modern medicine keeps us healthy, and we play better and we play longer."

Some play until the very end. In 1975, Bill Davis played a game as catcher, went home and died in his sleep at the age of 92. In 1969, an 83-year-old player named Lee Morrison dropped dead on the field. His teammates agreed that the field was a pretty good place to pass away.

There are concessions to age. Each team is allowed 12 men on the field instead of the traditional nine. Twelve can cover more ground than nine. To prevent collisions, there are two first bases, one for the runner and one for the fielder. Runners don't actually have to tag home plate to score. If they come close, good enough.

Errors are not counted. A batter who reaches base safely, no matter how badly the ball is misplayed in the field, is credited with a hit. The scorekeeper, Jane Case, used to keep track of batting averages. Batters were always complaining when she judged their hits as errors. Fielders, on the other hand, were disappointed when she charged them with errors on balls that could have been hits.

"These guys have big egos," Paul Good says. "It's simpler not to use batting averages."

So far this season, the Kids have won 20 games and the Kubs, 19. If one team gets four games ahead, players are traded to even things out. And each October the Kids and Kubs hold tryouts. Last fall about 50 hopefuls showed up. Only five made the rosters.

Five is the magic number. Each year, about that many retire. It can be touchy because some players don't want to stop playing. It's Good's job to persuade them.

"Usually, nature takes care of the problem," he says. "The player just can't do it anymore and has to stop. But some of them won't admit it's the end of the line. I remember I told one guy he should hang it up. He said, 'If I have to quit, I'll die.' What can you do? We let him play."

On the beach

The sand, roaring across the beach in the gale, stings like birdshot against the skin. You call to the boy, walking in front of you, but he doesn't turn. He can't hear, not in this wind, which threatens to carry both of you into the sea oats.

You want to show the boy something. Shiny and black, a fossilized shark's tooth lying in the damp sand has caught your attention. You hunker down, and reach, and an even stronger gust hits, and the surf suddenly rushes for your shoes, and you have to retreat. This is no time for wet feet.

The first, and probably last, good cold snap of the season has arrived from the north, with winds strong enough to uproot trees. It's the worst and best time for a day at the beach. It's cold, wet and miserable. It's also exhilarating.

The sea, roiled and nasty, thunders toward civilization, toward you and the boy. Wind breaks off the tops of waves and hurls them like misshapen cream pies. Your sunglasses collect salt water and sand. How will you ever locate fossils?

Fossils – ancient shark's teeth – are why you and the boy have come. Venice Beach, about an hour south of Tampa Bay, is the best place in Florida to find them.

Dark, ancient fossiliferous sand, carrying secrets of the past, shifts endlessly with wind and tide. The next wave may reveal a tooth a hundred centuries old – or one that broke away from a prehistoric shark's jaw millions of years ago.

"Here's one," yells the boy. He has found a scattering of shells a dozen feet from the surf. Mixed within the rubble, in plain view when your eyes adjust, is a curved black tooth, barely wider than a lima bean.

It looks like weaponry from a tiger shark, dead for ages. Some experts believe tiger sharks came along six-million years ago. How long has this tooth lain here? Maybe since the last full-moon tide. Perhaps it was here, in the open, when Spaniards stepped ashore. You're just the first to hold it in your hands.

Fossilized shark's teeth are found all over the planet – anywhere covered at one time by the sea. Montana has deposits of shark fossils. You can find shark's teeth on mountaintops. But it's especially exciting to find them here, on a deserted, undeveloped beach, in a gale.

You and the boy are a good mile from the nearest building, Sharky's Restaurant. Behind you are sand dunes, sea oats, palmettos and stubby pines. The sea reveals nothing of civilization. It's too rough for sailboats. You can't even spot an oil tanker on the horizon. The ocean, at least the surface, must look as it has since the beginning of time.

"The ocean is a wilderness reaching around the globe," Thoreau wrote in *Cape*

Cod, "wilder than a Bengal jungle, and fuller of monsters, washing the very wharves of our cities and gardens of our seaside residences. Serpents, bears, hyenas, tigers rapidly vanish as civilization advances, but the most populous and civilized city cannot scare a shark far from its wharves."

The Gulf is, and has been, loaded with sharks. Tiger sharks. Sand sharks. Lemons, bulls and hammerheads. Great whites, the bad boy from Jaws, visit the deepest water. And once there was a true monster.

The *Carcharodon megalodon*, larger than a boxcar, first patrolled the gulf more than 25-million years ago. It was probably the largest carnivore on Earth. You can tell by the teeth. They are triangular, serrated and, in some cases, eight inches long. The jaws that contained eight-inch teeth were six feet across. They could consume an adult dolphin or seal in a single bite.

But something happened within the last 50,000 years, something unpleasant for *Carcharodon megalodons*. They vanished, and nobody seems to know why. Only teeth remain.

You would like to find a megalodon tooth, of course. Every year, hundreds of people pick them up here, sometimes people as inexperienced as yourself. They happen to be walking along, in the shallows, and look down at the right moment.

On a nice sunny day, or on the day after a storm, beaches here are rich with shark tooth fanciers. Some wade. Some scoop sand with screened boxes and sift for teeth. Others stand, back to Gulf, and let the tide rearrange the sand at their feet. When a tooth appears, they pounce. Megalodon teeth, the big ones, are worth hundreds of dollars at area shell shops.

You and the boy walk along the stormy beach, eyes tearing against the wind. "Find anything?" you shout at a man who carries a sieve. He looks at you in the way native Floridians always look at tourists who have asked stupid questions. He knows you saw him taking off his shoes. He obviously just started. You wish you had asked anything else.

The boy, risking wet feet, challenges the surf. Every time a wave retreats, he charges, looks quickly for a tooth, and then outruns the returning volley. Ah, to be young again.

You stay higher on the beach and only a degree or two more dry. As you watch the sea, 20-foot palm trees tumble ashore, here and there, like Tinker Toys. Where were they uprooted? Texas? Louisiana? North Florida? A boat that hit one of these tree trunks would be swallowed by the sea.

You kneel.

You paw through shell. Here's a small, needle-like tooth. It could come from a sand shark or maybe a mako. You push it hard against your skin. This ancient tooth could draw blood. You put it in your pocket.

Later, on the drive home, you feel it sharp against your thigh when you fish in your pocket for toll money. You think about throwing a fossilized tooth into the toll basket at the bridge. Perhaps ancient people used shark's teeth for currency.

But you're a civilized guy. You drop in four quarters and head over the bridge.

Keith

When I was a boy, growing up in Miami, I did stupid, crazy things that could have gotten me arrested, hurt or killed. I liked to climb the roof at night and throw water balloons at passing cars, and when that lost its novelty I hurled guavas and other tropical fruit. One night, a couple of teen-agers whose car I smashed with a guava chased a friend and me over fences, through bushes and into back yards where dogs snapped at our heels. We somehow escaped.

One night, a friend and I built a dummy, and, hiding behind a bush, threw it in front of a passing car. The car screeched to a stop, and an elderly man got out, shaking, certain he had killed someone. I am still ashamed.

By the time I was 14 I was a fishing fanatic. I fished for snook in a canal that passed through a golf course in Miami Shores. I had to trespass to fish, but I was good at climbing high fences, and I didn't mind running from the cops. The cops would take you to the police station, call your parents, and confiscate your tackle. They never caught me.

Sometimes I wish I had been caught. If I had, maybe I would have stayed away from the golf course once and for all. Maybe Keith would be alive, and on those nights when I lie awake in a cold sweat I would no longer hear him screaming.

I went back last week. Visiting Miami on business, I had a couple of hours to kill and drove to the golf course. I walked along the first fairway, crossed a bridge that spanned the canal, passed under the railroad trestle – and then stopped when I saw the dam.

I was staring at the dam when a golf course groundskeeper drove up in an electric cart. "What are you doing?" he asked. I told him I'd come back to the scene of a tragedy that has haunted me for life, a tragedy my mind continually dredges up whenever I am depressed or I start worrying about the safety of my own sweet children. Death is no abstraction to me. That a lot of people live to old age is, I know, a matter of luck, of being in the right place at the right time. I am afraid to trust happiness.

"I remember it," the groundskeeper said. "I lived across the street from the sixteenth fairway. I remember all the excitement. It was awful."

"I was there," I said.

"Kids still sneak on the golf course to fish," he said. "I chased ten away already this afternoon."

"Take it from me," I said. "It's no place to fish."

I walked along the 11th fairway and looked at the sign on the fence at the dam.

"Danger," it said. "Automatic Gates Open Without Warning."

I introduced the twins, Keith and Kent, to fishing. We were 14 and in ninth grade. Kent was tall, thin, and, like me, a nerd who didn't know how to dress and blushed whenever a girl approached. Keith was short and built like a bulldog, with big bones and a neck about as wide as his shoulders. He got into a lot of fights at school, and when we played football, he always wanted to play tackle instead of touch. Nobody could bring him down.

It was a Sunday morning. My parents were at Mass. I met Keith and Kent at the golf course fence, and we climbed over. It was March, a little early for snook, but we wanted to try anyway.

Kent did his casting from shore; Keith and I stood together on a little walkway at the front of the dam. From there, you could cast under the dam and reach the spot where water and minnows trickled in from the other side.

Keith threw his yellow Creek Chub Darter lure under the dam. It got snagged on the floodgate, the mechanism that opens and closes to regulate the flow of water. Keith cussed and said, "I'm going to unsnag my lure." It was the last thing he said to me.

While I continued casting, Keith climbed over a guard rail, to the other side of the dam. He lay on the floodgate and reached inside to recover his lure. There should have been nothing to it: Just lean in, get your lure, get out.

The tide, at that moment, must have reached its highest point. Suddenly, the dam roared to life. Gears turned, machinery rumbled and the floodgates began opening. That was when Keith screamed.

Actually, it was a shriek. I still don't know how it happened, and I don't know if I can adequately explain it, but what happened was his upper body somehow got pinched between the floodgate and the rest of the dam. He could go neither forward nor back. As the gate came up to allow water to flow from below, life was squeezed from Keith. I'll tell you what he said, though it doesn't mean as much unless you can imagine how he shrieked.

"Mommy, mommy, mommy. I don't want to die. Oh, God, I don't want to die."

Kent and I leaped the railing and tugged on his legs, which were kicking, but we couldn't haul him out. Pretty soon his legs stopped kicking.

Kent sprinted to the clubhouse a half mile away for help. I stood crying at the dam, until two doctors, playing golf, ran over to see what happened. One reached into the dam and took Keith's pulse. "He's gone," he said.

A doctor told me to go home; there was nothing I could do. At that moment I wanted nothing more than to go home and cry in the arms of my parents. I pitched my tackle over the fence, jumped on my bike and pedaled home as fast as I could, my lungs almost bursting with effort. In my front yard, I jumped off the bicycle, while it was still rolling, and ran into the house screaming for my mom and dad. They were still at Mass, so I went into their bedroom, fell to my knees and prayed loudly for a miracle I knew was not going to happen.

Keith, my friend, a boy my age, was dead.

Nothing would bring him back. Ever.

The signs and smells
say "spring"

Over at Redington Long Pier, spring has arrived. Everyone knows that. Just take a stroll on the 1,024-foot pier that juts into the Gulf of Mexico at Redington Shores and check it out.

The Spanish mackerel are running, as they do every spring here in West Central Florida, and they are being landed by the fish-pole brigade.The flounder are showing up, in the sand next to the pilings nearest the bait house. At night, look down where the pier lights shine in the water. Ever see such nice, fat snook? The tasty game fish show up every spring.

"The thing is," says Don Rosenberger, the pier's 65-year-old bait monger, "that when you see them suckers in the light, you ain't gonna catch 'em. Snook are too smart."

Yet it's nice to see them even if they aren't biting. Up North, when groundhogs cast a shadow, spring has sprung. In Florida, we look for snook in the lights.

There are other unmistakable signs of spring, of course.

Jacarandas, bursting with their purple-blue flowers, are putting on a show along Florida streets. On lakes, alligators are stirring, moving through the cattails, staking out territory, preparing for mating season. So are snakes. Hikers in the woods are seeing black snakes and even diamondback rattlers.

Gopher tortoise babies are crawling out of their burrows to eat wire grass, and swallow-tail butterflies are flitting about the impatiens, zinnias and jasmine. And did you notice what just flew over the pinetops? It's a bald eagle, talons gripping a mullet that will feed baby. Ah, spring.

Even people who are indifferent about the natural world sense the new season. During winter, our roads are crowded and even more dangerous than usual. In the spring, we can breathe just a little easier. Spring has arrived when finding a parking place at the mall is a snap. On the beach, it's easy to find a spot for book and blanket. The awful traffic that made getting to the beach so unbearable a month ago is now only a memory.

Over at Redington Long Pier, you know it's spring when you can find a place to stand without shoving fellow fishers aside. Last month, anglers stood elbow to elbow at the pier railing. Some tourists, fishing for the first time, threatened to snag ear lobes with errant casts.

Now the regulars, their ear lobes intact, have reclaimed their pier. Don Rosenberger is selling fewer shrimp, renting fewer rods and answering fewer silly questions. ("No, sir. The reel goes on the bottom of the rod and not the top.") But he also has more time to spar with the old-timers who would be disappointed if he acted too polite.

"Got any big shrimp?" asks a gray-haired regular who smells of fish and sweat and is sure he could catch a trout if he had a nice, fat shrimp for bait.

"None of your damn business!" roars Rosenberger, who of course lets the anxious angler peek into the bait tank.

Nobody takes offense at Rosenberger's snappy patter. It's spring, after all. The weather is warm, and the fish are biting. Old friends are seeing old friends for the first time since fall. Has anybody seen Flounder Joe? Yeah, he was here yesterday. Caught his supper. Flounder Joe is something, ain't he?

That's how it is when the regulars show up at the pier in the spring. Nobody seems to need a last name. Flounder Joe. Old Art. Eddie. Larry. Even Rosenberger, who has worked at the pier for 13 years, who sees the same people every day, can't provide last names. Who needs them?

"Well, Arthur," he says to a regular, who is pulling a shopping cart full of fishing gear off the pier. "Don't lie to me, dammit, don't lie. What'd you catch?"

Arthur looks embarrassed.

"I got two keepers. I got two cutoffs. Just bit through my line."

Spanish mackerel don't get very big, but their teeth are impressively sharp. When they get away, a cut line is usually the reason.

Come summer, everything will be different. While springtime fish are as gentle as the season, summer fish are as wild and cantankerous as an afternoon thunderstorm.

"When it gets hot, we'll start to see tarpon," Don Rosenberger says. Tarpon grow as big as an adult man and 10 times as strong. Five summers ago, a deputy sheriff named Cal subdued a 172-pound tarpon at the pier. Cal, fortunately, was big and strong and had eaten his Wheaties.

In the spring, you don't have to be big and strong to enjoy the pier, though. A good mackerel is 15 inches long. A decent flounder measures a foot. Most springtime regulars are elderly men and women. They don't want to spend two hours wrestling a tarpon.

The regulars arrive in the morning, wearing aprons, carrying tackle boxes and rods and their lunches. They stay until late afternoon, or until the fish stop biting, or until the sun gets too hot. This is how it has always been.

"We've even had 'em die on the pier," Rosenberger says, looking confounded. After all, the sign at the pier entrance says, *The Gods Do Not Subtract From The Allotted Span of Men's Lives The Hours Spent Fishing.*

"About two years ago was the last time," Rosenberger says. "This guy, who had been helping me fix á net, walked down the pier, talked to his friend, and then come back into the baithouse. He dropped dead in that doorway. We called him Whisker Bill. If he had to die, though, this was a nice place to go."

Whisker Bill's picture is taped to a bulletin board inside the pier's baithouse. He poses next to some fine redfish. There are also photos of a woman named Monica and a grouper, Little Joe and a tarpon, and a woman called Virginia with a doormat-sized flounder, six and a half pounds.

"I was fishing straight down in the water by a piling," Virginia says, and points to the very piling that surrendered the flounder. Summertime anglers, competing for elusive snook and tarpon, are secretive. But flounder fishers, perhaps made mellow by spring, are generous with advice. Of course, Virginia will show you where she got the big one.

Virginia is 66, and her husband, Frank, is 68. Five years ago, they retired here from Illinois. Two years ago, they discovered the pier. Now, they fish just about every day. They like the fishing, but they seem to enjoy the people even more. Everybody is so nice.

"There's no cussing out here," Virginia says. "We're not cussers. We don't like cussing."

What's there to cuss about? The sky is dark blue. Pelicans glide above the water, looking for minnows. Somebody down the pier, the big guy with the Penn reel, just got a mackerel, a really nice one. The flounder are down there, somewhere in the sand, waiting for Virginia's bait. Flounder broil up fine when covered with bread crumbs.

It's spring, a good time to be alive in Florida.

Barefoot Stew

When Stew McDonald wakes up in the morning, he is not in the habit of putting on shoes. Shoes hurt his feet. They make them hot. Shoes impose on his sense of freedom. Could anything be more ridiculous than wearing shoes in Florida on a glorious spring day?

"Take a look at a baby sometime," he says. "You put shoes on a baby, and the first thing the baby does is take them off. It's a natural thing. Babies don't like restrictive clothing."

Neither does a certain 63-year-old Tampa resident known as "Barefoot Stew." McDonald, a former professional water-skier, auto racer and film industry location scout, goes barefoot almost everywhere.

When he drives his car or rides his motorcycle, he wears no shoes. When he goes to a dance at the Gulfport Coliseum, he is nattily dressed from head to pant cuff. When he flies commercially, his feet are often quite naked. Last time he visited Bern's, Tampa's famous steak restaurant, he wore a tuxedo – but no shoes. "If I wore shoes into Bern's, Bern Laxer would probably faint," McDonald says.

"That may be true," says the restaurant owner. "Stew McDonald is one of a kind. He may not wear shoes, but he doesn't look like a slob. When he comes into the restaurant, without shoes, he probably adds something to the life of everybody who sees him. It's a giggle. It's nice that we have people who are brave enough to do what they want."

McDonald, a true eccentric, always has marched to the beat of a different drummer – barefooted, of course. Born in New York but raised in Florida, McDonald began his war against shoes during the Depression. Although he owned a pair or two, many schoolmates were less fortunate. It seemed wrong for him to embarrass poor classmates with his wealth of footwear, so on the way to school he hid his shoes under a bush. After school, he put the shoes back on to fool his mother. He doesn't know if she ever guessed his secret, but she must have suspected something: When you go barefoot, you get tough feet.

Stew McDonald's size 11s are thick with callouses. His feet look tough enough to hammer nails. "I've stepped on nails, and usually they don't hurt me," he brags. "A thumbtack can hurt if it gets you just right, but hot pavement and glass don't bother me." Sand spurs? He laughs at sand spurs.

As a World War II bomber pilot, he often flew sans Army Air Corps boots. After the war, when he became a stock car racer, he wore protective clothing, but it was bare feet that laid pedal to the metal. "I thought I had a better touch on the accelerator with bare feet," he explains. His barefoot fetish also won him publicity and the nickname "Barefoot Stew."

In 1949, when a new water-skiing sport was born, McDonald knew he had found heaven. He was among the first half-dozen people to learn how to water-ski barefooted. He entertained thousands at the Cypress Gardens tourist attraction, taught movie star Esther Williams to ski and even had a small part in one of her movies, *Easy to Love*. The role required neither words nor shoes.

Barefoot Stew is tall, white-haired and handsome. He is also divorced and, some would say, available. But women, he laments, are often unfortunately nervous in the presence of a grown man who refuses to wear shoes. On first dates, he usually wears them, at least until he gets to know her better. Then off they come. "Sometimes at a dance, a woman will say she is afraid to dance with me because she doesn't want to step on my feet," he says, scoffing at the excuse.

"One woman asked why I didn't wear shoes. I asked her why she wasn't wearing a bra. I didn't mean to embarrass her, but she got the point. It's freedom."

Some people, of course, delight in the idea of a shoeless adult. Perhaps they remember childhood, when they ran barefoot through the grass and nobody thought ill of them. Every once in a while, an adult who spots McDonald's uncovered feet confesses envy.

"I tell them all it takes is guts," he says. Barefoot Stew has plenty. You can tell by his house. It is full of papers, souvenirs and trash that in places goes from floor to ceiling. Among other things, he washes milk cartons and squashes them flat and doesn't seem to throw them away. He says in the future he plans to take advantage of the city's regular trash pickup. But that's another story. Barefoot Stew would much rather give advice about going barefoot in Florida than talk about his trash. It's spring, after all. Barefoot season has begun.

"If you're worried about what people are going to think about you not wearing shoes, ease into it at first," he advises. "Go shoeless to a friend's house and see how it goes over. Drive your car without shoes. If nothing else, kick off your shoes the moment you get home. But go barefoot."

Some people, of course, think he's weird. McDonald feels sorry for them.

"We have an uptight society. People put a lot of needless pressure on themselves today. Wearing shoes is part of that needless pressure. It's strange. On one hand, anything seems to go when it comes to fashion. At a party you are likely to see a woman in a three-piece suit standing with a man in jeans. But people are a lot more conservative in other ways. In the '50s, and '60s, going barefoot was no big deal. In the 1960s and 1970s, it all changed. I think it was the hippies. Hippies were dirty with long hair and ragged jeans, and they went barefoot. Hippies gave bare feet a bad name."

Now there are signs in some restaurants warning customers to wear shirts and shoes. McDonald usually avoids such picky establishments, though he says he can usually calm down a worried waiter by promising to keep his feet hidden under the table. Three times police have cited him for driving shoeless. He goes to court and wins. "There is no such law," he says.

Commercial airlines are tougher on bare feet than any tack. "Most of the time, I can just walk on. Nobody notices. Only depressed people look down." On occasion, a cranky flight attendant looks down and gets even more depressed. Last time it happened, McDonald was manager of the U.S. Barefoot Ski Team, on his way to Munich with no shoe in sight.

"The stewardess took my bare feet personally," he says. "She threatened to throw me off the plane in Atlanta." McDonald eventually agreed to wear a pair of embarrassing booties that were embossed with the airline's label. "They say one size fits all. But they don't."

McDonald owns two pairs of shoes. He had another pair, but someone at a water-skiing banquet stole them and had them bronzed. He wears his unbronzed shoes in desperate situations, such as funerals and weddings and when he visits his sister in Washington, D.C.

"She's one of those people who gets uptight," he says. "When I'm going up there she says make sure you shave, bring nice clothes and wear shoes. When I go to Mass with her, I wear shoes, though I'm pretty sure Jesus never wore them."

The spring game

The oak tree beyond the right-field fence is blooming, and behind the left-field wall, the tattooed roofer roams, waiting to catch home-run balls to sell to fans strolling along Bayshore Drive. Inside Al Lang Stadium, the singing hot dog vendor is letting loose with an early *Take Me Out To The Ball Game* while the dancing beer salesman is already blowing into his harmonica.

Old men gum peanuts and talk of the old days. A child leans over the box seat railing and snares an autograph. Two elderly sisters from Toronto walk up First Street from their downtown hotel and find good seats behind the plate. The air smells of cigar smoke and coconut oil and Tampa Bay. From the field comes the welcome crack of Louisville Slugger belting ball. Spring has sprung.

"Is there anything that can evoke spring," novelist Thomas Wolfe once asked a group of baseball writers, "better than the sound of the ball smacking into the pocket of the big mitt, the sound of the bat as it hits the horsehide?"

The answer, in my opinion, is no. Nothing evokes spring for me today better than baseball, and nothing, when I was a boy, evoked spring as much as what my baseball cards called the national game.

Spring was the good time because of the baseball. Period. The big-league teams came to town and if you asked your dad enough times, maybe promised to mow the grass and sweep the sidewalks on Saturday, he would agree to take you.

Where I grew up, that meant the Baltimore Orioles, who trained in Miami, but I was a White Sox fan, and they seldom traveled to Florida's east coast. When they played the Washington Senators one Sunday in Pompano Beach, I hinted and then begged and my dad said okay, baseball today after Mass, but next Saturday you clip the hibiscus bushes.

We hit the turnpike, parked in a muddy field and rushed into a great old spring training ball park, where you sat on wood bleachers and could even talk to real ballplayers before the game when they visited the concession stand for Cokes and franks.

I was 13 years old in 1962 when I got the autograph of future Hall-of-Fame shortstop Luis Aparicio. As he signed, I held his hot dog. Many years have passed, and I have married, graduated from college and watched my own babies come into the world. Holding Little Looie's red hot still remains one of life's biggest thrills.

Al Lang Stadium, 1984. On the field, the White Sox take batting practice. Sportswriters and photographers swarm at the wire batting cage. I study a Sox pitcher named Richard Dotson, who won 21 games last season. Today he pitches against the Cardinals. Pitchers seldom bat in Dotson's American League, but they do in the National League, so Dotson steps into the batting cage for a couple of practice swings before the game.

"Is that Dotson?" asks an elderly man to my right. I nod yes. He says, "He looks bigger on TV."

"What paper do you work for?" I ask.

"Oh, I don't work for a paper," whispers Al Price, 69, retired banker. "I sort of just walked on the field to take a few snapshots. Nobody stopped me."

Only in spring training.

Ballplayers lean on bats and spit tobacco juice at their teammates' shoes. Chicago coach Davy Nelson shouts insults at anyone who will listen. White Sox manager Tony La Russa, arms folded, eyes squinting in the glare, studies a rookie.

His name is Joel Skinner. A catcher, he was selected the most promising player in the minor leagues last season. His fielding and throwing are major-league caliber now, but people are wondering if he can hit the curve. Skinner slams an easy batting-practice pitch over the left-field fence. And another. Then, bad luck: He fouls a ball off the screen, then dribbles a grounder to second. Cursing softly, he slams his bat on the plate, conscious of La Russa's stare. Will this mean another year at Denver?

"It's different for veterans," says Red Schoendienst, the 61-year-old St. Louis coach who spent 12 seasons as Cardinals manager. He played a big-league second base 14 years and made the all star team nine times. He sits in the dugout, eating stew from a Styrofoam cup. "The veterans, they're relaxed. They know they'll make the team. The pressure is on the kids. They're trying like hell. In their minds is one thing: 'Am I gonna make the club?'"

A fan pokes his head into the dugout and shouts, "Red! You're a gentleman and a scholar! You're like fine wine: You get better with age!" Schoendienst laughs and waves and says, "Where was I?

"Yeah. When you come to spring training, you'd better not be thinkin' about lay-ing on the beach. At least I never was. Of course with my skin" – Red's fair skin probably burns under a naked light bulb – "I stayed away from the beach anyway. Hell, I used to wrap a towel around my neck during spring training to keep off the sun. But what I'm saying is that in spring training, you'd better be thinking about winning a job. We got a 40-man roster but we only take 25 players north. So you work all day. Your time is your own after a game or practice, and you might pick up a fish pole and try to have fun, but if you're a kid tryin' to make the major leagues, all the time you're thinkin' about what you done wrong that day."

Sports writer Jerry Izenberg once wrote that watching a spring training game is as exciting as watching a tree form its annual ring. In one respect, he was right – who wins or loses is unimportant during spring – but in other ways the viewpoint is false and cynical. Baseball, as columnist Red Smith once suggested, is dull only to people with dull minds.

In Spring, baseball – and life – are meant to be savored rather than endured. Past indiscretions are forgiven. Forget last year. This may be the year. You take things as they come. Stop. Smell. Listen. Here's the pitch. Strike one. You look up and watch the plane fly over, dragging a restaurant advertisement through the sky. What's the stadium look like from way up there? George Hendrick takes strike two. Will Dotson waste a pitch? Geez, it's hot. Give me your ticket. You fold the ticket stub and place it between your eyeglasses and the bridge of your nose. A fabulous nosecap, it prevents a painful sunburn. High and outside. Ball one. Got time for a hot dog?

"Hot diggetty daaawwwgs, you all! Chicken lips! Cold dogs!" yells the vendor. He is Tommy Walton Sr. 53. The Voice, he calls himself. The singing hot dog man. He makes his grand entrance in the third inning. Then he stops and belts them out in a powerful baritone: *Take Me Out To The Ball Game, Amen, He's Got The Whole World In His Hands.*

"I like spring training better than regular season," says Walton, who makes a tour of major-league ballparks during summer. "You go to a major-league ballpark and you got to hustle. There's so many people you got to mind your Ps and Qs. In the spring, you can have fun with the people."

"You sing beautifully."

"Thank you," he says. "I've been singing all my life. I started when I was a little boy in the Church of Christ on 20th Street. That's where I was baptized and that's where I started singing gospel.

"One day I came down to the stadium. I needed a job. I had a pregnant wife. I went to the boss and he was afraid to give me a job 'cause he thought the younger guys would run me over. But I am the best. I been all over the country in most of the major-league stadiums and I am the best."

Other stadiums feature entertainers dressed as chickens or Indians. They give away bats and hats. Scoreboards explode with fireworks. Strippers bolt from the stands to plant kisses on outfielders. In the spring, at Al Lang Stadium, vendors strut their stuff. As Tommy Walton sings and peddles his dogs behind the first-base dugout, isn't that Honest George Houff, 39, blowing his harmonica, tap dancing and drumming his hands against his body as he sells beer in the box seats behind the plate?

"My seventh year here, yes it is, seven big years," he says, talking as fast as a liner to third. "Yeah, baseball. Baseball. The great game. I love it. We have the best hot dogs in the world and the best beer and this is the greatest game and the greatest fans and the greatest stadium, whoo, whoo, yeah. Excuse me, I'd like to talk, but I got to go and sell my beer. Yes, sir. Yes, sir. See ya later."

Honest George's beer sells for a buck a cup. The Voice gets a buck a hot dog. And outside the park, standing in his accustomed spot, Buddy Merchant, 31, is doing business as usual.

Buddy Merchant patrols the outside of the park with his Franklin fielder's mitt. He works for the Tarheel Roofing Company, but earns cigarette money by selling people baseballs that are hit over the fence. A cigarette dangles from his lips. His feet are bare, his head is covered by a baseball cap that says USA. Tattoos grace his biceps, including one that proclaims "Mom." Last season he got two standing ovations at Al Lang Stadium when he flagged down two enormous home runs struck by the Mets' Dave Kingman. He caught them on the fly on Bayshore Drive. Then he took an eraser, cleaned the scuff marks from the balls, and signed Kingman's autograph. He got three bucks for each ball. He once made $146 on a single afternoon.

"I've been doing this since I was eight," he says. As he speaks, his body is turned toward the stadium, his senses alert to cues that might tell him a ball is on the way. "Of course, the best time is batting practice because the pitchers are grooving them in for the hitters to hit. When the game starts, you don't get so many home runs. But you get a lot of foul balls."

"Why are you standing here?" I ask. Merchant's position behind the left-field foul line, across the street from the stadium, strikes me as wrong. "You can't even see the batter," I go on. "How do you know where the ball is going to go?"

"You listen for the ball hitting the bat. Then you look up and watch the fans in the stands. From them you can tell where the ball is." When a home run soars over the fence, the footrace begins between Merchant and the two younger men to reach the ball first. "I'm gettin' older, and I smoke, so I don't have the wind no more," Merchant says. "But I still get my share. And believe me, it's a lot better than it used to be. There used to be a lot of people tryin' to get to the balls. There was this one guy who was really good – the best – until he got hurt."

"What happened?"

"He was runnin' for a ball and his feet slipped on the gravel. He slid under this parked car but his arm caught on the bumper and his arm got tore nearly clean off. I mean, his arm was just hangin' there. He couldn't get no help neither, so he run to the hospital on his own. They say he made it in time."

In the spring, when baseball comes to Al Lang Stadium, talk is cheap. And talk, in many ways, is as much the game as hits, runs and errors.

"I seen some baseball in my days," Charles Carney, 80, says. Arthritis in his knees makes walking painful – unless the walk is to a baseball game, where he seats himself 25 rows up, sips a beer, peruses his scorecard and talks baseball.

"I'm a Pirates fan. I seen Pie Traynor play way back in the '20s and '30s. You're too young to remember Pie. You ever hear of him? Pie Traynor was the greatest third baseman ever. You could double down the third base line and he'd still throw you out. And he was playin' back when they had to use them old, flat gloves. Today, they use bushel baskets for gloves and still don't catch 'em all. Of course, you're listening to an old man talking now. The ballplayers today, they're good, too."

Sitting above Carney are the Toronto sisters, Blanche Jones, 82, and Kathleen Ruddy, 76. They live at the Bishop Hotel on First Avenue North and they walk to as many games as they can manage.

"I like to be outside in the spring," Blanche explains. "That's one of the things I like about spring training. You sit in the stands and listen to the chatter and the shouts and smell all the ballpark smells and the weather is wonderful."

"We're Toronto Blue Jay fans," Kathleen says. "Last year when they played at Al Lang I gave a note to the batboy to give to the Jays in the dugout. The note said, 'You got some Toronto fans here today so please play your best.'"

"And they did," Blanche says. "They beat the Mets in a close game."

"I had to miss my shuffleboard today," Kathleen says. "But baseball is worth it."

The pitch comes in, low and outside. Ball one. Spring has sprung. All is right in the world.

Greetings from Florida

In the world according to postcards, water sparkles and palm trees sway in gentle breezes. There are no awful traffic jams, no crushed beer cans littering the sand, no cockroaches keeping things interesting on the beach at sunset. In the postcard world, every sunset is gorgeous and reason for living in Florida.

Tom Brown, the postcard man, has always appreciated a good sunset. He knows how difficult they are to capture on film. Snap the camera too soon and the picture is bright. Too late and it's night. A perfect sunset lasts only a blink of a camera eye.

"A good picture is a matter of luck," he says.

Brown, a 47-year-old Clearwater resident, is no sunset dilettante. Last fall, after admiring several picturesque dusks, he drove to Clearwater Bay with his Linhof camera. He pointed the camera toward the palm trees and the Belleair Causeway and the western horizon. The sun fell, and the sky filled with golden light, a golden light that turned little clumps of dull gray clouds into majestic purple puffs. Only then did his finger depress the shutter.

He put the resulting picture on a postcard. You can walk into 375 stores in Florida and find the sunset postcard he calls "Largo, Florida." You can also find his postcards of the Don CeSar Resort, the Sunshine Skyway bridge, palm trees, boats, pelicans, shark's teeth, Key lime pie and beaches, beautiful beaches.

"What I do is try and take pictures from a tourist's point of view," says Brown, who moved to Florida from rural Illinois in 1947.

Tourists, Brown has learned, want cards that help them remember where they've been and what they've done, or, better yet, they want something to show off to their frozen friends back home. In West Florida alone, tourists buy an estimated 15-million cards every year.

Brown's cards, which portray Florida as a heaven on earth, appeal to people. Last year, his Clearwater company sold two million postcards of Florida scenes that ended up in tourist scrapbooks or the mailboxes of snowbound Yankees. Greetings, the cards advertised. Greetings from Florida.

"Give me a chance to make a photograph that includes water, blue skies, palm trees and white sand," Brown says, "and I've got it made."

He has made such romantic postcards for a while now. A former wedding photographer who "just about starved to death" in that competitive undertaking, Brown bought his postcard business 13 years ago from Ward Beckett, one of the old-timers of the trade. "I still starved," Brown says with a grin.

Brown looks well fed now. He owns a warehouse filled with a million cards. He owns three delivery trucks. He employs sales people. He and his wife, the company's vice president, have seldom been busier because business seldom has been better. The tourists are here, and they are buying the traditional postcards. Hotels, pelicans, palms, beaches.

"If something works, why change it?" asks Brown, a quiet gray-haired man who chooses his words carefully.

Several times a year he does change his postcards. Usually they're cosmetic changes – a different colored border, perhaps, or larger lettering – but more frequently he feels the need to reshoot old photographs to account for the state's explosive growth.

Old postcards of Clearwater Beach, for example, show the northern tip of the island as undeveloped sand. The northern tip is no longer undeveloped. "When I was a kid, it was a place teen-agers parked," he says. "If you parked there now, you'd be in somebody's yard." Brown updated his photo.

Once or twice a year, Brown and his cameras make trips to take new pictures of old subjects. He sets his camera on a tripod and starts shooting when the light and conditions are right. On other occasions he rents a helicopter for the aerial shots featured on many of his cards.

"I like helicopters," he says. "Helicopters hover. Helicopter pilots take off the doors and let you lean out. You can get good shots."

Airplane pilots usually won't take doors off. Airplanes fly too fast. Brown has been critical of airplanes since the day his rental stalled while he photographed Clearwater Beach. "I told the pilot to slow down. Well, an airplane can only go so slow. Don't think I wasn't surprised when I felt us start to drop." The pilot, happily, knew his job and brought the aircraft out of the stall. Brown knew his job, too. He got his picture.

Brown has taken half the pictures used in his 300-postcard selection. In that, he is different from most other Florida postcard entrepreneurs, who often buy photos from free-lance photographers or import photos from outside the state.

Brown would rather take pictures himself. In 1980, a few weeks after a freighter knocked down the Sunshine Skyway bridge over Tampa Bay and 35 motorists died, Brown grabbed his camera, rented a helicopter and headed for the bay. "I felt funny taking pictures because of the tragedy," he says. "But people kept asking me for a postcard showing what had happened to the bridge." The resulting before and after postcard, showing a healthy bridge and a damaged one, still sells more than 100,000 copies a year.

Four days a week, Brown climbs into a truck filled with 300,000 cards and sees that racks are filled. Popular cards such as the Skyway are hard to keep in stock. Others gather dust because they are duds. Brown looks embarrassed when he remembers the time his postcard of Redington Beach was identified by a customer as Indian Rocks Beach.

"You do make mistakes," he says.

Sometimes tourists want a card that Brown doesn't have. They want a card of a bikini-clad woman being pursued by a hungry alligator. They want a card of a young muscular man wearing skimpy trunks and a knowing grin. Brown buys them from other companies – if they don't offend his taste.

148

"There are some cards I couldn't get away with selling at all in the Tampa Bay area," Brown says, rolling his eyes. "They might work in a place that attracts a younger crowd like Daytona Beach. Here, I'd get run out of town. This is a conservative area."

Brown prefers to stick with the tried and true, the natural scenery of Florida. Unfortunately, it's getting difficult to make pictures that portray the state as a tropical paradise. Natural Florida, at least in urban areas popular with tourists, is disappearing due to development and pollution.

Years ago he could walk outside on the day following a cold front and find crisp, clear skies that always looked nice on postcards. Now he's as likely to find a brown haze caused by automobile exhaust.

He tries not to get discouraged, though. It is spring, after all, a time for hope. Vegetation damaged by winter freezes is showing green. He hopes to get out soon and shoot some palm trees, maybe on the beach, with sparkling water in the background. It'd make a nice postcard.

Greetings from Florida, such a card would all but shout. Greetings from Florida.

Possums

ST. PETERSBURG   4/15/91

E*at more possum!*
In North Florida, you see that bumper sticker on the backs of rusty Ford pickups and shiny new Cadillacs. Country folks have always been ahead of us city mice when it comes to wildlife appreciation.

Nobody I know in urban Florida sups on possum. We've become dainty eaters in the big city, snobs if you will, afraid to put the unknown into our bellies. Eat more possum? Scaredy cats, some of us are repelled by the very sight of them.

And possums are easy to see just about anywhere in urban areas. They trot across our roads after dark. They raise families in our yards. Possums remind us that at least some wildlife survives – thrives – in the asphalt jungle.

Possums, in fact, may be more comfortable in our cities than *Homo sapiens*. We have to pay for food and shelter, after all. Possums just take possession.

As we sit inside our air-conditioned homes, watching the latest *National Geographic* special about the Amazon Rain Forest, the great outdoors comes alive in our back yards.

Possums grin at us through the windows, eat the cat's food we forgot to bring in and then sneak into our attics before sunup. They enjoy the life of Riley.

Riley is the name I probably should give the big fellow who visits our yard every evening, hoping to scavenge something out of the cat's dish or compost heap.

Riley is so fat he waddles. From nose to tail he's about 30 inches long. My mother once spied him on the deck and shrieked: "A giant rat!"

With his round brown eyes, whiskers and hairless tail, Riley does resemble a rodent on steroids. But he has far more charm. Rats can't hang by their tails from tree limbs. And when rats play dead, they are.

I scare Riley off my backyard deck when I see him. I consider this possum education more than cruelty. Although I welcome his company most of the time, I don't want him getting domestic or possessive about my house.

Possums, raccoons and squirrels – "weed wildlife," a biologist friend calls them – have taken to city life like crabgrass. Leave your home's crawlspace open and they will crawl in. Forget to repair the ventilation screening on your roof's overhang and they will climb the nearest oak, yodel like Tarzan and swing into your attic on a clump of Spanish moss.

There they will raise a big family and you will not like it. Possums and raccoons tend to be loud and messy. Once settled, they are as stubborn about leaving as your spouse's relatives.

150

The way to solve a possum or raccoon problem is to physically remove them. This involves renting a live trap from a feed store (or borrowing one from animal control), placing it on the ground nearest their entryway and hoping for the best.

If you get lucky, release your trappees miles away, rush home and board up wherever they entered your house in the first place. Otherwise they or another furry family may continue to use your home as a Holiday Inn.

I have yet to evict a possum or a raccoon from my homestead, though sometimes I worry about the muffled late-night footsteps coming from above. I prefer to think there's a hoedown on the roof than a raccoon in the attic.

Mother raccoons do visit our yard, usually with offspring who are almost too cute for words. If they get to the cat's dish before I bring it in – fine, they have won. Let them eat. But we never deliberately feed them.

Raccoons, even when slightly domesticated, can be dangerous pests. Just ask me.

Last winter, as I walked through a city park, a raccoon trotted over, unafraid, grabbed my leg, and nibbled my shin as if it were an ear of corn. Clearly someone had fed the bad-mannered fellow, who got riled when I did not offer a handout.

I have no plans to bite, or be bitten, by a possum. And there have been ample opportunities. Last fall, when I saw a small possum heading for the cat's dish, I opened the door, stomped my feet and said "Raaahhhhhh!"

Possums, who don't like to be yelled at, always take the most direct route off the deck, even if something is in the way. This one tried to squeeze through an orange crate – I didn't think a kitten could do that – and got trapped.

He hissed when I approached, and then, just in case I didn't get the point, opened his mouth wide to reveal sharp teeth. When that failed, he shut his eyes and keeled over. I like it when a possum plays possum. Cliches live.

Anyway, I lifted the crate, he came to life and sprinted into the dark. I laughed.

But he who laughs last laughs best. (Writing cliches is like eating peanuts.) Let me tell you about The Revenge of the Possums.

One night, after the witching hour, when all was quiet and lights were extinguished, I stepped onto the deck to do some stargazing.

Looking through my telescope, I sensed movement near my feet, something large and white that was not starlight. Whooeeiiiooo. It turned out to be the world's most nearsighted possum about to blunder into my legs. We identified each other about the same time: I filled the night with terrified whoops and he with hisses.

I leaped backward, almost tripping across the Adirondack chair.

He jogged in place for a moment, kind of like the Roadrunner in that cartoon, and vanished noisily under the deck.

Satisfied that a coronary was not forthcoming, I returned to the telescope and tried to concentrate on Orion's Belt. Concentration is difficult when you hear a possum directly below you, sniffing indignantly. When I sniffed, I could smell him, too.

As the odor of wet, musky animal filled my nostrils, I never once thought of possum stew. Instead, I visualized him sneaking up behind me and biting my ankle while I focused in on Betelgeuse.

Defeated, I slunk into the house.

Later, while waiting for sleep, I heard him crunching his way through the cat's food. Heard something else, too. I swear it was giggling.

A family tradition

TARPON SPRINGS   5/17/87

The old man was talking about the glory days, when the river was filled with boats overflowing with hearty young men from Greece who would don heavy diving suits and drop to the bottom of the Gulf of Mexico to harvest sponges.

"There were so many sponges," he said in a heavy accent. "But then..."

The old man talked about how sponges were killed by the blight called Red Tide, how scientists discovered a way to make synthetic sponges, and how the young Greeks left the business of their fathers to make a better living as painters and carpenters and who knows what.

The old man, Antony Lerios, did not abandon the sponge business of his father. He did machine work to make a living, it is true, but he never forgot the old ways. When he got the chance, he built deep-sea diving helmets.

At 95, he is at it still. He is building helmets and passing on his skills to his grandson. "There's not much of a demand for handmade diving helmets anymore," said Nick Toth, as his grandfather puttered around the shop where they repair boats and engines when there is no helmet work.

Outside, you could hear the humming of saws from the boatyard next door, and you could see mullet jumping when startled by shadows of pelicans flying over the Anclote River. Toth said, "But I'm glad I know how to make helmets. It's satisfying work."

Toth is 32. He is tall, muscular and modern. A University of Florida graduate with a major in political science, he once had dreams of teaching college. Instead he found he enjoyed the profession of his Greece-born grandfather.

Antony Lerios moved to Tarpon Springs from the old country in 1913. His father was a sponge diver, and his brother worked on the sponge boats. Antony could fix almost anything, including diving helmets. When the city's most prominent builder of helmets died, Lerios filled the demand.

He has built them for 40 years, and he sometimes is credited for improvements that have been incorporated into modern helmets used by salvage, sponge and Navy divers. Lerios tapered the base of his helmet, the breastplate, to make it lighter and less cumbersome. He simplified his helmet by making it one piece instead of two.

He changed the angle of the port holes so a diver could better see sponges growing on the bottom. He changed the location of intake valves, so that air blowing into the helmet would keep the glass clear. He relocated the outtake valve so a diver could more conveniently clear the helmet of excess air. He managed to accomplish all of this and make the helmet look beautiful, too.

152

"I was a diver in the Navy," said Nick Galanses, one of several old divers who visits the shop to reminisce. "I still dive every once in a while for sponges or to do underwater salvage. These are wonderful helmets.They're one of a kind."

Antony Lerios is short and dark skinned, and behind thick glasses his brown eyes miss nothing. He drives a rusty Ford to the tin shack in the morning and works until noon. After lunch, he goes home and naps so he can be strong enough to help at the shop in the afternoon. He is known to work weekends.

"A long time ago, I try to teach three young boys how to make helmets," the old man was saying. "But they not like to work so hard. I like to work hard, and so they leave me. Now they dead. I still alive."

And working as hard as ever.

"I work now almost 80 years. People, they not believe me that I work all the time. I do, I do. I feel good. Work is good for you."

Most of the time, he and his grandson work on boating equipment for commercial fishermen in the shop that smells of oil, hot metal and sweat. Under the dim light cast by four bare bulbs, they fix bent propeller shafts. They straighten rudders. They repair diesel engines. They can do about anything when it comes to boats. But on rare occasions, somebody comes in and wants what they are famous for.

Building a diving helmet, the way they do, is a complicated task. It takes 150 hours – about four weeks if they were to work straight through. Every piece, from wing nuts to valves, is built with copper and brass, and by hand. Every needless scrap of solder, used to seal portholes and seams, is sanded or removed. They charge $3,000 for their helmets and don't advertise.

"We've sold helmets to divers all over the world," Nick Toth said. "They're a good functional helmet. They're good when the water is murky, when there is a strong current, when you have to work around an underwater construction site where you could get hit by a piece of lumber or steel drifting along the bottom. They're sort of like a construction hard hat."

Many people who order helmets no longer dive, or never did. "There are people who just want the helmets to look at," Toth said. "These helmets are part of the past."

A past that, in Tarpon Springs at least, may be gone forever. But who knows? A sponge blight has hit the Mediterranean Sea, and old spongers like to believe that Tarpon Springs will rise from the dead to reclaim its prominence.

If it does, Antony Lerios will be there, and if he isn't, his grandson will.

Antony Lerios died in 1992.

Another paradise for Big Bill

CUNNINGHAM KEY   6/10/80

Sometime soon, a bunch of Tampa Bay shrimpers will get together to say good-bye for the last time to Big Bill Tuerffs, the Pa Kettle of Pinellas Bayway's Cunningham Key. They will anchor their boats off the key and then Bill's wife Martha will scatter her husband's ashes in the bay.

"When the tide comes in," Martha says, "it'll wash Big Bill onto Cunningham Key. That's what he always wanted."

Big Bill, the well-liked shrimper and proprietor of Bayway Bait Tackle, died Saturday. It happened after Bill and Martha snacked on sweet rolls while waiting for their chili to warm. Bill, sitting in his favorite chair, dozed off while watching television. He jerked awake and asked his wife, "Did I snore?" Martha said yes. Bill never could stay awake in that chair. He giggled, and then his heart stopped. He was 61.

"He was never sick at all," said Martha, who suffers from emphysema. "We had a plan. I was going to live until Bill was 95. Then he'd have a year to chase women before he'd die. He always promised to take care of me. I never called Big Bill when he wasn't there to answer me. But now..."

Now Martha, who is 58, does not know what to do. Her new landlord has plans for tiny Cunningham Key, which is connected by the Bayway to the Pinellas County park, Fort DeSoto. The Tuerffs were supposed to move in six weeks. The Tuerffs, who had lived on the key 16 years, had not found a new residence.

"Bill was upset about having to move," said Martha, grieving at her dining room table with her 25-year-old son, Billy Boy. Her 28-year-old daughter, Deborah Jo Van Fossen, would soon arrive. "I think the thought of moving was what killed him."

There weren't many couples like Bill and Martha, who called themselves "Ma and Pa Kettle" because of their casual lifestyle. Junked cars often littered their yard and watermelons grew in mounds of dirt. Their five dogs and two cats snoozed in the shade of the porch. Customers had to ring a doorbell for service. Martha was often out back looking at the water and Big Bill, who shrimped at night, liked watching television in his undershorts. The bell gave him the chance to pull on his trousers before welcoming a customer.

He was a large and tanned man with a sandy thatch of undisciplined hair. He was as quiet as his wife is talkative. He loved his wife and often told her. They raised up three good children. Big Bill was somewhat of a child himself, Martha liked to say. She often accused her husband of having a Peter Pan complex because he did not want to grow up.

He was a simple man with simple pleasures. He liked to take the dogs with him in the boat while catching shrimp. By the hour he liked to stand on Cunningham Key and watch the sunsets and the Skyway Bridge and the birds. He always said he wanted his ashes scattered on Cunningham Key. After the cremation this week, when the tide is right, Martha will abide by her husband's wishes.

"Everybody loved him," Martha said. "He was the Godfather of the Bayway because he solved everybody's problems."

Big Bill and Martha's many friends knocked on the Tuerffs' door Sunday and Monday as the word spread across the waterfront. "Big Bill dead? What? I can't believe a heart attack could kill Big Bill." And these people, the shrimpers and fishermen and friends, visited Martha to pay their respects.

"There wasn't anybody like him," said fisherman Van Hubbard. "I spent a lot of happy times out there at Cunningham Key when I was a kid. Bill was a man who would truly give you the shirt off his back."

"I can't believe he's gone," said Lillian Ernsberger, who with husband Karl operates concessions at Fort DeSoto's Potter Pier. "Bill and Martha have been so good to us. When they didn't have shrimp to sell, they'd send their customers to us. They'd tell customers to buy their shrimp "off those kids' at the pier. Kids. I think Karl and I are older than they are."

Bill and Martha met when they were kids in Indiana. Bill was 18, big and strapping even then. "He was mine since I was fourteen years old," Martha said Monday. "We got engaged when I was fifteen. He used to kiss me on the forehead every day. When I was seventeen we got married. We were married thirty-nine years."

They moved to St. Petersburg from Indiana and found life hard. Big Bill couldn't buy a job. Martha ran a modest store in their home and sold vegetables and old clothing. Then she got a job at a department store and Bill found work at Fort DeSoto Pier.

In 1964 they opened the ramshackle bait shop at Cunningham Key and lived in a modest house on the premises. "This is our Garden of Eden," Martha liked to say. "We found paradise. Our life is an elixir. We drink from it all the time."

There were bad times out at Cunningham Key. Their property was visited by hurricanes and floods. They lost one baithouse to a waterspout. The same storm dropped a cold drink machine into the mangroves.

Then last year they got into trouble with the health department, which accused them of operating a campground without a license. They successfully fought the charge in court. "Like Ma and Pa Kettle," Martha said, "we rolled with the punches."

Big Bill would shrimp at night, give his catch to Martha in the morning and go to sleep. Martha would sell the shrimp to fishermen for bait. The Tuerffs operated a casual place. Next to the cash register they kept a book filled with the best ribald jokes told by customers. They always threatened to write a book about the bait business called *Cold Coffee and Warm Beer*.

"Big Bill always had some kind of project going," his wife said. "But he never finished anything. We always figured we had forever. He probably wouldn't have finished anyway. He had real big hands and he was real klutzy. He couldn't pick anything up without breaking it. I never minded. He was a nerd. But he was my nerd."

Martha Tuerffs passed away three months after saying goodbye to her beloved Bill. Her ashes were scattered off Cunningham Key.

The road to ruins

ST. PETERSBURG   4/15/92

The wind blew across Boca Ciega Bay into Abercrombie Park, where Mac Perry picked a sea purslane plant, poked it into his mouth and chewed thoughtfully.

"It's salty," he said, walking along the shore. "It's real salty, isn't it? They probably seasoned their food with this."

Near a discarded Dr Pepper can and a pink plastic cigarette lighter he found other salty plants, beach carpet and sea blite, and tasted them. He plucked a leaf from a bay tree, crushed it between his fingers and inhaled the pungent odor. Bay leaves probably spiced up many a seafood dish.

"This must have been a paradise," Perry said as a jet roared over Tampa Bay. He had driven the half mile from his home near busy Tyrone Boulevard to this quiet Pinellas County park. He stood among the oaks and the pines and looked at the bay and imagined how it was when the Tocobaga people lived here.

When the first Spanish explorers came ashore 500 years ago, the Tocobaga were here. On the shores of Boca Ciega Bay they lived in huts covered by palmetto-thatched roofs. They probably grew corn and squash and shot deer with poison-tipped arrows, but mostly they gathered food from the bays and bayous.

Tocobaga were imposing. They wore seabird feathers in their black hair and tiny fish bladders as earrings. They wore necklaces fashioned out of the fish backbones and bracelets made from olive shells. They carved designs into their skin and colored them with vegetable dyes.They paddled about in dugout canoes constructed from trees. They lived according to the rhythms of nature.

There may have been 7,000 Tocobagas in the Tampa Bay area when Panfilo de Narvaez and his men splashed ashore looking for gold on Good Friday, April 15, 1528. There may have been as many as 500 living in what, 464 years later, is Mac Perry's neighborhood near one of St. Petersburg's busiest intersections. Where the Tocobaga beat drums and prayed to the Great Mystery, today's bass-heavy car radios wage a sound war against the rumble of passing trucks.

"Not many people know they're living in what was a major village," Perry said. "I was talking to some people at a condominium down the road and they didn't even know there were ever Indians in Florida."

Perry, 52, has been doing his part for public education. Last year he produced a booklet about Tampa Bay Indian history for the conservation organization he directs, the Coastal Wildlife Club. He developed his research into a four-part television documentary series that was broadcast on local cable stations.

The native people constructed high ceremonial mounds for chiefs. They piled discarded shell and animal bone into neat garbage mounds. They buried their dead in mounds, too. For those who take the time to seek them out, mounds offer a kind of history lesson.

"Mounds were everywhere," Perry said. "But most of them were lost."

Developers used the shell-ridden garbage mounds as road fill. Unscrupulous collectors excavated burial and ceremonial mounds for museum exhibitions and souvenirs. Old-time West Florida residents may remember when Bayfront Medical Center in St. Petersburg was the Mound Park Hospital. The hospital was built on the site of a big village with seven mounds.

Today, only a scattering of mounds under state, county or city protection survive in greater Tampa Bay. The best preserved, the Safety Harbor Temple Mound, can be explored at Phillippe Park in North Pinellas. It was 20 feet tall and 162 feet long. Tocobaga, the chief of the Tocobaga people, probably lived on the top.

"For the most part, the history of these people has been wiped from the face of the Earth," Mac Perry said. "That's hard to understand."

Perry has always tried to educate himself about Pinellas. Born in Virginia, educated at VPI, he moved to St. Petersburg and became the county horticulture agent in 1969. Curious about his new home, he read histories and talked to aged residents who piqued his interest with stories about what Pinellas was like.

A Renaissance man of sorts, Perry painted landscapes, performed music and wrote a series of Florida books. His most recent, *Landscaping in Florida* – a *Photo Idea Book*, was published by Pineapple Press in 1990.

He and his wife Faye and their two children live near Park Street in an unusual house. They keep their Christmas tree up all year because they like it. Shelves, groaning with science and history books, display animal skulls and American Indian memorabilia. Their home is a shrine to the people who are no more.

Their house, like many in the neighborhood, sits atop a Tocobaga garbage mound about 15 feet high. Perry can walk under his house, paw through shells and find ancient whelks, scallops and clams thrown away by early Floridians.

"We had a major village here," Perry said, driving through the Parque Narvaez neighborhood. The stream behind Perry's house, now polluted by storm runoff from city streets, once was a source of clean drinking water for the Tocobaga. Boca Ciega Bay, now too dirty to support some shellfish species, provided food and tools for the early people.

The Tocobaga built a ceremonial mound and a plaza. Both are gone. Their garbage mounds paralleled the bay's shoreline. With few exceptions, most were bulldozed or covered with houses or St. Augustine grass now trimmed by ungrateful, gasping men who must haul lawnmowers up and down them.

"This neighborhood should have a sign or a plaque," Perry said. "I think we should shine a light on what we had here. It's history."

The village had two burial mounds, including the final resting place for 500 bodies, according to archaeologists. One burial mound in the neatly landscaped neighborhood is under a house. The other is beneath a parking lot and a fence. The fence is covered by graffiti advertising a popular heavy metal band and one young man's sexual yearnings.

It was a big village, according to historians. It stretched about a mile along Boca

Ciega Bay from Tyrone Boulevard south through Abercrombie and Narvaez parks – the sites of several large mounds hidden today among the oaks and palmettos and empty beer cans and pizza boxes.

"For at least a dozen millennia, a succession of native peoples extracted what they needed from the land and sea of the lower Gulf coast without destroying the environment that sustained them," wrote Raymond Arsenault in his history, *St. Petersburg and the Florida Dream*. "They probably would have gone on in this way indefinitely had it not been for the advent of the European age of exploration and discovery."

Nobody knows for sure exactly where in Greater Tampa Bay Panfilo de Narvaez actually landed. But some people believe it was in the vicinity of Abercrombie Park and Boca Ciega Bay. They believe his force – five ships, 400 men and women, horses, dogs and supplies –sailed through Johns Pass, sighted the village of the Tocobaga and came on in.

A small scouting party was met by friendly Indians, according to the only Spaniard who kept a diary, Cabeza de Vaca. The next day, when Narvaez and a larger party waded ashore, the Tocobaga people were gone. From other native people, the Tocobaga probably had heard about the Spanish lust for gold, slaves and religious converts. And they'd hid.

In the spring of 1528 – five minutes away from modern Florida's Tyrone Square Mall – Narvaez claimed for Spain the village, the bay and all surrounding lands. Then he moved inland. According to historians, he eventually discovered another village, where a battle broke out between the people of the old and new worlds. A Tocobaga chief, Hirrihigua, was wounded in the face. His mother was hacked to death and fed to dogs.

During the following two centuries, as many as 100,000 native people from the Florida Panhandle to the Florida Keys may have perished from warfare and European diseases for which they had no immunities. In the 1700s, people from what was known as the Creek confederacy, from Alabama and Georgia, migrated into the mostly empty Florida interior. They came to be called the cimarrones, or "people of distant fires." Floridians know their descendants as the Seminoles.

"I like to just think about what it was like," Mac Perry said, driving through his neighborhood. He turned onto a congested road, Tyrone Boulevard, and followed it to the VA Medical Center at Bay Pines in St. Petersburg. He wanted to look at the mounds behind the hospital. He wanted to show me the Tocobaga memorial inside a building.

The Suncoast Archaeological and Paleontological Society built the small display housed in a glass case. There were arrow points and the shells the Tocobaga used as tools. There was a bust of a dignified-looking warrior. Perry stared into the eyes of the statue.

Just outside the automatic door, a terribly thin man with a tube in his arm sat in a wheelchair, smoked a cigarette and coughed like death.

Perry nodded a hello to the sick old veteran. Then he climbed into his truck and drove away, swallowed by the rush-hour traffic of the 20th century.

Medicine man

TAMPA   5/22/88

Bobby Henry needed to chop down two nice cypress trees in the Everglades. He builds canoes out of cypress. Cypress dug-out canoes are perfect for cruising through the thick sawgrass, a perfect platform from which to gig frogs and shoot deer.

"When I was a boy," he says, "my daddy and I even slept in our canoe."

That was a long time ago. Henry, the manager of the Seminole Culture Center in Tampa and a medicine man, is now 51. Today, few of his people know how to make dugout canoes. The old people who remember are dead or dying. He says the young ones either care nothing about old traditions or think there's no one to teach them. Bobby Henry wants to teach them.

"The canoe was very important to my people," he says. His Seminole people were hunters and fishers who required canoes to travel the grassy waters of the Everglades. Without a canoe they went hungry. Without a canoe, they had no alligator hides or frog legs to trade for the fabric, wool blankets and beads owned by white merchants. The canoe was to their culture what the horse was to the Plains Indians of the West.

"My father taught me how to build the canoes," he says. "His father taught him, and his grandfather taught his father."

Bobby Henry this year will teach Danny Wilcox, a young Seminole who lives on South Florida's Brighton Reservation. He and Wilcox will burn out the insides of a cypress log, then start carving the canoe with special curved knives. They will keep it on the Tampa reservation.

Henry hopes to build a second canoe for use in the Everglades, where he still hunts. There, a dugout canoe comes into its own. He stands in the back, propelling the boat forward with a pole. Its wide and heavy end breaks through thick sawgrass that would stop traditional canoes dead.

"My people need to know how to build the canoes," Bobby Henry says. "Danny went to school, and he can read and write English, but he lived in the city and never got to learn much about the old ways."

Bobby Henry has coal-black hair, brown eyes and wears colorful Seminole clothing. He is married and has five children. He was born in the Everglades near the settlement known as Ochopee, and speaks with an Indian accent. He remembers the old ways. He grew up in the woods and swamp, where a boy never had to worry about things like math homework.

"I just learned things natural. How to build canoes. How to handle myself outdoors. Fishing. Frogging. I was hunting alligators before I was ten. I never did go to school."

Things are different for young Seminoles today, and Bobby Henry has mixed emotions. Some go to school on the reservation or off the reservation to learn to read and write the English language. But as they assimilate into modern society, they experience temptations that never existed for Bobby Henry.

"When I was a boy, in the swamp, I felt close to God because I was close to nature. Children who stayed in the swamp were never tempted to steal or cheat or do wrong. My uncle said, 'You go to school, you will learn stealing and cheating. You don't belong there. Schools are for white boys.' I didn't believe him then, but I sometimes believe it now."

In the latest issue of the *Seminole Tribune* newspaper, there's a front-page story about vandalism on a South Florida reservation. Parents are asked to keep an eye on their children. Drug and alcohol abuse, already a problem for other Americans, also threaten the Seminole young. Bobby Henry doesn't know the answer to the problem. He just knows it must be hard to be a young person torn between two cultures. It's hard to be an adult, too.

"I guess it's a good idea for our young people to go to school, so they can get along in the other world. But I also think it is good if they don't forget the Indian ways."

The Seminole Culture Center is a good place for people of all races to learn about native people. An eight-acre compound includes a museum containing Seminole artifacts and history. At craft areas, elderly women sew traditional clothing. Men carve cypress sofkee spoons used for cooking a cornmeal drink. Boys play their version of stickball, using whittled rackets.

Ponds contain garfish, bowfin and turtles traditionally eaten by Seminoles. Alligators sunbathe in large pits. Gators have long been used by the Seminoles, first as food, then as a source of hides for trading. In the 1920s, when the land boom brought thousands of people to Florida, Seminoles began wrestling alligators at roadside stands for tourist dollars.

"I guess I was eleven or twelve when I started wrestling alligators," Henry says. "My daddy brought me to town, and I saw other children wrestling for dimes and quarters for ice cream money. I wanted to get into it, too."

A compact, muscular man, Henry still mixes it up with alligators in the pit at the culture center. "I would rather leave it for the younger men," he says, watching the alligators and smiling. "But sometimes we're short, and I'm needed. I would like to retire with all my fingers."

It is safer to build canoes.

"My daddy and I would go into the swamp and find the tree we'd need. We'd cut a ring around it. Eight months later, the tree above the ring would be dry enough to work. We'd cut it down and make camp. We'd stay there the two or three months it took to make the canoe. We didn't have no calendar, but we'd time things so we'd be finished with the canoe during rainy season. Then we'd float out."

He and his father lived in the canoe during hunting time. Bobby shot animals with bow and arrow. They gigged frogs for the delicious legs. Eventually, they poled the canoe out of the deep swamp to the Tamiami Trail, the two-lane road that twists through the Everglades. There, they'd trade with whites. Bobby's favorite trader was a Miami baker who bartered bread and butter for frog legs.

For a lot of modern Seminoles, Bobby's stories are ancient history that have little relevance. Bingo and tobacco shops have brought the tribe a modest prosperity. James Billie, the tribe's ambitious leader, entertains plans for large Seminole farms, cattle ranches and aquaculture.

Bobby Henry agrees there are advantages to joining mainstream America. But he intends to do his part to keep alive the old traditions, too.

"There is no sense in forgetting the past," he says.

Life is a garden

Down at Green Bean Gully, near Lettuce Lane, Jewett Cook avoided twiddling his thumbs. He had them wrapped around a hose.

He was watering his strawberries, his pineapples, his zucchinis. The sun beat upon him like a ball-peen hammer. Ho hum. Gnats buzzed his face like fighter jets. Gnats, shmats.

Jewett Cook, 76, put down his hose and walked over to a dirt road named after a vegetable. He nibbled the head off an asparagus spear and said, "When I go home in the summer, to Illinois, some of the fellas they look at me, and they ask, 'You twiddlin' your thumbs in Florida?' "

He spat on the ground to emphasize the point he was about to make. "I say, 'No, sir. I don't twiddle my thumbs. I don't have time to twiddle my thumbs.' "

Green thumbs and twiddling seldom mix at the Tillers and Toilers, the vegetable garden club at Sun City Center, the retirement community south of Tampa.

These aren't backyard gardens the club's 37 elderly members are fooling with. In a four-acre field next to a softball diamond, Tillers and Toilers have plots no smaller than 15 feet wide and 75 feet long. Some have four plots.

Tillers and Toilers garden like men and women possessed. They prepare the soil with a club-owned Rototiller machine. They hoe and weed. They compost and mulch. They pray for rain, and when rain arrives, they pray for sun. They gnash their teeth over nematodes. They curse corn-stealing raccoons. They sweat a great deal.

"It's a lot of work," said Cook, a former Illinois seed company owner who has been a club member for going on two decades. "But it's fun, too."

For some, it's more than fun. It's their lives. Before some of them sign a real estate contract at Sun City, they want to know if they can have gardens. They had gardens wherever they lived before, or else they always wanted a piece of earth they could work and call their own.

For some, gardening is a way to guarantee their refrigerators will be filled with fresh produce. For others, a garden provides physical and mental therapy. For some, gardening is a form of self expression: My tomatoes are bigger than your tomatoes! Working with the soil, under the broiling sun, others have discovered talents they never knew existed.

Norm Evans, 80-year-old retired auto body repairman, stopped weeding his carrot patch long enough to explain: "Sometimes I'm here eight hours. I'm one of those fellas that has to be doin' something all the time. Understand? What I do is garden. I guess I've always had it in my blood. I just never knew it."

He spent his adult life in Pittsburgh. Repairing auto bodies was a good business, but it allowed little time for hobbies. He and his wife – they have been married more than five decades – moved to Sun City in 1984.

One day he saw the fellows cutting grass near the softball fields. When he stopped to help he learned about Tillers and Toilers. He joined and paid the $7.50 a year plot rental fee. Pretty soon he was perusing seed catalogs and looking with disdain on the vegetables the supermarket had to offer.

Norm Evans grows rhubarb, carrots, potatoes, green beans, cucumbers, peppers, papayas, bananas and pineapples. He digs ditches so that heavy rain will drain from his plot. He builds little fences to keep at bay the lettuce-eating rabbits. He drops to his knees to pluck out offending weeds. He brought to his garden a sink, connected it to the water pipe, and now he can wash his vegetables just in case he needs to give some away.

"You can't come by this garden and go away empty-handed," he said. A moment later, he was filling a plastic bag with red potatoes. "And you like green beans? Try some of these green beans. Ever see a zucchini like this? I wish I had some lettuce to give you. Last year I had lettuce this big. You never saw such lettuce."

He held his hands apart. Norm Evans grows lettuce the size of beach balls.

George Swan, a 75-year-old retired accountant, grows pumpkins the size of medicine balls. Last year he produced the largest Sun City had ever seen. The orange marvel tipped his bathroom scales at 105 pounds.

"I'm trying to grow some melons, too," he said, walking carefully among his vines. He had honeydews coming in. He had sugar baby watermelons. His butternut squashes were nothing to sneeze at. "But I'll tell you: It's work."

Jewett Cook had to agree.

"You can't let the work go for even a day," he said. "You have to keep up with it. Or it's going to overwhelm you."

Years ago, there was a waiting list to be a member of Tillers and Toilers. But now there is more garden space available than there are gardeners willing to do the work.

"I think it's because people are younger when they retire now," George Swan said. "There are a lot of forced early retirements in business nowadays. The last thing some of these young retired people want to do is hard, physical work. They come out here, and see the golf courses, and they know that sweating in a garden is not their bag."

"And you sweat," said Cook, spitting for emphasis. "That's where the toiling part of the Tillers and Toilers comes in. Oh my, yes."

"A lot of people think they want to garden," said Swan. "But they give up when they see how much work it is."

Some garden to the very end, until their legs or backs give out or their hearts finally give up and quit. And some move away from Sun City and their gardens, as wrenching an experience as that can be.

Over near Asparagus Alley, Jewett Cook and George Swan were shaking their heads about a man who had to do that. They were looking at one of the finest-kept plots at the garden. A sign in front of it said: *Doc's Vegy Clinic.*

Doc was nowhere to be found.

"Doc is moving back to Kentucky for family reasons," Swan said. "He's put so much work into this. It's a real shame."

Dr. William Epling, retired, started working on that wonderful garden two years ago. He brought in top soil. He built a wooden frame around his topsoil to keep the nematodes out. He put a fence around and over his sweet corn to thwart the raccoons.

He grew the best raspberries, blackberries and blueberries in Sun City. When he moved to Sun City, Sun City had to guarantee him a garden. Now his garden was reverting to the club.

"I went by for one last look this morning," Doc said. "I'm going to miss my garden. I'm going to miss my garden a whole lot. But I just know the fellas will take care of it for me. My garden is in good hands."

Watermelon man

Clyde Bumgardner looked plum worried about his watermelon.

"It should be bigger than this," he said, shaking his head. The watermelon, growing among the vines behind his Levy County mobile home, weighed about 50 pounds. Fifty-pound watermelons disappoint Clyde Bumgardner. He grows the largest watermelons in Florida. Last year he produced a state-record 146-pounder that measured about three feet long and more than four feet around. Bumgardner has grown them bigger, but last year was the first he ever bothered to register with the state.

Florida, of course, is known across the nation for its tasty watermelons. Motorists start seeing them at roadside stands in May, and supermarket shoppers find them through July. But they are modest melons, for the most part, small enough to be carried by a skinny teen-ager to a church picnic.

It takes a wheelbarrow to move a Clyde Bumgardner watermelon – a wheelbarrow operated by a strong person. Here in Levy County, a North Florida farming community where watermelon appreciation comes easily, folks still talk about the 170-pounder Clyde grew in 1988.

But now, hunkered down among the vines, he was frowning. "I don't think I got very good seed this year," he said. "I don't like the shape of this melon." An artist when it comes to watermelons, Bumgardner likes his to be symmetrical. His current melon was asymmetrical. Worse, the stem was off center. Off-center stems are notorious for breaking before fruit is ripe.

"Well," he said, "I can only hope."

Clyde Bumgardner, 73, likes to leave nothing to chance. He is not a professional farmer, but he is a perfectionist. Back when he was a coal miner, a merchant marine and an air-conditioning repairman, he wanted things to be just right, too. Now retired, he's a first-class fussbudget about his hobby: growing watermelons so big they probably could be hollowed out and used as canoes.

"I don't know why I do this," he said, walking among his vines in blue jeans and sneakers. When he bent over to remove a dead leaf his bare back looked almost black from the sun. "There's no money in it. I guess I do it because I enjoy it, and it gives me something to talk about."

In this neck of the woods, folks claim Bumgardner is the world's worst named man. No bum gardener, he should be called Wisegardner. Back when he lived in Ohio, he grew apples so big they required both hands to eat. "One apple, one pie," was his credo. He once grew a 29 3/4-pound cantaloupe, which would have been a

Florida record by 13 pounds had he entered the state contest. Instead, he gave the prize melon to his best bass-fishing buddy.

Right now, in his back yard, he has corn that may be as high as a small elephant's eye. Florida is not known as a peach state, but he grows peaches so juicy they have to be eaten over the sink. He carries around photographs of past watermelons and citrus trees that made him proud.

Some summers ago, as he and his wife drove through Arkansas, they passed roadside stands that seemed to overflow with 100-pound watermelons. Impressed, Bumgardner promised that one day he was going to grow mighty watermelons, too.

In 1985, he started experimenting. One of his first big watermelons weighed 90 pounds – and it was a species known more for taste than size. Then he got his green thumbs on seeds from a Carolina Cross. In 1985, in Hope, Ark., Ivan and Lloyd Bright had grown a world-record 260-pounder from Carolina Cross seed. Bumgardner buys his seeds from the Brights for $15 a dozen.

"It's easier to grow big melons in Arkansas than Florida because they got better soil," Bumgardner said. "And they don't have the problems with weather and bugs that we do. But you can do okay here."

Bumgardner has. He has grown a 170-pounder, two 162-pounders, a 156-pounder and a mess that would flirt with 140. Nothing smaller is worth the effort it takes, he says, and it takes a lot of effort.

In February, Bumgardner plants seeds in small pots and stores them in a kitchen cabinet warmed by a light bulb. When the weather outside has lost its chill, he puts the little plants into the ground, in soil he has prepared with care.

No ordinary dirt will do. Bumgardner works a fertilizer called 10-10-10 into the ground, adds dried animal blood and a tad of cottonseed meal. Then he buries into the rich soil his *piece de resistance*: a bunch of mullet heads. "The Indians used fish heads to grow corn," he said. "That's good enough for me."

The vines grow on plots that measure from 50 feet to about 100 feet long. From April to July, Bumgardner practically lives in his watermelon field, stewing about aphids, drought, wind, crooked fruit and other bad deals. He also carries a ruler in his back pocket to measure melons. In May, watermelons grow quickly. He's had a couple that put on two inches a day. His current prize, the one he frets about because of its asymmetrical shape, grew 10 inches in a recent six-day period.

The kinds of watermelon people buy at stores are usually harvested after about 70 days. Clyde Bumgardner likes to wait 120 days for his. The longer they're in the ground, the bigger they grow. Some people will tell you that giant watermelons are tasteless, but Clyde Bumgardner is here to tell you different.

"They're delicious," he said. "Now I like to put a little salt on mine. Really brings out the sweet."

When he is sure his melon is ripe, he telephones the county farm agent, who drives over, takes measurements and weighs the prize. The county farm agent registers the watermelon with the state farm office in Gainesville.

When the agent leaves, the fun begins for Clyde Bumgardner. He maneuvers a wheelbarrow under the watermelon and carries it to his trusty Buick. He opens the front door and slides the melon into the passenger seat. "It's the most delicate moment," he said. "I'm always afraid I'm going to drop it at that point."

But he has yet to drop one, and he has never smashed a melon against the dash though he never protects the precious cargo with a seat belt. Chauffeuring the melon around the county, he shows off what he's done. His mechanic is always mighty impressed, as are his friends at church, who usually get to feast on the melons. One melon fed 50 a few years ago.

It's satisfying to feed friends, he admits, but it's even more enjoyable to astonish strangers. He remembers fondly the day he drove his biggest melon ever to the farmer's market, where somebody who didn't know better had a 70-pounder on display. The king of the watermelons opened the door of the Buick to reveal 170 pounds of prime melon.

"It's good for the ego," Clyde Bumgardner said.

All good things, alas, must end.

"For a few days I show the big melon around," he said wistfully. "Then I lean it up against the house and look at it myself. I say to myself, 'I wonder if anybody will come by and see it today?' But eventually, I know it's time to give it away. I like to keep that watermelon around as long as I can. I don't want to part with it."

Clyde had nothing to worry about. Six weeks after this column published, he harvested a fine 155-pound melon.

Dewey's trees

The black finger bothered Dewey Paulsen, who trims trees for a living. In his business, a dead branch is removed to save the rest of the tree. It was only natural that he figured the same applied to a useless fingertip crushed in a log-splitting accident.

"It was dead all right," he says now. "It was blacker than a mummy's finger. It had to come off."

Dewey Paulsen has nothing against doctors, understand. Some of his best customers are doctors. He simply hated wasting a doctor's time on a mere dead finger, what with the really sick people in town needing medical attention. Dewey walked into his St. Petersburg back yard, clamped the offending finger in a vise, and amputated the dead part with a hack saw.

"It didn't hurt," Dewey says. Dead fingers feel no pain.

"He came into the house and said, 'Here, Mom. Catch,' and I did," Vivian Paulsen remembers. She fielded her husband's severed fingertip.

"I still have that finger somewhere," Dewey says. "But I don't know whether I could lay my hands on it or not. I did show my hand to the doctor later and he said he couldn't have done a better job himself. And what finger I got left is stronger than the good fingers. I get this nub under a log and it's mine."

Dewey Paulsen does not each quiche.

At 78, he may be the toughest man in Florida. At a time when androgynous musicians are contemporary heroes, a man's man like Paulsen is as rare as an Indian head penny. For four decades he has been an urban lumberjack, cutting down trees, hauling them away, putting up with everything from menacing thorns to heavy limbs that conk him on the head or come crashing down upon his fingers. Ask anyone: Dewey Paulsen is a treeman's treeman.

He wakes up before the rising sun, does some of the most physically demanding labor known to man, drives home at dark, and crawls into bed early. The owner of Dewey Paulsen Tree Service is also a ex-professional wrestler who lives inside the body of a physically fit man 30 or 40 years his junior. As he tosses a limb onto the truck, the muscles beneath his damp, white T-shirt shift like snakes in a gunny sack.

Cutting trees, he quotes the Bible. He eats no red meat or pork. He drinks no alcohol, carbonated drinks, coffee or tea. Fruit juice, milk and water are beverages of choice. He does not smoke – "I had a cigarette, a Chesterfield, when I was seventeen and it made me so sick I prayed to God to let me live"– and is not known to swear.

The only thing old about Dewey Paulsen is his poor hearing. "You listen to loud chain saws as long as I have," he says, "and after a time people got to speak up a little." His face, though lined and tanned from years spent under the Florida sun, has the character of an old live oak.

"He's some man," says his wife, who married her husband when he was 46 and she was 20.

"You got to work hard to keep up with him and I'm not ashamed to admit it," says Nick Cohoon, a Paul Bunyanesque fellow of 36 who works for Paulsen.

"Dewey's amazing," says Jim Rahe, a rock-hard 53-year-old treeman and one of Paulsen's best friends. "Almost 79 and he's still going strong, cutting trees with a chain saw."

Dewey Paulsen is still cutting trees with chain saws because spring is a good time for hardy men of his calling. Winter freezes kill or damage trees that need trimming in the spring to survive. The streets are alive with the sound of chain saws.

"Business has been good," Paulsen admits cheerfully. Behind him, Jimmy Cohoon, 40, stands in a cherry picker high above the ground and saws limbs from a big melaleuca behind a funeral home. "Back in '62 we had a real freeze," Paulsen says. "Three days straight it got down to nineteen. Lot of work in '62."

Cutting trees, Dewey tells people, is in his blood. His father was a lumberjack in Iron City, Michigan, before moving his family to St. Petersburg in 1910. Peter Paulsen was also what some people might call a tough cookie. "When a log came off the ramp, and it was a cull, he'd throw a cant hook in it and swing it off the line – all by himself! I don't know how he could do that himself, but he could. He knew his trees, and he was big and strong."

Unlike his father, Dewey Paulsen is a small man, five-feet-seven or so, but his arms bulge with sinew and vein, his stomach is flat and his chest is still impressive. "My chest used to be a lot bigger," says Paulsen, a St. Petersburg resident for more than seven decades. "When I was younger and went to the beach, I never passed a person who didn't turn around and take a second look. My waist was twenty-eight and my chest was forty."

Muscles rippling, chest sticking out, Paulsen was never timid about demonstrating his prowess. "I could lift the front end of a Cadillac – fifty-two-hundred pounds! Once my brother-in-law was sittin' in a Buick Six – you know how big a Buick Six is – and he said, 'I'll bet you couldn't lift this.' "

Dewey won the bet.

"Oh, I could lift anything. I never needed a jack."

Paulsen enjoyed matching his strength against other men. That's what attracted him to professional wrestling. Known as "The Iron Duke," he wrestled in Tampa and St. Petersburg. For publicity he allowed people to strike his stomach with heavy sticks. "It never hurt," says Paulsen, who quit the sport in the 1930s before his right ear could become completely cauliflowered.

Franklin Roosevelt was president when Paulsen cut his first tree for pay. An old man who trimmed trees for a living needed help from a strong, young fellow. A carpenter, Paulsen for the next seven years earned extra money as a treeman. Married in 1951, looking for a dependable profession, he began his own business.

"Back then it was much different," he says. "You didn't have a chain saw then. You had a cross-cut saw – the kind lumberjacks would use in tandem to take down a big tree – and you had a hand saw, an ax and some rope. I always liked the ax. I could chop wood like a house afire. Sometimes I'd get a worker who was a little slow, and I'd keep up with him, chop just as much wood with an ax as he could with a chain saw."

The chain saw changed the business. It made things easier, but it made a dangerous business even more dangerous.

"When you use a chain saw, you got to be concentratin' every minute," says Dewey, and his worker Jimmy Cohoon nods vigorously in agreement. "You can't have all kinds of things swirlin' through your mind except what you got to do."

One day, a chain saw bit through a branch and then his shoe.

"The night before I'd trimmed my toenails. If I hadn't, the saw would have caught the nail and ate up into my foot. I was lucky."

Paulsen at times has been less fortunate. Bee stings have sent him to the hospital. Falling limbs have struck him on the head and cracked his plastic helmet. "The only time I have ever had headaches."

One needs only to glance at his hands to know their owner does not work at some soft, office job. The middle and index fingers of his left hand look deformed, twisted. It happened when a heavy limb fell and crushed his fingers. "I told the fella above me not to hold the rope too tight," he says, as if that explains everything. Then he adds, "But he did, he didn't give me a slack rope, and that broke the branch. I didn't get my hand out of the way in time."

The tips of the right index and middle fingers are gone, or as Dewey describes them, "nubs." It happened late in the day, and he was tired, but he kept working, routinely feeding limbs into a hydraulic machine that splits logs into firewood. "I don't know how to explain it," he says, sheepishly. "I just had my hand there and it came down. I put an old rag around it and said, 'Come on. We got to go to the hospital.' " It was a few weeks later that he performed his hack-saw surgery. He was 67.

"You know, I just don't feel pain. I've broken my nose four times and it never hurt. When I was younger, I told my sister to throw me a dresser drawer, and she did, only she didn't throw it even, and it caught me on the nose and broke it. It was real crooked. Few years later, I was helpin' move a buzz saw, and a crowbar we were usin' hit me right across the nose. Three days in the woods, I cut fifty cords of firewood, and I get my nose straightened out – and I don't have to pay a doctor a cent."

The day begins early. He wakes before light and is fed a lumberjack's breakfast by wife Vivian. He may be a small man, but he packs away a bowl of oatmeal with bananas and raisins, and follows that with eggs, grits, whole wheat toast and fruit juice. Swallowing a handful of vitamins and a garlic pill, Dewey Paulsen is ready to face the world.

"Biggest tree I ever had to cut was a big banyan," he says. "It took a whole week. The trunk was ten foot in diameter! We hauled it to the dump and a few weeks later, it started growin' again. That was a tree."

He takes a break from trimming the melaleucas, or punk trees, reaching branches toward the telephone wires. He puts down the Poulan chain saw and says, "Thorn trees are the worst, though. You can't get away with a job without gettin' scratched. I've had men take one look at a thorn tree they had to chop and walk away. Those Florida Holly (Brazilian pepper) are not too easy either. They got branches goin' every which way and you got to cut past them to get at the big parts. This guy once, I gave him an estimate, only he thought he could do it by himself, and what happened is he got poked in the eye. He said, 'Dewey, I should have listened.'"

It's a familiar tune whistled by Dewey: If only the amateurs had listened to reason and let professionals do the job.

"This lady calls me one afternoon and asks me to finish a job her daughter started, only her daughter can't finish on account of she fell off the ladder and broke her arm. This man, a friend of mine, who was always talkin' about the money he had and the houses he owned, he thought he'd save money by trimmin' his trees himself. He started cuttin' and fell down and killed himself."

Jimmy Cohoon, one of the two Cohoon brothers who works for Paulsen, steps into the cherry picker that lifts him into the sky. His burly younger brother, Nick, stays on the ground to help Dewey. Jimmy cuts, big limbs fall. Nick steps forward, holds the felled limb above the ground for Dewey, who starts his chain saw and makes a cut less than three inches from Nick's hand. Nick doesn't flinch. Dewey is no Babe in the Woods.

So it goes the whole morning. They work with economy and rhythm. Cut, fall, cut, stack, cut, fall, cut, fall, stack. They take a short break for lunch – Dewey eats two egg-salad sandwiches, nuts, two bananas and three apples – and pick up their chain saws again. When they are finished, they all pitch in and toss the heavy limbs into the truck. It's backbreaking work, but Dewey Paulsen, whose next birthday is No. 79, leads the attack.

He doesn't want anyone thinking he's an old man.

"Dewey's never going to retire," his wife says later. "If he retired, he'd die. It's that simple. He'll cut trees until he drops."

"I'm lucky to be alive"

Dave Noonan probably will be discharged from the hospital soon, if all goes well, if the physical therapy sessions continue to work. Each day he does 300 exercises to strengthen the leg that is black and puffed. He does leg lifts, his face grimaced with the pain, and then he spends time in the whirlpool bath at Manatee County's Blake Memorial Hospital.

"I'm sore," Dave Noonan said. "With this leg I just can't get comfortable."

Three weeks ago, while tarpon fishing near Anna Maria Island, Noonan almost lost his life – and then his leg – when he was hurt by a giant sting ray.

He still cannot bend the right leg. The leg is still swollen and the dying flesh behind the knee is black. The one-inch hole in his thigh was made by the barb of the ray. Next to the hole is the six-inch scar left by the surgeon who operated to save Dave Noonan's life and limb.

The three of them, tarpon fishermen, were in the boat and waiting for the tarpon, Dave Noonan said the other day, trying to explain how the ordeal began.

Six lines, baited with pinfish, were in the water, and Noonan and Bob Smith and John Banfield were talking about tarpon at 12:30 p.m. Banfield got a bite, set the hook into what he thought was a tarpon, but instead hooked the sting ray. Banfield took his time playing the ray, a large one that stretched nine feet from nose to tip of tail and weighed about 150 pounds.

Banfield got the ray to the boat and Dave Noonan, who has caught many rays, got ready to cut the line. There is nothing to it. Gaff the ray in the wing, transfer the gaff to the left hand, hold the ray in the water next to the boat, clip the line with pliers held in the right hand. Watch the sting ray swim away.

Dave Noonan gaffed the ray in the wing, pulled it to the boat, transferred the gaff to his left hand, and then reached down to clip the line. He wanted to clip the line close to the ray, so the fish would not have to drag heavy line through the water when it swam.

But before he could clip the line, it happened. The ray jumped, actually left the water, and swung about. The 10-inch barb, located near the base of the tail, penetrated at least six inches into Dave Noonan's right thigh. Just as quickly, the ray withdrew the barb with a snap of its tail. Noonan screamed and dropped the gaff and his pliers as the sting ray flopped back into the water.

A sting ray barb is serrated, like a saw, and is meant to damage. It is covered with a sheath of skin that ruptures when the barb is delivered. The rupture releases a venom made of proteins and amino acids that causes great pain, throbbing, shooting

172

pain. Although seldom fatal – only two of 1,097 reported cases died within a five-year period during a recent United States coastline study – the venom can affect the heart and respiratory, nervous and urinary systems.

But the thing that almost killed Dave Noonan was not the venom. It was the barb.

A sting ray barb isn't designed to come out easily. The teeth of the barb are backcurved, to cut and tear when withdrawn, and Dave Noonan got it bad. The barb severed the main artery in his leg, and Dave Noonan sat down in his boat to bleed to death.

"Listen, I'm lucky to be alive," he said, sitting in his hospital room. He is 34, a partner in a remodeling company that builds cabinets. A Pasadena resident, he likes to fish for tarpon during the summer. He said, "I'd be dead right now if it weren't for the guys that were with me."

Nobody panicked. That was the thing. When Dave Noonan went down, blood pumping from his leg, John Banfield and Bob Smith wrapped a towel just above the wound. A tourniquet. They told Noonan that everything would be fine even though they knew things would not be fine.

They didn't know the way back to the marina. They aren't familiar with Anna Maria Island, which is located west of Bradenton and southeast of Egmont Key near the mouth of Tampa Bay. Only Dave Noonan knew the way back to the marina.

"I felt that I was going into shock, but I couldn't afford to faint," Noonan said. "If I did, I was a dead man. So John held my head up so I could tell Bob which way to steer the boat."

Dave Noonan screamed on the way to the marina. He isn't ashamed for anyone to know that. Imagine a hundred bee stings, or the stinging wound inflicted by the dorsal fin of a giant saltwater catfish. The venom from the ray was "a thousand times worse than that. It was unimaginable."

They got to the marina in five minutes. The rescue squad arrived about 10 minutes after that and stopped some of the bleeding with a pressure bandage. The ambulance arrived five minutes later. By 1:00 p.m., Dave Noonan was at the hospital. He'd lost four pints of blood by the time he was wheeled into the operating room where a surgeon awaited.

"He was very much in danger of bleeding to death," Dr. Rodney Adams said. "He was in definite danger of losing his leg."

Adams opened the leg and sewed together the severed femoral artery, a blood vessel about as thick as a man's little finger. The operation took 90 minutes and for three days Dave Noonan recovered in the intensive care unit.

His leg swelled until it was 18 inches around. The leg below the knee blistered and the skin turned black because for at least 30 minutes during the ordeal, before Adams repaired the severed artery, the lower leg was deprived of oxygen and blood. "I thought they were going to have to amputate," Noonan said.

But most of the dead black skin fell off, the swelling decreased, and the feeling returned to his leg.

Dave Noonan is using a metal walker right now, and he seems to get along all right. He does not know how long before he can walk without it. He is exercising daily and taking whirlpool baths and his leg is sore. He is tired of television, particularly daytime television. He is tired of the hospital. He does not know how long he will be out of work. He does know the sting ray will cost him and his insurance company about $6,000 before the ordeal is over.

"But I'll tell you something," he said. "As soon as I can, I'm gonna be fishing again. Maybe I won't be able to stand up and fight a fish. At least not for a while. But I'll be able to run the boat for somebody else. I just won't mess with another sting ray."

Mullet Mary

MADEIRA BEACH   6/5/79

Joey, tending bar, kindly told the watermelon salesman to get lost. "I don't want to have to pick up the seeds," Joey explained. "I let people eat watermelon in the bar and then other people complain about seeds sticking to their shoes."

Mullet Mary, sitting at the bar in the early morning, cared nothing about the watermelon. She was not hungry. She sipped her beer and lit a cigarette.

A big window fan blew the smoke out of Madeira Beach's Charter Center Tavern, a Gulf Boulevard bar frequented by commercial fishermen. The television was tuned to a rerun of *All in the Family*. While other patrons focused on the fuzzy black-and-white picture and the watermelon saga, Mary spoke of the fish.

"My husband and I ate a lot of mullet," she said. Mary and her husband Gray Giles once were two of the best to work Tampa Bay waters. "It was mullet and grits during hard times. You eat mullet, baby, or else you starve. Breakfast, lunch, dinner. I ate so much mullet my stomach went in and out with the tide."

Joey, tending bar, didn't want to hear about disturbed stomachs. She wasn't feeling so good. "Please, Lord," Joey prayed. "Please let me get over this hangover. I promise I'll never do it again."

When nobody arrived to help, Mullet Mary offered Joey some advice based on her 52 years on earth. "Have some more hair of the dog. You'll feel better."

But Joey poured herself a coffee instead and listened to Mullet Mary tell stories.

"I guess I mullet fished 15 years," said Mary, who sometimes wears a yellow T-shirt identifying herself as Mullet Mary. "You always had either too many mullet or not enough mullet. Too many mullet and the bottom falls out of the market. Not enough mullet and you don't make no money. You go out in the boat and all you get for your trouble is a red neck and a hungry gut."

Mullet Mary retired six years ago after her husband died. She tried fishing alone, but it was hard, and her sons were afraid when their mother went out in the boat. So now Mary builds traps for commercial fishers who catch blue crabs.

"I made 17 traps this week," said Mary, a tanned woman with short black hair. "See that blister there? That's from holding the wire cutter. I can do one trap every 45 minutes once I get my wire laid out."

Mary nursed another beer. She turned for a moment to watch two men playing cribbage at the end of the bar, but her mind was still working on the blue crabs. "Gray and I used to run about 200 traps during the summer. I used to catch crabs and pick the meat out for rich folks who didn't want to pick their own. I also bootlegged oysters until the game warden caught me."

But most of the time, she just netted mullet or pulled crab traps.

"Gray and I had some great days, baby," said Mary, who moved to Pinellas County from Cleveland in 1954. "Sometimes the water would be black with mullet. We could hardly pull the net. We'd catch so many mullet the fishhouse would restrict us for the rest of the week. But sometimes we'd get catfish. They'd get caught in the gill nets and you have to pull 'em out by hand. Catfish are useless. God, I hate catfish because of them spines. They hurt you. Sometimes those catfish would be holding their eggs in their mouths. That was something to see. They looked like peeled grapes."

Talking about ugly catfish reminded Mullet Mary about her other dislikes. "One day I pull a trap and see this big green thing in there that looks like a snake. Greener than Joey's shirt. I take it to Sonny Aylesworth's seafood place. Sonny's the aces, baby, when it comes to fish. He told me it was a moray eel. I'd never seen one before."

Mullet Mary said how she didn't even like to think about snakes. "No, baby," she said. "I got bit by a copperhead when I was a kid back in upstate New York. Then when I moved here 25 years ago I got hit by a diamondback rattlesnake. We had a trailer back there behind Babe's Drive In. I step out to get the cat out of the car before she has her kittens. I step on the snake. It hit me but I jumped and it didn't get any power behind itself. All I got out of it was two pin pricks. The poison ran down my leg into my shoe."

Life on the waterfront generally was safe. But Mary remembered the night she fell overboard. "I tripped over a rope and fell in by Big Bird Key. I made a big splash and Gray said, 'Damn, I thought you was a porpoise.' "

She and Gray once netted a dolphin my accident. "It was a baby and it got caught in the net. We were trying to release it and the mother was hanging around, crying. You could see tears. When we turned her baby loose, she stayed around, slapping the water with her tail. She was thanking us."

Mullet Mary encountered few sharks. "But we saw some, honey, especially up near Clearwater," she told Joey, a Chicago native who was afraid of being eaten by sharks. "We didn't see hammerheads," Mary said. "Just regular old sharks. You know some people eat sharks? The hell with that. I'll stick to mullet."

Mary's many friends still bring her mullet. She likes to roll them in cornmeal and salt and pepper and fry them in a pan. She likes grits on the side, and a cold beer from the tavern, where she can meet commercial fishing friends and talk about old times on the water.

"Gray and I, we had a ball mullet fishing. We found all kinds of stuff. A big Bible once, floating in Boca Ciega Bay. And once I saw this glove in the water and reached down to pick it up. Gray said, 'With your luck, there'll be a body attached to it.' But there wasn't. I never saw a body in the water. But we saw plenty of dead dogs and cats that people'd pitch off the bridges."

The reluctant mariner

The sea was a romantic place to Henry Black when he was a boy. He liked standing on the rocks and watching the big ships sail Tampa Bay toward the Gulf. He liked listening to the merchant seamen talk about where they had been and where they were going next. And at night in bed he could hear the fog horns blowing as ships headed to sea.

He could read books about the sea, and he could stand on the dock and catch snapper and blue crabs before breakfast, pretending he was a commercial fisherman making a living from the banquet the sea set forth.

So it was no surprise when Henry Black ran away to sea. Where else would he have gone? He was 14 when he sneaked one night aboard an old freighter, crawled behind some refrigeration units and remained hidden until Tampa was far behind.

His actions seemed wonderfully romantic to him in 1924, like something from a library book or a colorful story you'd hear outside one of those taverns that always line waterfront roads. Looking back today, he wonders why he did it. Now the idea of running away to sea strikes him as plain foolishness.

"If I had my life to do over again, I'd have gone to college and become a lawyer," is what Henry Black says about the subject.

At 75, Black lives within two blocks of the waterfront. He sits in a rocking chair and watches *As the World Turns* on his color television. Rocking steadily, as if nudged by a gentle wave, he talks instead of another kind of soap opera – the sea that first attracted him and then finally repelled him. He is too young to be described as an ancient mariner, but he is a reluctant one who no longer entertains idyllic notions about Mother Ocean. Or so he says.

"What was it I loved about the seas? Nothing," he growls now. "It was a job I started when I was a boy, and I got good at it. So I stayed at it."

He stayed 36 years. Except for a year spent as a cowboy, he never considered doing anything else. Yet for every warm memory, there are others he would as soon forget. In the North Atlantic, where he served on a ship carrying military supplies, he once saw the aurora borealis, the single most astonishing sight his eyes ever beheld at sea. But because it was World War II, and German submarines and airplanes were looking for convoy ships to sink, he mistook the northern lights for an enemy raid. He rang an alarm, and had to live with the embarrassment.

At his career's end, when he was captain of a Tampa Bay tugboat, his abilities made him both proud and a slave. There was an eight-year stretch when he had only

177

two days of vacation. Like a doctor on call, he went nowhere without expecting a summons to do work only he could do: "Captain, a ship is aground. We need you to pull her off the bar."

He remembers drunken captains, treacherous currents, long periods away from his wife and children. At sea, he used to see the kinds of sunrises and sunsets that landlubbers can only dream about, but he also experienced terrifying storms that threatened to send the old rust buckets on which he sailed to a graveyard in the deep.

A stocky redhaired man with Popeye's forearms, Black has been blessed or cursed with a good memory. He is unsure which, but the memory does come in handy when he talks to children about his life. His tales of the sea and long-ago Florida are part of a Hillsborough County folklore program designed to introduce schoolchildren to old ways of doing things.

Black, who can remember when Tampa Bay's cities were fishing villages, shows how he builds cast nets, his hobby for more than 40 years, and tells about the fish one can catch in those nets. But once in a while, when the schoolchildren hear how he spent his working life at sea, they get the look in their eyes he has seen in a lot of people who meet him.

And then he knows what Herman Melville in *Moby Dick* described as "the mystery about this sea" has gotten to them. Like a lot of romantic city dwellers who live on the shores of big water, they are thinking about what a nice life it must have been, feeling the rise and fall of the waves and the ebb and flow of the tide. They are imagining the cries of the gulls and smelling the salt spray but forgetting, as Samuel Johnson once wrote, that ""being in a ship is being in jail, with the chance of being drowned.''

"Going to sea," Capt. Henry Black tells schoolchildren and anybody else who asks, "can be be a beautiful thing. But it can also be a hard life."

Born in Tampa in 1910 to a fireman and a homemaker, he remembers spending as much time on Tampa Bay as his parents would allow. They were never more generous than in 1922, the year the Blacks moved to Port Tampa. Living so close to the seaport, he never tired of watching ships, swimming naked and catching heavy fish on handlines until his arms ached. But the Huck Finn life ended with his daddy's second marriage. He and his stepmother got along like shark and porpoise.

"When she tried to work on me with a broom handle, that was when I run off and stowed away on a ship."

The ship was the *MS. Muncove*, a freighter. Henry Black, finished with eighth grade, asked for a job. There were no jobs, but a nice man, the ship's oiler, told him to come back after dark. That night the oiler stowed him behind refrigeration units and covered him with a mattress. The boy avoided the captain until it was too late for the ship to turn back. The captain said he'd let him off in New York, but when the mess boy quit, he had a job.

"You grew up quick," he says now in that drawl of his. "They treated you like a man. As long as you could do a man's job."

He shipped out for a year, a 14-year-old seaman, and he enjoyed it. In fact, his taste for adventure was not yet satisfied. When he returned to Florida, he hitchhiked to the Everglades and became a cowhunter, the state's version of a cowboy.

"It was kind of rough, but it was fun. This was up around the lake (Okeechobee). The job was finding cattle. They'd be scattered everywhere, and you'd bring 'em back or brand 'em or slaughter 'em if they was fat enough. You'd put the meat on a wagon on top of a bed of palmettos and cover it with a sheet and bring it back."

On nights he failed to get back from the prairie, he covered himself with a blanket to protect himself from biting insects. Trying to breathe air instead of mosquitoes, he would pray for daylight.

"Snakes? Lord, yes I saw snakes. Rattlesnake and moccasin are out there. I got snakebit once by a moccasin. This was a period before I went back to sea. I was pulling catfish nets on the lake. The moccasins used to get in the net and eat the little fish. Then they'd get too fat to pass through the net mesh and get caught. So you'd have to pull 'em out. Anyway, one bit me by the thumb. This fisherman, he squeezed the wound until the blood poured out and then rubbed tobacco all over it. I never did get sick, but it sure hurt."

S nakebites seldom occur at sea, which may be a reason he returned to Port Tampa. He was still a teen-ager when he shipped out on a tanker, first as a seaman and eventually as chief mate. The ships on which he served called upon ports in the Soviet Union, China, Japan, Korea, the Philippines, Italy, Iran, England, France, Spain, Argentina, Colombia and Africa, but by then the thrill of the sea had worn thin. He was the reluctant mariner.

"My favorite port was Tampa."

There were great hurricanes, including one that tore a hole in his ship and filled the engine room with water and his mind with thoughts of death. The ship, a 400-footer, managed to stay afloat. He remembers another ferocious storm with 20-foot waves that slapped a mess boy from the stern, then deposited him on the bow – frightened but alive.

During the war, Black was mate on a freighter that set sail for the Panama Canal. The captain and most of the crew went ashore and got drunk. Black, the reluctant mariner, took the ship through the Panama Canal and into the Pacific.

After the war, he found a job at Port Tampa that he hoped would allow a normal family life. This was important to him and Alice, his wife. He had missed the birth of Betty because he was aboard a freighter off Cape Hatteras. He had missed Louise's birth because he had been aboard a Gulf of Mexico barge. He had made the birth of the boy, Henry, but then had to go to sea. That was how it was for a seagoing man. Home one day. At sea the next 45.

But things were going to be different, he thought, on the *SS Neptune*, a steam-driven, 117-foot tugboat. He would come home nights. He would see the wife and kids. He worked as deckhand and in the fireroom, where he shoveled coal into a firebox and endured 120-degree temperatures. And one day he was promoted to captain.

"As it turned out you were on call twenty-four hours a day," he says now, sounding bitter. "If I went to the drive-in, they'd page me. 'Capt. Black, please report to Port Tampa. There's a ship stuck on the St. Petersburg Turn.' And I'd drive my truck sixty miles per hour down Bayshore, take out the tug and go get the ship off the bar."

Relatively shallow, Tampa Bay can be treacherous. Ships must travel 40 miles of narrow, winding channel from the bay's mouth to the port in west Tampa. Currents in some of the narrowest channels sometimes reach eight knots, which is more than even the Gulf Stream can muster.

As a tugboat captain, Black was paid to help maneuver the ships through the channels to the port. And when ships ran aground, a common occurrence, it was often his job to free them, sometimes in frightening weather.

Bad weather has accounted for many Tampa Bay tragedies, but none more tragic than the Skyway Bridge accident in 1980. Capt. Black had retired when the bulletin came over his radio the May morning a tanker struck the bridge. But he has never stopped thinking about the accident. The pilot tried to take his ship through the bridge in a blinding rain and crashed into pilings instead. Thirty-five motorists were killed when the bridge collapsed.

"I sure felt sorry for the captain," Black says. "There's a lot of pressure on a captain. People don't know that. Sometimes I wonder what I would have done in that situation, and what I'd have done is not try to go through that bridge. When the weather is so bad you can't see in front of you, you put your engines on full-speed astern. You try to stop. You assume the worst."

Capt. Henry Black finally came ashore for good in 1958. Since his retirement, he has found time for things he always wanted to do. For friends he builds and repairs cast nets that are used to catch mullet. Sitting before the television in the rocker, he weaves pieces of monofilament net together by hand.

He continues to enjoy fishing, but generally only where water is fresh. It is strange, after so many years at sea, but since retirement he has discovered seasickness. If the bay is rough, and the wind is behind him, the smell of gas fumes coupled with the rocking boat makes him ill. He would rather spend his time on a quiet lake, or, better yet, on terra firma, growing in his garden okra, turnips, collard greens, bell peppers, eggplants and tomatoes.

But one odd thing. Two or three times a week, Henry Black climbs into his car and drives west on Ingraham Road until he reaches the port. There he looks at the ships and the water.

What is it about the sea that does this to a man?

He doesn't know.

Walking

Virginia Edwards is good at sauntering. She neither hurries nor dallies as she walks through the woods, and if something catches her eye she stops for a closer look and says something about it. In an age when most of us are anxious to get somewhere fast, sauntering is a lost art.

"I like the woods," she said, stopping to admire a green fly orchid that hung from the lower branches of a live oak. "I like walking a lot."

Henry David Thoreau, the New England philosopher who wrote *Walden* a century ago, would have enjoyed her company. He was an early master at sauntering, not to mention a lonely guy.

As he wrote in his essay, *Walking*: "I have met with but one or two persons in the course of my life who understood the art of taking walks daily – not to exercise the legs or body merely, nor barely to recruit the spirits, but positively to exercise both body and spirit, and to succeed to the highest and worthiest ends by the abandonment of all specific ends – who had a genius, so to speak, for sauntering."

Virginia Edwards, 46, seems to have that genius. Yes, she is exercising in her walks. Yes, she feels renewed by her walks. But she does not hike specifically for exercise or mental renewal. They just naturally happen when she follows her legs into the woods.

Several times a week, she invites other people to accompany her. She often leads hikes for the Florida Trail Association, which has long promoted the art of sauntering. The prime sauntering season in Florida begins in the fall and lasts through spring. From October through May nights are cool for slumbering backpackers, while the days are often mild enough for sweat-free hiking.

Edwards, a Florida native who has played in the woods since she was a girl, enjoys overnight sleepouts as much as the next person. But she finds more pleasure in daily hikes where she packs a canteen of water, a lunch and saunters for a few hours.

Eighteen of us accompanied Virginia on her hike into the Withlacoochee State Forest in North Central Florida. Most of us were city people from the crowded coast. Youngest among us was a 37-year-old Bradenton woman who was eight months pregnant with her first child. A 78-year-old Clearwater man, whose bulging muscles were testament to a life spent sauntering, was our senior member.

We had met at a McDonald's restaurant in Brooksville – yes, things are different now than in Thoreau's day – and driven in caravan to Robins Park at the forest's edge. At 9:38 a.m. we walked onto a sandy trail that weaved three miles through pines, oaks and sweetgums.

It didn't take us long to forget our city roots. The air smelled not of auto exhaust but of the heady perfume of the forest: pine needles, wildflowers, fresh air. As Thoreau wrote of the woods: "I come to it as a hungry man to a crust of bread."

Virginia Edwards, a short, sturdy woman with black hair that was hidden under a Florida Trail Association cap, led the way at a pace that was neither fast nor slow. Sauntering is like that. It automatically provides time to stop and smell the wildflowers or inspect a fallen leaf or admire how a twig seems to resemble Richard Nixon.

"A lot of people who live in Florida now, especially in the cities, don't even know something like these woods exist," she said quietly. "Walking here is such a nice way to get a taste of nature. You feel refreshed when you're through."

Virginia and her husband live in New Port Richey. The woods closest to their growing city seem to get smaller and smaller all the time. Development is moving in like a full-moon tide. "Every time I drive over here I see more subdivisions along the highway," she said.

But there are remaining pockets of wild left in Florida, and during the past two years Virginia has sauntered about 1,000 miles through them. The Withlacoochee State Forest is a favorite haunt.

"I like to see some of the large pine trees here," she said. The pines of Robins Park, where we sauntered, had been spared by chain saws. Some pines, more than a century old, towered over us. "Nothing stands up more free from blame in this world than a pine tree," Thoreau wrote.

Virginia stopped to study one that had been punished by lightning.The entire tree, top to bottom, had been hollowed out, as if someone had tried building a dugout canoe from a standing tree. "And it's still alive," Virginia wondered aloud. "It probably will live for several more years."

We gathered around her to listen. She didn't shout like a drill sergeant, or lecture us like a college professor. "I don't know Latin names," she said, pointing out live oaks, beauty berries, sweetgums and poison ivy. "I just know common names." Good enough. Having grown up on the edge of the Withlacoochee forest, she knew more than the rest of us.

"This is a wild plum tree." She had stopped again. "The fruit is edible, though kind of sour. The roots were used to make a tea by people with asthma. My father did, and it worked for him."

Walking on, we saw a button-sized crab spider. Virginia warned us to duck around the web of a golden silk spider, though we needed no warning. The spider, non-venomous, was as wide across as a coffee cup.

A few minutes later we saw walking death – a poisonous black widow, its carapace as smooth and shiny as a hearse. Virginia made no attempt to kill it and neither did we.

Sometimes Virginia sees a lot of wildlife. Deer jump trails ahead of her. Alligators grunt from swamps. Bobcats caterwaul in the distance. This was no such trip. The woods revealed themselves in more subtle ways. Wind rustled through trees. Squirrels chattered. Birds chirped. Virginia told us to listen to the cries of a pileated woodpecker. We weren't disappointed.

Sometimes the city intrudes. On one walk, she discovered a 1989 Camaro in the deep woods of the Richloam Wildlife Management Area. It was resting on concrete blocks – tires and T-top removed. "The auto dealer didn't even know it was stolen," she said.

We saw no vehicles on our saunter, happily, and saw no other party. We saw a Spanish bayonet shrub, though, and Sabal palms and a tree house in a giant live oak. A scaly lizard leaped across the trail, and a blue jay hollered at us from the trees. Some people, accustomed to a city's faster pace, might long for the mall, or movie theater, or rock 'n' roll concert after an hour or so of sauntering. But we, who were trying to simplify our lives – we who were trying to get into the spirit of sauntering – found our time with Virginia eventful enough.

We were back at our cars by early afternoon. Virginia took out a bowl and ate a tomato and lettuce salad. She reached into her pack, withdrew a portable hammock and strung it between two little pines so she could rest. She had an extra hammock, she said, if I wanted to borrow it. But I didn't have time.

If I wanted to avoid Tampa's notorious afternoon traffic on my way home, I needed to leave immediately. "The mass of men lead lives of quiet desperation," Thoreau wrote, without once ever having to drive on Interstate 275 through Tampa during rush hour.

Heading back on the interstate toward my life in the city, passing through the concrete canyon that is Tampa, I thought of the woods, and the art of sauntering, and the kind of woman who carries not one hammock but a pair.

Wheels of fortune

Jack Owen never uses a megaphone when he gives his gossipy bicycle tours of Palm Beach. He speaks so softly tourists beg him to talk louder. Instead, he tells them to get closer and hear better. On The Island, as wealthy residents call this place, shouting or even loud talking is frowned upon. Palm Beachers value discretion.

Right now Owen is wearing a pith helmet cooled by a solar-operated fan and telling a story softly and discreetly. He's astride his bicycle behind the mansion owned by the late Henry Flagler, the zillionaire who carved Palm Beach out of a mangrove swamp a century ago. Owen relates the history of the Flagler estate, a building that is about as big as your basic Don CeSar hotel, and he talks about the luxurious railroad car Flagler used to ride to Florida.

Then, quietly, he mentions the word "cathouse."

No self-respecting tourist wants to miss anything having to do with a cathouse, especially a cathouse on Palm Beach, and they draw around him.

"Some of the best-fed cats on the island exist on the scraps thrown out after social doings at the Flagler estate," Owen says in his British accent.

The tourists groan.

He pauses, for effect, and then delivers what his tourists really want: pure, unadulterated gossip about a different kind of cathouse. He points out another mansion, the one across the road from the Flagler estate, where "legend has it Mr. Flagler visited for liaisons with women who were not his wife."

"Ooo la la!" says a middle-aged woman from the seat of her 18-speed all-terrain bicycle.

Owen, 53, gives this tour winter and spring. On Saturday morning he meets a small group of cyclists at the lushly tropical Brazilian Court Hotel and leads them on a slow-paced 12-mile ride past mansions, estates and fountains. He passes on gossip, at least the kind he hopes won't get him into hot water with rich residents, and throws in a little history, too.

Owen, the author of *Palm Beach – An Irreverent Guide,* figures he is performing a public service. Every winter and spring, he contends, Palm Beach is besieged by out-of-town visitors who want the scoop about the Kennedys and the Trumps and other rich people with front-page names. Palm Beachers don't want to take their out-of-town guests around; they don't want to appear as if they are snooping on their neighbors. So Owen has filled the void.

"So far, I haven't gotten any complaints," he says, puffing triumphantly on a Viceroy.

That's because he is discreet. He tries to keep his tour groups small because small groups on bicycles are less likely to draw attention than large groups. And while he talks about millionaires who live behind the 20-foot, broken-glass-topped walls that surround some mansions here, he is careful not to mention names of anyone who may be alive and litigation minded.

He says nothing catty about Donald Trump, or Trump's $5-million estate, Mar-a-Lago, which has 118 rooms, 13 bathrooms, a bomb shelter and its own nine-hole golf course. Though Trump is a public figure, and a sitting duck for gossips, he's also one powerful dude. Owen also lays off the infamous Roxanne Pulitzer divorce trial that shook Palm Beach a few years ago. Peter P., Roxanne's ex, is still around.

"I don't want to take the chance of being sued," Owen says. "Sometimes it's better not to use names."

Owen is careful not to stop in front of famous homes to deliver his quickie lectures. He brakes his bicycle three blocks away from the Kennedy estate and merely says it is coming up on the left. Then he leads his group discreetly by. It wouldn't do for Rose Kennedy to catch him peeking through the bars of her front gate.

Owen, who was born in England, lives in working-class Lake Worth, but he makes his living in Palm Beach, and it pays to be discreet. He locates rare books for people who can afford them, and runs a catering business for people who can afford to throw big parties. In the past he has also captained yachts for owners who didn't wish to be bothered, and once was an editor at the *Palm Beach Daily News*, called the Shiny Sheet because its high-quality paper leaves no ink stains on the satin sheets of socialites who breakfast in bed with their favorite journal.

"I didn't last long on the Shiny Sheet," Owen confesses. "I tried to put real news in the paper."

Owen learned his lesson. On his bike tour, he seldom attaches names to the really hot gossip. Pedaling, he points out a home owned by an oft-married woman who is said to be attracted to young men. "At her last wedding, according to reports, she offered a toast to a future husband – who hadn't been born yet." Owen delivers the zinger in a monotone, punctuating the sentence with a dull period instead of a flamboyant exclamation point.

He shows his tourists the modest abode owned by The Island's most successful real estate agent, who sold $22-million in property last year. It features an 18-car garage and a fully operating Italian restaurant for entertaining friends.

"And what I'm going to show you next is not the Second Coming, but I want you to remember it later."

The Not-the-Second-Coming is an eight-foot-high cherry laurel hedge intended to shield a waterfront home from prying, tourist eyes. A moment later, Owen and his tour group glide past a 60-foot-high cherry laurel hedge that surely was manicured by the Jolly Green Giant, or, at the very least, a very brave gardener in a crane.

"Now this is what I call a Palm Beach hedge," Owen explains. "It seems odd that people who spend zillions on their mansions spend zillions on hedges to hide those mansions. But that's Palm Beach."

More Palm Beach fact and legend follow. He says you can tell when King Hussein of Jordan is visiting his Palm Beach home by the dangerous looking men in three-piece suits who stand outside and whisper into walkie talkies.

The owner of another home on the route gave his children $40-million each to get started in life, Owen says, without editorial comment.

Moving along, Owen says that a hippie lived among the fruit trees of this estate until he was hit by a Rolls-Royce while riding a bicycle through town. Next thing anyone knew, the hippie had a one-way, first-class airplane ticket to Hawaii. He didn't have to pay for the ticket himself.

Jack Owen's tour lasts about two hours. Shortly after noon, he leads the parade of cyclists back into the gardens of the Brazilian Court, the hotel where one of the late Robert Kennedy's sons died of a drug overdose. Owen says nothing about the tragedy.

"We don't even use the K word around here," he says.

Daisy's place

The lunchtime crowd sent Daisy Byrd sweating behind the counter, where she tossed on the grill the ground beef patties and onion slices that soon filled the little room with a heavenly aroma.

"You want cheese and tomato on that or what?" Daisy called over her shoulder.

The sweaty guy in the loud Hawaiian shirt said yeah. What the hell. You come to Daisy's place, you get your cheeseburger all the way.

The cheeseburger came on a little paper plate with napkins. The drink came in a can. You want a cup, go to the McDonald's in town. Nothing is fancy about Daisy's place, a dilapidated fish camp-restaurant called the Bridge Shack on Ringling Causeway in Sarasota County. It was built by J.J. Crowley in 1929, a year after the bridge was constructed over New Pass, and it looks its age. The old fish camp looms crumbling over the water like a haunted house on a cliff.

It was hot outside and even hotter inside the L-shaped room despite fans that moved the heavy air. Daisy and her helpers, Edie and Doris, ran themselves ragged, filling orders, the way they always do. The five lopsided bar stools were taken, as they always are, with hungry fishermen, construction workers and a few red-nosed tourists. There were no available seats at the tables, which rocked to and fro with every elbow because of the uneven plywood floor. The only level spot in the joint was claimed by the Aladdin's Castle pinball machine in back.

"This is a casual place," said Daisy Byrd, 59, who is as casual as her establishment. People accustomed to dining at corporate fast-food franchises sometimes open Daisy's screen door and ask if they can come in without shirt or shoes. Daisy laughs. She tells them they can come in wearing less.

"People come because it's comfortable," she said between grilling burgers. "They can let their hair down here. I tried to make improvements once. Painted the floor green and covered the bar stools and even fixed the roof 'cause I ran out of pots to catch the leaks. People gave me hell. They wanted it back the way it was."

Sometime soon the moment dreaded by Daisy and her customers will arrive. Soon, Daisy will say goodbye to her friends and turn off for good the hamburger grill that made her famous. Then she will leave the Bridge Shack – a Sarasota County landmark – before the bulldozers roll in.

Progress.

A new bridge, necessary to service growing Longboat Key, is needed because of heavy traffic. Daisy's place is located on the right-of-way and is owned by the state.

"I knew it was coming," said Daisy Byrd, who began managing the fish camp with her late husband Dan in 1946. "I psyched myself to prepare, but I'll miss it. How can you spend thirty-six years in a place and not miss it?"

Progress. And there's nothing anybody can do about it.

Daisy and her lawyer drove to Bartow to talk to the Department of Transportation people, but the news was just as Daisy expected. Daisy's late husband Dan had somehow forgotten to get a lease for the fish camp. They didn't have any rights at all, they were told. They were squatters on DOT property.

Dan and Daisy were that kind of folk. They didn't pay a whole lot of attention to paperwork. Married in 1941 in Tennessee, they moved to the Panama Canal because they wanted to live where it was warm. It was there that Daisy got her nickname. She is an attractive woman now, but she was considered a knockout then, with her blond hair and short shorts and bare feet. People told Blanche Byrd she looked like Daisy Mae in the funny papers.

When World War II ended, they moved to Florida, where the fishing was good and the climate mild. They found paradise at the fish camp at New Pass Bridge. For $80 a month they lived at the camp and worked the drawbridge while Dan got to fish.

What a fishing hole it must have been. One glance at the yellow pictures on the back wall reveals as much. There are pictures of Dan with giant cobia and jewfish caught at the bridge. Dan, gone four years now, loved his fishing. His mind went bad, Daisy says, and he took his own life. The fishing pictures are what remain of him.

"I never did much fishing," said Daisy, who sells frozen bait, bobbers and beef jerky from a busy counter. "Never cared for it. But I sold so much tackle and talked to so many fishermen I ended up knowing something about it."

Although uncomfortable on the water, she is an expert in the kitchen. The Daisyburger, as some customers call it, has made her famous in Sarasota County.

"I don't do anything fancy," she explained, drinking iced tea. "All I do is use a lot of TLC – tender loving care. I use good, fresh meat and fresh ingredients. Good Swiss cheese. No wilted lettuce or onions. I never slice the tomatoes 'til right before I put them on the bun. Lot of these places, they cut their tomatoes too soon."

Daisy's burger fame extends beyond the beery fishermen who use the bridge. Publications have dispatched writers to sample her fare. Rave reviews have generally followed. Some of those yellowed clippings hang on Daisy's warping walls, next to the sting ray barbs and wild hog tusks and the paper sign that says, *Eat a live toad first thing in the morning and nothing worse can happen to you the rest of the day.*

"It's been a good place," Daisy said the other day, after the luncheon crush. "It never got us rich, but it gave us enough to get by."

Daisy will retire soon, a little earlier than she hoped, but she has plans. She's got a place to live in Sarasota and intends to travel some. Her future, she hopes, is bright.

That can't be said for the Bridge Shack, the place she spent most of her life and raised two good children and loved a husband. The Bridge Shack will come down soon. Customers are already bidding for the bar stools and the grill.

By summer, people who want a decent cheeseburger will be out of luck.

Daisy will be gone.

Daisy went out of business during late 1982; her Bridge Shack came tumbling down in early 1983.

Henry's butterflies

Creeping through his backyard on his knees, Henry Swanson stalks butterflies. It is tough going, what with a cup of honey water in one hand and the forefinger of the other hand extended and dripping honey, but the man has found his personal Nirvana. He is feeding butterflies and all is right in the world.

Bees hover and light upon his hands. He brushes them aside. Leaves cling to his bare knees. He ignores the leaves. A red admiral butterfly is poised on the lawn, and Henry Swanson, God willing, is going to sneak as close as he can.

"I get pretty excited," he says, finally close enough to offer his dripping finger to the red and brown insect that coyly opens and shuts its wings a half-inch away.

Swanson is 62, and to hear him tell it, butterflies have saved his life. Retired, he used to have an important and stressful job. For three decades he was the agriculture agent in one of Florida's fastest growing places. In Orange County, which contains Orlando and Winter Park and Disney World, Swanson believed part of his job was warning people about the perils of growth. This, it turned out, was harder than he thought.

He told people that quality of life is directly dependent on a healthy environment. He told farmers how they would eventually lose their land to development. He gave speeches warning that Florida will become a desert if water is managed poorly. Few people wanted to hear his talk of doom, though, so Swanson worried himself sick instead. Among other things, he developed ulcers and insomnia.

Then he discovered butterflies. The ulcer is under control. A pillow feels good under his head again. Life is better.

"I think God sent me those butterflies," he says.

For eight years he has fed them in his backyard. He talks to them and photographs them. He believes they are intelligent. He wears a butterfly patterned shirt when he makes speeches about them. When a speech means an overnight trip, Henry Swanson arranges for a neighbor to watch his butterflies, and calls long distance for a report. These and other confessions are contained within the 74 pages of his book, *Butterfly Revelations*.

It is one of those books filled with exclamation points, but that's the way Henry Swanson even talks about his butterflies. If he doesn't watch himself, he gushes. Butterflies fill him with a sense of wonder! They make him want to share his pleasure with the world! Isn't it great the Florida Legislature declared April as Save the Butterfly Month!

What is it about butterflies to make Henry Swanson go on like this? Well, Swanson's butterflies are wild creatures, not trained dolphins from Sea World. His red admirals can come and go as they please, and it has pleased them to visit his yard almost daily since 1977.

The reasons are unclear, but Swanson finds them fun to think about. What is it about his yard? It must be something – butterflies don't daily visit the neighbors. Are butterflies directed to his Norfolk Avenue home by the 20-foot wide sunbeam that cuts through the laurel oaks and strikes his lawn every afternoon? Or is it the honey he spreads on his fingers or on the white lawn chair?

Do red admirals that feed in his yard pass on the information genetically to their offspring? He thinks they do. Freshly hatched butterflies are always showing up. How do they find out about the nightly honey banquet? And why no visits by other kinds of butterflies?

"It's hard to prove anything," he says. On the other hand, entomologists for years have followed the 2,000-mile migrations of monarch butterflies from New England to Mexico. Ornithologists get misty eyed talking about the swallows that return yearly to Capistrano. How do homing pigeons home? How do sea turtles find their way back to natal beaches? The natural world is filled with many wonders.

Henry Swanson witnesses wonders almost daily. Depending on the season and sunlight, his butterflies flap erratically out of the sky, circle his yard, then land on the chair, the ground, or even Henry. Although he neglected to keep records until 1977, the saga began in 1976, when a butterfly landed on the head of his grandson. Henry and his wife laughed. Imagine. Of all places to land. A baby's head.

Henry Swanson began studying up on butterflies. The red admiral, he learned, is a common butterfly of the northern hemisphere. It is about two inches across at the widest point and dark brown in color, with white blotches at wingtips, red bands on the forewings and red borders on the hindwings. It breeds twice a year, the female laying eggs on thistle leaves. The egg hatches into a caterpillar, which spins a chrysalis, the cocoon from which the insect later emerges as a butterfly. Then it apparently goes looking for Henry Swanson.

The butterflies came at a good time for him, at the end of a long public-service career of which he had become weary. Swanson was born in West Palm Beach, graduated from the University of Florida, and became an Orange County extension agent at a time when agriculture was still king. But over the years things changed, and Swanson is one who says the change was not for the better. He predicted the end to Central Florida's peaceful agrarian way of life.

"I felt like Paul Revere. I wanted to yell, 'Growth is coming! Growth is coming!' Why tell a farmer how to spray his crops if there's going to be no land to grow crops on in the future?"

When Walt Disney World opened in 1971, the whole county exploded with growth. Dairies, ranches and citrus groves were sold at high profits to developers who built shopping centers, homes and condominiums. Swanson even wrote a book about what happened, called *Countdown for Agriculture in Orange County*.

"I had an ulcer. I couldn't sleep. It felt like my hair was on end all of the time," he says.

Then butterflies arrived, and the metamorphosis of Henry Swanson began. He retired in 1978. *Butterfly Revelations* was published in 1979. He has sold more than 2,500 copies and donated $8,000 in profits to his church, which seems right to him, since he believes a higher power sent butterflies to calm him down.

When thoughts of environmental disaster depress him, Swanson has his butterflies to comfort and amuse him. Sometimes there are as many as 10 at once. Red admirals, he says, are so aggressive they will chase a bird or an airplane shadow. The birds and airplanes are unaware, of course, but what of it? And some drink so much honey they become honey drunk and refuse to leave his yard even at dark. Like a thoughtful bartender, Swanson gently nudges them on their way.

Swanson's greatest pleasure is introducing friends and strangers to the pleasures of butterflies. What time is it? It is 4:00 o'clock. The butterflies should be here any minute, he tells the skeptics squatting in his yard. Four o'clock arrives. No butterflies. A minute later they do show up, and Henry Swanson breathes easier.

Some people, watching Henry Swanson feeding butterflies, are delighted. Some are frightened. Like what is this? Black magic? In the face of Henry Swanson and his honey-trained butterflies, some people lose the power to reason.

Take what happened on a Saturday morning early in Swanson's butterfly career. He was working in the front yard when he watched a car park across the street. The people who climbed out were wearing Sunday clothes and carrying Bibles. Henry Swanson is a religious man himself, but he had been working hard and felt too sweaty and tired to receive missionaries. He quickly retired to his backyard.

There he saw a butterfly. Grabbing his honey, he knelt before it. He was kneeling and feeding it, totally absorbed, when the two Bible-carrying women found him. Embarrassed, Swanson explained about butterflies. Now they looked embarrassed. When he told them how the Lord had sent him butterflies, the missionaries excused themselves and departed.

"They never offered me any literature or even told me the purpose of their visit," Henry Swanson says.

God works in mysterious ways.

An old-time gas station

WILDWOOD   **3/24/91**

Used to be you could have a grand time when you drove around Florida. Why, you were likely to pass just about anything from a gospel revival tent to a big old alligator creeping across the road. And when you stopped for gas, then the real fun began.

Gas stations in old-time Florida were more than places to buy fuel. They were often country stores, roadside zoos and gossip centers rolled into one. While a pimply juvenile delinquent pumped petrol into your chariot, you gabbed with the grease-stained mechanic and then walked out back to admire the rattlesnake pit.

In old-time Florida, gas stations had it all.

Well, as you might have noticed, Florida has gotten modern. And so have the "service stations." In their sameness, they have become as dull as our homogenous shopping malls and restaurants.

Most are air-conditioned inside. Most don't even have mechanics. Some charge you for air. In the big ones along the interstate, you can often buy yogurt and lottery tickets from clerks with manicured nails. And some of these modern "service station" restrooms look as if they are scrubbed two, maybe three times a day.

It's not right, I tell you. It's just not right.

In old-time Florida, even gas station restrooms were an adventure, with their overflowing johns, suspiciously grimy seats and lack of toilet paper. Now, hell's bells, even the toilets are boring.

But I am happy to tell you that there is one area that is keeping Florida's old-time gas station tradition alive.

Here in North Florida, in the town of Wildwood, where I-75 meets the Florida Turnpike, where semi-trailers howl, where the speed limit is only a rumor, you can stop for gasoline, get a peek at baby alligators, buy a nice bullwhip, think about acquiring a swell shell lamp for your favorite aunt, gulp a couple of hard-boiled eggs and then rush for a restroom that might make you a tad nervous, depending on how you feel about cigarette butts floating in the wash bowl.

Ah.

Real gas stations live.

"Most people, they're mind-boggled when they come in here," said Debbie Farkus, owner of the Texaco A Day in the Country Trading Post just off I-75. "They're used to other kinds of places, other kinds of stores. They buy their gas and come in, and well, you can see their eyes get big. This is old-fashioned Florida."

Debbie Farkus grew up in Wildwood, a small town that has always catered to

192

motorists. Every day, according to the Department of Transportation, about 65,000 vehicles rush by on the way to somewhere else. Near the interstate exit, gas stations – the old-fashioned kind – line State Road 44. At just about any of them, you can buy oranges, pecan logs, coconuts, cowboy boots and other treasures you won't unearth at Disney World.

Debbie Farkus' station, with $700,000 in inventory, is the largest and most colorful. You know that the moment you pull up. Giant horns from Texas steers hang from the outside walls. There are totem poles, carved by sensitive artists with chain saws. There is a life-sized, cigar-store style Indian sitting on a chair next to a bin of oranges. And there is the sign few tourists can resist:

Live Baby Gators.

Well, there is one baby gator, a two-footer, in an aquarium, under a sign that warns: *Do Not Put Hands In Alligator Tank. He Bites.*

"He's the drawing card around here," said Ms. Farkus, who has gotten used to alligators during her 37 years in Florida and seems a bit mystified about what all the fuss is about.

"But I'll tell you. People like everything about gators."

She buys alligator products from area alligator farmers. At her old-time gas station, you can buy alligator skulls, alligator claw back scratchers and alligator teeth necklaces. Animal lovers might complain that selling alligator parts is tacky, but old-time Florida was a tacky place.

"People like our snake products, too," said Ms. Farkus. She sells belts. She sells hats. Hand over $400 in cash, and you'll go home wearing a cowboy hat made from rattlesnake hide. She'll sell you a stuffed raccoon for $250.

"You'd be surprised who buys what," she said. "People you wouldn't expect to buy something like a shell lamp – rich people – will buy a bunch of shell lamps. People'll buy anything that looks like Florida to them."

They buy cans of "Genuine Florida Sunshine." They take home bags of "Florida Sand." They claw for their wallets the moment their eyes behold the glory of cypress stump clocks.

"And I have what has to be the largest collection of turquoise anywhere."

The old-time gas station owner also peddles a passel of "I survived a Shark Attack" T-shirts and "Daddy Went Fishin' And All I Got Was This Lousy Hat" baseball caps. Near the cash register, not far from the cypress knee carved gnomes and paintings of Plains Indians, are the *Jesus!* license plates. Two steps away, customers can pick up a couple of the aerosol cans that contain Bull---- Repellent. How Great Thou Art meets Great Balls of Fire.

But that's how old-time Florida, and the Deep South, have always been. It celebrates the holy and the hell raiser at the same time, often in the same place. It's nice to find that a little piece of history still exists, even if you find it at a gas station.

Down the road, on U.S. 301, I stopped at another Texaco Trading Post, the one that advertised "Claxton Fruit Cakes." I was in no mood for fruitcake, but my stomach was growling like an old she bear.

I had a fine lunch. If you're in the neighborhood, I recommend the hard-boiled eggs and pickled sausage.

In search of solitude

Alone.

I'm riding my bicycle on an isolated beach in the Florida Panhandle. It's a wilderness preserve within St. Joseph Peninsula State Park. Shells are crunching beneath my tires, and the horseshoe crabs are scuttling along the tidal line. I haven't seen another human being in an hour. Haven't heard a human voice except my own.

I'm alone, as alone as you can get in real Florida, and it's a strange feeling. I'm frightened and exhilarated at the same time.

I love seeing nothing taller than a pine and hearing nothing noisier than a screeching osprey. The only visible building is 10 miles across St. Joe's Bay. The nearest telephone is six miles away at the park office.

Alone.

I sing an old Marvin Gaye tune to the rufous-sided towhees chirping in the palmetto thickets. I can sing it as loudly as I want and nobody – nobody – can tell me to pipe down. Ah, solitude.

I am also a city boy, a city boy who likes his comforts, a city boy who, despite himself, is nervous about being completely alone in the wilderness of Florida. What if the raw oysters I ate for lunch give me hepatitis? What if I suffer an attack of pancreatitis? What if my lungs clog with sarcoidosis? Or, more likely, what if I fall off my bike and bust a collarbone?

Who will bring me morphine? A turkey vulture? I forgot to tell my wife and kids where I was going and when I would return.

I've canoed and hiked in the Everglades, and got lost briefly on several occasions. I was nervous when it happened, but I was close to a trail, accompanied by other people, and confident that nothing would happen other than an adventure. Here, in wilderness solitude, it's me, myself and I.

In Florida, there aren't many places left to get lost in. The Everglades and the Green Swamp, I suppose, could swallow up a person who forgot to tell where he or she was going. The Ocala, Osceola and Apalachicola national forests might lose a solitary hiker or two. I probably could get lost in Tosahatchee State Preserve if I had to. But probably not. Florida has been tamed. I hum another bar from Marvin Gaye.

Stop the concert! Tracks on the beach!

Raccoons. You can see where they walked to the water to – what do raccoons do at the water? Do they wash food before eating? Maybe, but not in salt water. A mystery. Well, perhaps not. Here are the scattered legs of fiddler crabs. The raccoon was probably on a fishing trip.

I wish I had my fishing pole. About a 7-foot spinning outfit, equipped with 8-pound test monofilament line and a TT MirrOlure with a green back and speckles, would be perfect. I could wade out to where the grass starts, where the water deepens, and plug for spotted sea trout. You throw the MirrOlure out, let it lie briefly, and work it in slowly. The idea is to make the plug look like an injured fish. Big fish eat small injured ones. In nature, nothing injured ever survives.

Thoreau recommended that everyone learn to hunt and fish, because hunting and fishing taught important lessons about nature. He also expected people to give up hunting and fishing when lessons were learned. Sometimes I am sure my days as a predator are behind me. Other times I long for a fishing pole, a MirrOlure, and a good teacher.

I like wading. I like to feel the warm water slide past my ankles and knees to my waist. Wading, you feel as if you are entering the womb of the Earth. You also become a potential member of the food chain. What happens if a shark swims up behind you in that wilderness water and bites a chunk out of your left calf? You bleed to death in solitude.

Alone.

Thinking of lacerated calves, I climb aboard my bike. The tires are fat, but they still sink into the sand. I am in the lowest of 15 gears, pedaling hard, and barely moving. Ahead, a hawk – I think it's a red-shouldered hawk, though I could be wrong – flies along the beach. It doesn't fly over water. Hawks don't like flying over water. They know their limitations, too.

What's that? Farther ahead, 200 or 300 yards at most, an animal trots off the beach and into the woods. I've seen tracks of deer and fox. I pedal as fast as I can – and my bicycle computer says I'm going 4.5 mph – to the spot. There's a path, made not by the feet of humans but by paws and hooves of animals. It goes through the spartina grass, over the dune, past the sabal palms and into the pine forest beyond.

I leave the bicycle on the beach and follow tracks. They are unclear, but I think they are made by a fox. Climbing the dune, I skulk into the forest. Then I stop and suck on my hand.

When I was a boy, I read in *Field and Stream* about how you can attract foxes and bobcats by imitating the sound made by a distressed rabbit. Sucking on your hand, the author advised, approximates a wailing rabbit and brings in the predators.

The glorious results of a misspent youth.

"Help me! Help me!" my rabbit/hand squeals. Blue jays and squirrels, apparently aggravated by the ridiculous sucking sounds, raise an unholy racket.

I wipe my soggy hand and press on, press on into the woods for two, maybe three minutes. My God, the forest is lovely. I adore pines. I adore palmettos. I adore the idea that I don't have to share these woods with anyone.

Then I start thinking about my favorite childhood movie, Walt Disney's *20,000 Leagues Under the Sea*. Remember when Captain Nemo allows Ned Land a visit to a tropical island, warning him to stay on the beach? "Cannibals," Nemo says, "live in the jungle."

Within one, maybe two minutes, I'm back on the beach, on my bicycle, heading toward my air-conditioned rental cabin, thinking about what can happen to solitary adventurers who forget their limitations.

Like many city-born baby boomers, I'm a college-educated specialist. I'm good at my work, but don't ask me to hammer a nail, unclog a toilet or survive in the wilderness. I'm more comfortable in the woods than most city people – I love to hike, cycle, canoe, fish, bird-watch and look at wild flowers – but I would hate to depend on my own resources in an emergency. I don't think I can build a fire by rubbing together two sticks. What side of the tree does moss grow on?

Search me.

And what should I do in case of snakebite?

If something bad happened, while I was alone, I don't know if I could get back in one piece. The only thing I know I could do, for sure, is write a lucid account of my last hours.

"To whoever finds me," I'd scrawl into my official reporter's notebook, and go on to relate the sad story of my demise.

"The driftwood I thought would make a dandy walking stick turned out to be a sun-bathing eastern diamondback rattlesnake. The fangs got me once on the forearm, when I picked up the snake, and once on the buttocks, when I tried to run away. I was able to suck the poison out of my arm, but I haven't figured a way to suck the snake venom from my own bleeding backside.

"Wish you were here."

summer

Summer bludgeons and caresses

ST. PETERSBURG   6/24/87

"Here in Florida," Marjorie Kinnan Rawlings once wrote, "the seasons move in and out like nuns in soft clothing, making no rustle in their passing."

That certainly is true of fall, winter and spring in Florida, and it even may be true of summer if you live, as Rawlings did, on Cross Creek near two lakes in a cool cracker house under shady oaks. But I suspect literary license in her beautiful words. When Rawlings had to work outside in the summer, I'll bet she swore like a sailor.

The summers I have known in Florida did not come like nuns in soft clothing. Summer comes like a barroom bully, kicking open the door and breaking a beer bottle on your head. Our longest season, summer stays and stays and stays. Last year it said hello in May and didn't wave goodbye until early December.

The sun beats down hard enough to give headaches, and the heat sucks the air out of our lungs. Collars wilt followed by the will to do anything but sit in the air conditioning.

Thunderstorms and hurricanes remind us of the power of nature and our own fragile existence. Ferocious mosquitoes, kept at bay by a mild winter and spring, are renewed by the summer rains and sample our flesh every time we step out-of-doors to light our barbecues. Our dogs have fleas.

Afternoon rains and nighttime humidity act like tonic on our lawns, and many of us mark summer's arrival and departure by its effect on our grass. Summer is the season in which we are forced to battle our lawns every week.

I cut the grass last week, and I'll cut it again this week. I will fortify myself with cereal, oranges and coffee, and cover my neck, arms and legs with sunscreen, and then I'll walk outside and confront the bane of summer — the lawnmower.

I will add oil to the lawnmower and wipe my hands on my pants. I will add gasoline to the lawnmower and spill some on my shoes. After five hearty pulls that threaten to dislocate my shoulder, and as many Anglo-Saxon swear words as I can muster, the lawnmower will sputter and die.

Maybe I won't have to mow after all, I will think, and then tug the starter cord once more for good luck.The lawnmower will roar with good health. I will mow. It will take an hour out of my life today and an hour out of my life next week and an hour every week until summer ends in six months, but I will mow.

In summer, lawns spring eternal.

Yet there are cures for the blues of summer – if you are brave enough to leave the cool of your house to find them.

We find relief in swimming pools, lakes and springs in Florida. The beach is poor in summer, because the sand is too hot and the salt stings the skin, but a dip in fresh water is as refreshing as a kiss from a small child.

Springs are especially so. In Florida, spring water, bubbling from deep inside the earth, averages about 70 degrees. Walk in, a step at a time, if you dare, but it's easier to get a running start and jump. The cold will take the breath away.

Going barefoot in the summer will help you stay cool and transport you to earlier, innocent days.The trick is to pick your times. Mornings are best. Walk outside for the paper in bare feet and the wet grass will wake you.

Don't walk barefoot on pavement in the summer. The pavement is hot enough to burn your feet through flip-flops. Mirages, looking like ponds, rise ahead as you drive the interstate. When the afternoon rains arrive, mirages turn to steam.

If there's any kind of breeze, the coolest place to be is on the water. I canoe.

In summer, as I canoe, I watch for blue crabs. You can catch them in shallow water on a string tied to a chicken neck, and boil them and eat them, but I'd rather look. Blue crabs are delicious, but boiling crabs raises the temperature in what may already be a hot kitchen, and peeling crabs is work. I prefer to poke at them with my paddle and watch them raise their pinchers like boxing gloves. When I was a boy, a blue crab grabbed my ankle and drew blood.

I usually bring my fishing rod when I canoe. Absorbed with fishing, I don't notice the heat as much. In the summer, the shallows of Tampa Bay are filled with palm-sized pinfish. They are accomplished bait stealers, and you should be careful when unhooking them. They extend their spines like needles. So do saltwater catfish. Their spines are coated with a toxin that is painful if you are careless and get pricked.

When I catch catfish, I use pliers to unhook them, and throw them back in the water before they can do damage. The best way to avoid catfish and pinfish is not to catch them in the first place. Instead of natural bait fished on the bottom, where sluggish catfish dine during summer, I use a fast-swimming lure they can't easily catch.

I employ something called a Love Lure, a rubber-tailed doohickey that must look like a super-charged live shrimp to a trout. Paddle across the shallows to the edge of a deep hole and anchor. Cast your Love Lure into the hole and start reeling. If a trout is home, he'll usually bite.

A trout is good to eat, though in summer the flesh turns mushy if you don't put it on ice quickly enough. But some finicky eaters won't eat a summer trout – period. Summer trout, I should warn you, often contain worms in their flesh. A biologist once told me the reason, but I have forgotten. Trout worms, which look like tiny pieces of string, are harmless when cooked, but I still flick them out with the tip of my fillet knife for the sake of appearances.

In the summer, I usually fillet my trout under the orange tree in the back yard because of the shade. I'm a poor fish filleter, but I can get by if I don't have to do too many fish, which usually is no problem. I remove fillets from each trout and put them in a bowl of ice. Then I walk out into the yard and dig a hole.

I bury trout carcasses in my yard, partly to spare the nostrils of the man who picks up the garbage, but mostly because trout carcasses make fine fertilizer.

Trout carcasses make grass grow green and lush.

Trout carcasses give you and your lawnmower something to do for the rest of summer.

200

Growing up

"I am haunted by waters."
– from Norman Maclean's *A River Runs Through It.*

It begins early when you grow up in Florida, where salt water laps at the mangrove-covered shoreline only a block from home. One morning, while you play with toys on the living room floor, your dad wakes early, sips his coffee and asks the fateful question.

"Want to go fishing?"

Outside, the sun beats down so hard that Key West should be black and blue. But the heat means nothing. You are five years old, and you have seen those little gray fish swimming near the pilings, and you would like to look at them close, maybe hold one in your hand. Of course you want to go fishing. You put away your toys and take a small step into another world. With your dad.

He is a pianist who once fronted a small orchestra that cut demo records and played big band music in modest Chicago nightclubs. He called himself "Ernie Bergen" and wrote some of his own material, including *Candy Girl* about the candy saleswoman who later became his wife, my mom.

Now he is 35, and the music career dream is about over. In Key West, he plays piano in a scary joint on the waterfront, and his audience is drunken tourists and grizzled shrimpers just back from the Dry Tortugas. Broken beer bottles are jabbed at exposed jugulars. Calloused fists split sunburned lips. The balding man at the baby grand smiles and attacks only the keyboards.

Don't shoot him – he's only the piano player. The best dad a boy could have.

He borrows a skiff and we fish with cut bait for little gray snappers. I use a cane pole and he employs a heavy conventional rod and reel better suited for huge grouper. His night work means we have afternoons free for fishing, so we spend hours dangling mullet chunks from bridges and seawalls. He teaches me how to bait my hook and how to unhook a snapper without being pricked by fins. He unhooks the catfish, which have venomous spines, and he does not complain when my hook snags on the bottom.

We bring home long stringers of tiny snapper for mom to admire. She still has the photograph, yellowed with age.

Twenty-nine years later, I am driving through the Keys with my own wife and children. At the Baltimore Oyster House, I turn north off U.S. 1 and head for the bridge that connects Big Pine with tiny No Name Key. I tell Peter, my seven-year-old, that the modern, concrete span is still called Old Wooden Bridge.

"It's not wood, Dad," he says, as he and his oldest sister fish from the bridge for small sharks.

"It used to be. When I was a little boy, it was all wood and you had to watch where you stepped because the wood was rotten and would break."

"Did you fall in?" he asks. He already has noted the presence of large barracuda.

"No. We were careful. But we used to fish here a lot. My dad and brother and I used to catch good fish here."

"Do you miss Grandpa?" Peter asks.

"A whole lot."

Biscayne Bay, which separates Miami and Miami Beach, was a wonderful fishing hole in the 1950s. Development and pollution had not turned our part of the bay into the cesspool I sometimes think it is today.

We lived in a small frame house two blocks from a canal that led to the bay. Dad, who had quit the music business because he could not support his family, had taken a job managing the kitchens at a famous Miami Beach hotel.

It was about as close to show business as he could find. Once, up close, he saw Frank Sinatra, who dropped by the Fontainebleau Hotel kitchen to compliment the chef on the chicken cacciatore. One afternoon, in the Boom Boom Room, he sat to play the white grand piano for a small audience that included several dishwashers, busboys, waiters and a familiar-looking stranger who wore a lot of jewelry. "Mr. Ernie, he play good," announced the Cuban dishwasher. Liberace nodded.

Dad worked six days a week; on Saturdays we fished.

We had no boat – two weeks of seasickness aboard a World War II ship curbed his desire to own one – but you needed no boat to catch fish in those days. A boy and his dad needed two spinning rods, eight-pound-test line, some hooks, a bucket of live shrimp, a rope stringer and a piece of rocky shoreline that yielded fish.

"Get the net! Get the net!" he yelled one morning as he fought a large pompano to shore. Instead of scooping his prize, I pounced upon it as a lepidopterist might net a butterfly. The line popped like a firecracker.

He did not swear. We caught more fish. All was forgiven.

I would like to believe my life was shaped by those hours we spent on the water together. From him I learned an appreciation for nature that guides my life today. Not that he was prone to philosophizing like Robert Young in *Father Knows Best*. My dad was what people might call the strong, silent type. I often told him he would make a terrible interview. Like Fess Parker in *Davy Crockett*, my first hero, he was quiet until provoked, choosing to lead by example.

Offended by cowardice, he once grabbed a teen-aged hoodlum by the collar and recovered sunglasses stolen from my best friend. On another occasion, he jumped into his car and chased two men who had robbed a convenience store. Only later did he learn gunshots had been fired at him.

On occasion his anger was directed toward his oldest son. There were times, when I was growing up, that our relationship was less than sweet. My grades were poor, my hair too long, my hours too late, my radio too loud, my tongue too sharp.

But on Saturdays we were fishing companions, united by a common purpose.

Catching fish was our goal, I suppose, but I like to think our fishing turned into something more important. From fishing, I learned to appreciate nature in ways other members of the television generation could not. For a few hours on Saturdays I was a participant in a complex system that included the sun, moon, tides, minnows, shrimp, snapper. You wanted to catch a snapper, you had to think as a predator.

Fishing sharpened the senses.

The snapper bit today and not last Saturday, dad might explain, because a rising tide allowed the fish to come into the shallows, where our baits could reach them where they hid under the rocks. The full moon pulls on the water kind of like a magnet pulling a paper clip and creates the high tide we want. The fish stay in this area because of the mangroves. When the leaves fall, they start to rot on the bottom. Tiny sea animals show up to eat them. Crabs show up to eat the tiny animals, and snapper come to eat the crabs. It's like the House That Jack Built.

My dad was as smart as Davy Crockett.

When I was 14, we began making monthly trips to the Keys. What a paradise it was. From shore you could catch a five-pound snapper on one cast, and a three-foot barracuda on the next. From any bridge you could see 100-pound tarpon and 25-pound jack crevalle. On shallow water flats you could see the tails of feeding bonefish when they suddenly stopped swimming and began grubbing for crabs.

"It was beautiful, Bea," he would tell mom upon our return. "God, it was beautiful." The phrase became a family cliche.

But even then, in the early 1960s, the odor of irresponsible development was in the air. Dredge and fill, mangrove destruction and "No trespassing" signs ruined Key Largo for us. We headed west, down the Keys, to look for new fishing holes.

We eventually settled on Big Pine, about 30 miles from Key West. Camping during vacations, we caught hundreds of snapper and small sharks, and got our first good looks at diminutive Key deer, which have adapted to the harsh environment and grow no larger than German shepherd dogs. When we had to go home, my seven-year-old brother cried.

The long-distance call in 1982 reached me as I was finishing a column at the newspaper where I work. The caller was Marty, my brother. His ordinarily cheerful voice was choked with emotion. As he spoke, I could feel blood draining from my face.

"It's about dad," Marty said. "He went to see Dr. White yesterday because he thought he had a strained muscle in his side, but Dr. White said his spleen was enlarged and sent him to the VA Hospital for tests. They think dad has leukemia."

The last eight months of his life were spent mostly in the hospital. Each chill was a crisis. Fevers lasted weeks. Chemotherapy gave him strange rashes. Diarrhea sapped his strength and robbed him of dignity. His depression was total.

"He won't fight at all," Mom said. "That's what scares me."

His lack of fight was frightening and bewildering. I was frightened for him, and, I know now, my own mortality. I wanted him to give us all courage, but he could not. Never very good about articulating his feelings, he would not discuss the possibility of his own death; his father's son, I was too uncomfortable to ask. Instead, we talked baseball, music and fishing, and it was comforting to us both.

When I told him how much his grandchildren – Kristin, Peter and Katie – enjoyed fishing, the sparkle returned, briefly, to his eyes. He was pleased.

Three days before he died, I dressed him and brought him home from the hospital. He wept when he saw the children, who initially were frightened by his sickly appearance. But later, they warmed to dad, who expressed approval when Peter walked into the house to show off a small bream he had caught in the canal on a doughball.

"Look what I caught, grandpa."

"Nice fish," said my dad. Two days later, at the age of 64, he was dead.

The Keys, when I vacationed there last month, had changed much from when I was a boy. US 1 from Key Largo to Marathon is a 50-mile nightmare of fast-food joints, shopping centers and obnoxious billboards. Papa Hemingway, who always tried to be the man's man, would hardly recognize Key West, its streets filled with flower children and business slicksters who now stuff time-sharing condominium literature into the hands of tourists. Big Pine, always my dad's favorite, is changing at a slower place, but it's probably destined to become just another generic Florida city.

"See that canal?" I ask my children. "My dad and your Uncle Marty and I used to catch huge snapper in that canal. It was unbelievable."

A "No Trespassing" sign now guards the canal.

"We caught a real big grouper in that canal. Somebody used to keep a dolphin in a pen."

A house on stilts now sits on the site.

"Remember when that German lady came up to kick us out of there?" asks my brother Marty from the back seat. "Dad heard her accent and answered in German."

My dad, who spoke four languages, talked the German lady into letting us stay. I speak no German and don't remember where the German woman lived.

"Remember when dad waded into the water to net the grouper?" Marty continues, "and the big barracuda came up..."

I finish the story.

"When dad saw that barracuda he jumped out of the water like a missile launched by a submarine."

We giggle at the memory.

After a while, time does heal some of the wounds. Thinking back on the 33 years I was privileged to known him, I am comforted now by memories of our happy moments together, which finally have begun to replace the horror of the final months.

Sometimes, usually in late afternoon, when the light is soft and I listen to the sweet, high voices of my own small children as they catch pinfish or crabs, the memories come back with startling clarity. I see my children, and see the ghosts of myself, and my brother, and my dad, as we once were, fishing, so long ago.

Made in the shade

Up here in the country, smart folks appreciate a good shade tree. Just take a gander at Tim Johnston. Driving along Great Oaks Drive here in Citrus County, an hour from Tampa's bustle, he slows his ancient Chevy Nova, cranes his neck at an impossible angle, weaves briefly into the wrong lane, and stops dead in the road.

"Look at that one!" he says, pointing. What has caught his attention is a tree known as a live oak, one big enough to hide an entire back yard. Its lowest branches are so heavy they come close to scraping the ground. The tree top seems almost tall enough to threaten any passing Piper Cub. The shade is as inviting as your granddaddy's old swimming hole.

"That's as pretty an oak as I think you'll find," says Johnston, and his foot taps the gas pedal once more.

Johnston, 53, is crazy about good shade trees. He works for Citrus County as the horticulture extension agent, and when people have questions about trees and other plants, Johnston is the person they ask. He puts on seminars from one end of the county to the other, answers telephone calls and even has a TV show. Whenever he has the chance, he talks up the value of big, shady trees.

Citrus County is probably the West Florida capital of shade trees, especially oaks. Though development is happening quickly, more than 60 percent of the county's 629 square miles still is shaded by trees. Pinellas, where I live, has lost 84 percent of its forest to houses, shopping centers and pavement. It is also as hot as Hades.

But Citrus seems cooler. And prettier. Thanks to its trees, the county has what must be the most beautiful road in Florida. The one-mile section of State Road 48 that leads into tiny Floral City is lined by 85 behemoth oaks that were planted only two decades after Robert E. Lee surrendered at Appomattox in 1865. Driving on the quiet two-lane byway is like slipping through an oaken tunnel into the past.

"If you want to get killed around here," says Tim Johnston, "just do something to these trees. People love them."

Citrus County's road department gives State Road 48's prize oaks a careful pruning from time to time. The Floral Garden Club of Floral City watches over such projects with a stern eye. Recently, club members planted some young oaks to take the place of the few that are getting long of tooth. Four times a year, the club also picks up litter along the road. In the shade, it's a small chore.

"The Florida summer, in my opinion, is a good introduction to hell," Johnston says. "But our county is a lot cooler than, say, a city like St. Petersburg. We don't have all those buildings. We have trees."

Shade.

Florida natives such as Johnston seem to be born with a natural love for shade trees. They know shade trees help keep Florida summers bearable, cut down on air-conditioning costs, break up the monotony of having to look at buildings, and provide breathtaking natural beauty. In the dog days of summer, a good shade tree is as refreshing as a sip of homemade lemonade.

But some newcomers to Citrus, and to other counties, know nothing about natural shade. They arrive from Chicago or New York or Miami or some other big city where buildings outnumber trees, and automatically reach for the air conditioner. Who needs shade? They are apt to cut down their trees – if developers haven't done so already.

But not if Tim Johnston can talk to them first.

"I'm not going to change the world," he says, driving on."I have no illusions about that. You can't undo every dad-blamed wrong in the world. But I'll tell you: If you can educate people about saving trees you can do more than all the laws on the books."

Johnston grew up in on the shores of Tampa Bay. He was born in St. Petersburg's Mound Park Hospital, now called Bayfront Medical Center. In the 1940s, he used to hunt in the woods near Big Bayou and fish for trout in adjacent waters.

Across the bayou was Lewis Island. Lewis Island, when Johnston was a boy, had one house and four eagle nests. It also had a cornfield. Johnston's father used to trap raccoons that ate the farmer's corn. Today, Lewis Island is called Coquina Key. Lots of people live there. There are no eagles. There is no cornfield. A good shade tree can be difficult to find.

After high school, Johnston studied biology at the University of the South in Tennessee. "Then I went into the Navy and didn't bother to get out for twenty-one years." When he did get out, his home Pinellas County was too crowded for him.

He moved to rural Citrus and started a nursery, which he says "was an exercise in starvation." He quit the nursery business and went to work for the county. He is glad he did. He likes being an extension agent. He likes talking to people about trees.

"Now that's an oak and hickory hammock," he says, driving past Good Counsel Camp. "The hammock is interspersed with cypress and sweetgum. There's some magnolia, and some laurel oak, but the dominant tree is live oak. We have fine live oaks in the county. Now there's a good hickory! Well, it's not that good. You can see where lightning hit it."

His vehicle, with 99,000 miles on the odometer, creaks around the next bend in the road.

"Now that stuff hanging from the oaks is Spanish moss. Spanish moss is a relative of the pineapple. It gets nourishment from water vapor and windblown nutrient particles. Spanish moss doesn't hurt the trees. Some people don't like Spanish moss. But, hey. It's a free country."

A drive with Tim Johnston goes like that. When he sees something he likes, he points it out. If he sees a chance to educate, he educates. Listen: That canal over there – steamboats used to carry citrus down the canal to the Withlacoochee and on to Yankeetown for shipping to the north. Citrus County, he adds a moment later, no longer has much of a citrus business because of freezes. And the insects known as wood borers, he confides quietly, aren't the problem everybody thinks.

Slowing, he looks to the left and points. A pretty passel of oaks has won his eye.

"Oak hammocks are what we call climax forests," he says. "If we burned everything to the ground and started from scratch, eventually we'd get oak hammocks. But first we'd have grass. After a while, persimmon and pines would come in. The pines would eventually dominate. Then the oaks would come on in. Eventually the oaks would shade out the pines. And then you'd have an oak hammock."

Daniel Boone, who knew his way around the woods, might enjoy chatting with Tim Johnston about oaks and pines and shade. Especially on a Saturday or a Sunday when Tim and his wife, Marlene, have their eight children and seven grandchildren over for barbecue.

Out there on Turner Camp Road, behind his mobile home, he gets his fire going in the barbecue pit and roasts a hunk of deer that he may have hunted himself. And he usually blackens a nice, fat mullet. He prides himself on his blackened fish.

Then Tim Johnston and his family pull up chairs and talk about hunting and fishing, and eat like royalty. Not in the air-conditioned mobile home. Outside, in the shade of Mother Nature's own trees.

The significance of ice

APALACHICOLA 8/23/87

The significance of ice is lost on most people. Or so Willie McNair believes. He is sure that ice is another one of those conveniences modern Floridians take for granted. You want ice, walk over to the freezer and get ice.

"Folks don't give ice a lot of thought," is the way McNair puts it, and he sounds both sad and surprised.

McNair, 30, has given ice a good deal of thought. He is curator of the museum that honors the inventor of the ice machine, the late Dr. John Gorrie of Apalachicola. Consider the question that comes to McNair in the night: What if we had no way of artificially making ice? How would things be different in Florida?

We'll, we'd have to ship ice from Canada or some other freezing locale, the way Florida pioneers did. But what if ice were scarce – or too expensive to ship? Then what?

McNair can tell you what. Our cold drinks would be warm. Much of our food would perish. There would probably be no such thing as summer cookouts. Hangovers induced by drinking warm beer would not be relieved by ice cubes applied to foreheads. There would be no ice cubes.

And would there be modern refrigeration, or modern air conditioning, if somebody first hadn't figured a way to make ice?

No, without the ability to make ice, Willie McNair tells people, there might not be a Florida as we know it. The Sunshine State would deserve to be called the Swelter State.

"Without John Gorrie," McNair says, "things sure'd be different."

Gorrie, McNair will tell you, was one of the world's great unsung inventors. His story is fascinating and ultimately sad. Gorrie lost his money and his health while trying to convince the world of the significance of ice. He died unappreciated.

A physician, Gorrie developed a crude air-conditioning system to cool malaria patients in the 1830s. His system involved using a homemade machine to blow compressed air over ice into hospital rooms.

Gorrie imported his ice from New England, but when shipments were late or in short supply, his patients suffered. One day, probably in 1842, something strange happened to Gorrie's steam-driven air compressor. By mistake, the machine was left running all night. In the morning, ice clung to its pipes. By happy accident, Gorrie had invented an ice machine.

"He got the patent on May 6, 1851," Willie McNair says. "Patent number 8080."

McNair, who never got to go to college, remembers such obscure facts. In the years he has managed the museum for the Department of Natural Resources he has tried to learn all he can about Gorrie and Apalachicola.

In a good year, only about 3,000 people visit the one-room, red-brick building in Apalachicola's historic district. By comparison, about 20,000 people visit Disney World every day, something McNair might not like to admit, except for the fact that Disney World goes through a lot of ice made possible by John Gorrie's invention.

At the John Gorrie Museum, McNair does everything. He takes the small admission charge from visitors. He explains how Gorrie's ice machine worked and shows them a replica. The machine's basic principle is used in modern refrigeration. Gorrie's machine heated gas by compressing it, cooled it by sending it through radiating coils, and then expanded it to lower temperature further.

"The original is in the Smithsonian," McNair says, sounding proud. Then he shows museum visitors a model of Gorrie's air-cooled hospital room and points out the displays about old and new Apalachicola. He asks them to write their names and addresses – and any thoughts about the John Gorrie Museum – into a visitor book. A typical comment is "How interesting! I had no idea."

Gorrie, who was born in Charleston and educated in New York, came to Apalachicola in 1833. He liked the idea of practicing medicine in an exciting seaport city. Cotton, lumber and seafood were important industries in the town of 3,000, but after dark it could be a harrowing place. Not because of the gambling and prostitution that thrived, but because of the hellish mosquitoes that swarmed at dusk out of the marsh.

Nobody knew malaria was a mosquito-borne disease. Gorrie's theory was that malaria was caused by swamp gases. He recommended swamps be filled (an unfortunate way he helped change Florida) and claimed patients could be made comfortable by cooled air.

It took Gorrie almost 10 years to refine his ice machine. Although he had the patent, he said nothing publicly until June 1851, when he told his best friend, botanist Alvan Chapman, "I have made ice."

One month later, Chapman told Gorrie about a banquet to be held that night in the town's largest hotel. The banquet's host was worried about the embarrassing possibility of having to serve guests warm champagne because of a town ice shortage. At the banquet that evening, Gorrie enjoyed his career's shining moment.

"I can see him now," Chapman later wrote. "He was of medium height, with a large head crowning a stout frame, sallow complexion and dark hair and eyes. His countenance was usually serious, vexing to sadness, seldom lighted with a pleasing smile. Never with laughter."

On this night, Gorrie smiled and laughed. He ordered the banquet hall doors opened, and when they were, gave the signal for the waiters to carry in the champagne – champagne covered with ice made by a John Gorrie machine. He was regarded as a worker of miracles.

Gorrie's friends predicted great wealth from his invention, but Gorrie, by most accounts, was an indifferent businessman who cared more about helping to cool the sick. Nevertheless, he went looking for financial support. Finally, in Massachusetts, he found a wealthy backer. Before even one machine could be produced, Gorrie's benefactor died.

Gorrie traveled the country again in search of funding, but he found nobody willing to take a chance. In fact, many considered him a lunatic. One northern newspaper thought it necessary to warn its readers: "A crank called Dr. John Gorrie down in Florida claims he can make ice as good as God Almighty."

Gorrie, with no money and no hope, returned, humiliated, to Apalachicola.

"By then even his friends had turned against him," Willie McNair says today. "He'd been the mayor and he'd founded the church, but I guess maybe they thought he really couldn't make ice in large amounts. Anyway, he shut himself off from the world, stayed in his room, would barely eat, wouldn't see no one. He died a few weeks later on June 29, 1855. They say he had the biggest funeral Apalachicola ever saw. He was 52."

His remains are buried across the street from the museum in a little park. McNair tries to keep the grave neat. He cleans the stone monument that bears the dates of Gorrie's birth and death. McNair says the date of death is wrong on the statue, but there's nothing he can do except tell people the facts and hope they appreciate them.

"Folks say they're glad he invented the ice machine and all," McNair says, "but I don't think they realize that he's responsible for a lot of our modern ways. It's incredible when you think about what ice has meant."

Every day, Willie McNair thinks about John Gorrie, and the significance of ice, and what he would say if the door opened and there stood the doctor.

"I'd say 'Dr. Gorrie, thank God for a man like you.' "

Stuck on sandspurs

ST. PETERSBURG   9/16/90

A lot of people, and I am one, will tell you Florida isn't as good as it used to be. Our state has too many people, and too much traffic and crime. Pollution and development have loused up some of our best woods and waters.

But one thing has improved, thank goodness. We seem to have more sandspurs than ever.

Just about any beach is loaded with the little devils. So are the open, sunny patches of any decent park. Your yard, if it is like mine, is probably home to a good many. Since sandspur plants thrive in disturbed areas, our roadsides are lined with them.

It's fine with me.

Like cockroaches and summer thunderstorms, sandspurs serve as a constant reminder that we have yet to totally conquer natural Florida. We can control mosquitoes, for the most part. We can escape summer by ducking into the air-conditioning.

But take off your shoes, and sooner or later, the tiny spiked flower at the end of a sandspur plant is going to find the most tender part of your foot. And you're going to say ouch.

There is probably nothing wrong with that.

"We need the dark to appreciate the light," David Crewz told me the other day, and I found myself nodding in agreement. "Having sandspurs really makes you appreciate the roses."

Crewz was not knocking sandspurs. He admires them as much as I do. A botanist for the Florida Department of Natural Resources, he is an expert in coastal vegetation. While sandspurs are found throughout Florida, they are most common along the coast. The other day I watched Crewz pluck a sandspur stalk, admire the spiky flower and then bury it. I think he was hoping that more sandspur plants would sprout.

Sandspurs are a member of the grass family, Crewz will tell you. There are 25 varieties throughout the world, and 11 in the United States. Florida has seven species, more than any other state. The most common, usually found near the coast, is *Cenchrus incertus*. A great name for a great plant.

What good are sandspurs?

It's a question I hear from time to time, usually from a new Floridian who has gotten off to a rough start at the beach. "Ah, yes," I say, leaning back at my desk. "The sandspur question. Well, sandspurs represent the real Florida. They are a member of the grass family. Under my electron microscope, the spikes on a sandspur look kind of like asparagus spears." I usually stop about then, because the new Floridian is

211

looking at me as if I were Cliff Clavin, the insufferably boring mailman from Cheers.

"Sandspurs do serve a purpose," Crewz explained the other afternoon. "They are a vegetation that tends to anchor sand dunes in place."

Without sandspurs and other vegetation, in other words, our already threatened sand dunes would be gone with the wind. Perhaps the best place to admire sandspurs in West Central Florida is Fort De Soto, a huge Pinellas County park at the mouth of Tampa Bay. "A very good population," Crewz said.

Park management, according to Crewz, cultivates sandspurs by constant mowing. "Sandspurs are what we call pioneer vegetation," he said. "After an area is mowed, they're among the first vegetation that returns. They grow fast. If park management mowed less at Fort DeSoto, sandspurs eventually would be crowded out by other vegetation such as sea oats."

But mowers mow at a frantic pace.

"Walking around Fort De Soto in flip-flops can be dangerous."

Evolution has blessed the sandspurs. They are survivors. Mow sand dunes and sandspurs will have a picnic. Build a road and sandspurs soon will be ready to puncture your knees should you have to change a punctured tire on the roadside. Bulldoze the woods and sandspurs will be the first plant to reappear. And they may show up at the bulldozer's next stop.

Sandspurs spread by hitching rides on whatever brushes against them. A fox, passing across a dune, catches a sandspur in its fur. A mile later, the fox stops and scratches the sandspur away. The sandspur falls. Seeds drop. A new sandspur colony is born.

"Sandspurs catch on the treads of bulldozers the same way," Dave Crewz said. "Bulldozers spread 'em like crazy."

So do people. Picture this: It's late in the afternoon. You sit and take off your shoes. Gotcha! Sandspurs, in your shoelaces, are now sticking in your fingers. Swearing, you remove said sandspurs. You drop them carefully into the garbage. The next day the garbage is transported to the landfill. A week later, a new sandspur plant sprouts among the spinach cans. A month after that, the mature sandspur plant at the landfill catches the tail feathers of a laughing gull, which flies that evening to Passage Key, where the seeds fall.

Help! The sandspurs are coming!

"I think it's possible," said Crewz, "that we have more sandspurs in Florida now than ever before."

I am not threatened by a growing sandspur population, even though my feet, hands and buttocks have been punctured by thousands of them over the years. Sandspurs are good.

Let me tell you how good. The other evening I walked to the water with my favorite fishing rod, knowing I would probably have to share the bayou with other fishers. But I had it to myself, I think, because of the huge field of sandspur plants between the pavement and the trout.

A private fishing hole, in modern Florida, is a rare and valuable commodity.

If you accuse me of planting those sandspurs I'll deny it.

Hooked on tarpon

Two hours in bed and still sleep will not come. Lying on your back, you stare at the ceiling fan. You hear a raccoon drag the cat's dish on the back porch and a barking dog in the distance. At midnight the sounds annoy like a dripping faucet.

Another hour passes without slumber. Then two more. Your brain begins the countdown. If I go to sleep now, I'll still be able to get an hour and a half. You count sheep, but they gradually lose shape and evolve into jumping tarpon. You have never been able to sleep the night before a fishing trip.

At 4:00 a.m. you give up, crawl from bed and eat a light breakfast. You walk into the backyard and check for rain. A sliver of moon hangs high in the southeast, not far from the planet Jupiter, but you focus on Mars, glowing red over the banyan tree. Then, out front, you hear the rumble of a truck's idling engine.

Larry Mastry has arrived. It's time to fish for tarpon.

Stevie Nicks is singing on the radio when you climb into the truck. Mastry turns her down and gets to the point. "I didn't catch anything yesterday. I was going real good for a while, but yesterday they just wouldn't eat. They just turned off."

Mastry is a muscular man in his 30s. He owns a tackle store and belongs to a well-known St. Petersburg family that has dominated the tarpon fishing scene for half a century. His uncle, John Mastry, died of heart failure while fighting a tarpon. Larry's father, Mike, once caught the biggest fish in the Suncoast Tarpon Roundup, a tournament that has filled every summer since 1934. Brothers and uncles and cousins have made reputations on their ability to catch tarpon.

At the age of seven, wearing a special harness that helped hold the fishing rod, Larry caught his first tarpon, a 68-pounder. At 15, he hooked a 102-pound tarpon that towed his boat for three hours through thunderstorms before surrendering. Mastry has won money in tarpon tournaments, caught hundreds of fish and lost thousands. In this summer's competition, he has fished six hours a day four times a week and caught and released 24 tarpon – more than all but one of the other 900 contestants.

You roll across the Skyway Bridge, which spans Tampa Bay, towing the boat, and he looks at the clouds on the western horizon. Thunderstorms have plagued his fishing all week, and he has been menaced by waterspouts almost daily. You turn west at Bradenton and head for the beach. Sarasota Bay, you hope, will hold tarpon.

Like the pelican, the tarpon is one of Florida's great natural resources – with one obvious difference. It takes no effort to experience a pelican; just walk to the nearest salt water and look. To fully appreciate a tarpon, you must first work yourself into decent physical condition, learn the habits of the fish, be fortunate enough to hook one and strong enough to catch it.

The tarpon is perhaps Florida's top game fish, known for strength, endurance and the ability to leap from the water. A distant relative of the herring, the tarpon is long, thick and silver with large eyes. Tarpon have no food value, so almost all are released alive. Last night, before your pitiful attempts at sleep, you reread novelist Thomas McGuane's description of the fish:

"The closest thing to a tarpon in the material world is the Steinway piano...the tarpon, when hooked and running, reminds the angler of a piano sliding down a precipitous incline and while jumping makes cavities and explosions in the water not unlike a series of pianos falling from a great height."

You like the part about tarpon making big cavities in the water, but pianos are too sluggish to ever be mistaken for tarpon. A tarpon on the end of your line is more like a gargantuan fire hose, squirting out of control, spinning and twisting this way and that, as unapproachable as a very angry python.

Considered too big and wild to be subdued on humble rod and reel, tarpon were harpooned in the 1800s. Then, in 1895, somewhere on Florida's West Coast, a man named William H. Wood became the first to catch one on conventional tackle. It began a sport fishery that endures today.

Since then, the heaviest caught on hook and line weighed 283 pounds. A 218-pounder was landed in Tampa Bay in 1973. Larry Mastry caught a 175-pound tarpon in 1985, his personal best, though he has hooked and lost much larger ones, and landed smaller fish that tested his strength, endurance and stomach.

"In 1980, I fought one in the Manatee River for three hours," he tells you. "This was during the hottest part of the day. I had a little kid on board with me, and I kept asking him for water, I was so thirsty. The only water I had was from melting ice in my drink cooler, so he was giving me that in a cup.

"Well, I'd been drinking the water for hours, while fighting the fish, when I happened to look in the cooler. There was a dead pinfish floating in the ice water. I'd been sucking down that fish water like it was coming out of the ground.

"Well, three hours pass. I have no energy. My hands aren't working. I've been drinking fish water. I finally get the fish close enough to the boat to try and gaff it. I stick him with the gaff. The rope holding the gaff breaks. So I lose the gaff and the fish falls back in the water and I'm fighting him again.

"Now I have a worthless kid on board, hands that don't work and no gaff. I get the fish in again and this time I put my hand in his mouth and try to pull him in by his tongue. It's too slimy; I can't do it. I put my hands through his gills. That doesn't work either. Finally, I get out this big stringer and work the rope through his gills, and haul him into the boat. One-hundred and thirty-two pounds. I'd never want to go through that again."

Dawn on Sarasota Bay. Mastry puts out two anchors to hold his boat steady near Longboat Key. A stiff breeze blowing from the southeast rocks the 20-foot boat and carries the scent of land. Laughing gulls drift over us, wondering if we have brought food. Minnows dimple the water's surface, creating what Mastry calls "nervous water." He hopes nervous water means hungry tarpon are present under the minnows.

If they are, he expects them to swim by the boat before the incoming tide turns. He says we are in perfect position. The water is deeper here, and the tarpon use the channel beneath us as a highway across the bay.

Listening to him, you look toward the high buildings of downtown Sarasota and wonder if tarpon will survive continuing development as the state grows. If these fish do disappear one day, you tell yourself, the quality of life will have fallen another notch.

Perhaps tarpon will be luckier than the Florida panther, on the road to extinction because of development, or the king mackerel, devastated by commercial fishing excesses. Though some fishers kill big tarpon for vanity, or to enter in tournaments, most anglers today estimate their weight, take a quick photograph, and release them.

Tarpon also seem to be a hardy lot and tolerant of human-caused factors that have whittled away the populations of other species. An ancient fish, they have survived for thousands of years. Among other things, they have evolved a primitive lung that allows them to gulp oxygen at the surface when water quality is poor.

Mastry is watching for rising tarpon right now. His boat has an eight-foot tower that enables him to see great distances and deep into the water. Shading his eyes, he sees no tarpon.

Undiscouraged, he climbs from the tower and opens a cooler, where menhaden lie on ice. Menhaden shad, as large as a man's foot, are good bait. Now he takes down a nine-foot fishing rod from a rack. The reel is spooled with 300 yards of line with a breaking strength of 50 pounds. At line's end is six feet of wire and a hook honed to razor sharpness. He hooks the dead menhaden through the eyes and casts it into Sarasota Bay. He does the same with seven other rods.

Then he waits.

Tarpon fishing is a waiting game, so you tell fish stories. You talk about the one big tarpon you have caught, an estimated 135-pounder, that took 40 minutes to land before you let it go. Mastry, the guide that day, remembers it well. He laughs when you tell him your arms were so tired you needed both to lift a Pepsi to your lips.

Mastry tells of the time he gaffed a tarpon that almost drowned him. "The fish was still green, not tired at all I mean, and he dragged my upper torso under. I mean, I wedged my legs between the engine and the stern to stay in the boat."

The gaff snapped before any bones.

You tell of a man who was not so fortunate. He gaffed a tarpon that ignored him and continued swimming. The angler hung onto the gaff and was dragged the length of the boat, where his ribs struck a metal railing and cracked like potato chips.

Mastry tells tales of hooked tarpon that jump into boats. This rarely happens, he adds, and has never happened to him, but it does happen, so you think about it every time you have a tarpon in the air.

"I knew this guy it happened to," Mastry says. "After he set the hook the fish came out of the water and landed in the boat and went nuts. The guy, he got the hell out of the way. The tarpon blasted a hole in the liner of the boat, beat his way around the center console, smashed the coolers, and finally jumped out. Then the line broke."

You can't top that one, and you forget to tell the story about the Largo lure maker named Harold LeMaster who fought a tarpon up and down Clearwater Bay for 18 1/2 hours before the hook broke. Mastry has heard that one before, anyway. Everybody who fishes tarpon in West Florida has heard the story. It made the national fishing magazines in 1952.

"Tarpon have so many ways of beating you," Mastry says, drinking a Pepsi. "They can wrap the line around their bodies when they jump and break off. They have a cast-iron mouth that's hard to set a hook in. They'll clean you out, take every inch of your line. I've hooked about a hundred fish this year, but have caught about 20 percent. They're tough."

When the strike comes at 7:21 a.m., you are leaning against the drink cooler, and wondering how long a human, namely you, can go without sleep. In other words, you are unprepared when the rod suddenly snaps down in the holder, bends almost in two, and line buzzes from the reel. You react sluggishly, moving as if chased by a grizzly in a dream, but Mastry skips by you, jerks the rod from the holder and sets the hook.

The fish, when it feels the sting, flies from the water, wild and furious, a Steinway-piano-out-of-control-firehose-grizzly bear-python rolled into one, contorting its body into a "U", then falling and firing into the air again, shaking its head, gills rattling, making your mouth open and eyes pop.

Then the line breaks, and the rod relaxes, and Mastry falls back, and you look at him, and he looks at you, and then you both stare at the nervous water where about 120 pounds of tarpon just disappeared into the foam.

The old man and the sea

BIG PINE KEY   7/10/88

I want to catch a great white shark: You know, the bad boy who ate all those bathers in the movie *Jaws*. I want to pull hard on the heavy fishing rod as white death, as I happen to call this shark, dives to the bottom, shaking its massive head, lifting me from the fighting chair and then dropping me until my backbone aches.

I want to be drenched with sweat and smell the salted air, as the bearded white-haired captain who looks like Hemingway shouts directions.

"You almost got him! Pump! PUMP! PUMP THAT ROD, YOU IDIOT!" he will bellow, and I will not be insulted, because this is how big-time fishers talk when a great white shark is on the line.

I want to look into the 18-foot shark's round black eyes as it breaks surface, and see those deadly jaws instinctively open and crunch shut as they search for what antagonizes them. I want to yell with triumph when the mate finally throws the flying gaff into white death, slips the rope around a stern cleat, and then commences to pound my back in congratulations. Because we've got him.

I want to go below deck then, splash cold water in my face, and gaze into the mirror to see if I have somehow become a different man.

Back on deck, I want to hear the captain on the radio, talking to shore, alerting the media, saying that some skinny St. Petersburg man just bested a world record great white. As we draw closer to Bud 'N' Mary's Marina, I want to see the television lights and cameras waiting.

I want to be able to say to my kids, "Well, what do you think of your old man now?" Their eyes shiny with pride, they will wordlessly embrace me if they know what's good for them.

Heck, it could happen, I daydream – if only I could get to the Keys, where they have been seeing, hooking and even catching great whites all year. Let me at them.

To anglers, the great white is the Holy Grail. The largest fish ever caught on hook-and-line was a 16-foot great white that weighed 2,664 pounds. Commercial fishers, using nets, harpoons and rope, have landed even larger ones. A 21-footer that weighed 7,000 pounds was once taken off Cuba. A 7,000-pounder could swallow an adult man whole. And great whites do.

The most infamous shark attack in history, which inspired Peter Benchley's *Jaws*, happened off New Jersey in 1916. In a 10-day period four people were fatally attacked and several others maimed by the same great white. And it was only an eight-and-a-half-footer.

Cold water sharks, great whites rarely have been reported off Florida's coast. Until this year. Off the Keys, great whites have been on the prowl. One charter boat returned to dock with a 686-pounder. Another landed a 455-pound great white.

At least six others have been seen. One boat hooked and lost an estimated 1,000-pounder. The shark was considerate enough to postpone its escape long enough to allow a boat passenger to make a video that later made the TV news in Miami.

Visit the Keys, drive by marinas, and you'll see the signs: "Monster Fishing! Match Your Strength With A Maneater!" Keys anglers, inflamed with the idea of tangling with a great white, have gone shark nutty. Some aren't satisfied fishing for them on rod-and-reel. One brave/foolish diver made the front page of a Miami newspaper by spearing a 1,000-pound tiger shark, another species reputed to enjoy gnawing on human flesh.

I wouldn't mind catching a tiger shark, I daydream, but I would rather catch white death. I never kill a fish for vanity, because I think it's wrong, but if I ever caught a great white, I might be tempted to break my policy. A stuffed great white, jaws agape, would look neat above the fireplace.

It's time, I tell the wife and kids, to go to the Keys.

But first I make a telephone call to the marina where a boat docked last February after catching the 455-pound great white. Sometimes even I get lucky: I find myself talking to a mate who works on the Huntress II. His name is George Sarley.

George tells me Capt. Bill Hegland was fishing in 700-feet of water for mako sharks on the fateful day. Makos are smaller, more streamlined and more beautiful than their great white cousins. A few years ago, when makos were discovered off an area called The Hump, many boats began fishing for them in earnest. This year great whites apparently joined the makos.

"I think maybe the great whites have always been here," George says. "But nobody knew it until we started fishing for makos."

He says the captain at first thought the big fish at the end of the line was a mako, even though it was an odd color. Makos are an electric blue; the big boy thrashing at boatside was slate gray – and mean.

"It took a bite out of the transom," George tells me over the phone. "The damage was bad enough that it cost some money to repair. And the mate who gaffed it, well, when he reached for the line to pull it closer, the shark extended its jaws – kind of like the monster in *Alien* – and took a snap at him. Missed him by inches."

I have a feeling I am going to make great white history before the week is over.

Threatening gray clouds pile high on the horizon as we cruise the Overseas Highway, also known as U.S. 1. I don't care about scary clouds. Not when almost every marina or fish camp we pass boasts some kind of mounted shark or concrete facsimile of a shark. I count two concrete great whites that must measure 20 feet in length. They have girths wide enough to hide a Japanese subcompact.

The rain starts. Rain won't last forever.

The wind picks up, whipping Florida Bay to a white-capped frenzy.

We arrive at the motel. We wait for the weather to clear. I line up a few stories to write in the meantime.

On the day I'm on an interview in Marathon, the weather breaks. I am not at the marina when the boat leaves, taking my family offshore to great white waters. One of my children claims to see a shark; her siblings sensitively claim she is a dirty liar.

They catch a boatful of tasty fish known as dolphin, though. Dolphin fish are different from dolphin mammals, so I feel no guilt as I eat a plateful of dolphin meat at supper. Hemingway's Old Man, Santiago, ate raw dolphin to give himself strength during his battle with a blue marlin. I will need strength for white death.

The weather front has finally escaped to the Bahamas. The skies are as blue as the gulfstream. But nobody I know who owns a boat is heading for the sharking grounds offshore. The fools! They're chasing dolphin and tarpon when there are great whites to engage.

I have no boat, and I don't care. I will do the impossible: I will catch white death without a boat.

We pile into the car, drive 30 minutes, stop at our favorite Big Pine tackle store and buy steel wire leaders and steel hooks and mushy mullet, ripe and stinking, just right for tempting the beast. Back in the car, we drive two blocks, turn north, follow the road, see a Key deer grazing, pass a mobile home village, then park at the bridge.

"We're going to catch us some sharks!" I announce, rigging rods, cutting bait, giving orders. And nobody dares to argue.

A few minutes go by. I study the water. Let the others watch birds. Somebody has to be prepared. Then, it appears, just as I knew it would. Wearing special sunglasses that allow me to see under the water, I detect a shadow moving across the bottom.

"Shark!" I yell. "Shark!"

Ahab never sounded better.

Six lines are fired in the direction I point. Lines cross and snag. Brother shouts at sister. Sister screams at mother. Various death threats are exchanged. Shark picks up bait. Line screams from reel.

Shark on! Do you hear me? Shark on!

"What kind of shark is that, daddy?" asks the eight-year-old.

I look at her. I want to tell her about white death, and 1916, and world records, and glory. But she is too smart to believe the green sluggish four-foot creature is the *Jaws* of bad dreams. I have to tell the truth. I tell her it's a fat zero on a scale of 10, a stinking nurse shark.

"Oh."

Someday everything will be different, I daydream on the drive home. Someday my luck will change, and the old white-haired captains at the marina will be talking about me as they drink their rumrunners at sunset.

"When it comes to great whites, you is the king," they will say, and I will have to agree. I is.

Then I will challenge them to arm wrestling. The cowards, of course, will refuse to compete, but I will graciously buy the next round of rumrunners anyway, because that's the kind of real man I am. When I sleep that night, I will dream of lions.

The bat tower

The mosquitoes during the day were bad enough to test the strongest of men. When Fred L. Johnson had to work near the swamps he burned coconut husks in a smudge pot and prayed the smoke would keep mosquitoes at bay. Sometimes he still had to scrape them off his arms with his hands and knock them from his back with banana leaves.

At night you stayed indoors unless you were plum crazy.

"After dark was when they got real bad," says Johnson, recalling the Florida Keys of his youth. "When dark came, if you went out on the porch and put your hand on the screen, the mosquitoes would gather outside on it. When you moved your hand, you'd see the imprint of your hand – the imprint made by mosquitoes clinging to the screen. You didn't dare go outside. They'd suck you dry."

Johnson is 79. Retired, he lives in Key West, his birthplace, where mosquitoes today are controlled by powerful poisons sprayed from airplanes. But for many years before the Keys were developed, before heavy-duty pesticides were invented, Johnson worked for a wealthy Sugarloaf Key landowner who wanted to make a tourist paradise out of what he considered an uncivilized hell – by getting rid of mosquitoes.

His name was Richter Clyde Perky. He envisioned a Florida Keys heaven-on-earth covered with tourist resorts and people eager to part with money. Perky also believed mosquitoes had to be eliminated before his dream could come true.

In 1929, Perky directed Fred L. Johnson to build the strangest edifice the 100-mile-long Florida Keys have ever known. Using expensive pine and cypress hauled from the mainland on the Flagler railroad, and plans acquired from a Texas eccentric, Johnson walked into the mangroves and built Perky a 30-footer tower – to house bats.

"The idea was to build a tower to attract bats that would eat mosquitoes," says Johnson, who worked 14 years for the now deceased Perky, who spent more than $10,000 on his fly-by-night scheme. "At night the bats were supposed to fly out of the tower and eat up the mosquitoes.

"As far as I know, we never had the first bat in there."

Today, the bat tower rises from the edge of a mangrove swamp behind the Sugarloaf Lodge resort, about 17 miles from Key West. One drives past the resort, turns north at the tennis courts and heads a quarter-mile down an incredibly potholed rocky road that dead-ends at the tower, which looms over the swamp like a windmill missing its blades. Repaired in 1981, listed on the National Register of Historic

Places by the National Park Service in 1982, the tower still stands tall and true – and batless.

"I can't say it's worthless," says Miriam Good, whose husband owns the Sugarloaf Lodge. "Everyone wants to see it. It's good for business."

For many years the tower has been talked about and written about by people who repeated tales that grew with every telling. The instigator of innacurracies was often R.C. Perky himself, a clever promoter who took advantage of his tower's nonsuccess to create a legend he hoped would publicize the resort he eventually built.

Perky was a jovial man given to wearing white linen suits custom-made in Cuba. He appreciated white lies as well. With a straight face, he liked telling travel writers how he sailed to Cuba to collect bats for his tower. Watching their pens fill notebooks, he told how hundreds of island luminaries, entertained by the Key West High School band, gathered to witness the elimination of mosquitoes, once and for all, in 1929.

When nightfall arrived, Perky went on, and bats fled the tower, they were eaten by mosquitoes.

In an alternate version, his uncooperative bats simply returned to Cuba never to be seen again. In a story that continues to this day – the tale is printed on the Sugarloaf Lodge dinner menu – "...A professor named Platt, Felonious by first name, conned Perky out of $10,000 to create the ultimate in mosquito control."

It makes good copy.

"I don't know how they came up with all that stuff," says Fred Johnson, the only known survivor who participated in the birth of the bat tower. "It didn't happen that way."

R.C. Perky was a Spanish-American War veteran and businessman who moved to South Florida to take advantage of a building boom in 1908. He was attracted to the Florida Keys, which were linked in 1912 to the mainland by a railroad built by Henry M. Flagler. In 1917, Perky bought property and a sponge farm on what later became Sugarloaf Key.

His sponge business went badly. His empire was so vast and inaccessible he found it hard to discourage poachers who sneaked onto his property to steal the sponges he grew on underwater racks. Ambitious, he eventually abandoned the sponge business to develop his land in 1928. With his superintendent, Johnson, he built a large house, a plant to generate electricity, and made plans to develop a fishing lodge. But first he felt the need to deal with mosquitoes.

Perky had read a book called *Bats, Mosquitoes and Dollars* written by Dr. Charles Campbell of San Antonio, Texas. A health officer said to be dedicated to the extinction of disease-transmitting mosquitoes, Campbell believed the bat was man's most potent weapon. He wrote that a single bat could eat 1,000 mosquitoes a night. If enough bats could be concentrated, Campbell wrote, they easily could take care of any mosquito problem.

Campbell, who had noticed bats roosting in silos and belfries, got the idea of building a tower. He built his first at Mitchell's Lake, Texas, in 1911. Inside the tower were hundreds of compartments for roosting bats. Bat guano, a valuable fertilizer, would slide down a metal chute into waiting trucks. Campbell, who tried to consider all the angles, believed a typical tower annually could produce two tons of bat droppings.

But his *piece de resistance* was a bat bait whose ingredient he kept secret.

Campbell's Texas bat tower, according to documents stored at Key West's Historic Preservation Board, was a success. Bats roosted in the tower and helped control mosquitoes. The Texas Legislature in 1919 recommended him for a Nobel Prize. Campbell failed to win, alas, but he did put up for sale his bat bait and bat-tower plans for a cool $500.

At Sugarloaf Key, R.C. Perky, plotting against mosquitoes, took notice.

"Mr. Perky was a smart man," Fred Johnson says. "He sent a man to Texas to check Dr. Campbell out. The man we sent brought back a favorable report. Campbell told us that if we had bats on the Keys – and we did...they used to roost on the telephone junction boxes and knock out the service – then they would be attracted to the tower."

In early 1929 Johnson began construction. He sank four sturdy posts into a poured concrete foundation. Around each post he placed metal guards to keep snakes and raccoons away. On top of the posts he built the tower. The outside frames were longleaf pine. The shingles were cypress. Inside were hundreds of pine slats for the bats, and a metal chute to transport bat guano to the ground. Nothing was painted. Campbell said bats would be repelled by paint.

"We used the best of materials," Johnson says. "Ten-thousand dollars was a lot of money in 1929."

Then, on Flagler's railroad, a 50-pound box of bat bait arrived. Johnson remembers the pungent moment. "It really smelled bad," he says. Following Campbell's directions, Johnson installed the box, drilled it with eight holes and covered it with distilled water. The water activated the bait.

"When the water hit the bait, the smell was unbearable," Johnson says. "It was so bad you had to get out of there."

Despite the odor, Perky dedicated his bat tower "to good health" on March 15, 1929, according to the crude inscription scrawled and barely visible in the cement beneath the tower. But no bats arrived. And that summer a bad storm roared through the Keys, deodorizing the odoriferous tower.

"We tried to contact Dr. Campbell for more bait," Johnson says. "But his son told us he'd died. His son said he didn't know how to make the bait bait. I think it was made out of ground bat organs, but Campbell's son said the one secret his father took to the grave was what exactly went into his bat bait.

"And that was the end of it. We never had any bats."

Well, maybe not the end. A terrible hurricane blasted through the Keys in 1935, knocked down Flagler's railroad and killed 400 people. The bat tower endured. The Overseas Highway, U.S. 1, was built over what remained of the railroad bed, enabling thousands of people to drive to the Keys, bringing progress. Before Perky died in 1938, he built his resort, and modern technology controlled his mosquitoes. And back there by the mangroves, the tower endured, waiting for bats.

It still waits, behind one of he Keys' most modern lodges, which offers guests miniature golf, an airstrip and a seaplane base. Sitting in the bar, sipping a beer, is the owner of new paradise, Lloyd Good, talking about it all.

"Naw, we don't have any mosquitoes here," says Good, who knows the value of good publicity. "We've got a governor now whose state is free of mosquitoes."

What about bats?

"Oh, I've seen bats around here. Late at night. Sitting on these barstools."

Fireflies

Nightfall catches most of us modern Floridians hiding in our air-conditioned living rooms, curled up with our televisions, fighting boredom.

Dr. James Lloyd, who is never bored, feels sorry for the rest of us. By surrendering the night we have lost the chance to communicate with fireflies.

"Anybody," he says, "can do it."

An entomologist, Lloyd has been talking to fireflies for nearly three decades. When fireflies light up his neck of North Florida, he uses a small flashlight to blink back at them. They respond. Fireflies think he is another firefly interested in mating.

"I usually can get them to land in my hands," he says.

Lloyd, 56, works at the University of Florida, where he is known as a world authority on firefly behavior. An admitted eccentric who sometimes quotes poetry in his firefly chats, he is a nocturnal wanderer whose field trips to remote woods have been interrupted on occasion by suspicious police looking for drug dealers or game poachers.

"I end up doing lectures about fireflies," Lloyd says. Hard-eyed lawmen have yet to drag him to jail. "Most people have loved fireflies since childhood."

For him, fireflies are more than a way to make a buck. He likes fireflies. As an animal behaviorist, he finds them an ideal subject: Flash a light at them and they react. As a nature lover, he finds them mysterious: Like many people, he is enthralled by their blinking.

"But I'm no expert on how they do it," he says, though he can explain.

Chemicals in their bodies, called luciferin and luciferase, create a yellow-green light when they interact. Fireflies can somehow produce the light at will, using it to attract mates. Yet some learn to mimic the light of other firefly species. Many an amorous male has been deceived, then devoured, by a clever female of another variety.

"Oh, what a tangled web we weave, when first we practice to deceive!" Lloyd wrote in one of his many scientific papers, quoting Sir Walter Scott, who probably never had fireflies in mind when he wrote *Marmion*.

Though Lloyd was born in rural New York, where fireflies light up the night, he never thought they would become his destiny. He was more interested in fishing, hunting and music. After graduating from New York's Fredonia State College with a science degree, he headed for the University of Michigan and graduate work. His plan was to learn about animal behavior. He needed a creature that was plentiful and relatively unstudied. The more he watched fireflies, the more he was fascinated.

Sometimes he shares his enthusiasms with entomology classes, dragging out what he calls his "dog and pony show," complete with firefly slides, firefly flight-pattern diagrams, firefly flashlight-blinking demonstrations and readings of firefly poetry. "Ah, the cunning fireflies!" is one old Japanese chestnut he uses."Being chased, they hide themselves in the moonlight!"

When he finishes teaching his classes, he often disappears into the moonlight himself. And not always because he needs to complete his firefly field work.

"You don't spend 3,000 nights in the field over 30 years just to get more data."

He has enjoyed flickering fireflies in Thailand, Indonesia, New Guinea, Jamaica, Columbia, Canada and Mexico. He has studied them in Maine, Missouri, Virginia and most Southeastern states. In his opinion, North Florida is the best place on the continent to see them. He's counted 35 species around Gainesville alone, and they're active practically all year.

Many urban Floridians, alas, miss all the excitement. For one thing, they have no interest in the natural world or they are afraid to go outside after dark because of crime. And in some places fireflies are hard to find.

In big cities, a nature buff needs luck to see a firefly. Fireflies, like some other beetles, spend much of their lives in the ground. In urban areas, much of the ground is covered by asphalt. Lawns are sprayed with insecticides to kill chinch bugs. The air, during mosquito outbreaks, is fogged with poisons. Nights are lit up by street lamps. Lloyd considers all these city trademarks bad for fireflies.

There are about 2,000 named species of fireflies in the world, and probably 1,000 varieties that have yet to be named, and they all behave more or less differently. Trying to sort them all out, trying to figure who is blinking at whom, and what it means, has been Jim Lloyd's career task.

"Hell, nobody can know all this stuff," says Lloyd, contemplating all those blinking beetles that inhabit every continent but Antarctica. "I guess life is about finding out how dumb we are."

But he has tried his best, and now, if things go smoothly, the world will enjoy the fruits of his labor. He is putting together a 1,000-page treatise based on everything he has learned about firefly behavior since he began studying them as a graduate student in the early 1960s.

He has 3,000 pages of field notes to interpret. He has 7,500 specimens, kept in 50 drawers at Gainesville's American Institute of Entomology, to refer to. Then he has to write the book.

"I want ordinary people – not just entomologists – to be able to use it," says Lloyd, who's written firefly articles for *World Book* and *Encyclopaedia Brittanica*. "I want people to be able to take it outside and refer to it. If the firefly blinks this way, or that way, I want people to be be able to read how to answer them. And to know what kind of firefly they've been talking to."

Why should people bother? Because firefly watching is much more interesting than television, in Lloyd's opinion. Because firefly watching is a nice way to renew interest in the natural world. Because fireflies are there.

"If you want to study mammals you might have to sit two hours in the woods and be lucky to see a squirrel. If you want to study deep-water fish you have to go down in a bathysphere. To look at fireflies you just go outside at night. They're perfect research animals. You don't need any technology."

Lloyd, who got his doctorate in entomology from Cornell, is not big on technology. Oh, he uses some of the latest electronic wonders, but overall he thinks technology has discouraged amateurs from practicing science. They think they need expensive equipment to be real scientists, when all they actually need is curiosity, their eyes, and maybe a little flashlight if they want to experiment with fireflies.

"A lot of the stuff I've been doing amateurs could have been doing," Lloyd says. What has Lloyd been doing? He's gone out into the night, watched fireflies light up, observed how other fireflies responded to the light, and drawn conclusions.

Firefly behavior is complex. Some can imitate the blinks of other species. Others blink at different altitudes: A low altitude blink means something different than a high blink. Some fireflies hide in the bushes, wait for a low blink of another species, and home in on the light like a sidewinder missile. While firefly watching may be an innocent pastime for humans, it's nerve-racking for the insects. It's a jungle out there.

Last summer Lloyd put 8,000 miles on his pickup truck during Florida field trips. He doesn't complain. He says he likes the woods at night and he likes the solitude. For the record, he has never been bitten by a snake, stepped on an alligator or fallen into a ditch during his nocturnal wanderings.

"I have not even run into a seductress," says Lloyd, a born romantic.

For the most part, his most memorable encounters have been with random homeowners troubled by the appearance of Lloyd in their woods or pastures after dark. For some reason, many property owners are afraid of a grown man who talks quietly into a tape recorder while twirling across a firefly-filled field holding several fishing poles on whose ends small lights glow.

The lit-up poles allow Lloyd to mimic firefly flight patterns. At least that's what he tells the spooked homeowners, who usually are accompanied by the police.

"I've been made to leave a couple of times," he says. "But most of the time I get to stay. People are pretty nice about what I do."

A night at the opera

RICHLOAM   7/10/91

Dark comes early to Withlacoochee State Forest. The sun dips behind the pines and the shadows lengthen and the night creatures reveal themselves. Armadillos crash through the palmettos. Bats flit over the dirt road where wildlife biologists Lenela Glass-Godwin and her husband, Jim, have parked their pickup. The Godwins are creatures of the night, too. They have come to listen to the opera.

"Hear that?" asks Lenela.

"Pig frog," Jim says.

The Carusos of the night are serenading. They are grunting and creaking and pinking and oinking and chirping and making a noise that sounds like a thumb playing across the teeth of a comb. They are doing everything but ribbetting.

"Frogs don't ribbet," Jim Godwin says quietly.

"No, that's pretty much a Hollywood fantasy," Lenela agrees.

No matter. The important thing is that a froggy concert is taking place here in Sumter County and the Godwins have orchestra seats.

"I love it out here," Lenela says. On a night as warm as a bloodhound's breath, as the mosquitoes whine and the humidity drips from the trees, Lenela is blissful. "You really experience the diversity of life after dark," she goes on. "It's ironic that most people are completely unaware what's going on outside their homes at night."

Public indifference to the night is one of Lenela's pet peeves. She is a non-game education specialist for the Florida Game and Fresh Water Fish Commission's Lakeland office. Her husband is a commission biologist and a professional nature photographer. Everything about the natural world interests them, but herpetology, which takes in the study of frogs and toads, is their passion.

"People should know more about toads and frogs," says Lenela, born in the Alabama country 29 years ago. "They tell you what's going on in the environment. What's going on is life."

Lenela, who taught at Texas A&M before joining the commission last fall, is trying to educate the public about the out-of-doors night, including frogs and toads. In recent months she has led nighttime hikes in the Tampa Bay area, written publicity releases about frog music, put together slide shows for civic groups and tried to do some frog PR when people call the commission's office in a panic or with stomachs growling. She is not the person to call for a good frog legs recipe.

Frogs, these days, need advocates. In much of the world, frogs and toads are under siege from development, pollution and habitat destruction. Many people, in their homes at night, hostile or ignorant about the natural world, neither know nor care.

REAL FLORIDA

"It's kind of strange," Lenela says. "And a little sad."

Some folks who call the commission don't recognize a frog when they hear it. They want an expert to check out the terrifying backyard sounds. Others don't want to put up with the amphibious Carusos and their wetland opera. The Godwins find it hard to believe that some people move from city to country and then complain about the racket.

"For some people, frogs are right up there with bats and snakes," Lenela says. She loves bats and snakes, too.

So does her husband, who is as quiet as she is talkative. Born in Arkansas 35 years ago, Jim Godwin spent happy boyhood hours patrolling the banks of the White River for snakes, turtles, frogs and other wild creatures. He never outgrew it. Part of his job includes surveying Southwest Florida watersheds for vertebrate life. It's also his hobby.

The Godwins, who met and married while Jim was earning his master's at Auburn, spend most weekends camping in woods throughout the state. "We bird, botanize and herp," Lenela says. Slowly they are learning Florida's natural history.

During the week, when office work restricts their travel, they leave their Lakeland home about sundown and drive into Central Florida's woods and wetlands. Good places to watch and hear frogs include the Green Swamp, state parks and forests, county and city parks and even back yards. Frogs usually like a little moisture.

In some places, though, frog and toad populations are on the wane, a worldwide phenomenon that alarms scientists. "The most popular theory is that pesticides are hurting them," Lenela says. Other reasons may be habitat destruction and global warming. Delicate creatures that eat mostly insects, frogs and toads may be among the first to suffer from the collapse of the food chain.

Herpetologists are usually the first to notice when things go wrong. If every frog in the Withlacoochee were to lie down and die, for example, the Godwins might be the only ones who would know. They almost always have the woods to themselves at night. "I guess most people would rather watch television," Lenela says.

She finds frog study more interesting than *Cheers*. Wearing rubber boots, she wades into a ditch along the road. She's a tadpole of a woman, an inch short of five feet, with short blond hair and an easy smile. Jim, wearing boots and a headlamp, is a bullfrog by comparison. He's about six feet, wears a beard and measures every word. While she talks, he sneaks away to explore a faraway ditch.

"Crooonk!"

There goes the pig frog again, singing bass and doing its best Tom Waits imitation.

"Diga-diga, diga-diga."

Introducing, on percussion, the pine woods treefrog. Jim Godwin listens intently, pinches his nose and repeats the call letter perfectly. The treefrog, which probably should think before opening its mouth, answers.

"It's male frogs that call," Jim explains. Male frogs sing to establish territories and to attract females who might, you know, be interested in hanky panky. Males sing their hearts out; females, overcome, swim, hop and climb to them. What follows is better left to the imagination.

"I'll tell you a romantic story," says Lenela, two months pregnant and watching her husband creep through the water like a heron. "Before Jim and I ever dated I had my eye on him. One night, when we were on a graduate school field trip, I watched him wading in a pond and stalking a frog just like he's doing right now. I thought 'Wow! Is that neat!' "

No doubt blushing in the dark, Jim continues stalking a green treefrog in the ditch. With his painstakingly slow movements, he resembles a wading bird on dinner break. Every once in a while, he stops and calls:

"Queenk! Queenk! Queenk!"

A green treefrog, feeling territorial or lustful or something humans will never understand, foolishly answers. Jim homes in. A moment later, he stops, stoops, gets water in his boots and snaps a green treefrog photograph for his files.

"I learned how to do frog calls when I was in graduate school," Godwin says after he climbs from the water. He learned his stuff by listening to serenading frogs, stalking them and then identifying them. There are at least a half-dozen calls in his repertoire.

People can learn without getting their feet wet. The Godwins recommend *Reptiles and Amphibians*, a Peterson Field Guide written by Roger Conant and Joseph T. Collins. The text includes "voice" descriptions. The Godwins also like *Voices of the Night*, a recording available from Cornell Laboratory of Ornithology in Ithaca, N.Y. From the safety of living room armchairs Herp Wanna-Bes can learn frog music.

Not that the Godwins ever feel anything but safe while in the woods. Jim blames himself for his only injuries: He has been bitten by non-venomous snakes while releasing them from game commission traps he uses in wildlife censuses. And a couple of times, while camping in the woods, he's been startled out of sleep by the screams of quarreling barred owls.

"You're safer here than in the city," Lenela says. The moon is rising, which means the frogs will begin quieting down. "I never feel afraid. If you keep your wits about you, if you use common sense, you have nothing to worry about. Only thing that can bother you here is man. And that hasn't happened yet."

Most of the dangers, such as they are, involve getting there. Tailgaters imperil the Godwins more than anything. The Godwins tend to brake for anything that slithers, creeps or hops.

"On the way home," Lenela says. "We may stop if we see some snakes."

A man called Frog

Florida is modern now, and Frog Smith doesn't like it. Why the other day, this city fellow drove by in a Japanese diesel truck, of all things, and Frog stood in his driveway, and listened to the hateful diesel rumble, and smelled the hateful diesel fumes, and he had to shake his head because it reminded him of how all the old trains are gone.

"Trains are diesel trains now," said Frog, sounding sad. "I liked the old steam locomotives. They were beautiful. A diesel train is nothin' more than a glorified car to my way of thinkin.' "

Frog, who is almost 91, has other dislikes. He is generally down on big buildings, development, too many people, air conditioning, poorly designed dentures and shoes. He yearns for the simpler days of old-timey Florida, when steam locomotives chugged through the woods to the sawmills, and people sat at campfires and told stories. Folks went barefoot, too.

Frog feels it is his responsibility to keep alive the old days, and he has done a fine job of it, through his primitive paintings of Florida scenes but mostly through his stories of pioneer Florida. Frog Smith, the renaissance man of Florida folklore, can tell you stories. And stories. And ...

"Didja ever hear of Bone Mizelle? He was a cowboy way back when, and he's the only cowboy on record in Florida to have picked up a wild cow in his arms and chewed his mark in the ear. The owner of the cow said he'd give him the cow if he'd do it – so he done it.

"Fort Myers is the only town on record to have bought a moonshiner a still. This was way back when it was a cow town. A bunch of wives got tired of their husbands comin' home late, so they had the moonshiner arrested, see. Well, the revenue agent took him and his still away in a boat, but the still somehow got lost at sea so there was no evidence. The agent had to bring the moonshiner back. At the dock waitin' for him was a brand-new copper still.

"Once a Fort Myers man asked me if I had seen a doctor around. 'My young son just stuck a nail in his foot,' he said, 'and I want to get him a tetanus shot to keep him from having lockjaw.' 'You needn't worry,' said I. 'I have probably stuck 100 nails in my feet and I never had lockjaw.' 'You can say that again,' said he, and went on in search of a doctor."

Frog is blessed with the gift of gab, all right. For 25 years, he was featured storyteller at the Florida Folk Festival in White Springs, where the museum has a tape recording of him talking about cowboys. The Smithsonian invited him to Washington in 1976 to tell stories of Florida folklore and display his pictures of old sawmills. Even Charles Kuralt, the CBS journalist, came calling on Frog for *On the Road.*

At his own expense, Frog has printed three books about Florida folklore, written a novel about old Florida and has produced a weekly column for the last 33 years for *Fort Myers News-Press.* He calls it "Cracker Crumbs."

Frog Smith is a cracker, which means an old-time Floridian, and proud of it, and when a man asked him once what'd he'd be if he couldn't be a cracker, he said "ashamed." His credentials are these: He was born in Pine Bloom, Ga., in 1896 but moved to North Florida in 1902. He first ran his daddy's steam locomotive when he was 8, got an engineer's job when he was 14, and over the next 75 years or so worked as a logger, pipefitter, oiler, boiler, mechanic, blacksmith, commercial fisherman and hunter of alligators and frogs.

During the Depression, Ernest A. Smith's family didn't go hungry. Not with all those frogs hopping around the Everglades. When neighbors found out how Ernest A. had caught enough frogs in one night to fill a barrel with frog legs, they started calling him Frog. Frog didn't care for the name at first, but now it's fine with him. In the phone book he's E.A. Frog Smith.

He's lived in Fort Myers more than three decades, in four different houses, three of which he built with his own hands. His current dwelling lacks air conditioning, of course, but it's comfortably cooled by a fleet of fans and just maybe Frog's flapping jaws as he tells stories about the paintings and testimonials and photographs that hang from his walls. A Frog never forgets.

Frog is a small rumpled man who has white unkempt hair, horned-rimmed glasses and a machine-gun style of talking that is part comedian, part country preacher and part historian. One topic flows into another, and one story evokes three others, and listeners have to work to keep up.

"I'm glad to be here, but when you pass 90 you're glad to be anywhere. I never smoked, I never drank and I never went with a girl 'till I met my first wife. We had a four-hour courtship but our marriage lasted 48 years. We rode a motorcycle all over West Florida back when there wasn't a paved road anywhere.

"I remember a lot from the last century. In Christmas of 18 and 99 Santa Claus gave me a billy goat and a cart and my daddy put me in it and the goat got loose from my daddy and run off way up yonder and I got skinned up good. We ate goat the next day, but I didn't like it.

"I had a TV show in Fort Myers about three months, but it run out and I run out, too. I been married three times, the last time for about a year now. Ethel lost her husband, and I'd lost my second wife after 17 years, so I figured we'd get hitched."

Frog recollects he has called at least 100 Florida locales home over the years. You name it, he has probably hung his hat there. He is stunned to see how fast the state has changed.

"It was a different place in the old days. Now take the sawmills. Sawmills built this state. They were everywhere, and each sawmill had a railroad to haul the lumber out of the woods to the bigger railroad lines or to the shipping ports.

"Lumber was the biggest industry in Florida, and now it's pretty much dead.

Why I haven't seen a yellow pine in this state in 40 years! I think second-growth pine is no good. You got to stand over it with a paint brush and a termite gun.

"Modern Florida uses too much water. There are places that used to be 20 feet under water that are bone dry now. When I was a boy, I once seen four boats steamed up and ready to go on the Suwannee River. You could wade across the same spot now.

"Used to be panther all over. One night I came out of the Caloosahatchee River from giggin' frogs and there was a 7-foot panther sittin' in my truck on my ice box. He took his sweet time gettin' off, but when I come back with my shotgun he was gone.

"I used to shoot rabbits for a livin', and you had to shoot 'em in the eye so as not to spoil the meat. I'd clean 'em as I walked along, to save weight. There was this bobcat that'd follow me and eat the brains and guts that got throwed out.

"Mosquitoes were really bad. Why once in Clewiston, in 19 and 35, they killed 11 hogs, seven cows and a mule!"

Frog no longer hunts or drives because of failing eyesight, but he keeps busy with his painting. About 10 or 15 years ago, as he recollects, he was sitting at home, feeling "bottled up" by a rainstorm, and he picked up a paper and drew a picture of a locomotive. His wife liked it, and he drew others, and when he added paint people liked them even better.

They were paintings of the old Florida Frog had known and loved. Sawmills. Locomotives. Steamboats. Plantations. Hunting trips. Two of his sawmill paintings hang in the Smithsonian, and he likes to brag that his paintings have homes in every state in the union "and even Athens, Greece." He gets $100 for each painting and it takes about a week if his hands feel up to it.

Painting is getting more difficult. Frog is an artist with bad hands. In 1918, when he was running the power plant, waterworks and ice house in Chipley, he accidentally touched a switch and received a 2,300-volt shock that knocked him out and permanently bent a finger of his left hand. In 1935, he was trying to remove a rat's nest from a pipe at a Clewiston sugar mill when the pipe fell, tearing ligaments in his right arm and hand. They pain him now and contribute to his already crippling arthritis.

"I'm not feelin' too bad overall, though," he said. "I've had a couple of heart attacks, but I got no real bad problem now. I hurt my back in the lumber business and had spinal trouble for 30 years, until I was instantly healed at a tent meetin'. That's why I believe in the Bible."

Snakeman

Todd Hardwick, ace trapper of escaped animals, is used to dealing with excited people. The other morning he jumped out of his truck to find a few wild-eyed folks running into a yard waving machetes.

"Where's the snake?" called Hardwick, whose South Florida business is catching animals that nobody else will catch.

A police officer – Hardwick also is accustomed to dealing with police – pointed. There was a 14-foot Burmese python hiding under a clump of soggy carpeting.

Burmese pythons aren't supposed to live in Florida. This one was an escaped pet of a young man who had just found out he needed a stronger cage.

Hardwick, blond, lithe and 27, crouched next to the soggy carpeting where the snake was hiding. He lifted the carpeting and petted the snake to calm it down. He made small talk with the police and neighbors to quiet their nerves, too. Among other things he wanted to gauge their courage. "A snake like this could break my ribs," he would say later. "You want to figure out if you got somebody who will help you if you need it."

Reassured, he reached down and picked up the snake. Just like that. It neither bit nor hissed. It coiled around his arms several times, but in a way that almost suggested friendliness.

Hardwick dropped the snake into a blue duffel bag and put the blue duffel bag onto the front seat of his truck. Then he headed for McDonald's and breakfast. In the drive-through, the woman who handed him his hash browns stared at his truck – a sign says "Who Ya Gonna Call? Pesky Critters Relocation Service" – and she stared at the duffel bag.

The bag was moving around like a Mexican jumping bean.

"You could tell she wanted to know," Hardwick said as he dug into his potatoes a few minutes later. "But she was afraid to ask."

Most people are fascinated by Hardwick's work. He is probably the most famous animal trapper in the world right now. If you read newspapers and magazines, if you watch television, you probably have seen him and Big Mama, the 22-foot reticulated python he caught under a Fort Lauderdale home last summer. Photos of Hardwick and the 250-pound reptile, a native of Southeast Asia, appeared on front pages all over the world.

Hardwick and Big Mama were on Johnny·Carson's *Tonight Show*. They were featured on Tom Brokaw's *Nightly News*, on CBS' *Rescue: 911*, and in *People* magazine. Tired of his celebrity, Hardwick shaved his beard, hoping to perform his work anonymously. Yet people still recognize him. A flamboyant man, he sometimes carries a .22 pistol in his pants and has been known to wear sharkskin boots.

"The only difference between me and John Wayne," he likes to tell people, "is that John Wayne is dead." And don't bother mentioning Crocodile Dundee. The Croc is a make-believe person. Hardwick, who grew up on the edge of the Everglades, is a living, breathing daredevil.

"If I can't catch an animal, nobody can," he said. "I get to see all the good action. I've got the greatest job in the world."

Hardwick started catching urban wildlife for a living in 1983. This followed years of not charging friends and neighbors for catching everything from rattlesnakes to raccoons in their yards and carports.

"When I was a kid, I couldn't get enough of animals," he said. "I didn't hang around the mall. I was in the woods." In high school, he was the prime suspect when bullfrogs showed up in the girls' toilets. In the Everglades, he caught snakes just for the thrill. His hobby was breaking horses for ranchers in Homestead.

"I always wanted to work outdoors and with animals."

South Florida is the place to do it. Despite 4.5-million people, there are wild animals everywhere. Raccoons and possums inhabit even the nicest neighborhoods. South Florida, meanwhile, is the tropical pet headquarters for the United States.

During 1987 and 1988, more than 1.26-million snakes, turtles and lizards from foreign lands cleared customs here.That included 18,150 ball pythons alone. Many of these animals are shipped out of state. Many are bought by South Floridians. Some escape or are illegally released by their owners into the urban environment.

Then Who Ya Gonna Call?

"The climate is right for a lot of these animals," said Todd Hardwick. "They thrive down here. Especially the big snakes. There are plenty of dogs and cats for them to eat. Plenty of raccoons. A python can grow four feet a year down here."

Pythons and boa constrictors are among the largest and most efficient predators on Earth. Although they are non-venomous, they suffocate prey in their squeezing coils and swallow them whole. A reticulated python can grow longer than 30 feet. Some experts claim that pythons and boa constrictors are reproducing in South Florida's urban jungles.

"They seem to be all over the place."

Last fall, Hardwick got a call from a construction crew that was having python problems near Miami International Airport. An 18-footer had fallen out of an Australian pine tree and landed on a bulldozer. The bulldozer operator, who was terrified of snakes to begin with, was still shaking when Hardwick arrived.

Hardwick ordered him back into the bulldozer and told him to pick up a fallen tree. Then Hardwick shimmied under the tree and recovered the injured snake. "It was hurt in the fall," he said. "It died a couple weeks later."

Hardwick, somehow, has avoided serious injury despite being bitten by horses, foxes, raccoons, ferrets, bobcats and non-venomous snakes. Only once did he need hospital treatment. That was from a possum bite on the wrist. He guesses he has received 45 rabies booster shots over the years.

"Hell, I could be bitten by Cujo," he said about novelist Stephen King's make-believe killer St. Bernard. "I'd pat him on the head and send him on his way."

But most animals don't menace him. The other day he caught a raccoon that somehow dropped through the ceiling of a nice Coral Gables home. The animal had eaten through the air-conditioning ducts, but it didn't try to eat Hardwick. At another home, he recovered a possum that had chewed its way through an attic television cable before climbing into a Todd Hardwick trap. It, too, was docile.

Hardwick released both animals into the woods of west Miami. "I refuse to catch all the animals that people call me about," he said. "I only get ones that threaten people or property, or when I think the animal will be killed by people."

Hardwick catches the animal, and then charges the worried homeowner a fee that depends on the distance he must drive, the effort and the danger. If the animal is an exotic, such as a big python, he typically charges nothing – but takes possession. He sells most of the pythons and boas he catches. Some are worth $500 or more. Last year he caught about 35. Once he caught five in four days.

He is not rich, but he is comfortable. He works seven South Florida counties, putting 850 miles a week on his truck. He plans to expand to Central Florida.

For now, South Florida keeps him busy enough. Recently he was called to Miami International Airport to round up 11 monkeys that had escaped a broken crate. It took 14 hours, and a couple of shots with a tranquilizer gun, but he got them.

Then he headed over to Homestead Air Force Base, where cattle crossed a canal and refused to surrender the runway. Jets were unable to land until Hardwick roped a belligerent bull and escorted him off airport grounds.

"I rode in the Homestead Rodeo two years ago. Rode a Brahma bull. You sit on him in the chute, and then you nod, and they open the chute, and you go out and try to hang on. The bull threw me and came inches from stepping on my throat. Now that was an experience."

Perhaps it was his cowboy background, or the caffeine-loaded Cuban coffee he drinks by the quart, that helped him face Miami's bison problem last year. An eccentric doctor near the edge of town had his own herd, which escaped one foggy night and naturally stampeded the turnpike.

Hardwick helped police move them off the road, but not before seven bison were killed by motor vehicles. Hardwick brought two very dead bison home and had their heads stuffed. They look down on him from his office wall.

"No sense in wasting buffalo," he said.

The buffalo made the national news, too. So did the time he caught a freak, snow-white raccoon. But nothing topped the press he got for catching Big Mama.

On a summer night in 1989, a retired Fort Lauderdale couple was listening to the rain fall when they heard what sounded to them like a terrified scream. David Spalding told his wife Ruth to stay inside while he went into the yard to investigate.

"It looked like three men were wrestling on the grass," he recalled the other day. "Then I turned on the light. The snake looked like it was 25 feet long. It had a huge raccoon in its coils." Moments later, the snake and the unfortunate raccoon disappeared under the house.

REAL FLORIDA

The first thing the Spaldings did was check their house for places a snake might enter. Satisfied that it would not join them in bed, they dialed 911. "We aren't afraid of snakes," Ruth Spalding said. "But we were afraid for the children next door."

Police officers answered the call. But for some reason they neglected to crawl under the house. The people from the local nature museum decided not to do anything about the snake either. Meanwhile, at least once a week, the Spaldings watched the snake come out at night and catch raccoons.

"It liked to hang out at the tool shed next to the mango tree," David Spalding said. Raccoons from nearby Hugh Taylor Birch State Park visited the Spaldings yard after dark to eat mangoes. Big Mama, apparently an escaped pet, had found heaven. She ambushed raccoons, crushed them in her coils and swallowed them whole.

So Who Ya Gonna Call?

Finally, in August, somebody called Todd Hardwick. He didn't believe a 25-foot snake was hiding under somebody's house. Most people, he has found, exaggerate a snake's size by two times. An eight-footer usually turns out to be four. It's human nature.

But he became a believer when the Spaldings showed him a piece of skin the snake had shed during a growth spurt. The skin was almost wide enough to wrap around a telephone pole.

"He and another man just crawled under the house," Ruth Spalding said. "I think it was the most frightening thing I've ever seen. I was sure we'd never see them again."

Hardwick had his own misgivings.

"I felt like I was a dragonslayer going into a dragon's lair."

He failed to find the snake.

"But I could smell it. There was a lot of feces down there, a lot of shed skin. You could tell he'd been living under the house for a good long time."

The next morning, Todd Hardwick returned with three able-bodied men.

"I wanted reliable people who would keep their cool if the snake grabbed me by the throat."

They carried rope, lights and garbage can lids to use as shields. They carried a powerful tranquilizer. The veterinarian who prescribed the drug said it might kill the snake, so to use it only during an emergency. "If a snake that big bit you, it would rake you right to the bone," Hardwick said. "If it wrapped you up, it could kill you."

The four men crawled under the house on their bellies. Fortunately, none of the snake hunters was a claustrophobic. Unlike crawlspaces under most homes, this one was catacombed with individual chambers. Hardwick and his crew had to crawl from chamber to chamber, using the holes dug by the snake.

They found the snake in a back chamber. While Hardwick's crew held his legs – so they could withdraw him quickly should the snake attack – he pushed his upper torso through the hole dug by the snake and peered into the chamber.

"She was coiled up about six feet away and flicking her tongue. She was real calm. That was the scary thing. By her posture she was saying, 'Yeah. Come on in and get me. If you've got the nerve.' I didn't like the confidence in her eyes."

Hardwick retreated from the snake's lair. Under the house, the four men developed a plan. Two men remained under the house to block the snake's exit. Hardwick

236

and an assistant crawled out from beneath the house and prepared to dig a hole under an outside wall closest to the snake. Meanwhile, South Florida's media had arrived in full force.

Hardwick dug his hole. As two men held his legs, he pushed his upper body into the snake's chamber. By now the snake was alarmed. "She was bouncing around like a Slinky." It slithered along the ground less than two feet below Hardwick. He decided now was as good a time as any.

When the snake got close, he dropped a snare over its head and immediately screamed for his helpers to drag him out. The snake, however, had other plans. It resisted with all its might, and for a sickening moment Hardwick felt his feet slipping inside his cowboy boots.

"All I could think about was being pulled into the dark by the snake, and nobody being able to help me."

But to Hardwick's surprise, and a little to his horror, the snake suddenly stopped pulling. Instead it came right at him. The snake's forward momentum, and Hardwick's hasty retreat, carried them into the yard. As media people knocked each other down getting out of the way, the snake coiled around Hardwick.

His friends and several courageous bystanders rescued him. Straining, they unwrapped Big Mama from Terrible Todd. Only then did the photographers, and the news camera, return to record the moment for posterity.

Hardwick stuffed Big Mama into a sleeping bag.

"That snake was worth millions to me in publicity," said Hardwick, who recently sold the prize to an anonymous collector.

People still send him newspaper clippings from Europe, Japan, South America and Australia. Even the *National Enquirer* did an article. "I was sure they were going to link missing spring break students to the snake," he said. "But they did what was probably their first factual story in history."

In bars, people continue to buy him beers and ask him to retell the story. He does, but he says he's getting tired of it. He wishes he could have a new story for them.

And he thinks he will.

Soon.

"There's a place in Miami," he said, "where there have been reports of a python, a giant, bigger than Big Mama. Reticulated pythons get longer than 30 feet, you know. One of these days I'm going to check it out."

The gator brigade

Joe Borelli, a human bloodhound in khaki, is on the trail of an alligator known to have a yearning for dog. Behind Timberlake Apartments in southern St. Petersburg, Borelli searches for clues. He stalks the edge of a lake, peeks through cattails and watches for ripples on the water's glass-calm surface. The gator must know who is on the prowl.

"Sometimes they disappear the moment you show up," Borelli grumbles.

Now he creeps into an enormous, overgrown Brazilian pepper tree that sprawls across the shoreline. Most apartment dwellers stay away from the scary jungle for fear of snakes. Borelli enters without hesitation. To him it looks perfect for alligators.

He steps over huge limbs. He knocks aside thick branches. He spreads apart leaves. Finally, he finds a culvert that drains storm water into the lake.

"The gator could be in there," he whispers. "I got a gator out of that culvert one time. Gators like culverts." The culvert's opening is as black as the eye of a water moccasin. Nothing is revealed.

"Hell," Joe Borelli says, voice louder now. "That gator could be just about anywhere."

Borelli, a crusty, white-haired, leather-skinned man in his 60s, knows the habits of alligators better than most people. Since 1978 he has been licensed by the Florida Game and Fresh Water Fish Commission to trap urban alligators where they menace people, pets and property in the state's most developed county, Pinellas.

When a Pinellas resident complains about an alligator, commission officers investigate. If a gator is certified as dangerous, Joe Borelli and his helper, son Joey, are notified at their Clearwater home. They climb into a red-orange 1980 Toyota pickup – it smells of rotting gator bait – and head for the appropriate lake, pond, canal, ditch or yard.

Joe and 28-year-old Joey capture gators sunbathing under clotheslines and in swimming pools. They nab them in garages and carports. Joe and Joey crawl under houses, mobile homes and docks to recover them. The trappers slither into culverts, throw their snares and drag out thrashing gators.

They haul the gators, alive, to Dade City, where a skinner shoots them, removes hides and butchers the meat. The Borellis sell the meat to licensed restaurants and the skins at auctions monitored by the state. In a good year, the Borellis catch about 100 alligators and make a comfortable living; in a bad year, they spend hours on the water and often get nothing but sunburn.

It is difficult, frustrating work. They catch fewer than half of the alligators for which they have permits. Most of the time, when they arrive on the scene, they hear the words alligator trappers dread most: "You should have been here yesterday."

When they get lucky, and catch one, they are likely to be swatted by the alligator's muscular tail or snapped at. On one occasion, an alligator put Joe in the hospital with a nasty bite. Joey, meanwhile, has been charged by enraged alligators. His quick reflexes saved his hide.

They love their work.

"I can't imagine doing anything else," says the senior Borelli, a lifelong animal trapper and a former commercial artist who once designed ads for Maas Brothers. "I got no bosses, no deadline, and I'm outside."

"I was with Kash 'N Karry for eight years," says his son, a barrel-chested Clearwater High graduate who wears an alligator's tooth on the straw hat that covers his jet-black hair. "I was going to get into management, but then I figured out I didn't want to be in management. I wanted to do this."

The Borellis are among 46 people contracted by the game commission to trap alligators in Florida. In 1978, the state started the program to control what biologists said was a growing alligator population in urban areas. Joe Borelli, who had trapped fur-bearing animals in Florida, New York, the Rockies and the Arizona desert, got one of the jobs.

"If you offered me a trip to the Super Bowl, the World Series, or Ocala National Forest, I'd take Ocala National Forest," he says. Though he was born in Brooklyn – his accent gives him away – he is most comfortable out-of-doors, stalking animals.

When Joe's parents moved to Florida in 1938, he knew he had discovered paradise. He remembers when there were bears in crowded Pinellas County. "Now that area is golf courses, houses and condos," he says unhappily. Today, the largest predator remaining in the state's most urban county is the alligator.

Florida has about a million of them, biologists say, and credit aggressive wildlife management for the large numbers. But things used to be different. Until 1962 there were no bag limits on the number of alligators that could be taken, and the species almost disappeared. A statewide hunting ban that followed, and national laws that prevented the sale of hides, allowed the alligator population to come back. Now, in some areas, there may be too many.

Although alligators in the wilderness are normally timid and easily frightened, urban alligators quickly adjust to people. If they are fed – it's a misdemeanor to feed one – they lose their natural human fear and become aggressive. They crawl into yards, chase dogs and even attack people. A swimmer was killed at a North Florida state park by a large alligator in 1987. In 1988, a child was pulled into a suburban Southwest Florida lake and drowned by an alligator that had been routinely fed by residents.

A small hunting season for alligators was allowed in 1988. Some 230 hunters killed 2,912 alligators. Trappers, meanwhile, were issued 7,979 permits to catch alligators and got 4,464. The Borellis trapped 110.

It's 10 a.m. on a steamy July morning. The security guard of the Timberlake Apartment complex stands on the lake shoreline and looks sheepish. The Borellis are here, and the alligator that has frightened residents is gone. It's a seven- or eight-footer and considered dangerous.

"There was a dog on the shoreline the other day," the guard says, "and the gator saw him from the other side of the lake. I had no idea gators could move so fast. He really came across the lake."

The dog escaped. Many alligators trapped by the Borellis have devoured dogs. Joe once saw a gator grab a dog and shake it so viciously the head was broken off. The Borellis recently bought a toy mechanical dog they hope will help them lure alligators close enough to shore to catch. They have yet to try it.

Their weaponry also includes tape recordings of chirping baby alligators. Sometimes a chirp will draw a charge from a female alligator that thinks her young are in danger. To a male alligator, a chirp is a dinner bell. They eat baby gators.

"Well, I don't see anything," Joey Borelli says. As his father walks along the lake edge, Joey scans the far side with binoculars. He sees nothing but ducks.

"This isn't that unusual," he says. "We usually don't get an alligator the first time out. We usually have to come out a couple of times. Unless we get lucky." Luck, of course, is relative. In June, when the Borellis arrived at a Lake Maggiore community to work, the alligator was on hand.

Unfortunately, it had crawled deep into a culvert. Residents said it was a sixfooter. Joey tied a line to a hook, baited it with a decomposing beef lung, and floated the whole shebang into the hole. The gator was not hungry.

Joey was determined. He attached a light to his hat and grabbed a 10-foot pole on which a noose was mounted. Ducking, he entered the culvert and moved ahead until, 25 feet in, his light revealed glowing eyes. The alligator looked bigger than six feet to him, Joey remembers.

He slipped the noose around the head.

"It's real hard to pull an alligator out of a culvert," Joey says, as his dad listens."They spread their legs against the side and use their tails to wedge themselves. What you do is pull with all your might, and when the alligator relaxes, you can move him a little."

In the culvert, all went well until Joey bumped his head and extinguished his light. At that very moment, the alligator stopped pulling. It meant one thing. The alligator was coming out, and Joey was in the way.

"That's when I heard him scream," says Joe, laughing at his son.

"I started backpedaling as fast as I could," Joey says. "I was really scared." He got the gator, which turned out to be nine feet, before the gator could get him.

"We've gotten them bigger," Joe Borelli says. "Sometimes the big ones aren't as feisty as the smaller ones."

They hauled a 13-footer from Lake Seminole. They nabbed a 12-foot-10-inch whopper behind Ruth Eckerd Hall in Clearwater. They caught a 12-footer behind the Lake Maggiore fire station in St. Petersburg. Joe says firefighters apparently were feeding it; firefighters considered the gator a pet.

"They didn't want us to get it," Joe says. But Joe and Joey did.

It's 11 a.m. at St. Petersburg's Lakewood Country Club, where seven-foot alligators have been sunbathing on fairways and making golfers nervous.

REAL FLORIDA

"We've had one on the 13th fairway," says the security guard. "And I think there's one on the 15th under a pepper tree."

Joe and Joey Borelli jump into their truck and follow the security guard. The gators are nowhere in sight. Joey checks out the lake shoreline through binoculars. Joe points out spots he has taken alligators in the past. "I don't think there's any water in Pinellas where I haven't gotten one," he says.

Not that alligators need water. Joe and Joey once caught a gator in downtown St. Petersburg, seven blocks from the nearest lake. Not long ago, they received an emergency call about the ultimate urban alligator.

During the night, a five-footer had sneaked into an open garage and crawled under a couch. Joe got his gator, as he has gotten other gators from under mobile homes and houses.

"I don't like going under houses," he says. One time, under a house, he had to catch somebody's escaped four-foot monitor lizard. "They're even faster than alligators."

Though Joe is flirting with retirement age, he's seldom overmatched. He is one of those people who seems to be tuned into animals and the elements more than humans. He wears a straw hat and a long-sleeved shirt and inevitably walks from tree to tree, staying in the shade and protecting himself against the sun. He usually won't check an entire lakeshore for alligators; experience has taught him that a wild goose chase rarely turns up a goose. He looks only in the most likely places. And when he finds an alligator, he weighs his movements carefully.

"If you lose your concentration, you're going to get hurt," he says.

Once, five years ago near the town of Oldsmar, it happened to Joe. He lost his concentration while dealing with a seven-footer. When he grabbed for its jaws, he somehow missed, and the gator clamped onto his right hand and held on.

"The thing you don't want to do is panic," Joe says now. "You have to be perfectly still." Two reasons for that, he explains. One, if you pull, you'll only tear your flesh. Two, if you upset the gator, it might do what gators do naturally when they catch prey. They start rolling to break apart skin and bone.

"I just looked at him eye to eye until he let me go."

Joe's got a scar near his thumb. An infection from the tooth and the dirty water put him in the hospital. He missed a month of gatoring.

At Lakewood Country Club, Joey asks the guard to call when the gators show up again. With lightning flashing, he and his father climb into their truck and head north.

It's noon at a subdivision called Starkey Heights. Joe and Joey Borelli stand staring at a wide canal. A 10-foot gator has scared residents. The alligator is gone now.

"He's been hanging around where the kids are fishing," says a man.

"He was lying on the bank, and hissed at a guy who rode by on his bicycle," says a woman.

"I seen him grab a duck," a man says. "I watched him carry it into the storm drain."

The Borellis are happy to hear about the culvert. The gator might be in there now. While Joey waits by the canal, Joe goes to the truck to get one of the beef lungs they buy from a Dade City source. Beef lung is perfect gator bait. One, it smells to high heaven. Two, it floats. Joe sticks a hook into the beef lung, adds a marshmallow for visibility and hands the rig to Joey.

Joey stands on the culvert, dangling the beef lung from a rope. He swings the bait to and fro for momentum, then pitches it into the culvert. "If the gator is there, he'll smell it," he says.

Joey spreads the rope across a bush where he can see it. Now he and his dad back away. If the gator hears them, it might not bite.

"All gators are different," Joe says, as his son listens. Some gators attack a bait immediately. Others swim up, sniff and flee. Some gators refuse to come near, especially if they see strangers watching from the shore.

"One time I was in this woman's yard, and I couldn't get the gator to come to the bait," Joe says. "She walked out her door, opened the gate, and the gator made a beeline for us. She'd been feeding it and the gator recognized her."

An hour passes. Still no gator. The Borellis tell alligator stories to the neighbors who have gathered to watch. They often work in front of an audience. Once, near Ulmerton Road, a television station helicopter filmed them. Their photographs, meanwhile, have been published in newspapers across the country. Men who capture alligators alive are a novelty.

The Borellis, especially Joe, dislike publicity. While many people are relieved when they catch urban alligators, others complain that what the Borellis do is a form of cruelty. The trappers are unashamed of their profession; at the same time they avoid the limelight that might invite controversy.

They let the game commission's publicity department explain the principles of wildlife management to the many Tampa Bay residents who learned about wildlife from Walt Disney specials, loathe hunting and buy their meat packaged neatly at the supermarket. Gators are trapped and killed, the commission says, because there is a surplus of alligators and nowhere to put them. Biologists say it is pointless to move dangerous alligators from an urban area to a rural area already crowded with alligators. The habitat supports only so many.

"You'd think we'd be thinning out the alligator population by now," Joe says. "But there are as many now as there were when we began trapping eleven years ago. I know we're not hurting the population."

That's about as close as he gets to making a speech.

Joey says, "We're private people. And what we do is really no big deal." There's nothing to give away their profession but their khaki trapper clothes and smelly truck. Joey has friends who don't know how he makes a living. "When they ask, I say I work with my father."

But these people at Starkey Heights seem relaxed about alligator trapping. They don't criticize the Borellis. They want to hear gator lore, gator stories.

Can a gator see straight ahead when opening its jaws wide? Joe doesn't think so. Do gators chew? Nope, Joey says, they tear.

Do you guys eat a lot of gator? Hardly ever. It's worth five bucks a pound; five bucks can buy five pounds of hamburger. For that matter, the Borellis don't own one pair of alligator shoes between them.

Do alligators really crawl into swimming pools?

"We get a lot of them out of pools," Joe says. Not just outdoor pools. Gators like screened-in pools, too. They bash right through the screening. They also climb fences to get into pools. Alligators have claws at the end of their feet that let them climb a chain-link fence in a heartbeat.

Still no gator in the culvert. Joey goes to the truck and returns with a snare. He sets it up in the culvert opening. The snare will catch any gator that tries to swim in or out. The Borellis will come back soon and check.

If they have their gator, they'll grab the rope attached to the snare and pull with all their might. Sometimes they can haul in a small gator by themselves. A big one is tougher. They have to drive the truck to the water's edge and attach the snare-rope to the winch. They winch in the gator, get a few more ropes around it and tape the jaws shut.

Then, with block and tackle, they lift the alligator into the truck. Alligators larger than 11 feet don't quite fit. If you ever see a gator tail protruding from the back of a red pickup, you probably are following Joe and Joey Borelli.

"The truck is better than the Volvo station wagon we used to have," Joey says.

It's 3:00 p.m. and overcast when Joe Borelli calls out the next destination: Serenity Gardens Cemetery on Indian Rocks Road. "People who have come to pay their last respects don't want to see alligators," Joe explains.

They park at the big lake. Joe, of course, has caught them here before and points out exactly where. In that culvert. By that oak tree. Near that bridge. No alligators are in evidence now.

"You shoulda been here yesterday," barks a cemetery employee.

Yesterday, an eight-footer crawled out of the lake and stopped in the middle of a road, blocking passage of an automobile. Today, ducks cavort on the lake – a bad sign. Ducks don't cavort where alligators play.

"This is how it is sometimes," Joey explains.

"It's a waiting game," Joe says.

"These people will call us," Joey says.

"Probably just when I sit down to eat," Joe grumbles. "They always seem to call at supper."

Two days later.

Noon.

Joe Borelli is sitting on the shoreline at St. Petersburg's Timberlake Apartments, the same place he and Joey visited the other day. Now he's holding a line, attached, he hopes, to the alligator. "We came back so I could put a snare over the culvert – the one hidden by that big Brazilian pepper – and I saw him," he says. He threw out a baited hook.

The gator took the beef lung, spit it out, and took it again. Then he went under. Joe has been waiting for Joey to bring a stronger rope and a snare. Here comes Joey. They're ready.

Joe pulls on the line, and it's clear something heavier than a beef lung is on the other end. Joe's thick muscles work against it.

Something white flashes in the murky water. It's the alligator's throat, exposed. Its jaws are yawning open. The gator is hooked solidly.

While Joe pulls, Joey uses a pole to position the snare around the alligator. The two men don't even talk. They don't have to. They've done this about 1,000 times since 1978.

Joey's got him. He hauls the alligator, thrashing, to the bank. A half dozen spectators, mostly security guards and residents, automatically step back. Joey seems nonchalant, though he is alert. He respects gator jaws and gator tails. He has been knocked down by an alligator's tail before.

Thirty feet from the lake, Joey stops with the gator. As Joey holds it still with the rope, Joe uses a pole to close the gator's jaws and pin them to the ground. Next Joe steps on the closed jaws, kneels, and grabs the jaws with his right hand. A gator has tremendous biting power but lacks the strength to open its jaws against resistance. With his left hand Joe wraps the jaws and the eyes with electrician's black tape. The gator stops struggling.

Now Joey straddles the gator. He ties the four legs behind the gator's back with rope. Hogtied, the gator won't be able to crawl in the truck. Joey whips out a measuring tape. This gator is six feet four inches. Joe attaches a game commission tag to the tail. It's tag No. 71, the 71st gator the Borellis have caught in Pinellas County in 1989.

They put their gator in the truck.

"You know what," Joe says, right before they leave. "Couple weeks from now, there'll be another gator in that lake to replace this one we caught. That's just how it is. Gators will get in through the culvert system. They'll walk on in. Hell, they'll cross busy streets to get here.

"There always will be gators."

Milt Sosin, reporter

MIAMI   7/15/90

Milt Sosin, the ancient and crusty reporter who covered the Kennedy assassination, earthquakes, hurricanes, revolutions and the lives of the famous and infamous, is acting this morning in a manner that might surprise the people he has growled at, intimidated or exposed in print during a half century of journalism.

The man known for his pit bull personality seems to be purring like a pussycat.

As he works his beat, covering the federal courts here for the Associated Press, he is nice as pie. He pokes his head into offices and makes small talk with secretaries. He chats with a lawyer in an elevator. He shares respectful words with a newspaper reporter outside a courtroom. With a charming smile, he even opens a hallway door for a sweaty man in a three-piece suit.

For Sosin, who is probably the best reporter you *never* heard of, charm is part of his giant bag of journalist's tricks. His job is getting information. Being chummy, though it may come unnaturally, could pay off one day: He may need these courthouse people to provide news that might lead to an Associated Press exclusive.

"It's no big deal," Sosin says later, sounding almost embarrassed. "They're just sources. You treat them right. You stop by and ask them if anything is going on, that's all. If they give you something you can use, you protect them. You never betray their confidences."

Sosin did not become a Florida journalism legend by being Mr. Nice Guy. He got there by guts and guile, by working hard and traveling far. He got there by an uncanny ability to be where news was taking place. A plane crashes and Sosin is on board. A hurricane changes course and strikes where Sosin is staying. The man who killed John F. Kennedy is murdered and Sosin is close enough to smell gunpowder.

"I know he wasn't at Pearl Harbor," says Howard Kleinberg, the former editor of the now-defunct *Miami News*, where Sosin was the star reporter for 32 years. "And I know he wasn't at the birth of Christ. But he was everywhere else."

Sosin is about 80, give or take a few years, and it's none of your business if you want exact numbers. Ask him his age and you're likely to hear the famous Sosin snarl. About his private life Sosin seems to be as sensitive as an injured rattlesnake.

"Why the hell would anyone care about reading a story about me?" he roars.

But in his professional life, Sosin was known for his dogged pursuit of people who wanted to avoid publicity or reporters. "Milton was the most abrasive, annoying, persistent reporter I ever saw," says retired *Miami News* columnist John Keasler, who worked with Sosin for 30 years.

Sosin was so aggressive that he was arrested, more than once, for interfering with police investigations. He was physically attacked by mobsters, who objected to his take-no-prisoners coverage of organized crime. He intimidated public officials, lawyers, timid editors and anybody else who got in his way.

He had the great reporter's gift of being in the right place at the right time.

In 1963, when John F. Kennedy was assassinated, the *News* sent Milt Sosin. Two days later, when Lee Harvey Oswald was murdered by Jack Ruby, Sosin was literally inches away. "My aged mother was watching on television," Sosin says now. "She turned to my sister and said, 'He shot Milt!' "

Sosin had more than an eyewitness account. Ruby had been helping him, giving him tidbits of information, drawing him diagrams of the Kennedy shooting for two days. Sosin's scoop was how a small-time nightclub owner had the run of the police station.

"Whenever there was a tragedy – a plane crash or a ship burning at sea – we always worried about where Milt was," says Edna Buchanan, the *Miami Herald* reporter who won a Pulitzer Prize. "He had this strange ability to be where news was happening. At a plane crash or something, our reporters might be waiting behind police lines – only to find that Sosin had been a passenger."

Other reporters were sure that hurricanes followed Sosin, who loved covering natural disasters with a passion. There's a famous *News* photo that shows Sosin calling in his hurricane coverage from an outdoor phone. Right after photographer Jay Spencer snapped the picture, a huge wave knocked both men down.

"How do you cover a hurricane?" somebody once asked Howard Kleinberg. His reply: "Give Sosin and Spencer a roll of coins and send them where the wind is."

Sosin covered earthquakes and revolutions, floods and fires, murders and parades. He posed as a homeless man for three days and wrote about his experience. He interviewed Winston Churchill and Fidel Castro. Meyer Lansky, the late and infamous mobster, called him "Milt."

Sosin's reporting was, and is, known for its accuracy, fairness and brevity. He never won the Pulitzer Prize, but he won tons of smaller ones. As a writer, he was no Leo Tolstoy, though if you added up his stories you would have a volume longer than *War and Peace*. And that would be an apt title for his work.

"He wasn't as good a writer as he liked to believe," says his former boss Kleinberg, who started working at the News in 1949. "He would give you the five W's – who, what, when, where and why. The basics. But nobody could hold his jock when it came to gathering information. He was the greatest reporter I ever saw."

Meaning no offense, Kleinberg talks about Sosin in the past tense. Sosin may be an old-timer, but he hardly belongs in a museum. For one thing, he's slim, tanned and fit. He has the shuffling gait of an ex-athlete. On the tennis court, he routinely beats younger opponents.

On the job, his eyes are piercing and alert under bushy eyebrows. His questions and remarks are as penetrating. With his jutting nose, and his ever-present pipe, he could be Sherlock Holmes' street-wise cousin. Sosin is good at mysteries, too.

When he retired from the *Miami News* in 1976, his colleagues sprang a surprise party. Sosin calmly reached into a back pocket, withdrew a story he had written three days earlier and started reading aloud. The story detailed all the secret party plans. Sosin had written the story in rhyme and verse.

His retirement lasted a day. One. Then he accepted a "part-time" job with the Associated Press. He generally works a 40-hour shift at one of Miami's most challenging beats. The federal court is not where a news organization sends a young inexperienced reporter or an old one with tired blood.

"He has the job as long as he wants it," says Sosin's editor, Will Lester. "He has the enthusiasm of a cub reporter. Milt generates news. He's quick. He's accurate. He knows everybody."

Two years ago, Sosin uncovered one of his best scoops. For weeks there had been rumors that the federal government was going to indict Panama dictator Gen. Manuel Noriega for drug crimes. The *Miami Herald* had reporters working the story, as did the *Miami News*, the *Fort Lauderdale Sun-Sentinel*, the *Fort Lauderdale News* and some smaller publications. The Associated Press had Sosin, his experience, his sources, his famous news nose.

"I was sure he had been indicted," Sosin says now. "But the U.S. attorney was keeping it secret. He wanted to announce it at a press conference. I made a few phone calls. All my sources said Noriega's name was on the indictment. I told The Associated Press to go with the story."

"If it had been any other reporter, I would have held the story," says The Associated Press' Lester. "But I have learned that having Sosin is like having a crystal ball. Half the time he knows things before judges do."

Milt Sosin, reporter, had himself another scoop.

"Don't make a big deal of me," Sosin growls. "I'm just a goddamned reporter doing a goddamned reporter's job."

He pauses.

"Understand?"

Sosin was born in Jersey City, N.J. "Know where that is?" he asks. "It's the asshole of the world." His mother was a homemaker and his father owned a stationery store. They encouraged him to do what he wanted. Even at an early age, Milt Sosin wanted to be a newspaperman.

"I didn't want a job where I had to work hard," he says without a smile. "I wanted to travel the world at somebody else's expense."

He studied journalism at New York University. He worked for a number of small newspapers in the New York area. When World War II began, he joined the Army. In 1944, after his discharge, he came to Miami in uniform. He wanted to live in a place where it never snowed. The *Miami News* hired him.

Sosin made an immediate splash. As the first reporter to fly in a hurricane-hunter airplane, he wrote a hair-raising account. "It was an old B-25, and I was in the nose, and it leaked. Back then we flew into the storm at low altitude. You really felt it. The winds would knock you down so low you thought you were going into the ocean."

Sosin was as flamboyant as his stories could be colorful. When reporting a story that involved flying, he often dressed as an aviator. Covering hurricanes, he might look like a New England lobsterman in a yellow slicker. Reporting from the Everglades, he could have been just another frog gigger.

"He had a wardrobe for every occasion," Kleinberg says. When the nation's space program began in earnest in the 1950s, the News dispatched Sosin, who had to expand his wardrobe to include spacewear. Colleagues say he would appear at the Cape looking more like an astronaut than the astronauts.

Don Wright, who won two Pulitzer Prizes for his editorial cartoons in the *News*, started his career at the paper as a photographer. Working with Sosin, he says, was an experience. "He was a swashbuckler," says Wright, now cartoonist for the *Palm Beach Post*. "He did everything with high drama. I flew with him a couple times when I had to take pictures. Of course he had his own plane. He would announce everything he was doing in a loud voice. LEFT REAR RUDDER. RIGHT REAR RUDDER. I guess it was his checklist he was going over, but he scared me to death."

When Sosin was assigned to the office, he came to work by paddleboat. He rode it across the Miami River.

When Sosin was reporting locally, he got around town in a Jaguar. Not just any Jag. Sosin always drove silver Jaguar convertibles.

"He was something to see," says Edna Buchanan, who sometimes competed against Sosin for the *Herald*. "You'd be at a fatal accident, or a murder scene, and here he'd come down the street in that Jag with his gray hair blowing in the breeze."

After work, Sosin often carried passengers in his Jags. He had (and has) a penchant for younger blond women who in unenlightened times might have been described as "bombshells." He was married once, but it failed, and after the divorce he seldom went wanting for female companionship. Sometimes, late at night, Sosin and a woman friend would stroll into the newsroom. Heads snapped around to watch. Sosin knew how to make an entrance.

He also knew how to make enemies. During the 1950s, when organized crime gained a foothold in Miami, Sosin was on the job. One day a mobster confronted him at Wolfie's, the famous deli on Miami Beach, and accused him of writing lies. Sosin ordered him away from the table. The mobster kicked Sosin in the shin and missed with a vicious punch.

"There was a period where I always checked under the Jag's hood for bombs," Sosin says. He also carried a .32. When he went dancing at the famous Fontainebleau Hotel's Poodle Room, then a favorite gangster hangout, Sosin liked making a point of handing his pistol over to the bartender.

"I just wanted them to know I had it."

Yet, in a strange way, the big-time criminals respected him. In the 1960s, one of Miami's most notorious bad guys, flamboyant jewel thief Jack "Murph the Surf" Murphy, granted him a series of exclusive interviews.

"He knew I was a fair man," Sosin explains.

Later, as a murder suspect, Murphy called Sosin and asked him to write a story saying that Murphy thought police should prove their case or get off his back. "I wrote it. He was arrested the next day. He was convicted, too."

Sosin even had a working relationship with Meyer Lansky, who was supposed to be the brains behind the nation's organized crime. Lansky granted his only interview to Sosin. Years later, when Sosin was working on a story about legalized gambling, he called Lansky's attorney and asked for another interview with the old mobster.

The attorney told him Lansky would never consider talking to a reporter again. Minutes later, Sosin's phone rang.

"Milt," said the voice. "It's Meyer."

Sosin enjoyed traveling. He reported from 46 countries. Vacationing in Mexico, he was probably the only tourist who delighted in the earthquake. Earthquakes made such good stories. In Cuba, before the revolution, he was arrested by machine gun-toting government soldiers who wanted him to stop asking questions.

Somewhere, in *Miami News* archives, is a photograph of Milt Sosin holding a machine gun, while one of his interview subjects, Fidel Castro, totes a typewriter. There also are photos of Sosin standing behind John F. Kennedy and Richard Nixon. There is a photo of Sosin with Winston Churchill.

"After the war, Churchill came to Miami Beach to paint. I knew where he was staying." Sosin and a photographer drove over. They walked into Winston Churchill's yard. A Scotland Yard officer objected, strongly, and ordered the newsmen to leave. Churchill waved them over.

Scoop.

There are photos of Sosin interviewing trapeze artists – as he sits on scaffolding 50 feet above the landing net. There are photos of Sosin in the cockpits of jet planes. Many Sosin stories involve planes. In one, Sosin's plane ditched in the ocean near Cuba. He always considered himself lucky. Firsthand accounts of plane crashes made good stories.

He had no patience with newsmakers who didn't want to talk. And he found ways to make them talk.

"During the Cuban Missile Crisis, the *News* sent Sosin and I to Homestead Air Force Base," says Jay Spencer, the former News chief photographer.

"Sosin walked up to a general and started asking questions. The general brushed him off. Sosin walked about 10 feet away and started pouting. Dramatically. It looked like he was crying. It was part of Sosin's bag of tricks. The general got flustered, walked over, put his arm around Sosin, and told him everything Sosin wanted to know.

"Then Sosin ran for the phone booth and started dictating."

The *News*, an afternoon paper that closed in 1988, prided itself on local coverage. When the *Herald*, a much larger morning paper, got a local scoop, Sosin usually was assigned to redeem the *News*. At 5:00 one morning, Sosin began such a redemption project, telephoning key sources all over Miami. Says former editor Howard Kleinberg: "One guy objected to Sosin waking him. Sosin not only chewed him out for not recognizing the importance of news, he chastised him for not speaking distinctly."

Sosin thought well on his feet. In 1968, Kleinberg remembers going through filing cabinets and discovering a bottle of rum. It belonged to Sosin. Although Sosin is a throwback to an era when reporters were almost expected to drink alcohol on the job, Kleinberg was dismayed.

"I called him on it," Kleinberg says. "Sosin explained that when he covered a fire, his feet sometimes got wet, and that a shot of rum kept him from catching his death of cold. I allowed him to have his rum. Who was I to tamper with tradition?"

REAL FLORIDA

In the newsroom, Sosin was a terror. Once or twice a year, he would resign and come back only when the offending editor had been dismissed, demoted or made to apologize. He can quote lead paragraphs that he says were ruined by stupid editors. Thirty years ago.

"When he phoned in a story, he was sure he had it all," says Ken Heinrich, one of Sosin's former city editors. "He was tough on people who were handling his stories. They hated to deal with him."

"Amateurs," Sosin called editors who let him down. It was, and is, his battle cry.

"He could get to you," Heinrich says. "He was needling me on deadline once, just wouldn't let up, and I knocked him over a chair with a phone book. I felt bad about it later. I think somebody must have put him up to it."

Sosin could be obnoxious on the job. In a group interview, he was all elbows, pushing his way to the front. "To work against him was formidable," says Charles Whited, now a *Miami Herald* columnist. "He always irritated me. Still does. To know Milt is to dislike him."

Colleagues say that if a radio or television reporter got a microphone in his way, he might ruin the broadcast with profanities. At an accident, or a crime scene, especially with deadline looming, he became even more aggressive. Sometimes the cops put him in jail to shut him up.

Former *Miami News* columnist Keasler tells a story he says illustrates Sosin's determination. "Sosin calls from the scene of a fatal accident and says, 'The dead man has a common name. I got to get a middle initial.' You can hear Sosin browbeating the cops in the background. Then the line goes dead.

"Sosin calls about an hour later. He says, 'The middle initial is T as in table. And I'm in jail.' Sosin had taken the wallet out of the poor, dead soul's pocket and gotten the initial. He was arrested."

Sosin says now: "Keasler says that? That's a ridiculous story. It must have been someone else."

But others say Sosin let nothing stop him.

"I love Milt – he's an institution," says the *Herald*'s Buchanan, known to be as hard-boiled as an Easter egg. "But there was one thing he used to do that turned me off. He liked to beat the police to the next-of-kin. Milt wanted to tell them that their loved one was dead. He thought he got the most honest emotions that way."

"Who said that?" Sosin bristles. "Edna? Ridiculous. Ridiculous. You going to print that?"

Milt Sosin no longer drives silver Jaguars. But that hardly means he has mellowed. He claims it's impossible to find decent Jaguar mechanics in Miami nowadays. "I drive an American sports car."

What kind?

He refuses to answer.

"I don't want to give them free advertising," he snaps.

Five mornings a week he drives his vehicle to the U.S. District Court near Miami's depressed Overtown area. Windows of many adjacent businesses are boarded or barred. Barbed wire fences surround parking lots. Walk into the federal court building and you have to pass through a metal detector. Many people have guns in Miami; Noriega sometimes appears in court here; federal judges in the South have been killed by bombs.

"You want Sosin?" asks the security guard at the metal detector. "Sure, he's here. He always is."

Everyone knows Sosin, the legend. Security guards. Lawyers. Janitors. Unannounced, he strolls into judges' chambers, tells them what the public wants to know, and maybe passes on the kinds of jokes that can't be printed in family newspapers. If he is working a story, he sits, asks sharp questions and takes notes on a yellow legal pad.

Unlike many modern journalists, Sosin hates tape recorders and most other electronic gizmos. A pen or pencil is good enough for him, and if his interviewee talks too fast, Sosin tells him or her to slow down. When he is satisfied with his information, Sosin heads for his office.

Associated Press has a 12-foot-by-22-foot office on the third floor of the courthouse. Sosin has a battered desk, two 1988 telephone books, a telephone and a tired-looking Royal manual typewriter he seldom uses. Sosin composes stories in his head and dictates. No computer terminals. No extensive rewriting. No suffering at the keyboard.

"He's so different from other reporters," says photographer Bill Cooke, who sometimes works with Sosin. "Most of them now are kind of yuppies in suspenders. They eat quiche for lunch, and they sit at their computer terminals and talk about the quality time they hope to spend with their kids. Sosin is the last of a dying breed."

Sosin, perhaps surprisingly, has a higher opinion of young reporters. He says he generally is pleased by the state of journalism. "Print journalists, by and large, are an educated lot. There's some fine investigative reporting being done." Broadcast journalism is another story. "Too many of those people can't report. They're rip-and-read artists." In other words, they rip off Milt Sosin's stories and read them with authority on the air.

"They aren't willing to do the work," he says.

Sosin lives for his work. Any new reporter at the Miami bureau of the Associated Press usually has to spend a day with Sosin. "They have a hard time keeping up with him," says Cooke. So do polished, veteran journalists.

"Three years ago, I had to cover the pope's visit to Miami," former *Miami News* columnist John Keasler says. "Security was tight. Up near the pope, there was a crush of people. I thought I was as close to the pope as anyone could be. Then the pope turns, and I swear to God, Sosin was behind him."

So how does Sosin do it?

Does he get help from the pope's best friend?

At the age of 75 or 80 or 85 or 90 – whatever his age – how does he continue to thrive in what is basically a young person's profession?

Sosin is spectacularly unhelpful.

Reporting is being at the right place at the right time, he says. It is knowing people. Asking good questions. Luck.

All true. But trite. From Sosin, you want more. You want him to boil down five decades of excellence in one wonderful sentence. But that may be too much to ask of a man who doesn't go in for even a penny's worth of dime-store psychology. Ted Williams probably couldn't tell you what drove him to be a .400 hitter, either. Pushed for information, Sosin says quietly, "You're a pain in the ass."

A moment later he says, "I never considered reporting as work. That's the truth. I never worked a day in my life."

Upstairs Florida

BALSAM, N.C. 8/2/87

Here in Florida, we don't know how to relax, and that's a sad thing. We are forever speeding around in our cars, and glaring at our watches, and looking for things
that will complicate our lives and make our hearts pound way too fast and loud.

We know it's unhealthy to live as Type-A personalities, so once a year we go on
a vacation and try to relax. Usually we don't relax on vacation. At best, we glare at
our watches while standing in line at the theme park. At worst, we stay home and
paint the house.

This time, I tell myself, vacation is going to be different. I want to go where my
family can smell flowers, where we can watch birds, where we can be bored if we
want to be bored, where we don't have to stand in line. We need to go where people
know how to relax.

We inch through Tampa during morning rush hour, and I fume at traffic that is
costing us vacation time. When the speed limit leaps to 65 and other cars roar by as if
we are moving at 33 rpm in a 45 rpm world, I grip the steering wheel tightly and
complain about the waste of gasoline.

Gainesville comes and goes. The rest stop near Jacksonville is clean, but
Jacksonville air smells of chemicals, and I fume about air pollution. We eat lunch in
the car to avoid unnecessary stops and unhealthful fast food meals. I swear at the
thunderstorms ahead. I wonder if we're making good time. I wonder if the mechanic
fixed the oil leak.

"Relax," my wife says.

Then we leave the interstate, and the less traveled road winds through small
towns, and finally, up ahead, we see hills and peach trees and know that we are close
to what the wonderful *Miami Herald* writer Al Burt once called "Upstairs Florida."

Upstairs Florida, the mountains of North Carolina, is where a lot of us from this
busy crowded state go for vacation. In the fall, many go to watch green leaves turn
red and gold. In the winter, many go to experience snow and risk broken ankles on
the ski slopes. During spring and summer, Floridians visit to escape the heat and to
relearn how to relax.

They know how to relax in upstairs Florida. It's all the porches and rocking
chairs and whittling. At the house we rent here, there is a huge porch and four rocking chairs, and we sit and watch the man across the dirt road sit in his rocking chair
and watch us watching him. If he's not whittling, he should be.

His name is Bill. Unlike many people who own houses here in the Carolina
mountains, Bill is not a Floridian. He was born in North Carolina, and has stayed. He

lives with his mother, in her 80s, and she cooks meals on a wood-burning stove, and he cuts grass at many homes on Balsam Mountain, and evenings they just sit on the porch, she dipping snuff and he sucking his pipe, neither of them saying anything, both of them just a messin'.

Messin' is a North Carolina word for doing nothing. "Messin'," writes North Carolina author Bob Simpson, "consists of things like sitting under a tree and looking, maybe braiding blades of grass, or counting a flight of birds. Serious ones might try to estimate the number of leaves in a tree, while the serious and lazy might only estimate the number of branches."

Small children are naturally good at messin', and we have brought some along. We go together for a walk up the mountain, because that's what you do when you come to upstairs Florida. The children mess as they walk. Look at this millipede, the boy shouts, stopping in his tracks. The girl picks a flower and wants someone to weave it into her hair.

We who haven't learned about messin' yet don't want to stop. We want to hike quickly, get the heartbeat up, maybe lose weight while we're vacationing. Even in upstairs Florida, it takes time to shed the curse of the city.

Hummingbirds help get us in the spirit. We have hummingbirds in Florida, but not like here, where they are as common, and not much larger, than bumblebees. We find two hummingbird feeders and fill them with sugar water. Wings buzzing, fleets of ruby-throated hummingbirds arrive at the feeders, hungry and feisty.

They fight over the feeders. From the front porch 20 feet away we watch through binoculars. Then we stand under the tree and watch from six feet. Our presence doesn't bother them, so we stand on a bench a foot below them for a true bird's-eye view. Hummingbirds don't care. They're about as relaxed as everybody else in upstairs Florida.

We have a television in the house, but we're too far away from the nearest station to get reception. The teen-ager is unhappy: Upstairs Florida, she is sure, is a dreadful place. Then she discovers the art of berry picking.

We don't have many wild berry bushes in Florida, but they do here, and she is good at finding them. She hikes up the mountain with a paper cup and returns, triumphant, with blackberries. On the Blue Ridge Parkway, where few people drive faster than 35 miles per hour because of the breathtaking views, she prefers to read. But at every stop, she looks for wild strawberries. Wild strawberries are good with cereal.

In upstairs Florida, a good thing to do after breakfast is walk down to the nearest railroad tracks and look for railroad spikes. Why? "You'd pay a couple of dollars for one at an antique store," a city woman and veteran shopper tells me. I am unconvinced, but I pick them up anyway, I suppose because they are there. In upstairs Florida, picking up railroad spikes seems quite sensible, about as sensible as putting pennies on the tracks. By afternoon, they'll be squashed flat.

We hike up the mountain after supper. The bad heat, such as it is, is gone from the day, and the rabbits and woodchucks are likely to be out. So is the horse down the road, which likes yellow apples, and beyond the horse is the high mountain, so strange to someone from the flatlands of Florida.

The road is steep, even by upstairs Florida standards, so it's essential to have a walking stick. We don't need walking sticks in Florida, unless we live in high-crime neighborhoods, but they are nice here upstairs.

We don't buy walking sticks; we find them on the ground. We don't want sticks too dead and dry, because they'll snap under our weight. A just-cut branch is fine as long as it reaches shoulder height, and we will whittle away rough spots to make it fit comfortably in hand.

On flat ground, a walking stick helps maintain rhythm. Going uphill, climbing rocks, or descending a slippery trail, it converts a human, as Colin Fletcher once wrote, from a shaky biped into a courageous triped. And who's afraid of bears? Not the owner of a walking stick. We don't see any bears, though dogs we encounter threaten to lick us to death.

In summer, night comes late to upstairs Florida. Around 8:00, the fireflies appear. They're bigger than Florida fireflies, but they also seem slower, and the children find them easy to catch and put into jars.

When it's finally dark, about 10:00, the fireflies are gone from the yard. They still light up the jar though, and for some reason their frantic blinking makes me melancholy. The children are inside the house reading, so it seems safe to rise from the rocking chair and open the jar.

What happens is the fireflies crawl to the jar's lip, flex their wings, and launch themselves into the upstairs Florida night.

Satisfied, I return to my rocking chair. It makes a creaking sound in the dark.

Frank's Pier

Nobody ordered hamburgers for lunch the other day, and that was good, because Frank Cavendish doesn't sell them anymore. He stopped selling hamburgers because, well, they were too good, the best in the country, according to Frank, and they created too much work. Frank sells hot dogs now, and he keeps the Alka Seltzer next to his antique cash register.

Frank even sold breakfast at his Rod and Reel Pier. But that was a long time ago. Those breakfasts were good, and that was bad, because it made Frank work too hard. So Frank dropped breakfast. If you want beef jerky, or a candy bar, or a package of crackers for breakfast, fine. Don't ask for more. Don't rock the pier.

The other day was typical at Rod and Reel Pier, which pokes into the mouth of Tampa Bay on the edge of the Gulf of Mexico near Bradenton. A typical day is something like this: Frank comes in about 7:00 a.m., talks to a few friends, sells a few beers and some bait, talks about shark fishing, drinks a few beers, talks through his public address system, sells a few beers, drinks a few beers and then maybe goes home.

Things have been slow lately. That's for sure. Frank Cavendish even shaved off his beard, the beard he used to dye a different color every day and sprinkle with glitter. Frank said, "Every day at 3:00 p.m. I'd dive off the roof of the pier house and wash off the dye. People'd come from all over to watch that. I shaved off my beard when everybody started wearing them. But it was kind of pretty while it lasted. Would you like a beer?"

Frank, who has tried to stop being a character, has even stopped shark fishing. He used to be famous for shark fishing, you know. Frank Cavendish, you may remember, once caught from his little pier a 17-foot hammerhead shark that weighed 1,386 pounds. Nobody has ever caught a hammerhead larger than that. But after catching 779 sharks weighing 150 pounds or more, shark fishing became work, so he stopped.

"I'm 69 years old," said Frank, standing at the cash register. He wore a T-shirt and plaid shorts. His feet were bare. "Shark fishing is hard on you. Besides, when the movie *Jaws* came out, there was too much excitement about sharks. Even youngsters who didn't know what they were doing were shark fishing. Dangerous business. I didn't want to hang up a shark anymore."

But when he shark fished, he meant business. He employed 70 feet of 6,400-pound test rope, tied it to a five-foot chain leader that was attached to a five-inch forged steel hook and used a 10-pound slab of stingray for bait. He'd leave his bait out all night, recover his shark in the morning and use block and tackle to hang it at the pier entrance to attract tourists.

Nobody fished for sharks from Frank's pier the other day. A few people fished for pompano, and a few for flounder and a few more for snook. Nobody seemed to catch anything. Most drank beer while watching black skimmer birds eat minnows in the water. A few bathers swam near shore. When one drifted under the pier, Frank barked into the rusty microphone that hangs from the pier house ceiling.

"Somebody tell that boy to get away from the pier. He's gonna get cut up by a barnacle on the piling."

One of Frank's customers found that funny. "I'm gonna tell her you called her a boy, Frank," the man said. "She must be a 44-24-36." Frank said nothing. He got somebody a beer, tossed a hot dog into boiling water and wiped his bald head because it was hot in the pier house even with the one fan blowing.

Frank Cavendish bought the pier 18 years ago. A successful salesman who had worked for the R. J. Reynolds Co., U.S. Rubber and Goodyear, Cavendish moved to Bradenton, where he was employed by Tropicana Orange Juice. Then he fell in love with the ramshackle pier at the end of Anna Maria Island, quit his orange juice job, bought the 30-year-old pier and tried to become a fishing bum.

"Things worked out real good," said Frank. "Too good. That's the thing. This has worked into a business. I didn't want that."

Frank's business was good the other day, even though fishing was poor. Frank peddled a few hot dogs and a lot of beer. People sat on revolving stools in the pier house, flicked cigarettes into overflowing ash trays, and people stood against the back wall under the Pabst Blue Ribbon clock. Some stood looking at Frank's bulletin board filled with clippings about Frank and fish he has caught, and they looked at the beer advertisement that, upon close inspection, actually says, "Enjoy a nice cold girl."

On Frank's shelves were bottles of suntan oil, cigar boxes, pipe tobacco, and crackers, peanuts and pretzels stuffed into large glass jars, and cans of tomato juice used in his famous Bloody Marys.

Hanging from the walls and ceiling of Frank's place were Coca-Cola signs, saw-fish saws, a barometer, a naked woman painting, a devil doll made out of a guitar fish, two shark jaws and photographs of Pittsburgh Pirate baseball players who visit Frank when training in Bradenton during spring. "We get a lot of pitchers with sore arms," Frank said. "Their managers send them here to fish. When they cast, they exercise their arms."

Looking through the salt-encrusted windows of the pier house, Frank's customers could watch and ridicule the stubborn anglers who hadn't yet traded their fishing rods for beer. At a table outside the pier house, one man cleaned what looked like mullet. He was watched by a lazy-looking man who leaned against the paint-chipped pier house.

Although the outside of Frank Cavendish's place badly needed paint, it will probably never see another coat. "I made $38,000 worth of improvements after Hurricane Agnes in 1972," Frank said. "I could have spent a lot of money to fancy it up. But it would ruin it."

Hurricane Agnes was unkind to the old pier. It buckled the deck, then covered it with 10 inches of water. Frank Cavendish won't forget the morning after the hurricane. He rowed out to the pier in a leaky old skiff, which immediately began sinking. Looking around for help, he spotted Salty Sol Fleischman, the former Channel 13 fishing broadcaster who lives on Anna Maria Island. Salty, on that wondrous day, was fishing for redfish.

"I yelled at Salty for help," Frank said. "He didn't come. He took pictures of me while I sank. I had to swim to shore."

Frank doesn't mind swimming. He often swims the 100 yards from the pier house to shore. But he no longer swims after dusk because of sharks.

"One night I dove off the pier and all of a sudden, I saw this old boy heading for me. I curled up in a little ball so he couldn't bite my legs. Well, he turned away from me but swatted me with his tail. A shark's tail is like sandpaper. That tail peeled me like an orange. It took four Manhattans and a box of Band-aids to get over that."

Talkin' about
the Wakulla River

WAKULLA SPRINGS   6/28/87

The river, the old elephant bones and the performing big-mouthed bass are waiting for Capt. A.J. Rainey, who climbs aboard his glass-bottom boat, cranks the engine and announces in a loud voice:

"Now a whole lots of this trip consists of me talkin'. I'm gonna tell you about the spring and the birds and the fish I call Henry. Now you watch that glass and listen to me."

A dozen passengers peer through the glass at Wakulla River and listen.

"Now under these waters, we got 14 different species of fish, only you're gonna see only three or four kinds," A.J. Rainey says. "I gots wild ones and tame ones and wild ones that come when I call 'em. Wakulla Springs. Yeah. Yeahhhhh! Wakulla Springs."

At Wakulla Springs State Park, 15 miles south of Tallahassee, boatmen have been giving this tour for more than 60 years. It is not the kind of tour one gets at our big theme parks, where guides are white college kids home for the summer who dress up and point out pretend rhinos and crocodiles. At Wakulla, guides generally are African American men who grew up on the river and know every authentic bass, bird and blade of grass.

Most of the tour is informative, but all of it is entertaining and an important part of Florida folk culture. The boatmen do a lot of talking, as Rainey says, but by long tradition they also chant and sing, sometimes in a stream-of-consciousness style that suggests a country preacher, sometimes within the context of a blues or gospel tune, sometimes in what could be a modern rap artist's rhyme.

"Rain, shine, sleet or snow," A.J. Rainey says, "We always be willin' to put on a show."

Rainey is a relative newcomer to the glass-bottom boat business, which has lasted in Florida since the end of the 19th century. He's 22 and has guided less than three years. But like other young guides who run tour boats on this river, he learned at the elbow of old-timers who learned their trade from other old-timers who are either dead or gone.

"We are talking about a very old Florida tradition," says Barbara Beauchamp, the folklife arts administrator for the Department of State. "Most everything that these guides learn and say – the sing-song patter and the chants – has been passed on orally for generations. That's why it falls within the realm of folklore."

Wakulla Springs is the perfect place for such a program. It evokes an old-timey Florida that's disappeared almost everywhere else. The 2,900-acre park is in the mid-

259

dle of a forest and swamp preserve that has stayed the same for hundreds of years. Deer, bobcat and even bear survive.

The spring is one of the deepest and most powerful in Florida. Every minute, 600,000 gallons of water gush from a cave hidden 185-feet below the surface. The skeleton of an ancient elephant, known as a mastodon, was discovered in the cave and reconstructed at the Florida History Museum in Tallahassee.

A few mastodon bones are still visible on the sandy bottom. As guide Rainey tells his guests, "We got a jawbone, a leg bone and a hip bone, too. We have 'em all at Wakulla Springs for you." Some early Tarzan movies were filmed here to take advantage of the clear water and beautiful surroundings. So was the late-show chestnut, *Creature from the Black Lagoon.*

Ponce de Leon was probably the first out-of-state tourist to sample spring waters. In 1513, he was certain that Wakulla Springs was the Fountain of Youth. Six years later, on a return trip to Florida, he learned of his mistake. He died from wounds inflicted by Calusa Indians in the Everglades.

Boat tours have been conducted since the 1920s. Luke Smith, who guided 40 years before his retirement, was famous for the colorful and rhythmic way he described underwater flora. "All sunken and undah watah greeeeeen is growin'." Wilbert Gavin's specialty was vultures. "Way out in the country now, some people refer to 'em as a country airplane. In some of those other places, they refer to 'em as the undertaker's helper."

Luke Smith taught Gavin, who taught Hawk Jackson, a current guide who has helped teach one of the new ones, A.J. Rainey, who today is piloting the glass-bottom boat called *Henry,* named after one of the springs' featured performers.

"Heeeeeere boys," he sings, sounding like he should be in church as he summons bass, bluegill and catfish within view. "This is a call to your convention."

As he sings he backs the boat toward deeper water. The fish, which have been milling below, turn and follow. "Heeeere boys. Come on this wayay. Come on this wayay. Straighten up now. Straighten up." Incredibly, the fish swim in a straight line and eat the food Rainey tosses.

"Now all these fish have got to make you fishermen sick," he says, reading the minds of passengers who are entertaining fish-fry fantasies. "These fish will cost you $500 a pound and five years in jail. We don't allow fishin' here.That ought to take the taste of fish right outta your mouth. I know it does mine."

He maneuvers the boat over the deepest part of the spring, where it's black and scary enough to harbor a monster or two.

"They say if you drop a copper penny down in here, it'll be silver by the time it hits bottom. You folks wouldn't have to worry 'bout going down there. It's the comin' up you'd have to be concerned about."

He says he has saved the best for last. He is going to show off Henry, the pole-vaulting bass. Passengers exchange glances. Is this going to be as fakey as one of those theme park jungle cruises? Rainey rings a bell and swings his boat over a cypress limb that leans across the sandy bottom.

"All right now, Henry," he sings, in the raspy voice of an old blues singer. "Meet us at the pole. I say all right now, Henry. Meet us at the pole."

A largemouth bass swims out of the weeds.

"Wake up, boy, 'cause you heard what I said." Henry calls. "I said wake up, boy. You heard what I saiiiid."

Henry hovers next to the pole.

"Jump iiiiit!" Henry darts over, turns on his side and rubs his body against the pole as he crosses. It's as if he is ridding his belly of parasites, but he does it every time Rainey sings the words "Heyyyyy now!"

If it's a trick, it's a good one, and like a magician, Rainey does not explain tricks. Most passengers probably don't want to know how or why Henry the bass is obedient. Knowing would spoil the spell Rainey has cast. Anyway, passengers look glum as Rainey heads for the dock.

"Hold on tight," he announces. "This is where the fun begins. Last time I brought the boat in, I hit the dock so hard and everybody got off at once. I called it the express."

He is teasing. He docks with only a gentle bump.

"I think somebody prayin' mighty hard."

Solomon's Castle

ONA   9/6/87

Howard Solomon is not bonkers. He is just unlike anyone you have met lately. Out there in a Central Florida swamp, where mosquitoes buzz and bullfrogs croak, Solomon has scavenged a bunch of junk and used it to build his dream home: an honest-to-goodness castle.

"I always was interested in medieval things," explains the man who has been called the Rembrandt of Reclamation and the da Vinci of Debris. "I started building this thing, and I built straight up. It turned into a castle."

Solomon's Castle, three stories high and open to the public, represents 15 years of hard labor. At 8,000 square feet, it is as big as a good-sized church. It has towers, flying buttresses, stained-glass windows and a dungeon. It has a drawbridge and a moat filled with alligators.

"Some people are surprised when they see this," Solomon says. He pauses dramatically. "Others think I'm nuts."

Solomon, a 52-year-old artist whose specialty is metal sculpture, is more like a Wizard than a cuckoo bird. When you visit him, and see the magic he has created in the middle of nowhere, you know how Dorothy must have felt when she saw the Emerald City. You know you're not in Kansas anymore.

Say you are driving across the state on business. Thinking of the work ahead, you're grumpy. As you near Bradenton on State Road 64, which cuts through Central Florida, two signs catch your eye. The big one – Orville Triebwasser Taxidermist – you ignore. The smaller sign you find intriguing.

Solomon's Castle.

A castle? In Florida? Curious, you turn south on 665 and step on the gas. Business can wait. You need a peek at a castle. What a narrow road, you think. Better drive slowly. Nice farm over there. Cows. Look at that red-tailed hawk on the wire. Hope the truck doesn't break down. Somebody's got a wonderful orange grove here. Wonder how it did in the last freeze?

A castle?

After nine miles, you encounter the next Solomon's Castle sign. You've come this far, so don't chicken out now. You turn left on a bumpy sand road that threatens to loosen every tooth. A black snake slithers across the sand. This is an adventure, all right. Hope it's not a wild goose chase.

Then, ahead, you see something. Through the oaks and pines, on the edge of a swamp, gleaming in the sun, is a mammoth silver structure that suggests some kind of carnival edifice.

262

You have reached Solomon's Castle. Who is this Solomon? Is he the son of Norman Bates?

Nervous, you walk through a dark entrance. It's sweltering inside, and smells of mothballs. Anybody home? Two armored knights, dummies both, guard a door. Yoo hoo. Your eyes adjust. You see something move. In the back, a skinny man with a beard and glasses rises from a table piled with tools. "Hi," he says. "I'm Howard Solomon."

The king of the castle is home.

The man who built the castle is not exactly the boy next door. That's the impression you get as he tells you of his life, which began in Rochester, N.Y., in 1935. When he was four, after all, he got his hands on his mother's razor blades and knitting needles and built a very respectable truck.

He hated school, and school hated him. "Teachers told my parents I was borderline retarded. They recommended putting me in a trade school. Said I'd never amount to much. My favorite class was shop. I was good in shop."

After high school graduation he joined the service. He spent hours putting together weapons and taking them apart. "I was one of those persons who could have done it blindfolded." After the Korean War, at his uncle's invitation, he visited St. Petersburg – and stayed eight years. Good with tools, he had no problem finding work at a time when Tampa Bay was exploding with growth.

In 1964, looking for a change of scenery, he moved with his wife to the Bahamas. Solomon knew he had found paradise. "In the Bahamas, nobody fixes anything because repairs are too expensive. So everything gets thrown away. I found a dynamite dump in the Bahamas." With other people's trash he constructed all manner of treasure. "That's where I first started doing sculptures," he says.

The Solomons returned to Florida in 1972. "We were looking for seclusion," Howard Solomon says. In a swamp located halfway between the little Central Florida cities of Arcadia and Wauchula he found seclusion.

"My plan was to build a large conventional building where I could work and store my tools and sculptures. When the bulldozer was finished clearing, I found out I didn't have enough room to spread out they way I'd wanted. I really had bought a swamp. So I built straight up. I had no plans to build a castle. It was just serendipity. Spontaneous."

For building materials he used junk he found in the woods, on the river, along the roads. He borrowed $19,000 for lumber. A couple of carpenters helped with the foundation, but he did the rest himself.

"When the people in town found out what I was doing, they wanted to see it. I opened the castle to the public. That's how we ended up making a minor Florida attraction out of our seclusion."

Though he does not advertise, about 20,000 people visit Solomon's Castle a year. Travel companies include it on their Florida tours. Central Florida schoolchildren bus in for field trips. Antique car clubs from the West Coast visit regularly. Bikers roar onto his property, like modern knights looking for a joust, and turn into pussycats.

Honeymooners drive over from Orlando and say they enjoy Solomon's Castle as much as the Other Magic Kingdom. And after a day at Walt Disney's playground, they like Solomon's prices, too: He asks a donation of a couple of bucks.

The king of the castle often conducts tours himself. It's one of his many trades. He says he can make a living, or has made a living, as a carpenter, woodcarver, electrician, plumber, machinist, welder, sheet metal worker, painter, paper hanger, sand blaster, mechanic, gunsmith and a cook. And to all of those he could probably add: comedian.

The Picasso of the Put-On takes you outside the castle, points to one of the towers, and says: "My grandmother is up there making chicken soup. In the medieval days, they used to pour boiling oil on attackers. Here, we use chicken soup. It hurts, but at least people get well soon."

He points out the stained-glass windows he made himself, and tells how he bought used aluminum plates from the Wauchula newspaper and used them to shingle the castle. He shows you the moat and says you can't see the drawbridge because it's under water. "It's a downbridge."

Inside the castle, Solomon leads you into an art gallery to his sculptures. You expect a few pieces, but what you get are 300 sculptures that range from simple to spectacular. They also make you grin. His work has been described as funny, impressionistic realism.

A lawnmower sculpture hangs by invisible wires from the ceiling. Solomon says, "It's for cutting really tall grass." He shows you a roller skate sculpture a yard long. "It's for Big Foot." The mother-in-law clock he sculptured has two faces.

He shows you a strange-looking turtle sculpture, a turtle that has been blessed with hair. "I call it the tortoise and the hair." He says his life-sized Fulton Fish Market truck sculpture can carry three passengers. "One passenger sits at the wheel, one pushes and one runs alongside."

A ship with iron sails is gravity-powered. "It goes straight down." A weird-looking bird sculpture, a Chigle, floats fiercely above the room. "A chigle is half eagle and half chicken," Solomon explains. "And it's terrified of landing." There's a car powered by a V-8 engine. Yes, just as you suspected: Open the hood and you discover the engine is constructed with V-8 juice cans.

The king of the castle wastes nothing.

"This is Lionel," he says, introducing you to a lion that looks mean enough to bite off your hand. Lionel was created from two scavenged 50-gallon oil drums, three 30-gallon drums and 70 pounds of welding rods. Lionel took 45 days to make.

A steam locomotive, large enough to carry a child, sits in a corner. Solomon built it with a valve trumpet, a lampshade, a 1910 Ford kerosene lamp, a transformer canister, a piece of Xerox machine, shock absorbers, beer cans and gravel. It runs.

"This was when I was in my evil period," Solomon says, entering a gallery containing home-made guns. One shoots toilet plungers. "For flushing out perpetrators." The hernia gun weighs 70 pounds. "It used to weigh 60 but I forgot to dust." Napoleon's pistol boasts an 18-inch barrel. "This is why he always had his hand in his coat." The gun for conscientious objectors has no trigger.

Now you go for a walk in the Solomon living quarters. Even there, things are a trifle skewed. He is probably the only person in Central Florida who can go from his kitchen to his upstairs bedroom by an elevator powered by car battery. In his living room, in front of the television, he also has constructed Florida's best conversation piece: Opening a trap door he reveals a grotesque sculpture of a torture victim.

"The dungeon," he says.

Outside Solomon's Castle, the shadows are getting long. You don't want to go home, or go to work for that matter, so you stand there in the yard and make small talk.

You will come back, you tell him, and you mean it. You'd like to spend more time shopping in his gift shop for items that include a tiny bird house that is actually a dwelling for mosquitoes. You want to see his castle when his adds the 35-foot bell tower. And you are looking forward to a meal at the 60-foot pirate ship-restaurant he plans to build in the moat.

"Sometimes when I look around, even I'm impressed," he says. "But my God! No wonder people think a madman lives here. I guess it is a little insane."

But you don't agree. Howard Solomon is not a fruitcake. He is just one of those adults who has refused to grow up.

Thank heavens.

Killer in the Keys

The Big Wind.

That's what Bernard Russell tells Florida Keys newcomers about. When they tell him they think it might be fun to experience a hurricane, he educates the pilgrims about big wind:

"You don't want to be here when a big hurricane hits. You want to listen to the experts who tell you to get out a long time before the storm gets here. If you're caught here, you're sunk. It's too late. You can't get out. You can't go out in the yard to secure your house. You have to sit there, and listen to a wind you can't believe. The wind howls and carries on and there's nothing you can do. Nothing. . . ."

In 1935, when Bernard Russell was 17, the most powerful hurricane in United States history swept through the Upper Keys. On Labor Day night, the unnamed storm, with its 250-mph winds and a 17-foot tidal surge, killed more than 400 people. The dead included 50 members of the Russell clan. Bernard Russell saw his mother and sister blown away into the night. A nephew was torn from his grasp. Only 11 Russells lived to see morning.

"There's nothing you can do if you're caught in a major storm," Bernard Russell, 74, says again. He sits in a chair in his Islamorada living room a block from the Atlantic Ocean, where balmy breezes rustle the coconut palms and fill the spinnakers of vacationing sailboarders.

"People don't know now what a major storm is like. And there are so many people here." There are too many, according to some folks. About 78,000 people live along the 150-mile chain of islands, which includes Matecumbe Key and its town of Islamorada. Add to that about a million annual tourists. Their lifeline to the mainland, for the most part, is a two-lane blacktop just a few feet above sea level. Civil Defense authorities figure it would take 30 hours to evacuate the Keys – if all went well, if there were no major road-blocking accidents or stalled vehicles on the 42 bridges or acts of stupidity or acts of God.

The Keys of 1991 are different from the Keys Bernard Russell knew as a boy. Russell, a retired cabinet maker, prefers the old Keys. They were unique. Today's Keys, in his opinion, are on their way to becoming just like cities everywhere.

"We even have a Burger King now," he says. "Everybody has Burger Kings. What we used to have is Mister Pete's. Sweetest hamburgers in the world. People used to get together there and talk. It was just a little neighborhood place. We didn't need a Burger King. Mister Pete's is gone."

REAL FLORIDA

He is uncomfortable talking against the progress that has brought so much prosperity to the Keys. But as a native, as the grandson of the man who founded in the last century what became known as Islamorada, he is protective of his Keys. He saw his island leveled in 1935 and helped rebuild it into a booming tourist area. He does not know if his Keys will survive progress. Progress can be more powerful than any storm.

"When I was a boy, my dad would say, 'We need six lobster for supper,' and I'd walk to the water and reach down and pick them up. Didn't need a boat. If I brought back seven lobster, dad would tear up my rear end. We didn't take what we didn't need.

"Now the lobster are on their last legs. Too many people taking them. Conchs – I cut my teeth eating conchs – now they're fished out. There used to be acres and acres of Key lime groves. People bulldozed them down and sold the property. Lot of the new people have no sense of what the Keys were like."

There are condominiums and $400-a-night hotels. There are huge marinas and outdoor "tiki bars" and gourmet restaurants galore. Offshore, the nation's only living coral reef is threatened by pollution and the anchors of thousands of vessels. Inshore, water scooters roar over the shallows and rout roseate spoonbills, great white heron and the bonefish that President George Bush tries to catch when he vacations here in the winter. The Keys boast a $450-million tourist industry.

"We're in danger of losing all the things that made the Keys unique."

Bernard Russell's grandfather, John Henry Russell, sailed to Key West from the Bahamas almost 150 years ago. By 1854, he had worked his way north to the key known as Matecumbe, a corruption of the Spanish expression "mata hombre" or "kill man," a prophecy fulfilled later by the big wind.

John Henry Russell, like most of the original Conchs, as early Key settlers were called, was more a farmer than a fisher. He grew pineapples for a living. So did his son, John A. Russell, Bernard's father, an ambitious man who also fished, raised chickens, grew limes commercially, operated a filling station, owned a grocery and was the island's first postmaster.

"Dad was an energetic man."

So was Bernard's mother, Catherine Louise. In addition to raising four children, she worked a garden and canned produce that would last a year. She made clothes and did some practical doctoring. During the Depression, the Russells never missed a meal. Neither did many of the other growing pioneer families, the Pinders and the Alburys and the Parkers.

"It was a magic place when I was growing up, a paradise," Bernard Russell says now. He's tan and stocky and talks in a country person's simple but lyrical way. Children worked to help their families, and attended a two-room school, but they also fished and played and developed a taste for homemade ice cream and candy.

And twice a day, Henry Flagler's famous train chugged through the Keys and provided free entertainment and brought the mail. Flagler, who helped develop Miami Beach and Palm Beach, completed the Miami-Key West railroad in 1912. In the morning, Bernard Russell and his family and friends met at the railroad station to gossip and to wave to the train. They did the same at night. Everybody flocked to the

267

waterfront when the ferry from Key West arrived bringing people and their cars. And after the cars passed, boys sometimes napped in the road.

There were hardships, but the Conchs were hard people.

"The mosquitoes were so thick you could catch them in your hands. Dad at night would set up smudge pots on the lee side of the house to smoke 'em away. If you needed doctoring, you had to get on the train to Key West, though my mother's herbs helped cure some sickness, too."

The Keys, a string of islands, some no more than a hundred yards wide, have always been vulnerable to big winds. Forty-three tropical storms have battered the Keys, killing and destroying, during the last century.

In August 1935, weather experts say, a storm formed off Africa and headed west across the Atlantic. By month's end, it was somewhere off Cuba and heading north. Miami started getting word of it from passing ships.

Within a 48-hour period, it grew from a minimal hurricane with 74 mph winds into the most powerful to hit the United States. It took a bead on the Upper Keys.

Matecumbe Key, the town of Islamorada and adjacent islands were almost bustling in 1935. President Franklin Roosevelt's New Deal had given 650 World War I veterans both homes and temporary work: They were building the highway that would eventually link Miami with Key West.

Hurricane forecasting was in its infancy on Sept. 2 when winds and seas began picking up higher than anyone expected. Worried federal officials supervising road construction called Miami. At 2:35 p.m., an evacuation of the Upper Keys was ordered.

In Miami, it took two hours to steam up the locomotive and assemble 10 cars for the emergency run. Meanwhile, the storm drew closer. The train left Miami and chugged through Homestead and into the Keys. At 6:50 p.m., in hurricane force winds, the train picked up a few evacuees about 20 miles north of Islamorada. As the train stopped, a loose cable, swinging violently from a pole, snagged the locomotive.

It took 80 minutes to clear.

The train headed toward oblivion.

When the train pulled into Islamorada at 8:10 p.m., winds were blowing 200 mph with gusts even higher, according to experts who later reconstructed the storm by examining the damage and what remained of weather instruments. The barometer plunged past normal 30.00 to 26.35 millibars, the lowest in U.S. history.

"We didn't want to ride out the storm in our house," Bernard Russell says now in a strong voice. He has told this story before because he thinks it's worth hearing. "Our house was right on the ocean where the storm was coming in. We decided to spend the storm on the lee side of the island in the house where we packed limes."

Bernard, his parents, three sisters, an uncle and his five children braced themselves.

"The wind, it was tremendous. You couldn't hear. And the pressure inside the packing house was so much greater than what was outside that the windows blew out."

At 8:00 p.m., Bernard noticed brown water oozing under the door.

"I didn't say anything because I didn't want to scare anybody. I knelt and tasted it. It wasn't rain. It was salt. I told my dad. He said we'd have to get out of there and go toward the train station, where it was higher. He said to grab a hold of somebody and not let go."

The Russells walked outside.

"My nephew was pulled right out of my arms. My mother went, too. I never saw them again. I managed to grab hold of the doorway. I felt the house start to rise up, like it was going to blow away, so I went into the storm."

It was so black he could see no more than a few inches.

"The wind and the water pushed me into the lime groves. I had no control. Something blowing in the wind stuck in my back and knocked me down face first into the water. I couldn't get up. I thought 'This is it.' Then the wind blew whatever was in my back out of my back and I could get up.

"I didn't know where I was. I just went with the wind and the water. The water got deeper. I crawled up on a trash heap and my foot caught. I couldn't get it out. I was stuck. The water kept coming. I stood as tall as I could and cupped my hands around my face to get air. The water was up to my face."

The water suddenly receded a few feet. Russell believes the tide broke through the fill on which the railroad was built. The bottled up water was allowed to gush across the island.

"I heard yelling. I shouted to whoever it was to keep yelling. I worked to free my leg and listened for the yelling. Finally I got my leg free and bumped into somebody. It was my dad. He'd only been a few feet away and couldn't get to me."

Russell's father was injured. A storm-driven projectile had sheared away one of his buttocks.

"We kept on going. Everything but the locomotive was blown off the track. Some of the cars were blown 100 feet away. We crawled into a car right next to the track and stayed 'till morning.

"When it got light, it was still blowing hard, and we crawled into the locomotive. We stayed there until the wind died down."

Survivors were greeted by a hellish scene.

It was like the world's most powerful bomb had exploded in the middle of the island. All but one of Matecumbe's 61 buildings were gone. The surviving building looked as if a giant sledge hammer had caved in the roof. Trees were broken off just above the ground. Russell could stand in one spot and view both the ocean and Florida Bay. Most train track was gone. Remaining rails were twisted into grotesque shapes. Flagler's $27-million railroad died at sea, too.

Bodies were everywhere.

Some people had drowned. Some were crushed by trees. Some were impaled by limbs or lumber. Some were tangled in the tops of fallen trees. They had tried to climb to safety. Others were decapitated by tin roofs flying at 200 mph. Some bodies were unrecognizable: The sand-driven wind had blasted away their faces.

"We were too in shock to even grieve," Bernard Russell says. He stops, takes a deep breath and continues. "I went over to where our house had been and there was nothing I could recognize. It was just a space.

REAL FLORIDA

"If you saw somebody you knew, alive, you were so happy."

Thirty members of the Russell family were never found. They blew away to sea. The body of a niece was recovered 40 miles away on a mainland beach. She was clutching her dead baby.

For months afterwards, bodies were discovered miles away on offshore islands. Thirty years after the storm, a developer dredged up an automobile with 1935 license plates. Inside the vehicle were five skeletons.

Two days after the storm, emergency crews arrived from Miami and Key West. One helper was author Ernest Hemingway, who took a look around and vowed never to write about what he saw. He kept his promise.

The remains of some of Russell's family were shipped to Miami and buried in mass graves. Most of the deceased, however, were cremated in pyres. Four mass fires were needed to burn bodies.

"I said, 'Dad, what are we going to do?'" Bernard Russell remembers 56 years later. "Dad said, 'All we have left in the world is our property. What do you want to do?'

"I said, 'I guess we have to start over. We're going to start over. We're going to dig in and start over.'"

The 11 remaining Russells started rebuilding. So did other survivors. Bernard joined the Coast Guard and then the Army. He married one of the Pinder daughters, Laurette. She had somehow survived the hurricane, too. They have been married 52 years. Unlike her husband, she dislikes even the thought of recalling her memories about the big wind. She lets him do the talking.

Bernard Russell became a talented carpenter. He could build anything, including boats, but his specialty was cabinets. As the Keys grew, as Islamorada's population surpassed 1,000, so did his business.

But he felt he owed something to the Keys. He became involved in public service and Civil Defense.

When Hurricane Donna roared through the Upper Keys with 150 mph winds in 1960, Bernard Russell and his family rode it out. As a foot of water lapped at his home's foundation, Russell helped protect lives and property against the second-worst hurricane to strike the Keys.

Russell founded the island's first fire department.

For more than 20 years he was in charge. When somebody needed an ambulance, the phone rang in his home. When he retired, his legacy included a fine building, 26 firefighters, three trucks and two ambulances. He is proud of his fire department.

He and his wife travel frequently in their retirement. Their only daughter lives in Central Florida. They also visit the Ocala area, where so many ex-Conchs have moved in recent years to escape tropical storms and the storm of people that progress has delivered into the Keys.

Bernard Russell has refused to move, though. During summer, during hurricane season, he can be found in his home in the Keys, less than a block from the U.S. 1 memorial to the 1935 storm and its victims.

270

"When we have a storm now, I take my wife to the mainland and I come back," he says, sitting on the memorial's steps. "I can't blame her for wanting to go. When she hears that wind whistling and roaring outside, it blows her mind."

After he drops Laurette off, he turns around and returns to the Keys.

"I have to," he says as traffic inches by on the highway behind him. "I may be needed. The thing I have always asked myself is this: Why was I spared? Why am I still here? I saw great big robust he-men dead on the ground. I saw little skinny children who survived. How do you put that together in your mind?

"I have to think the Lord has a purpose for me. I might be needed."

Wild man of the Loxahatchee

JUPITER   9/18/88

The early morning sun is already blistering hot on Trapper Nelson's Loxahatchee River. At least it feels unbearable to a city boy made soft by air conditioning. His T-shirt, soaked with sweat as he packs the canoe, will stay wet through the day.

Trapper Nelson, who was known as the "Wild Man of the Loxahatchee" before his 1968 death, didn't believe in air conditioning. For that matter, he didn't believe in electricity.

The Trapper, who fled New Jersey in 1931 to escape an urban lifestyle and the cold winters, wanted another kind of existence. Here on Florida's Southeast coast, about 30 miles from the mansions of Palm Beach, he found what he was looking for on what the Tequesta Indians called the Loxahatchee, or Turtle, River: isolation, wilderness and tropical heat.

Heat? What heat? Every morning, regardless of the season, he picked up his ax and cut firewood. Not that he needed much firewood. Cold spells in the swamp were brief. He cut firewood for exercise.

He stood six feet four and weighed a fatless 240 pounds. His stomach, rippled with muscle, looked like an old-fashioned washboard. As for his woodpile, what remains today measures 80 feet long and 12 feet high.

"He was one tough guy," Eric Bailey tells you. Bailey rents canoes on Indiantown Road, where your trip to Trapper's will begin. Born in Palm Beach County 51 years ago, Bailey grew up paddling the river. He knew Trapper. "He let me sleep on his land one night," Bailey says. "The mosquitoes ate me alive."

Trapper Nelson, you have read, favored roast possum. Thinking of that, you push your canoe into the dark water. The cypress swamp closes in around you as you enter his river world.

You have always wanted to paddle this river and visit the old homesite of Trapper Nelson, which has been restored by the state. The Loxahatchee, which begins in the Everglades and flows about 25 miles through Jonathan Dickinson State Park on its way to the Atlantic Ocean, has been designated Florida's only Wild and Scenic River by the U.S. government.

It deserves the designation – today. Maybe 10 years from now, when the coming development has taken its toll, the river will be just another cesspool. Today it is narrow and winding and beautiful as it slices through a primeval swamp where Tequesta Indians once hid from pioneers. Owls hoot from the treetops. Turtles watch from logs, which in low water block your passage. This is no river for casual paddlers.

272

REAL FLORIDA

You are paddling with a boy. He sits in the bow and you in the stern. It takes him a few minutes to get the hang of paddling in a narrow, meandering river in swift current. It takes you a while, too. You want to stop and admire the scenery, but if you gawk too much – isn't that an Indian mound on the right? – you end up bumping into one cypress root after another.

You portage around the first obstruction. The aluminum boat feels as heavy as an Indian's cypress dugout canoe as you haul it through brush that scratches your face and roots that bruise your ankles. Next time, you vow, you'll bring your 45-pound fiberglass canoe.

You shouldn't get lost here if you follow the current. But you worry anyway. A wild river will do that to you. You jump as three white ibis explode into the air just around the bend. Something else – something big – drops into the water, again just out of sight.

What if a cottonmouth falls into the canoe from one of the branches you have to lean under to pass? You have no snakebite kit. And you could never paddle back against the current. You have no choice. Go with the river. That's what Trapper Nelson always did.

The son of Polish immigrants, he was born Vincent Nostokovich in Trenton, N.J., in 1909. Nobody seems to know when or why he began using the name Nelson. It probably doesn't matter. What matters is that at age 14 he ran away from home, escaped into the New Jersey woods and trapped muskrat. He hopped trains and rode the rails west. He trapped small animals in Colorado and then disappeared into Mexico, where he was arrested for smuggling guns. Released from jail, he returned to New Jersey, tired of the winters, and headed for Florida.

In 1931 he settled on the Loxahatchee where it flowed into the sea. But there were too many people on the coast, and too many laws, and in 1936 he rowed nine miles upriver, built a cabin, planted fruit trees, trapped animals, sold their fur and ate their flesh. Trapper Nelson was home.

You feel less at home paddling your canoe through the swamp on Trapper's river, though. You are repelled as much as you are attracted. You marvel at the intricate webs constructed by the harmless saucer-sized golden orb spiders when they are high in the trees, but slap at them nervously as they brush across your face.Trapper Nelson would laugh.

Up ahead is a submerged log. You think you can paddle over it. Snap. The wooden paddle you have brought from home breaks in two. The boy laughs. You do, too. Stupid, stupid. Fortunately, you have a spare paddle, made of plastic and aluminum. At the next obstruction, you climb from the canoe, balance on the log and drag the boat over. Sweat runs into your eyes. It's work.

Trapper Nelson thrived on work. Once a month he gathered his furs and rowed them nine miles to the settled coast and sold them. He got $2.50 for a good raccoon pelt. A seven-foot gator skin brought $3. Three feet of otter fur was worth $15 – even during the Depression.

Trapper Nelson would take his money and treat himself to a civilized meal and pie for dessert. The whole pie. Then he'd climb into his skiff and row nine miles back home.

He was a hermit living a primitive life. But he was no backwoods hayseed. He read avidly, mostly paperbacks, and, when he could get it, the *Wall Street Journal.* Good in math, he was even better at business.

During the late 1930s, in fact, he began paying delinquent taxes on other people's river property. According to Florida law, he got title to the property if he paid taxes three successive years. When he died, Trapper Nelson owned 858 acres of riverfront. On paper, he was a millionaire.

Not that he lived like one. His home was a crude log cabin he built by hand. He slept in a small bed draped with mosquito netting. One of his few luxuries was a hammock hung from a picnic shelter.

He built the picnic shelter after he learned, in the 1940s, that Palm Beach millionaires, and their guests, would pay to visit his property and to meet him. Trapper knew how to put on a show. When he heard their boats approaching, he'd yell like Tarzan and swing on a rope over the river.

He sold the city slickers orchids and fruit. He built a small zoo and filled the cages with swamp animals. He wrestled alligators and walked among guests with snakes draped around his wide shoulders. For Trapper, it was a good life – until Uncle Sam beckoned.

Trapper tried to escape military service by getting married; the Army took him anyway. He became an MP on a military base on the coast. His wife, meanwhile, ran off with another soldier. It was another reason for Trapper to distrust people.

Paddling, you stop for a cold drink. You eat a banana. You consult a map. After two hours of paddling, you're tired. You hear voices. Looking ahead, you see two men who are actually paddling upriver, against the current. They shout: Did you see it? See what? They point.

You look up into the cypress. A bald eagle spooks and flies just under the canopy. Now you better understand why the Trapper loved it here. You dig your paddle into his river. An hour goes by, and the river opens, and there's Trapper's place, ahead.

Brad Melko, 38, is waiting at a picnic table. He's a ranger at Jonathan Dickinson State Park. He also lives on Trapper Nelson's property. He didn't know Trapper, but he has interviewed people who did. When you visit the Trapper Nelson Interpretive Site, Brad Melko gives the tour.

He shows you the cabin, which is about 60-feet long and 20-feet wide. The Trapper acquired a gas stove in his later years, and a refrigerator, but he never brought in electricity.

The park ranger also shows you the fireplace. After Trapper died, and the state got the property, rangers repaired the fireplace. Rock crumbled and out poured 5,050 coins totaling $1,829.46. Trapper didn't trust banks, even if the government insured the savings. He feared anything having to do with government.

He was right to be distrustful. In 1966, the man from the state health department came around and announced that Trapper Nelson's tourist attraction was a disgrace. He said the pit toilets were inadequate. He found the animal cages unsanitary. Fix things up or get out of business, he said.

Seething, Trapper Nelson built a restroom with real plumbing. He improved his animal cages. Not good enough, the health department man said. Not good enough at all.

Trapper Nelson stopped receiving guests. When they arrived, he greeted their boats with his .12-gauge shotgun. He told them, "I have no friends." He cut cypress trees so they blocked the river. For the next two years he lived as a recluse.

If you wished to see him, you wrote a letter. When he got around to the post office, which was seldom, he would write back if he wanted to see you. Usually he wanted to be left alone.

When an old trapper crony, Todd James, wrote in 1968, Trapper agreed to see him. They made an appointment to meet at the downriver home of a mutual acquaintance, John Dubois. Trapper Nelson never showed.

That was odd. Trapper was an eccentric recluse, but a dependable one. If he said he was coming, he was coming. Dubois went to Trapper's river camp. The camp looked pretty much as Dubois had remembered it. The only peculiar thing was the smell. The bad smell overwhelmed everything.

Trapper Nelson was lying in his hammock next to his shotgun. There was a huge hole in his chest. He had been dead for days. The animals had eaten their fill.

"The coroner ruled it a suicide," park ranger Brad Melko tells you. "Trapper had been very depressed and living in isolation for a while, so he could have killed himself. It's possible."

No one will ever know for sure. Some say he was killed by robbers who thought money was buried on Trapper's property. He also was the kind of man who makes as many enemies as friends. Murder was a possibility. Brad Melko says, "I kind of think he was shot by somebody else."

Thinking of a dead man, you return, subdued, to your canoe. The rest of the trip through the mangroved section of the river takes two hours. It's a tough paddle, against the wind and an incoming tide, and you're tired at the end.

Eric Bailey, the canoe rental man, is waiting at the appointed boat ramp. He loads the canoe on a trailer and drives you back to your car. Traffic is heavy on US 1, which is being widened to accommodate the hordes of people and the new condominiums and shopping centers closing in on Trapper Nelson's river.

As wild as a panther, as ornery as a black bear, as resourceful as an old she-coon, Trapper Nelson represented a Florida that is just about gone. As auto exhaust fills the bus, you find yourself thinking: Trapper, maybe it's good you aren't here to see this.

Caught
in a magic moment

FLAMINGO   **7/8/90**

My brother and I talk often on the telephone, and sooner or later we get around to the topic of fishing. He has a passion for tarpon and other large gamefish; I hardly fish at all anymore. Yet I enjoy hearing his stories, and we like talking about the fishing we did as boys in Miami.

Fishing was close to a religion for us. We weren't good about tumbling out of bed for school, but we had no trouble leaping up at 4 a.m. for fishing trips. We had no boat, but nobody needed a boat back then, or any fancy equipment for that matter, and we caught snook, tarpon, barracuda, snapper and bass.

Outstanding fishing was something we took for granted when we were boys in the 1960s. South Florida's water was relatively clean, and the marine vegetation that supports the food chain seemed to be in good supply. If my mother wanted a bass for supper, we walked to the nearest canal and caught bass. If she wanted a snook, we usually caught snook.

My brother still lives in South Florida, and he still experiences some pretty good fishing. But he has to work at it. He sometimes drives 100 miles to the Florida Keys, and then travels 40 miles by boat, with a guide, to catch something memorable. Things aren't the same.

"Do you remember the time. . . ?"

A lot of fish talk with my brother begins like that. If my son happens to be within earshot, he listens intently. At 14, he is as passionate about fishing as anybody can be about anything. He fishes in the morning, in the evening, and tries to squeeze in a couple of hours in the afternoon if his parents will let him neglect summer chores. At night he reads about fishing or works on his tackle.

My daughters enjoy fishing, but they can take it or leave it. To my son, at least for now, nothing is as important. He and his friend pooled their babysitting money and bought a $30 boat. It's a dingy, one of those little six-footers that sailors row from the sea wall to their sailboats, and the best you can say about it is that it floats.

On the weekend, they load their equipment and carry the dinghy – carry it – a half-mile. Once in a while, they manage to catch something, usually catfish or pinfish, and throw them back. Saltwater catfish and pinfish, which have little food value, are plentiful. Trout and redfish and snook, good-eating fish, are harder to catch than when when I was a boy.

Yet he never seems discouraged. He is sure that every cast will be the one that finally lands a great prize. When we drive together, his eyes take in the passing water and the possibilities. "I'll bet there's fish there," he says, pointing to a nice section of

276

mangroves. "What would you use? A jig or a MirrOlure?" Then he returns to the outdoors magazines he brought along to study. He reminds me of myself – as a boy.

I lost my love for fishing some years ago. I can't tell you exactly why. It may have been the fact that for a decade I made my living by writing about fishing, and that it became business instead of a simple pleasure. It may also have been that I started questioning whether fishing was an unnecessary cruelty in a world that is already exceptionally cruel to wild creatures. Anyway, hiking, birding and canoeing satisfied my urge to commune with nature.

But lately, since my son started living and breathing fishing, I have been reborn. I have been seeing the activity through his fresher eyes. There is an inherent cruelty to fishing – we impale them on our hooks, after all – but there is something magic about it, too. Nothing I know equals the electric moment when an angler feels the weight, and the power, of a big fish on the end of a line. You feel connected to the Earth.

Fishing, in addition, can be a doorway to understanding how living things on the planet work. An angler has to think like a predator to succeed. An angler has to understand the food chain, the tides – maybe even watch feeding pelicans for clues.

Every once in a while, an angler takes the life of a living creature. But only the most brutish kind of person takes it lightly. Most good anglers I have known release everything other than fish they intend to eat. There are still people who kill fish for vanity, but thankfully they are disappearing.

Most modern anglers are sensitive about the aquatic environment. When something goes wrong, they are among the first to notice and to speak up. Just as the illiterate shrug when zealots burn books, people who seldom leave their condo cocoons are unlikely to raise a fuss when developers and polluters destroy undersea life. The best of today's anglers, I am sure, are destined to become tomorrow's environmentalists. I am proud that my son is a fisherman.

When my brother and I were boys, we never thought about the environment. The fish seemed endless. Sometimes my heart weeps for my son and other children who love to throw out a line; environmental destruction has left them so little to catch. Maybe it's good that we have places such as Disney World. They substitute fantasy for flesh-and-blood experience.

But sometimes a boy gets lucky . . . .

I was in Miami recently, on business, when my brother set up a fishing trip for Everglades National Park. A friend of his, a guide, had a day off and was willing to take us. Did we want to go? For my son, it was Christmas in July.

I won't bore you with all the details. But we caught fish. We caught them on live shrimp, and on lures. We caught and released mangrove snapper, yellowtail snapper, spotted sea trout, sheepshead, ladyfish, jack crevalle, blue runner, pigfish, pinfish and two kinds of catfish. We saw dolphin rolling in the channels at Snake Bight, and we saw huge loggerhead sea turtles in Florida Bay, gasping for air. Twice black-tipped sharks grabbed fish we were reeling in and bit through our flimsy lines.

Late in the afternoon, my brother's friend, fishing guide Mike Romero, suggested we try to catch tripletail. Tripletail aren't gamefish. But tripletail fight hard. Hooking one is like trying to stop a four-wheel-drive truck by hanging onto the rear bumper. Though they are short and stocky, tripletail are also acrobatic. They jump.

REAL FLORIDA

My brother caught a six-pounder. I lost one when it broke my line on a channel marker. My brother lost one when it broke his line, too. I lost another when the hook fell from its mouth. My son, who wanted one so badly you could feel it in the thick tropical air, was left out of the action.

Then, minutes before it was time to head in, his rod doubled. His line twanged. His voice got high with excitement. He had one. He had a tripletail. We saw it jump. Romero, the guide, yelled. Big fish. Real big fish.

Romero coached him. Keep your rod up. Now point your rod down. Keep your line away from that channel marker! Put more pressure on him. Not that much! Boy, you can't rest. When you rest, your fish is resting, too. From the back of the boat I listened, and watched, and prayed. The thought that he might lose this fish, and be disappointed, was difficult to endure.

It took him 14 minutes to work the tripletail to the boat. But we had no net, no gaff, and we needed one for such a fish. Romero made a makeshift gaff out of heavy line and a big lure, and for a moment we thought it might work. But when Romero snagged the fish, we knew immediately our gaff was weak. The fish threatened to escape.

Desperate, Romero wrapped his hands in an old pair of pants, kneeled and cradled the fish in his arms. He could feel hooks biting into his hand. He cursed. He lifted. Then: tripletail in the boat!

Romero, one of South Florida's best guides, walked over to my son and slapped his hands in congratulations. I was surprised to feel tears in my eyes.

That night, at my brother's home, we ate some of the 19-pound tripletail. We ate it barbecued, jerked and with garlic and butter. My son announced that it was the best fish he had ever eaten. I had to agree. To me, it tasted as sweet as a warm memory.